ON MY WAY OUT II

ALSO BY RICHARD HAWLEY

FICTION

The Three Lives of Jonathan Force
Greeves Passing
The Source of Longing
The Other World
The Guru
Paul and Julianna
The Headmaster's Papers
The Headmaster's Wife

POETRY

Twenty-One Visits with a Darkly Sun-Tanned Angel
The Headmaster's Poems
St. Julian
With Love to My Survivors
Aspects of Vision

NON-FICTION

Forward and No Retreat: Two Centuries of Linsly School Life
I Can Learn from You: Boys as Relational Learners (with Michael Reichart)
Souls in Boxes
For Whom the Boy Toils
Reaching Boys / Teaching Boys (with Michael Reichert)
Beyond the Icarus Factor
Hard Lessons and Other Talks to the School
Papers from the Headmaster
Hail University! A Century of University School Life
Mr. Chips Redux / Miss Dove Redivivus
Seeing Things: A Chronicle of Surprises
Building Drug Free Schools
The Purposes of Pleasure
A School Answers Book
Coming Through School (editor)
Boys Will Be Men
Kiski: The Story of a Boys School
On My Way Out: a Reflection on Closure

ON MY WAY OUT II

A REFLECTION ON CLOSURE

RICHARD HAWLEY

Spun apart from the wheel of work,
Fidgety in their bird bones,
They grow old and full of questions.

—R.A.H., "The Poor in Spirit."

. .

ORCHISES • WASHINGTON • 2020

Library of Congress Cataloging-in-Publication Data

Names: Hawley, Richard A., author.
Title: On my way out II : a reflection on closure / Richard Hawley.
Description: Washington, D.C. : Orchises, [2020]
Identifiers: LCCN 2018033057 | ISBN 9781932535419
Subjects: LCSH: Hawley, Richard A. | Older men—United States—
  Biography. | Retired teachers—United States—Biography. |
  Preparatory school teachers—Ohio—Hunting Valley—Biography. |
  University School (Hunting Valley, Ohio)—Faculty—Biography. |
  Middlebury (Vt.)—Biography. | Authors, American—Biography. |
  Upper class families—United States—Social life and customs. |
  Aging—United States—Anecdotes.
Classification: LCC CT275.H4787 A3 2019 | DDC 305.26/10092
  [B]—dc23
LC record available at 2018033057

••

ORCHISES PRESS

P. O. Box 320533

Alexandria Virginia 22320-4533

G 6 E 4 C 2 A

PREFACE TO THE SECOND VOLUME

This second installment of *On My Way Out* continues a reflection on my progress to the end of life. In it my intention remains the same: to document the passage from full sentience and physical capacity to less and still less and then, perhaps, to none. I began this project in my 66th year when I became aware that, while feeling mentally alert and well enough physically, I was held overall in a distinctly new condition. Though still immersed in professional commitments and embedded in an engaging and demanding complex of personal relationships, I had a profound realization that I was no longer going anywhere—at least not going anywhere outwardly. This realization, while striking, was not upsetting. "Busy" as I often found myself, there was a distinct stillness at the center of my being, and it was out of this this new stillness that I began to live my days.

With the publication of what follows, I will have now chronicled seven running years of later life. One might suppose that in the course of so much introspection and almost daily self-inscribing that I would have come to "know myself" especially well. For me, the most interesting and energizing result of this work to date is that something close to the opposite has occurred; rather than confirming who I am, I am beginning to discover who I am. If I am not mistaken, I appear to be learning.

Quite a bit is documented in what follows: perspectives on the state of the nation, the culture, negotiating one's way through the complexities of modern commerce and media. There are the rigors and challenges and small satisfactions of daily living. As I advance into my seventies, there is inevitable physical deterioration, diminished social impact and overall effectiveness. Decline, certainly—but also, unmistakably, development.

I propose in several entries that what feels like new capacity and new perspective is in fact a consequence of the breakdown with age of some formerly adaptive mental structure. I am not, for instance, a more inventive piano player in my seventies because I have learned or disciplined myself to do anything new; I am a better piano player because certain brain hemisphere boundaries necessary to manage practical right-left distinctions in my prior life have broken down with age. In consequence, I have more trouble now making directional sense of the overhead signs on the Interstate. I am more likely than ever to utter the exact opposite of the word I intend. And, as luck would have it, I am more capable of playing different cadences simultaneously with my right and left hands on the piano. More generally, age-related breakdowns in prior discernments and certainties have opened up new—sometimes terrifying, sometimes beautiful--considerations of long familiar circumstances. In this second volume I explore what feel like new messages being transmitted from such unlikely sources as the rock face of a mountainside viewed from a train window, the furrowed brow of a mother ape suckling her baby.

The growing awareness that former discernments, convictions, and certainties break down with age, while temporarily unsettling, is also an opportunity the receive experience in a new unfiltered way. Breaking down prior mental structures is not the same thing as breaking the mind that holds them. I am not talking about dementia or any other kind of misalignment of mind and given world. I am referring to a renewed and enlarged beholding of the familiar, a condition that, with grace, comes with age.

This age-altered way of experiencing both internal and external data poses challenges, but challenges I am longing to meet. Former certainties and habits of interpretation are no longer reliable. The world has become at once less predictable and more interesting. In the course of chronicling what follows I have become aware of how I have in the past made my most mistaken calculations and worst decisions. Throughout my school years and professional life I have been regarded, especially in cultural and intellectual matters, as a "quick study." Put simply, I could from childhood onward feel my mind racing to find an assignable pattern in material put before me. When tested formally, I was quick to scan possibilities for what might pass as an answer, then assert it as the answer. When I was mistaken, it was because I hadn't stepped back far enough or taken enough time to determine what was necessary to draw a correct conclusion.

Today I feel no rush to closure; today I do nothing but stand back. Rather than bundling, shaping, and interpreting the day's data—the fall of light on the pine crests in the woods behind the house, the last grating utterance of Donald Trump from the White House lawn—I wait for the impact, feeling its force. A decade ago I would have been working those impressions into communicable categories, into opinions, into, were I in the mood, a poem or an essay. Today I am not so much "working on" daily experience as I am witnessing its work on me.

I come back to the notion of messages. Today, as never before in my life, I feel I am receiving messages, some of them urgent and beyond my present ability to integrate fully. Moreover—and this is something of an embarrassment for a lifelong writer to admit—my problem is words. As I attempt to explain in some of the entries to follow, the messages I feel are being unmistakably transmitted to me are not being transmitted in words. Trying to convey them to a reader in words feels too often like a feeble, failed approximation of what I have experienced, at best a distortion. I ask myself am I merely failing to convey the message? Am I failing to convey it because I have failed to get it? With respect to ultimate things, must words necessarily fail?

This being a book, one must hope not. To return to my motivation for even trying: I realized, beginning in my 66th year, that I am now held in an altogether new and different relationship to the given world: an all-being realization that I am living minute-to-minute, day-to-day in relationship to my certain end. The condition is in equal measure stirring and autumnal.

It has something revelatory to say, and I am listening.

R.A.H.
RIPTON
DECEMBER 2019

THE MAN WRITING THIS

The text that follows documents the developments in my life as I pass through the threshold of old age into the altered circumstances that inevitably bear on it, resulting in diminished and then lost function, with the attendant contraction in perception and effectiveness unto The End.

As noted in the preceding preface, this account of what I am calling my "end game" must be as particular as I am. It must register the particular place where I live, the places I am able to go, the people near and dear to me, and others who shape my circumstances. And while this extended exploration of my evolving experience is not, I hope, a mere diary, it must necessarily include responses to events and the occasional crises that compose the News, the Times.

If a little problematically, this account also requires some picture of my past—where, literally, I and all of this verbiage have come from. I began composing this narrative mid-way through my 66th year when it became clear to me that I was held in a unidirectional process that was unlike anything prior in my life.

The last thing I wanted to do was to write an exhaustive, and no doubt exhausting, autobiography. In other books, both fiction and non-fiction, I have made what I believe is sufficient reckoning with what my past experience has revealed to me. But because the particularity of my life and circumstances is essential to interpreting what I say about the stage of life I am documenting, some kind of summary of my past is in order—or so I have decided at age 73, seven years into the work. What follows is a brief and I hope helpful summary of who I have been.

I was born in the city of Chicago in 1945 to Robert and Kathleen Hawley. At the time of my birth, my father had not yet returned from naval duty in the Pacific, and my mother and my older sister had temporarily resumed residence in my grandparents' house in the city. After my father's return, our family moved to a suburb northwest of the city, Arlington Heights. I attended the public schools in Arlington Heights, all of them in walking distance of my house, in an era and in a setting that was completely continuous with the Norman Rockwell illustrations in the magazines our family subscribed to. In Arlington Heights, I felt safe, able on foot or bicycle and later the family car to go and do what I pleased. If I had been asked at any time during the years of my early schooling, I would have said I lived in the epicenter of a big, safe, country, and though a young country, the greatest and strongest in the world. Until the assassination of President Kennedy, I felt benignly *held* in the United States of America.

I was not an extraordinary boy, but I was lively. Though small and slight (then), I was mad for sports, was without much effort a good student, and, if narrowly, a passionate reader. I learned to play the piano, mainly by ear, and became facile, even a little precocious. My early friendships and loves went deep and were formative.

By a fluke I am sure no longer possible in college admissions, I was admitted to Middlebury College in Vermont, a transition at once overwhelming and life shaping. I was stirred past my descriptive powers by the rugged beauty of the college and the region. Living so intensely in a hive of my fellow students, I could barely focus on the academic program, which was hopelessly rigorous. Almost half the males of my Middlebury class flunked out or dropped out. For half my time there I limped along scholastically, but finally found my feet in political philosophy, and thanks to some very generous teachers, a light flicked on about the relatedness of cultural and historical developments. I was alternately lazy and busy at Middlebury. I became the editor-in-chief of the paper. As in my hometown, I formed sustaining friendships and entered into exciting amorous relationships, including one my junior year with a freshman woman, Molly Watson, to whom I may have proposed marriage within days of making her acquaintance and would ultimately marry.

While at college I resisted thinking about practical futures. My idea of a man's work was doing what your father did. My father bought and sold municipal securities for a bank. I knew I did not want to do that. I liked making music, writing, and being in school, so I went on to graduate school at Case Western Reserve University in Cleveland, and as I was completing a master's degree, made two consequential decisions. I married Molly Watson, and I took a job teaching government and history at University School, a private boys' school in Shaker Heights, Ohio.

For my first three years at the school, I was simultaneously studying political theory full time, at Case Western Reserve, where I earned my Ph.D, and at Cambridge University, where Molly and I spent a year while I studied as an M.A. student in theology in order to gain a perspective on my doctoral thesis.

Molly and I returned to Cleveland where I continued to teach and then to take on administrative duties at University School. Molly finished her undergraduate studies at the Cleveland Institute of Art, and we began to build a family, producing three daughters, Kate, Jesse, and Claire. I augmented my work at the school with published articles and books, many of them about school life, and in 1988 I was named University School's sixth headmaster, in which post I served, dizzyingly, busily, through my retirement in 2005.

That clear, possibly gilded seeming career arc, or story, though factually accurate, is far from the whole story and in fact is wildly misleading in excluding some of the most formative events in my life, especially those marking the later decades. In 1995, I commenced a consuming, sense-obliterating love affair with a young woman, Celeste, who was singing to my accompaniment at a series of weekend jazz gigs. I am not sure hindsight is adequate to convey the power, the feeling tones, and emotional stress of that decade in my life. To my reckoning now, the affair represented a dangerous but also enlivening counter life to the moral confinement and stressful demands of my school days. The affair was indescribably (at any rate, I will not describe it) passionate, but it was not merely lust. I cared—and care—deeply for Celeste, though our relationship challenged and obviated what I had believed were inviolate commitments to fidelity and prudence. At the time, I looked wildly to literature and to the experience of others for a sense of where I was in my—what?—free fall? Double life? All of it made more confusing by the fact that I had not lost a trace of love and gratitude for Molly, nor for a moment did I want to abandon or retreat from my family life. As my retirement loomed, my affair still largely a secret and unsuspected, Celeste and I were approaching a dramatic reckoning: we were going to be practically and geographically apart, as Molly and I were moving to Vermont. But this relationship-ending prospect was upended by Celeste's revelation that she was pregnant, paternity not in doubt to either of us.

So, a few weeks after Mr. Chips departed with great appreciative fanfare from University School, a fourth daughter, Lucia, appeared. And in an aggravating, schizophrenic manner I worked to attend to everybody in the unsettled constellation I had created: Molly and our children, Celeste and the baby, my extended family, my closest friends. The hurt and confused feelings of my near and dear, Celeste's fear of abandonment and ruin—her husband had left her—were a daily cacophony. I had upset and surprised everybody, and it was all my fault. I still loved all the people I had previously loved and thus tried to do what I felt was loving toward all of them. At what I thought must be the nadir of my misery, I decided I would perhaps be happier and my world more stable if I left Vermont and lived with Celeste in Cleveland. I did this for sixth months, even bought a house there for Celeste, the baby and me. While apart from Molly and treading water in the new arrangement, I realized I was emotionally drowning and, mess and recriminations notwithstanding, returned to Vermont and Molly, who miraculously, it seemed to me, was willing to have me.

And so it has gone. The account above I am sure has raised all manner of questions for readers, many of them answered in the narrative that follows.

R.A.H.

ON MY WAY OUT •• II

March 7, 2014: Today's *New York Times* included a long obituary of Sherwin Nuland, a distinguished surgeon, and a professor of medicine at Yale. He was also a writer, and some years ago when I was on a tear reading about old age, I read his excellent book, *How We Die*. The gist of the book is to puncture the illusion of the "good death," an easeful passage in which the dying person, untroubled by too much pain or other discomforts, exchanges final farewells and good wishes with loved ones. While some deaths are less agonizing than others, Nuland wrote in unflinching detail about what really happens in the end stages of cancer, heart disease, and other terminal conditions. The result of reading his measured, sobering account of actual deaths was, for me, to lower my own expectations of an easy exit.

The obituary made clear that Nuland's deep immersion in death and dying, as well as his vocational commitment to preserve life, was the result of an excruciatingly awful childhood. From his infancy on, his mother was seriously ill, finally succumbing, when Nuland was 11, to colon cancer. She died at home, and Nuland vividly remembered the putrid smells and bloody pads that emerged from the sick room. His father, who bore the name Nudelman, was ill himself. A Jewish immigrant and illiterate, he did menial work in the garment industry. Prone to violent tempers and at the same time physically diminished, he was both a disappointment and a terror to his two sons. Medical findings after his death revealed that, among other infirmities, he had been living for years as a syphilitic.

The story of Nuland's rise out of this unpromising household is not quite the stuff of Horatio Alger. In early mid-life, about the time of his father's death, he had a dramatic mental breakdown so severe that a lobotomy was considered before electro-convulsive treatment was adopted, successfully, instead. Nuland was not only able to return to his practice, he was able to soar professionally. And write about death, about facing death just as it is, whatever the circumstances of its visitation. *How We Die* proposed a reconsideration of the tendency of doctors to recommend unlikely life-sustaining treatments. Nuland admitted to having done so himself, unwilling to convey the ultimate bad news: you are going to die.

Nuland's life seems to me heroic. He endured unbearable suffering and pain throughout his childhood, finding light and purpose by shining in school. That he would not only dedicate his working life to mitigating pain but helping others to face it is an inspiration.

March 2-12, 2014: Throughout a paradisiacal stay in Key West I sensed that I must fortify myself in every respect for the babysitting duty M and I had committed to while Kate and Shad enjoyed a first-ever post-babies vacation in Hawaii. It was not really a vacation for Shad. He had been invited through his Second City contacts to emcee some sort of business conference on the islands. The gig was not only lucrative, it included luxury lodgings in a big hotel overlooking the Pacific. They had amassed free flight miles for Kate, so off they went, their first time apart from their daughters Anna Jane and Winifred, ages 4 and 1.

In some ways we were an unexpected pick for the job. Shad's parents, who live in Iowa and five hours from Chicago by car, visit Kate and Shad more frequently than we are able to manage. Both at their house and in Chicago they have seen much more of Anna and Winifred whom they adore. They would have gladly taken the assignment and may have been a little miffed not to be asked, but Kate, though fond of her in-laws, is concerned that they don't have sense of the kinds of food that are good for infants, whereas M certainly does, thus the invitation to us. Of course we accepted without a blink, but we, certainly I, did not underestimate the requirements of the job. The girls, again, are 4 and 1. Anna is potty trained, Winifred not. Anna goes to a preschool across town. She also has a dance class and some party invitations the week we are in charge. M and I have only tended them in the marginal ways grandparents do in the course of extended family gatherings. We had never been in charge of them--waking them, feeding them, changing them, bathing them, exercising them, amusing them--for a single day. Truth be told, although I find them irresistibly cute and engaging and M would be happy to be eternally in their presence, we do not know them that well yet. To ease the passage to their first week of life apart from their parents, it was agreed that we would arrive in Chicago a day and a half before Kate and Shad were to fly off, the idea being to get the girls familiar with us and for us to learn the driving routes to Anna's various commitments. A good plan, but it was foiled.

The entire country has had a devastating winter, but Chicago has been hit particularly hard by what the weather people are calling a "polar vortex." By the time we arrived in the city there had been 64 days of sub-zero temperatures. Adding to this the wind chill associated with Chicago's famous "lake effect," was often life-threatening. Travel all winter has been stymied with cancelled flights and impassible roads. We had booked a hard-to-get direct flight from Burlington to Chicago, but the day before departure--a clear and sunny day in Ripton—we received an automated telephone call saying that our flight had been cancelled; the proposed next flight was in three days. We knew we had to be in Chicago prior to Kate's flight out, so we considered driving—17 hours in the best of conditions, but as it turned out, the forecast was for the worst of conditions, rain, sleet, icy roads, intermittent blizzards. Our last hope was Amtrak, and it worked.

We booked a roomette on the overnight Lake Shore Limited from Albany to Chicago, a sixteen hour ride. The two and a half hour drive from Ripton to Albany was a little unsettling. We were not at all certain how the project ahead was going to go. I had ambivalent thoughts about the train ride. I love trains generally but had not been in a sleeper since my grandmother and I took the Denver Zephyr out west when I was twelve. M is more than ambivalent; she is dubious. One of her firm expectations of daily life is that she will have private, comfortable access to a toilet. This is by no means assured, given that the roomette's notional toilet, its receiving oval about the size of a football, is wedged, during the day, directly against one of the two passenger seats; at night it is inches away from the turned down sleeping surface of the lower bunk. I was in the mood to consider it an open-ended adventure. For again, I really like train rides. I like the gentle jostling as we chug along, I like the sweep of countryside and the back ends of settled areas and cities, the looming stations. I especially like all of that swooping by in ghostly shadow at night.

Moreover, we were pleasantly surprised by the extreme-- compared to any form of air travel--civility of the Amtrak attendants. On boarding we were introduced to our own "personal assistant," a sturdy woman named Melanie. She insisted on taking and stowing our luggage in the roomette, told us that she would summon us for mealtimes in the dining car, turn down our beds at night and make them up in the morning. Her own room was adjacent to ours and she said not to hesitate to ask for or about anything and said she would keep fresh coffee brewing and have juice and other bottled beverages available as needed. This promising introduction to the trip was reinforced when we learned that our meals in the dining car were included in the (surprisingly modest) ticket price. Better still, as we were approaching Syracuse, we made our way to the dining car for dinner, and it was not only clean and nicely appointed with stiff white linen table cloths and heavy plates and silver, the food--my roasted chicken, M's glazed salmon--was excellent, beyond typical restaurant quality and, after Key West, our standards were high.

So far, so good, but then as I considered retiring for the night I realized I had failed to pack the mouthpiece designed to prevent sleep apnea. A sickening dread. I cannot sleep without it. When sufficiently exhausted I fall into what would otherwise be the onset of sleep, at which point some bit of tissue in my uvula falls slack and closes off my breathing passages, causing me to snort and to awake. It is dispiriting and exhausting to spend an entire night doing this, but despite every improvisation of head position and mouth setting I could think of, that is how the night passed, obviating all the pleasure of the gentle clickety clack of the car, the romance of the dull yellow station lights looming and receding outside the window, its chilled face just inches from my nose.

We arrived at Chicago's Union Station about noon. Shad very nicely offered to pick us up and drive us to the apartment, but I wish we had been able to take a cab. He had a harder time negotiating the loop traffic than he had anticipated, and it was glacially cold waiting for him at the curb outside the station. I cannot remember another time when my face hurt more from the cold—and I am a Chicago boy. After a vigil of fifteen minutes or so, M had to go back inside the station lobby while I guarded the bags and watched for Shad.

The babies were in exuberant high spirits when we arrived, and it was very sweet to see them, but deep in my interior I had a foreboding. I knew that there was demanding work ahead and that in the course of the afternoon and evening before Kate and Shad's departure we would have to learn a lot of routines, including car routes to the children's various destinations and stocking the larder with necessary provisions. None of this would have been daunting were I fully myself, but I felt way off, punch drunk from lack of sleep, no energy, an ominous ache in my throat. More ominous, I noted immediately that both Anna and Winifred's noses were running copiously with the effluvia of winter colds. But it was important to be cheerful and upbeat for Shad's and Kate's sake. They were understandably apprehensive about leaving the girls for the first time and I think felt a little guilty about imposing the responsibility on us and being the unintended cause of our travel woes. We assured them all would be well and set about establishing comfortable relationships with the girls.

The nine days that follow are a blur. We called our Ripton cleaning lady Marilyn and asked if she could post my sleeping mouthpiece overnight, which she kindly did, but there was another night with practically no sleep. For me nothing is worse than rising from bed feeling utterly unrestored but knowing my presence and full attention are expected beyond the door of the bedroom. Anna and Winifred arise early, around six. Molly takes charge of Anna, seeing her through her morning ablutions, getting dressed, and eating breakfast before heading out in Shad's car for her preschool which is a twenty to thirty minute drive through rush hour traffic. The drop off to the school is a delicate business as there are hundreds of parents attempting simultaneously to deposit their children. There is no legal parking near the school entrance, and most of the children are too little to leave the car on their own and make their way inside. M negotiates all of this, not me, as I am back in the apartment, in charge of Winifred. She sleeps in a crib and announces her awakening with insistent calling from her darkened room. When I enter the room and turn on the light, she is at first confused and then apparently glad to see me-- thank God. The room is redolent of full diaper, and as I lift her from her crib and lie her down on the changing table, I realize it has been a while since I changed Lulu's diapers. Fortunately all the required gear is at hand--fresh diapers, moist wiping tissues--but I was neither quick nor efficient in my ministrations. I would learn in the course of the week that tiny Winifred is a prodigious eater with corresponding evacuations. This particular morning I was startled by the enormity of what was produced when I finally and clumsily managed to tear back the plastic tabs that bound the diaper. I do not recall such challenges with Lulu, certainly not the complexity of cleaning the adjacent orifices. I was certain my efforts were taking far longer than Winifred was used to, but she seemed agreeable enough as I fumbled through the process, all the while babbling gibberish. It may have been twenty minutes, even a half hour, before I was through. I managed to get her dressed, although when M returned she told me I had Winifred's outfit on back to front.

So began the days, and so deepened my fog and mounting sense of physical malaise. There was not a waking moment from the girls' rising through their bed time that they did not want or need something. Quite understandably they expected full attention. There was a good deal of reading to them, in Winifred's case often the same book a half dozen times in a row. The apartment is small, and Kate found a wall system composed of stacked black boxes, perhaps a dozen in all. Each box is filled with toys and stuffed animals, dress up clothes and art supplies. In the course of a day's play most of the boxes are hauled from their station, emptied and strewn throughout the sitting room area. At day's end I return everything to the boxes, restack them, and there is order again. During the day hundreds of items are strewn over the floor, so that one tip toes gingerly from room to room. The hardest sequence to manage is bed time. The girls eat an early supper at about six, then bathe together, after which M swaddles one of them in towels, I the other, we dry them in their rooms, dress them for the night, then reassemble for story reading. We look for any sign that Anna looks sleepy, then lie her down in her bed and sing to her. When she quiets, we leave her room and attempt to lay Winifred in her crib, but she resolutely never wants to do it. She wails when we leave the room, and M goes in to console her, holding her and singing to her in a rocking chair in the darkened room. I am lying supine in our bed, stupid with exhaustion, listening.

In the course of our stay my malaise deepens. With the arrival of my mouthpiece, I gain a little sleep, but the ache in my throat progresses to a cough and cold. I am probably feverish from time to time but do not take my temperature. After three or four days, there is a strange, labored quality to my breathing. I seem to be able to take only shallow breaths, and I have the impression that my throat and lungs are lined with what feels like fiber glass. It occurs to me that I get relief from this shallow breathing only when I go outside, especially when I walk a good distance, say to the grocery store from provisions. Then I realize that, chest cold aside, I am having an allergic reaction to Kate's cat, a large, suspicious creature called Azul whom Kate thoughtfully shipped out to her Iowa in-laws in anticipation of my coming. She also had her carpets and furniture steam cleaned to mitigate the cat dander, but there it was. I took some over the counter allergy medicine, but it did not agree with me. As the end of the week approached, it was hard to imagine feeling worse. Moreover, it rankled me that M was doing more of the heavy lifting than seemed fair to me. Yet despite my physical decline, there were sweet compensations. I was pleased by the clear comfort the girls seemed to feel in our presence, their willingness to approach us cheerfully and suggest play, reading, snacks, or a spell of their favorite video, the animated Pixar film, Frozen. They seemed cheerful at meals, playful in their evening tub, glad to see us in the morning.

I cannot imagine a relationship like this being formed in any other circumstance. They call me "Popsy," and this pleases me. I find ways to surprise them and to make them laugh. Anna is precociously articulate, and she has a rich inner life, characters in her imaginary world often intermingling with daily reality. One day she tells us that school was interrupted by the appearance of Prince Hans, a problematic character in Frozen.

An indelible, favorite moment from day five: we have bathed the girls, and I am carrying Anna swaddled in oversized towels to her room to dress her for bed. I am holding her in such a way that we have intimate eye contact. She stares at me with a look of what seems to me humorous affection, then says, "Popsy, I think you are a little bit disgusting," and we both erupt in laughter. The phrase becomes our joke for the duration of my stay. I realize, despite my physical decline, my love for these children is bottomless.

March 15-20, 2014: As we are due to depart Chicago and fly home, the forecast for Vermont grows ominous: huge snows and hurricane force winds expected. Not even waiting for the airlines to cancel, I book a return railway ticket. I am desperate now, a serious upper respiratory infection, a constant, hacking cough, complicated by the constricted breathing due to the cat allergy. The train leaves at nine at night and arrives in Albany the next day, mid-afternoon. My hope is that by the time we arrive, the storms in Vermont will have abated and the roads clear enough to drive home and not hole up in some upstate New York motel. As expected, the flight was duly canceled, and had I waited until they told me, I could not have booked a sleeper on the train.

The ride east was mainly grueling, bad chest, fever chills, and constant coughing, M too. I sleep poorly in my berth, but doze periodically through the following morning and afternoon. Out the window Buffalo, Rochester, Syracuse are partly voided by snow drifts. I notice that as we near Albany the roads visible from my window look clear and drivable; we will at least be able to make a start toward home. My friend Gary emails me on the hour from Middlebury. The morning report was white-out blizzard conditions, police urging all to stay off the roads as all surfaces are iced over and the wind is creating zero visibility conditions. By afternoon the snow has stopped, but the roads in Addison County have not yet been salted and cleared. Late afternoon, as we leave the train in Albany, the Vermont roads are said to be snow-covered but with caution drivable. We decide to do it.

In the event, the New York State roads were mostly cleared, but once in Vermont, it was packed snow over ice, forty miles of this between Fair Haven and Ripton. We proceed cautiously at half the speed I would drive on a clear road. Fortunately we encounter few cars. After dark the temperature falls steadily from a few degrees above zero to 9 below as we turn into our drive. Pulsing stars and intense moonlight tint the snow a lovely blue. Mercifully, the driveway has been plowed. The snowbanks created are several feet higher than the car. We have to shovel a pathway to our back door—feathery powder—in order to get inside. The house is chilly. Without a bite to eat, without unpacking, we collapse into bed.

I had agreed with Celeste that I would drive to Cleveland the next morning. Given the circumstances, she understands I cannot. Believing, or at least wanting, my respiratory troubles to be in decline, I decide to drive west the following day. This is a mistake. The roads were better and Interstate 90, normally blizzarding from Syracuse to Buffalo, was clear, but I was far from well. When I reached Cleveland at nightfall, the congestion was thick in my chest, and I knew the kind of coughing that would follow. I was not fit for company, but there I was. Celeste had made a restaurant reservation for dinner, which I endured but could not enjoy the evening out. Back at the house, I made straight for bed.

A fitful night of coughing, serial bouts of sleep with lurid dreams in which I failed to meet all kinds of commitments. In the morning my right eye was sealed shut with a kind of goo. I had to pry the lids apart with my fingers. The goo had hardened along my eyelash to a composition with the feel of sea salt. When I looked in the mirror the whites of both eyes were reddish brown. Celeste forbade Lulu to come into the room and wake me, as is our ritual, and I gained perhaps an hour's rest before facing the day.

I am sure my ceaseless coughing and generally impaired condition dampened what would otherwise have been Celeste's very high spirits, as this was a special weekend for her. She was about to celebrate her 49th birthday, resolving that this coming year would represent a fresh approach to life. To symbolize that fresh start she decided to have her head shaved. She did this in conjunction with a national fundraising effort in aid of cancer research. The venture was called St. Baldrick's Day, after an Irish saint, commemorated on the Saturday before St. Patrick's Day. Men and women and children all over the country would, after securing cash pledges from friends and family and neighbors, report to designated centers to be shorn. Celeste had raised an impressive $3,000 in pledges, which she was donating in honor of her late mother. Giddily transported by the prospect of her transformation, Celeste was barely in the waking world on the appointed Saturday.

The mass shearing was to take place in the Cleveland Heights municipal recreation center. Celeste insisted that Lulu and I accompany her and log every minute of the procedure on camera and iPad. The designated room was chock full of people, mainly mothers and children. Beyond a registration table were offerings of sheet cake and cups of sugary soda. Behind a line of eight or nine male and female barbers busily shearing heads, a woman with a microphone stood on a chair and all but inaudibly made a case for the project, praising the various participants and updating the amount of cash pledged and received. Celeste told me this woman was mother of a seven-year-old diagnosed the previous year with leukemia. The room was noisy with the shrieking of children, rather a carnival atmosphere, and it was unbearably warm for me. At one point while Celeste was waiting for her turn to be shorn, I made my way out of the room, and found a bench in a cool recess of the building in order to gather my wits and cough in relative solitude. Celeste found me at once and in some agitation insisted that I return to the shearing room. Clearly my witness was important to her. Fifteen or twenty minutes passed before her name was called and she was seated before a barber, the only attractive young woman among the hair cutters. The woman with the microphone introduced Celeste by name, read the dedication Celeste had written to her mother, Dina, and the total she had raised in pledges—significant applause, as no other individual had raised as much. Lulu holds the iPad in video mode and I ready my phone camera as Celeste's shearing begins. She is clearly elevated with feeling, her eye contact wavering between desperation and exhilaration. Celeste's hair is long, lustrous, rather unruly brunette, descending, when let down, to her shoulder blades. Unbeknownst to me, before the cutting began, one of the senior barbers asked if her hair could be saved for the making of wigs, her hair qualifying for selection both because of its quality and because it had not been treated or dyed. Also unbeknownst to me, Celeste had managed at the last second to negotiate with the cutter something rather less than a shaved head. For twenty-one minutes Lulu and I carefully document with our devices the transformation from long-haired woman to short-haired woman. At each stage, she looks remarkably different, always attractive but attractive in a distinctly different way. I waited with uneasy fascination for her to become shaved bald, but it didn't happen. Just as she reached a rather fetching boyish look, hair shaved up close behind her head and up the sides but with a bit of bangs in front, the cutter tidied her up and set her free. The effect was striking. Celeste, while far from bald, was clearly transformed. It would no doubt have been an expensive procedure in a salon. She has always looked to me an indeterminate age, certainly nothing like forty-nine, but now she clearly looks a younger woman. Her face has good bones, nicely defined cheeks, good chin, and these are now more prominent. Even before she left the barber's chair, I could see she was pleased by what she saw in the mirror. The other women surrounding her admired her extravagantly. She had achieved what she most wanted: a transformation, but without the dramatic oddity of temporary baldness. In any event, Celeste was exuberantly happy.

Before I arrived, sick, Celeste had made a restaurant reservation for the three of us at a favored downtown restaurant for this evening. I tried to be something other than a gloomy coughing specter as we attempted a cocktail hour before driving downtown, but the malaise had contracted me into myself. It was a raw, windy Sunday night, and once seated in the restaurant we realized we were the only diners. In that sepulchral setting I did my best to be agreeable and to keep Lulu amused, but it was a very muted dinner. Poor Celeste, eager for a celebration.

Another night of terrible, household-disturbing coughing, and in the morning it was determined I must see a doctor. Fortunately my old Cleveland doctor, the saintly Debra DeJoseph agreed to fit me into an already crammed schedule of appointments. Five or six years ago, I was granted a similar last-minute appointment for an identical bronchial crisis. In the waiting room, I caught Debra's eye as she stepped out of the examining rooms to consult with her receptionist. It was not my time yet, but as she waved hello, I told her this could be very easy, in that I was in exactly in the same condition as I was the last time she saw me. She laughed and said, "I'm afraid we can't just Xerox this." Later when I was examined it was established that my lungs were clear of pneumonia, and I was given an antibiotic and a codeine cough medicine. It felt good to have a concrete remedy in hand.

That night before I got into bed, I took a swig of the cough medicine. The prescription was for a teaspoonful every four hours or as needed. In my reckoning my swig approximated a teaspoonful. Awakened by coughing some hours later, I took another groggy swig, what may have been a few hours later, another. This final dose sent me into a series of hallucinatory half-waking dreams in which I negotiated at breakneck speed all kinds of crises. When I attempted to rise and dress, I felt I was standing on deck of a ship tossed by heavy seas. I could barely keep my balance walking. Concerned that my bug had progressed into new, worrying symptoms, I gave the cough medicine bottle a close look. My swigs had consumed half the bottle. I had induced an opiate swoon. Idiot.

One of the most compelling reasons for making this trip was to see Lulu perform a solo song in her school's variety show. The evening of the performance I was worried that I would disrupt the proceedings with my cough, but my concern was allayed when I realized the general atmosphere in the auditorium was fairly raucous and that coughing would hardly be noticed. There was quite a series of numbers—tentative sawing away on tiny violins, not quite audible recitations, singers veering away from the tune and rhythm of the attempted song—before Lu took the stage. Clasping the microphone with authority, she belted out a Taylor Swift pop hit. Lulu was plenty loud, in tune, lyrics audible, but what carried the performance was her assuming the posture and the plaintive facial gestures appropriate to the song's pining after love gone wrong. I was touched by the fact that, at eight, Lulu is an eager, unselfconscious performer. May that never change.

The next morning, probably to Celeste's relief, certainly mine, I headed off, through light snow flurries, on the long drive home. I tried to reassure Lulu as she was dressing for school that the next time I saw her I would not be sick and coughing and that we would have days of furious fun. I don't know if my condition improved at all in the course of driving back, but it was a terrific relief to know that I was no longer bothering anybody.

March 21-April 5, 2014: I make firm resolves to restore my underperforming body to vigorous health. The solitude and regularity of routines in Ripton should serve me in this. First commitment: a serious diet. It would be good to cleanse the system after this bout of respiratory distress. I could also stand to lose fifteen or twenty pounds. Imperfectly monitored measures of moderation have not served me well. I have to do the real thing, the very astringent Dr. Rau diet, a regimen of mainly fruits and vegetables and unprocessed grains. M and I have done it before, M for cleansing, I out of curiosity. It is a challenge, especially for the first week. For one thing, there is not much to eat, and absolutely nothing in the saline, savory category I find most satisfying. But once you get going, confidence builds that you can stick it out. Several years ago, when M and I did it the first time, I was impressed that, unlike practically every dietary scheme I had tried before, I actually got thinner pretty quickly. Very reinforcing. So here I go.

Morning: a cup of vegetable broth (instead of coffee or tea), a "green drink" (blended smoothie of banana, apple, and kale), a few spoonsful of unsweetened oatmeal. Lunch: a soup of vegetable broth with the constituent vegetables left in, a mélange of squash and kale. Supper: a baked potato, broccoli and cauliflower. There are variations, including quinoa, millet and brown rice. I feel altered at once, not necessarily in a good way. Eating less and eating this restricted regimen does not feel too great a hardship, as my appetite has not been strong since the onset of my sickness. I mainly feel weak, digestion a bit uncertain, and generally relieved when a meal is over. It is hard to know what to attribute this slightly impaired condition, whether the ravages from having been sick for two weeks, the digestive impact of the antibiotics prescribed, or the new diet. Impossible to determine, and I decide I do not care. By the third or fourth day, it is clear that I am losing weight. I can see a new gauntness in my face when I look in the mirror, and I can feel a detectable absence of pressure against the waistband of my slacks when I buckle my belt. I don't like to weigh myself, especially when dieting, but I am weighed whenever I go to the doctor. I was weighed when I went to Dr. DeJoseph in Cleveland, and I was weighed ten days later when I checked in with my doctor here. Both times I was wearing winter clothes, shoes, and my pockets were full, but between the two appointments I had apparently lost eight pounds. Encouraged by this, I have held fast to the rigors of the diet— truer even than M who occasionally toasts a thick slice of wheat bread and tops it with butter and peanut butter.

The Rau diet forbids alcohol, and I thought this might create a pang around the news hour when I would typically prepare a substantial, unmeasured cocktail. Again, the receding illness or antibiotics may have been a factor, but I have not missed or wanted booze at all. I also have a feeling alcohol may have played a bigger part in my weight gain than any other element of my food intake. In any event, moving into the third week, the diet no longer feels like any kind of imposition. The respiratory distress has at last receded, and I have finished the ten-day course of antibiotics. I am two belt notches and one pants size to the good, and I feel I have entered that stage of dieting in which I no longer feel I am feebly enduring a deprivation. Today I feel aggressively, and a bit vainly, in charge. I think I will continue with this program until I see a good reason to change it. Might I, for instance, become too thin?

My second positive resolve to restore my health was to check with my doctor, William Barrett, about what should be done about my navel, which over the past decade has progressed from a puzzling enlargement to a distinct bulge. Apparently there has been a breach in the muscle wall, and the navel has become herniated. It will be a good idea to have this corrected surgically, Dr. Barrett suggests. The little bulge causes me no distress beyond an annoyance that it is there, but Dr. Barrett outlines a number of serious troubles that could lie ahead. We schedule an appointment with a local surgeon, Dr. Fuller, who, like Barrett, assures me that I have no serious problem but it is best to correct the hernia, so Monday morning, April 7, I will rise early, shower and scrub my belly with a special soap, eat or drink nothing and report to Porter hospital, where I will be knocked out and surgically corrected for about an hour and a half. If all goes well M can drive me home an hour or so afterwards. Sounds very straightforward. I have never had a surgery. Will report.

April 8, 2014: I am sitting gingerly upright as I type this, so as not to stress the wound from yesterday's operation. The surgeon, Dr. Fuller, the anesthesiologist, Dr. Calhoun, and a handful of nurses prepared me thoroughly for what would happen, and it happened just as they said. M drove me to the hospital, where I registered and was sent to the surgical center. I undressed, donned my gown, and the nurses hooked up the IV apparatus to the back of my left hand. Another nurse shaved my belly and asked me to inscribe my initials on my belly button with a purple felt pen—this apparently so that there is no doubt about the location of the procedure to be attempted. At first the IV drip was just a hydrating solution and antibiotics, but once wheeled inside the surgery room, the anesthesia was introduced into the same port.

Everybody who spoke to me was cheery and brisk, which I took as a promising sign. I was not aware that the anesthesia was actually being introduced until Dr. Calhoun peered down at me and said I should be feeling very sleepy. I did not feel especially sleepy, although I was aware of a great peacefulness as I stared up into the concentric circles of fluorescent bulbs overhead. Then everything progressed into a kind of agreeable blur. I listened to the surgeon and the nurses bantering as they went about their ministrations on the nether side of the curtain separating my upper and lower body. I was in a pleasant mood as I felt a very gentle prodding in the vicinity of my navel. The impression was of fingertips tentatively probing the skin about my belly button. It was impossible to imagine anything invasive, anything like *cutting*. At one point, it occurred to me that I could contribute to the banter, and I made a point or two, which seemed to surprise no one at the working end of the table. The procedure was completed in about an hour and a half, but it felt to me like a very few minutes.

M was waiting for me in the recovery room. The nurses chatted with us for a while, telling us about the pain medications we would pick up at the pharmacy. I was still anesthetized enough to be able to put my clothes on without any noticeable discomfort. I felt clear headed as we walked out of the surgery center in the direction of the car. I was told I should not attempt to drive for a week but, mistakenly or not, I am sure I could have driven us home. We picked up the prescriptions and once back in the house, I made myself comfortable on the yellow room sofa, answered emails, read and dozed till dinner time. The whole business seemed eerily easy. Getting ready for bed later, I was aware of a tenderness along the incision, the seam bound together tightly with a clear circular bandage. There was some discomfort in the course of the night, a kind of insistent stinging, but nothing that could not be endured. I slept only intermittently, my thoughts returning to the orderliness and ease of the procedure. I had not known what to expect. Never having been operated on before, I suppose I carried a bit of my childhood notions into the proceedings.

When I was a boy the idea of "operations"—cutting into the flesh and manipulating or removing things inside—was the most repellant, frightening thing I could imagine. The very design and integrity of the body implied the wrongness of cutting into it, spilling blood and exposing viscera so clearly meant to be contained within. I was not aware of consciously bringing any of this revulsion into today's procedure, but I think it must have been at work even as I outwardly did my best to make it a pleasant, or at least undramatic, experience. And while Dr. Fuller took pains to tell me exactly what would happen in the course of the surgery—how the incision would be made, what muscles and tissues would be manipulated, that a mesh screen would be inserted inside my navel and stitched into place-- I refused to picture any of it. Before the procedure was scheduled I had made my own mental picture of what would be done. The parted muscle wall that had allowed intestinal tissue to come forward and make a bulge would be sewn together, keeping the innards in. I wanted it to be that simple. And I wanted it to be over. God bless those dutiful, skilled, and disciplined people who know better.

April 14, 2014: First shirt-sleeve warm day of the year. Beyond the back deck the river is brown and frothy, moving fast down the mountain with the last of the winter's snow melt. Soft air and bright sun make it impossible to stay indoors so, belly wound be damned, I hike the three-mile loop around Ripton and can feel the sun on my face for the rest of the day.

In the afternoon I drive myself to Porter hospital to have my incision scar checked by Dr. Fuller. I unbutton my shirt. He probes the incision up and down, presses in, asks me to cough, asks if I feel pain (no), have I needed pain medication (no), any problem moving about (no), bowels moving (yes), comfortable driving (yes). In two minutes I am on my way.

In the evening I address the Hawthorne Society of Middlebury on the plight of boys in the contemporary world. I was invited to give the talk months ago by my old college dean and now friend Dennis O'Brien. The Hawthorne Society is the vestige of a literary society formed in the 1840s originally composed of the president of the college and various dignitaries from the town, the pastor of the Congregationalist Church, president of the Bank, etc. Today, while membership is still selective and self-generated, it seems a looser

collection of college staff and townspeople. Average age appeared to
be mid-seventies. Dennis, who presently presides over the Society,
confided to me over a recent luncheon that he would not be
disappointed if the group decided to disband and, as he put it, "recede
back into the nineteenth century."

The Society meets at The Ilsley Library in town. M decided she
would like to come, and so we arrived and greeted many of the
venerable members before the talk began. I decided to mix in bits of
my own work with boys at University School with the past half
century's concerns about boys failing to thrive generally, concluding
with the positive findings from Mike Reichert's and my recent studies
of effectively teaching boys and of the centrality of relationship in the
process. In hindsight, a bit too much to cover in 45 minutes, but I got
through it without, I think, losing my listeners. Their questions after
were thoughtful, and they were generous in their praise of the
presentation. The night before I had an anxiety dream in which I was
giving the presentation not about boys but about the novels of Anthony
Powell—to a group of inattentive ten-year-olds at some sort of indoor
recreation center. By dream's close, the boys had all scampered out of
the room to play ball, and I was left alone holding the sheaf of my
remarks in my hand. By comparison, my actual talk was something of
a pleasure. I left the library hoping that I would continue to know some
of the people M and I had met.

April 19-26, 2014: A full week of Lulu, her spring vacation from
school. The theme is excursions and adventures, which suits me after
what has felt to me like a period of convalescence since my umbilical
surgery. We ignore weather forecasts and proceed as if it is high
summer: zoo, aquarium, two different water parks. At first I beg off
joining Lulu on the roller coaster-like water park slides where from
atop a high platform you descend in an inner tube through twisted
watery chutes at colossal speed before splashing down in a shallow
pool at the base of the structure. Lulu is mad for these, and by the
second day I relent and join her, quite glad to realize that the exertion
places no special strain on my incision wound. It is clear that I am

healed. Lulu and I bob up and down in a simulated wave pool. By days' end she has tried every ride and game in the park. Later, showered and a bit dressed up, we dine at leisure, all treats allowed. Lulu eats the little she is going to eat—a French fry or two, a few bites of steak—within minutes of our arrival at the restaurant. We pass the time playing hangman. Back home and in pajamas, we play poker and other card games. If Celeste is tired and wants to go to bed early, Lulu and I read a few chapters of a book about a sad girl and the closeness she feels to dolphins. Our last night together we somehow get on the subject of dancing, and we watch on-line video after video of Fred Astaire doing his famous numbers, some solo, some with Ginger Rogers or Eleanor Powell. Lulu is transfixed. A good sign. In fact, a very good week. I feel invigorated, healed, back in the world. On the plane home it occurs to me that Lulu was not for one minute moody, unpleasant, fussy, angry. That is an achievement in an eight-year-old. Upon rising until retiring in her bunk quite late, she is sunny, funny, full of questions and ideas. She speaks well, articulates clearly. I could look into that face and listen to that voice forever. What a blessing—strange blessing though it may be—for me to have this love at age 69.

April 29, 2014: Just below the frantic surface of the daily news—a disappeared Malaysian jetliner with all aboard, murderous tornadoes sweeping up through the southern states, Russia's steady incursions into feeble Ukraine—is a kind of melancholy reckoning, expressed by a variety of pundits from different angles, to the effect that the prevailing order, what has been called The American Century, is dissolving. Two days ago the *NY Times* reported that the American middle class is no longer the world's wealthiest. A day or two before that the Times carried a long piece on how, after a half century and billions expended, our War on Poverty has posted no victories. The essay focused on McDowell County, the poorest county in West Virginia, passed over coal country where the grim subsistence living conditions of poor whites stimulated JFK and then Lyndon Johnson to launch a sweeping series of federal aid programs. Today, the denizens of McDowell County are if anything worse off, public assistance providing most of the income. Children who manage to graduate from high school and attend college leave the region for better prospects. Those who stay become mired in alcohol, meth, and other drugs. Most of the young men do jail time. All of that seems very isolated and local, but I suppose the McDowell County conditions are not far removed from those just off the paved roads in Ripton. Last night's NBC news included a finding that American high school graduation rates have *risen* to eighty per cent—and this was represented as a positive finding.

Dreadful, featherweight columnists like Maureen Dowd of the *Times* fills her column with junior high sniping at President Obama for being weak and unmanly in not forcibly opposing the land grabs of Vladimir Putin in Ukraine and in otherwise failing to make the world right for her. Whereas David Brooks, who actually *thinks* about social movements in historical context, invites Times readers to see our historical moment as one in which the United States, since World War II the dominant force in global affairs and the leading proponent, despite all bad guesses, errors, and contradictions, of democratic political process and individual liberty, is being brought low by "a thousand cuts." The cuts in question consist of the likes of the Russian incursion into Ukraine, the Egyptian military's dismantling of its duly elected government, the persistence of a noxious regime in Syria in failing to yield to or make peace with its revolutionaries, the teetering regimes in Iraq and Afghanistan, nearly certain to descend into sectarian warfare and repression in the aftermath of the U.S.'s military presence. There are other "cuts" from African rogue states, from Indian Ocean pirates, from China's new willingness to claim Pacific islands as their own. As Brooks points out, none of these "cuts" is in itself worthy of massive expense or substantial military intervention. We have neither the resources nor the will to resolve all of these conflicts. And because we do not, there are new incentives for both established and rogue regimes to move on the less powerful and to gain advantage. There is no longer, Brooks proposes, a real or perceived world hegemon. And thus our news is the progress of "death by a thousand cuts."

It is sobering for me, entering true old age, to think of the nation losing status, losing momentum, losing prosperity, losing purpose. I would be pleased to have someone tell me all of that is just a projection of my own decline. And I would gladly accept that verdict, if it were not for the fact that the decline in question is no construction of mine. It is the news of the hour, just behind the missing planes and tornadoes and earthquakes. It is cut after cut after cut.

When I taught Roman history to the ninth graders of University School, I liked to linger on the reign of the Antonines through Marcus Aurelius, the so-called Pax Romana when Roman law, Roman buildings, Roman roads, Roman culture were uniformly dominant throughout Europe and the Mediterranean. I liked to imagine some Roman magistrate quartered comfortably in a villa in Britain or Spain or the Levant--imagine his certainty that this Pax, this regime, was eternal. Not unlike me, assuming the continuity and rightness of liberal democratic life from my cozy outpost in Ripton, Vermont.

May 1, 2014: Another brain worm from the daily news: there has been a botched execution of a condemned man in an Oklahoma federal prison. The European firms that manufacture the chemicals used in the death-bearing injections have apparently decided they want no part of what they believe to be the inhumane business of capital punishment and have stopped shipping. In consequence the prison authorities in Oklahoma improvised what they thought might do the trick in executing a man convicted of the murder of a woman he had brutally assaulted, shot, then buried alive. Civilian witnesses to his ultimately lethal injection reported that it did not go as planned. It took nearly three quarters of an hour to kill the man, and some of the observers said the condemned man looked visibly uncomfortable, appeared to suffer. An attorney connected to the deceased described his late client's ordeal as "torture." In today's news European states are apparently in an uproar over such penal savagery. For the past two days the picture of the murderer—a scowling, unshaven visage, almost certainly a police mug shot—has been all over the front pages and TV news programs. Oklahoma prison authorities have launched a "thorough review" of what went wrong. Capital punishment adversaries are calling for a moratorium on all scheduled executions.

What is wrong with me that I cannot feel that a significant wrong has occurred in this instance? If we are going to execute vicious killers with lethal injections, I agree that the process should be as quick and painless as medicine can devise and that it was unfortunate that the Oklahoma murderer suffered more than he might have. But I am unable to see it as a significant misfortune. I am not opposed to executing vicious killers. In fact, when their guilt is determined beyond a doubt, I think it would be a great service to society and to them to dispatch them immediately. Considering the alternatives—firing squads, electrocution, hanging—lethal injection seems both a quick and humane method of ending a life. It is what, truth be told, physicians and nurses do every day with the graduated doses of morphine administered to patients in pain and near death. Moreover, as I have observed these ministrations given to my mother, I believe that doctors and nurses are very good at it. As I have written already, the two injections given to put down my dog Vickie—the first to anesthetize the site of the final, lethal injection—caused not a twitch of discomfort in Vickie as I held her in my arms, and she was gone in an instant. This procedure involved no foreign laboratories or exotic chemistry. Why was it so hard for the Oklahoma prison staff?

But the bigger question: why has this killer's somewhat prolonged death stirred people's hearts and minds? Is it some quantifiable amount of underserved pain he endured? That he suffered? Are vicious killers to be spared suffering? Does it matter that he was not intentionally made to suffer, that he was not "tortured," that the faulty injection was mistake? I wish I could talk to someone passionately upset by the Oklahoma incident. I would want to ask for whom and what are they feeling. To those opposed to executing anybody for anything, I would want to ask if they think something precious and sacred is being killed, or if they feel biological vitality is itself sacred and precious. If so, is death always an insult, always a mistake? If it is not mere vitality, but something sacred and precious within that person, I would want to ask if they think that sacred and precious quality can be killed along with the person. I agree with Socrates who at his trial chided his prosecutors for thinking that if they executed him for being devoted to the truth, they could somehow extinguish the truth that had so inspired him. What exactly is the wrong that the Oklahoma murderer suffered in his delayed execution? And how momentous a wrong is it?

I asked at the outset "what was wrong with me" in being unmoved by the account of this execution. It is not a rhetorical question. There could well be something wrong, and I would honestly like to know what it is. I was alternately frustrated and amused that my father, as he progressed into his eighties, became an ardent advocate of capital punishment. From his sunny study in Walnut Creek, California, he would write long, strident letters to the local papers and to the San Francisco dailies admonishing politicians, police, prosecutors, prison authorities to "get on with it," stop wasting tax payers' money on housing and feeding deadbeat killers for years and years, etc. Occasionally he would send me copies of the letters. I would ask him, "Why does this concern you?" "Do you *know* any condemned killers, know anything about them or their lives or their circumstances? Why are you so suddenly angered about this?" He had no answers to these questions. My asking only deepened his conviction that so many clearly rotten people—killers—were biding their time, unkilled, in California prisons. Exasperated, I let the matter drop. So perhaps I am merely growing into my dad, which sheds little light on the rightness or wrongness of his convictions.

May 2, 2014: Living for forty years in Cleveland might have taught me to be patient in waiting for spring to make its mark, but no. Is it just age that makes me long for a reliable softening of the air, buds, first leaves, a crocus, a daffodil? Frost: "Nature's first green is gold / Her hardest hue to hold." We are now into May, and the Ripton air is still icy hard. The woods are a monotonous brown-gray. Driving down the mountain to Middlebury, there are still clumps of grimy snow clutching the incline just beyond the berm. It is time, it is past time, for more light, for breaking through this wintery drear. Florida was rich and sensuous, the sun and heat like a gluttonous meal, but it did not carry. I returned to the north with murderous bronchial flu. Frost called this hiatus "mud time," and I'm sure mud is prevailing in pastures and unpaved byways. Mud mood prevails all day.

Yes, I think it is age, as in how many more springs have I got coming? Is this non-arrival a hint of the ultimate non-arrival, that destined season I will never see? For the time being, *pax* Eliot, April is not the cruelest month / breeding lilacs out of the dead land / mixing memory with desire, etc. April was winter and mud time, breeding nothing out of the dead land, and May is so far crueler. I walk the dreary dun-colored loop around Ripton. Temperature in the 40's, lowering clouds, intermittent rain. The river is the color of coffee and cream except where it froths up icy gray over the rocks. Hardscrabble. All of Vermont is playing hardscrabble.

May 10-12, 2014: Another visit with Lulu and Celeste, this one en route to California where I will see Claire in action with her students, then spend time with sister Ginny, our first time together without the subtext of caring for our parents.

Two and a half glorious, distinctly big city days with Celeste and Lu. After so much lingering winter chill in Ripton, it is bright and humid and warm in the midwest. No matter how much clothing I shed, I am steamy warm. But it is welcome. We visit the aquarium where Lu is rapt, obsessed with photographing the exotic, eerily lit fish with my phone camera. We go to the zoo, where the twin highlights are a solitary polar bear swimming endless identical circuits around an aquamarine pool that is part of his constructed "habitat." Celeste wants to think the bear is exuberant. I am certain that it is depressed to the point of madness and is discharging that awful energy in its relentless laps. There is a glassed viewing place below water level where the enormous bear's face swoops by inches from ours. Celeste believes the bear is hungry for contact. I think the bear is hungry for the viewers behind the maddening glass wall.

The other riveting attraction is a mother ape with two adorable babies. One baby, almost certainly a boy, is climbing and swinging on great stalks of bamboo. The other baby is nursing at its mother's breast. The mother is seated, legs extended before her, her back erect. Her baby kneels between her legs, mouth to her nipple, an arm dangling around its mother's neck. The mother is motionless, her great head canted down over her baby as if in deep reverie. At this moment I am dumbfounded that there was ever a time when observers did not immediately see that apes were ancestors, not some safely "lower" gradation of being. This is not a sentimental thought. In clear sunlight, something in the atmospheric particles connecting the nursing mother and child to me conveys a bond, a certainty of our relatedness.

We also take in a touring Broadway show--*Motown*--which is goose-bump stirring from beginning to end. I marvel again that there can be so many talented performers, men and women who can combine the virtuoso singing and dancing and acrobatics demanded by these shows. I am transported and happy to notice that Lulu seems to be as well. This may be our fifth Broadway show, and she is just eight. Lucky Duck.

All the rest of our time seemed to be spent dressing up for, finding, and then dining at fancy restaurants. Lulu's selections run only to buttery noodles with an occasional taste of steak, but she senses the elevation of these bustling places, and we enjoy ourselves. I try but fail to keep some semblance of my astringent, mainly vegetarian diet. I also have cocktails and wine, in a spirit of what the hell.

While I am with Lulu I have the impression that she is somehow printing herself onto me as a photograph might be melded into a collage. She is in every agreeable sense a little girl of eight, but there is an ageless, intelligent directness to her company that seems to forge a deep wordless connection. I feel it all day and wonder if she does also. Love that girl (as her mother tells me seventy times a day).

May 12-14, 2014: At Union Station in Chicago I board Amtrak's California Zephyr from which I will disembark near daughter Claire in San Francisco. I have been looking forward to this trip, especially west of Denver where the train ascends through the Rockies. All is well as I board, the roomette sleeper with just me in it feels commodious. I like the familiar jostle and sway as the train makes its way through the western suburbs, then exurbs with just a few tract houses and a name on an elevated water tower, then the flatland farms, the Mississippi, Iowa.

As the dinner hour approaches, I go to the club car for a bourbon on the rocks, which I take up to the glass vaulted observation car. Late afternoon sunlight on newly plowed fields skirting barns and silos and the occasional copse of trees shading a farmhouse.

I am seated in the dining car opposite an elderly African American man who is a retired professor of educational psychology at an Indiana college, and a man about my age in a ball cap, a builder from Battle Creek, Michigan. We get on easily, share our destinations, family details, try to summarize our work. At one point the professor and I realize we have some research interests —developmental psychology, the plight of boys —in common. There follows the exchange of writers' names, studies, books common to those kinds of discussions. After a minute or two of this, the builder says, very winsomely, "I'm just the opposite of you two. I don't read books, I don't write anything, and I can't even use the computer." We adjust the conversation in the direction of inclusiveness, in the course of which it emerges, impressively, that the builder has built a palace of a dream house for himself and owns substantial holdings.

As we finished our meal I, seated on the side of the table facing the forward direction of the train, noted ominously darkening sky approaching. The professor said that he had seen severe storms in the forecast for the region. In minutes the sky outside the window is blue-black, the glass streaming with the downpour.

Back in my compartment, I read and wrote emails as true night fell. I was under the impression that the storms had passed, but in the morning we were awakened with the announcement that the train was running late, mainly due to being slowed by severe weather — including a tornado we narrowly missed but which devastated a small Nebraska town lying along the tracks. Heading to the dining car to breakfast I was alerted by another amplified announcement that severe weather west of Denver had caused rockslides closing our route to

California. In consequence the train would be hitched to another train in Denver, and we would now proceed to San Francisco via Cheyenne, Wyoming, and Salt Lake City. Apart from the delay, I am disappointed that I will miss the spectacular mountain vistas promised along the scheduled route. Confirming this disappointment as we finally make our altered way out of Denver is how strikingly stark and featureless the city is, both its undistinguished downtown skyline and the miles and miles of low-slung industrial storage buildings and strip retail ringing the city center. I would attribute this impression to mood, except that this has also been my response to Denver on prior visits.

I have now been aboard the train for two and a half days. It is mid-morning, and I am sitting in the glass-all-around observation car taking in the sere khaki colored serrations of western Nevada under a pale cloudless sky. I am convinced that even more than walking or bicycle-ing —and of course more than flying —riding the train provides the deepest immersion in terrain. There is no distraction. You just look and look at thousands of contiguous acres of what you are passing through. Now, for instance, I can feel this seemingly eternal stretch of Nevada printing itself onto my nervous system, the way an image prints itself on photographic paper. This was also what I felt passing through the Iowa and Nebraska flatlands and the Martian wastes of Utah. Five years ago, I drove by myself coast to coast, and that drive wakened some dormant sense memories —especially the clean, piney smell of the West from the Rockies westward —and imprinted some new ones. This trip, perhaps because I am narrating in real time, is printing images into what I am certain will be permanent memory. There is something else going on, harder to describe, something active and alive in the visual conversation I seem to be having with the vistas illuminated before me. It feels as if there is a kind of affection in the transmission, not something wanting to be loved, but *offering* a kind of love. I know this is why I wanted so much to make this trip. I am trying to be open to this message, this transmission.

By late morning the train passes over the Donner Pass, the steep drop below the train window extending down to a jade green lake girded with pines, behind which a sequence of green hills rise before the tree line breaks, baring the humps and peaks of snow covered Sierras. I take pictures with my iPad camera, and they are faintly suggestive of the reality, but I cannot capture the heights or depths. When I view the images on my device, they are pretty enough, but misleadingly settled. I will forego the camera from now on and try harder to empty my mind of intentions and interpretations. Again, these vistas are sending something, offering something. The message is too big and too old for my tiny powers of reception, but I will try anyway to reduce what is happening to just the scene before me.

May 12-13, 2014: Though the extended train ride was a highly distinctive pleasure, it is good to relax in the comfortable rooms of my favorite San Francisco hotel, the Majestic, on the corner of Sutter and Gough. It is especially good to shower thoroughly and at length, unbuffeted by the movements of the train. I have not exercised beyond moving from roomette to dining car for three days, and the sunny inclines of San Francisco streets are a bracing corrective. Except to visit with Claire at her new apartment in the Sunset district and to dine with her, my principal desire is to walk until I am exhausted.

Friday morning I rise early and take a cab to Claire's apartment from which we drive over the Bay Bridge to the charter school in Oakland where she teaches its first graders, nearly all of them Hispanic. The neighborhood is down-at-heel residential. The school's modest but serviceable facilities occupy what had been some kind of church. We arrive a half hour before the children, and Claire is busy preparing paper material she will hand out to her students in the course of the school day. As the children arrive, they are supposed to wait outdoors on the school's concrete play space until their all-school morning meeting, but many of them shyly poke their heads inside the door of the classroom to greet Claire. While she is at work, I note a pleasing complexity of exhibits—student work, posters illustrating the Water Cycle, etc.—covering every wall surface and suspended from the ceiling. The rectangular room is organized into several distinct settings: a cluster of desks for composing and computing, a carpeted seating area for group instruction, a table and chair positioned for individual conferences or tutoring. Everywhere there are labeled bins of art supplies and other materials. The overall effect is visually stimulating, an impression that someone has taken great care.

The school day starts with the whole student body, grades K through 8, assembled by class in an enclosed outdoor courtyard, onto which each classroom door opens. There are a few general announcements, including that Ms. Hawley's father is a special guest today. I am given a loud cheerful greeting and respond with what I hope is a gracious wave. A lively young teacher of kindergarten leads the morning program from the metal steps joining the first and second floors of the school. There are two amplified songs to which the children are encouraged to dance, imitating the moves of their respective teachers. Some of the teachers seem to lack confidence in executing their dance moves, but Claire is an enthusiastic dynamo, and her students follow, gyrating with impressive attention.

It is hard to describe adequately what transpires once Claire and her students (and I) are gathered into her classroom. The children are excited that Ms. Hawley's (Meez Oley's) father has come to their class. They are uninhibited in disclosing things to me: "I *love Meez Oley. She is never mean, except sometimes when the boys are bad.*" When I first observed them lining up for morning meeting, they looked to be a homogenous group of small, coffee-colored children, for the most part nicely turned out for the day. Within minutes of watching them interact with Claire and with each other, each became distinct, and I quickly associated names and faces: Nahomy, Luis, Fernando, Ashley, Jocelyn, Carlos...

I know that a father's perspective could well distort my assessment of Claire's performance, but I am certain anyone in the school business would certify her a masterful teacher. She succeeded both in commanding expected behavior and in conveying instructions and subject content. I doubt that 22 closely gathered students at University School under my watch—in any grade, much less first— would have attended more closely and been more quickly responsive. Claire explained to me earlier that she has adopted an approach in which she more or less "narrates" continuously what is going on in the classroom. The narration includes her instructions to her students as to what they will be doing and how they are expected to be doing it from minute to minute, as well as her presentation of specific lessons and material. The flow of her narration breaks only when the children answer questions or offer observations. I am impressed that Claire is sharply observant of behaviors I fail to notice as the class goes about its business. Apart from her presentation of specific material, her narration is a series of praises. "Carlos, I like the way you were first to quietly take your place in line." "Luis is paying such good attention to Jocelyn as she describes her drawing." "Fernando is generously sharing his markers with Jocelyn." There is little doubt that these repeated praises—I heard not a single admonishment from Claire in the course of the day—have produced the attentive and engaged behavior so attractively apparent in her students. I was also interested in Claire's assigning an individual student to monitor the praiseworthy and problem behavior of classmates in the course of creating projects or participating in the all-school meeting. The designated monitor noted the desired and undesired behaviors on a pad attached to a clipboard and duly reported her findings to the assembled class at Claire's request. The children named, whether positively or negatively, responded with grave acceptance. This practice seemed to stimulate the children's awareness of their social impact, especially on the part of the designated monitor, an assignment shared equally by all of the students.

It did not surprise me that Claire is liked and likable in class. I believe she really loves each of her charges and has a ferocious commitment to their ultimate success and of the school's success. What did surprise me is how hard she works at it, how disciplined her planning and preparation, her ability to monitor with seemingly multiple eyes the children at work about the classroom. The climate created is affectionate and safe—to the extent that *I* wanted to participate and try my hand at the proposed projects. Foundational to the children's ease and willingness to contribute was Claire's masterful discipline and control of the process from the moment the first child entered the classroom.

May 17-20, 2014: Replete with what was a very satisfying spell in San Francisco I flew south to Los Angeles to spend three days with my sister and her friends. The prospect of spending hours on end with my sister, without the overwhelming subtext of caring for our parents, is both pleasing and strange.

A terrific heat wave—105 plus—has just broken in LA, and my days are breezy and clear under bright, sharp sun. I am reminded again how aversive and uninteresting I used to think Los Angeles was, including Glendale where my sister lives. I see now that the aversion was no more than my inability to reconcile the distinctive look and feel of southern California with my familiar and favorite places in Ohio and New England. There is really no continuity in the landscapes of the American Northeast and Southwest. It has taken me a long time, about 20 years, to open my eyes to what is there, and what is there when I arrive in Glendale is street after street of immaculately tended Spanish style homes, the stucco washed pink or mustard or khaki colored, roofs of tubular orange tile. The crisp air is pungent with eucalyptus. Tendrils of brilliant pink and red bougainvillea spill over the walls and rooftops of the houses and garages. The boughs of the jacaranda trees are thick with blue and violet blossoms. Through gaps in the branches ridges of mountains, their foliage burnt to dull gold, rise with surprising authority. In every way the prospect before me is as dramatic as Ripton in its most brilliant light, but as I gradually and gratefully learn, it is a different drama.

Glendale and Burbank have now through steady visiting over the years become something close to an alternate home. I can now comfortably navigate main arteries and residential streets. I have favorite walks, favorite restaurants. I know what shops sell what. With my sister and her friends, now my friends, as a social base, I could move in and settle in easily, as I might also in New York, San Francisco, Cleveland, Chicago, or Cambridge, England. Most of my friends, I think, have identified their lives within a specific place; with me it has become places.

My days and nights with my sister are a running succession of convivial gatherings, guests entertained at her house or gathered at restaurants. Ginny has discovered an intriguing bar called, I believe, The Red Door. It is located behind a commercial strip on the main street of Toluca Lake. You proceed through parking lots down what looks like an alley of garages and refuse bins to a...red door, recessed a few yards under an overhanging roof. No sign, no lights, just a dully painted red door. Inside it is almost impossible to make your way forward because it is so dark, but perhaps twenty yards ahead are the glitter of bar lights and bottles, also four oversize TV screens, each playing a vintage black and white movie—the Red Shoes, Dracula, City Lights, etc.—without the sound. When my eyes finally adjust I see that it is a spacious place, with comfortable seating, sofas and upholstered chairs clustered around low tables. There is also a substantial L-shaped bar with stools. When Ginny and I arrive, one of her friends, Jackie, is already seated and waiting for us. In the hour and a half or so while we are there, seven or eight of my sister's friends and colleagues drop in for a drink and lively talk. I immediately warm to the place. It is more spacious and comfortable than a typical bar, and it doesn't have the neighborhood cheeriness of a pub. Even when my eyes adjust, it is very dark, globed candles on the tabletops, the bar lights, and the TV screens providing the only illumination. It occurs to me that beyond the chatting faces huddled together in our group, I can barely see the other people scattered about the room, only the flickering of the candles at their tables. My trysting days are long over, but I cannot get it out of my head what a perfect place The Red Door would be for meeting a lover. The prospect has no present reason to stimulate me, but it does.

The Red Door aside, there is a good deal of drinking in the evenings in my sister's world. I may not have noted this if M and I had not stopped having cocktails before dinner at home. Weeks earlier when we began this abstinence—M in the interest of spiritual discipline, I hoping to accelerate weight loss —I thought I would feel a woeful pang at evening news time when we would typically turn on the TV, sip and nibble on something. Not only did no pang present itself, after a day or so it seemed unimaginable to have a drink before dinner. A drink, I felt, would make me want to take a nap. So abstinence proved to be no hardship—and I am certain it contributed to my losing maybe twenty pounds in just a little over a month. I could see no reason to remain abstinent during my brief visit in California though, as usual, I found my evening drinks, gin martinis, a welcome pleasure. I tried to monitor what particular effects and diminishments drinking caused in me, but it was hard to tell. I would be interested in what an external observer might report. My guess is that I am more animated when drinking, my voice a little louder. Also my piano playing may get sloppier, a crucial chord in a seldom played song missed or forgotten.

May 20-22, 2014: Home in Ripton, but not in my right mind for almost a day. I mistakenly thought it was a good idea to take a red eye flight home departing at 10 p.m. from Burbank, arriving at 6 a.m. at New York, with a few hours layover then a quick flight up to Burlington and home. I assumed I would sleep at least a little on the plane, possibly even doze at the airport during the layover, but I was wide awake for the duration. I arrived home in the thin, papery condition I recall from my college days when I would stay up all night, also unwisely, studying for some dreaded exam. I am clearly too old for this. I was in utterly unproductive recovery mode for a full day.

It occurs to me as I review my trip west that at least three times I recorded the impression that certain experiences—long hours with Lulu, watching a mother ape and her baby at the zoo, extended viewing of the western landscape from the observation car of the California Zephyr—seemed to be "imprinting" themselves onto my conscious-ness. What is novel in this impression is not the obvious fact that experiences do indeed impress themselves on one's mental interior and are thus retrievable from time to time, but rather that I seemed for sustained spells of time *aware* of the imprinting process, could feel it. Moreover, as I noted while passing through the Sierras into California, it wasn't a mere transmission of visual data to mental storage but also a *message* of some kind, an offering that seemed to carry with it a kind of affection. It was as if the panoramas passing before me were saying something like "this is an offering to you," an offering—considering the height and depth and beauty of what was passing before me—I knew I was incapable of taking in fully, though I strained in a very pleasurable, elevated state to take in as much of it as I could, which required shutting down interpretation, analysis and, to the degree I could manage it, the production of or attention to words.

This notion of experiences transmitting a message or *meaning* behind the sense impressions went deep with me. I cannot stop thinking about it. Logically, one of two possibilities would seem to be true: the experiences evoking the impression of meaningful transmission—a message—are either doing just that, or else I am projecting some inner need for such messages onto experiences that carry no such intention or perhaps, with respect to the mountain vistas, no capacity to transmit anything intentional. Assuming that the first alternative is true, that these experiences are conveying intentional, meaningful messages, then it is tempting to think that I have arrived at some new, advanced sensitivity—including the awareness that the world is in fact conveying all kinds of heretofore imperceptible messages. But given the rest of what I sense is going on as I age, I doubt that any new, higher, more refined powers arrive in one's advanced years. More likely, what look like new, clearer perceptions are the result of prior mental structures, those developed in youth to screen distracting stimuli from practical consciousness, having broken down with age, just as physical coordination, balance, and mobility break down. Certain breakdowns in prior adaptive function can produce positive benefits, as when in middle age the hemispheral brain dominance that made it difficult for me simultaneously to play different cadences and sequences on the piano with my right and left hands began to deteriorate, with the result that my piano playing became more dexterous and inventive. The "improvement" in my playing was the result of the degeneracy of a prior adaptation. Similarly with the experiential "messages" I seem to be receiving; far from indicating a new capacity to perceive, my prior ability to filter out distracting and practically unhelpful elements of experience may have at last broken down to the extent that mountains have been liberated from their prior categorization of great masses of inanimate rock well known to compose pleasing scenery—so that now mountains have become new, unfiltered data. Having lost my hard and early-earned preconception of them, mountains might now be anything, might be whatever they are saying.

Fully aware that even musing about such matters could be evidence of feeble-mindedness as the world reckons, I choose to take these new messages, however incompletely understood, seriously. While just an intuition at this point, I would not be surprised if at the very end of my life, that moment when all practical function, discernment and powers of discrimination have shut down, the full message will make itself known.

May 23, 2014: To celebrate improvements made to M's studio and gallery—track lighting, which enables each picture to be highlighted, and a handsome new sign outside announcing the True Water Gallery—we hold a party. The invitees include all the nearby friends we can think of, most of them artists themselves, about thirty people in all. Everybody comes! The plan was to have drinks and hors d'œuvres in the gallery followed, for those so inclined, by a sitdown dinner at the Inn across the street. The dinner posed a bit of a comfort problem with us, as the innkeepers quoted us a price per person for the meals and wine. Our initial thought was that people who elected to dine at the Inn would pay for themselves, but then that began to feel awkward. We hadn't mentioned paying for anything when we made our invitations. Would people expect to be treated or would they naturally assume, as I would, that their hosts should not be expected to pay for thirty people to dine out? In the event we decided not to ask anyone to pay and to eat the cost in a spirit of Happy Opening, and it was.

M's new paintings are mostly large oils of seaside scenes in Marion, dreamily evocative and atmospheric. My favorites were inspired by photographs she took early one morning. Awake at first light, she walked down the lawn of the Marion house to the water's edge. Daylight was just beginning to penetrate a fog that hung over the boats moored in the harbor, creating an effect that made the boats, parts of their masts obscured by mist, seem suspended in the air. M has become a very good painter of water in all kinds of light, and the rendering of the various boats, most of them familiar to me, is meticulous. I am not alone in finding these pictures haunting. Also on display were a dozen or so small oils of Marion and Vermont landscapes. These are inexpensive and tend to sell quickly.

In the event, our guests were duly appreciative of M's work. She made a significant sale of a large fabric landscape and, in the course of the Vermont Open Studio Weekend that followed our party, a number of smaller sales. The gallery event turned out to be pleasantly bibulous, and our party was almost raucously convivial as we moved to the inn for our dinner and more drinks. The food was excellent, contributing to a gladdening sense of Good Party, a reluctance to leave, and a few unneeded but very much enjoyed nightcaps in the inn's pub room.

A dinner party for thirty after which there was nothing for us to clean up. We walked across the street to the house, turned out the lights, and retired to our bed in elevated spirits.

June 9-15, 2014: M and I drive south to the Cape. Over the weekend we will disperse M's parents' ashes, half of them in the St. Gabriel Church courtyard in Marion, the other half into the sea in the middle of Buzzard's Bay. Even as we depart from Ripton on a bright crisp morning, we both know this is going to be a melancholy excursion.

The plan is to spend a night in Marion by ourselves in the old family house, then rise at dawn and drive to Provincetown where we will spend two days pleasurably idling and, in M's case, steeling herself for the final material farewell to her mother and father. Our solitary stay in the old house was a little ghostly. Months have passed since Molly's mother died, yet her presence and her husband's permeate the stilled atmosphere as we enter the kitchen. Housekeepers have kept the place almost disturbingly immaculate, the parental bedrooms and the beds in which each of them died have been carefully made, fresh flowers on the nightstands, as if awaiting Anne's and

Hoyt's return.

M and I have not been having evening cocktails of late, in my case for dietary reasons, but in unspoken acknowledgement of a special occasion, we each drink bourbon on ice as the evening meal is improvised. We find ourselves speaking in hushed tones and padding lightly about the quiet house. After dinner we watch a satisfying episode of the BBC's Call the Midwife series before retiring. As planned we rise early and head down the Cape. I feel as if I have somehow been holding my breath.

At first sight of the Provincetown dunes in milky morning light I am flooded with a rush of confusing sensations. For a time, perhaps twenty years ago, arrival in Provincetown produced the same sense of giddy liberation that arriving in Key West does. Like Key West, Provincetown is literally land's end and carries with it the restlessness of artists and writers who were happy to escape there. Both towns have also been safe havens for gay men and women so that open sexual identity and preferences are now normative. In both destinations I have always felt a pleasing mixture of civility and sexiness. Of the two, Key West is more rackety, but Provincetown carries its own vital force.

I have never been in Provincetown this early in the season. Most commercial establishments are up and running, although there are vacancies in the inns and B&Bs. The water is too cold for swimming, but it is good to hike the beaches and lie out in the sun. We are staying in the opulent Land's End Inn, perched on what must be the highest elevation for miles. Below, higgledy-pigglety eaves and chimneys flow down to the waterfront and wharfs. At day's end the declining sun strikes the white hulls of boats and the sandy far shore with a blazing clout. I look out over the harbor to the far shore and I cannot withdraw my gaze. It is if I am pulled out of myself, something I recollect at once from my past visits.

We spend easeful hours walking Commercial Street, stopping into galleries. M succeeds in placing a half dozen of her new paintings with the Thanassi Gallery which has shown her earlier work and sold a picture or two. We dine out extravagantly, taking our time. The salty air is welcome in my nostrils and at midday the hard sun feels good on my face. This is Provincetown, all right, but there is a decided Afterward about all of it. I am not going to discover anything I did not expect. I cannot imagine a surprise. The atmosphere is missing its old charge of sex.

Back in Marion the old house no longer feels ghostly and vacant. M's sister Lea has arrived from California and her brother Jacob and his wife Kristine have driven down from Portland, Maine. Molly's younger brother Dog and his wife JoAnn live just down the road, and all are at hand. We set about the agreeable, familiar business of planning and making meals. We have always gotten along, and talk comes easily over drinks before dinner.

The plan is to assemble in the courtyard of St. Gabriel's Church at the appointed hour on Saturday. It has been raining intermittently, and we are not sure how the interment of the ashes will go in the rain and not at all sure if we should head out of the harbor on Doug and JoAnn's yawl, The Swamp Yankee, to distribute ashes there. But the collective mood is relaxed, and in the event the sky is gloomy but there is no rain, and we are able, each one of us, to insert a trowel of Anne and Hoyt's ashes into a hole already dug for them. The courtyard will be sodded over after the interment. A small brass plate bearing Anne's and Hoyt's names and their dates of birth and death will be added to others lining the surrounding walkway. With appropriate solemnity but also with a measure of cheerfulness we complete the quiet service we had planned, including most of the prayers of the Episcopal funeral mass offered by a young bespectacled woman who is an assistant rector of the parish. Afterward we are invited to reflect or pray in the small chapel next to the courtyard, and we all do. The sanctuary of dark wooden pews and trim is illuminated only by what daylight penetrates the stained glass. I am struck by how right and welcome the quiet feels in this dimly bejeweled atmosphere.

A lowering, overcast sky continues to hover overhead, but still no rain. We decide to board the Swamp Yankee and without setting sail motor out of Marion harbor into the gray calm of Buzzard's Bay. Perhaps a mile into open water, Doug cuts the engine and we drift. I can see The Bird Island Light House over the starboard rail and beyond it the faint outline of the Sagamore Bridge spanning the Cape Cod Canal. The Swamp Yankee is a fine old wooden boat, about forty feet long and sleeping up to eight. In many ways it shows its fifty years. Its bright work could use paint and the quarters below look a bit tired, but it sits handsomely in the water. The gray over our heads and the gray of the quietly lapping waves against the hull seem to merge, and we grow quiet. Molly and her sister work the cap off the urns holding the remaining ashes. Testing the wind to make sure the decanted ash will not blow back into the boat, each Watson sibling takes a turn shaking some of the ashes from each urn into the sea. The ashes make a kind of swirling cloud, gray on darker gray, as they enter the water. Each of us tosses a few flowers in the direction of the ashes, and as the boat drifts away with the current, the flowers trailing behind us on the surface of the water seem to me a touching farewell. And I, who had spent nearly all my time in boats in these waters in the company of M's mother and father, find it impossible not to feel their presence, which includes their bottomless love for their children. It was not at all awkward that no one spoke as we motored back to land.

June 16-24, 2014: On Sunday after the interment I drive all day from Marion to Cleveland, Interstate 90 bearing steady traffic, much of it vacationers moving to or returning home from their getaways in the Adirondacks and the Finger Lakes. But the traffic moves, and I some-how arrive at Celeste's house as usual at the dinner hour. Both Celeste and Lulu are in animated high spirits, and it is determined that we dine at an upscale Mexican restaurant nearby. Lulu has a lot to tell me and to show me. She has, no doubt influenced by her mother, become highly fashion conscious—or better, she has developed a highly distinctive approach to turning herself out. She wants to impose personal touches on her outfits. This might involve sowing patches onto her tops and shorts. She has also learned a technique called "bow backing," in which she will cut open the back of a tee shirt or blouse and sew the loose halves back together with a series of bows. I am surprised she is so fond of this look, since one can only see the bows from behind her, but she is emphatically pleased and wears the same bow-backed tee shirt every day I am there. I am touched by her pleasure in this creation, and it is nice to see the lovely skin of her little back between the bows. It occurs to me that the bow-back effect would be very sexy on a developed woman, and I muse a little whether Lu might be aware of this. Though small for her age and showing no early signs of pubescence, she is precociously adept at getting herself up like a glamor puss. Her ears have been pierced since her infancy, and she has an array of striking earrings. Whenever possible, she applies lipstick and, if Celeste lets her, eye makeup. So painted, she looks to me like an appealing vixen, but I wonder if I should be concerned about signals she may be unwittingly transmitting.

As in prior summer visits, there is a whirlwind of activity from rising until bedtime. Celeste has a dozen home improvement projects, which require my assistance in, say, locating a new storm door, buying and planting flowers, hauling furniture from her late mother's house into storage. Lulu is on a girls' softball team, and we go to her games, cheering her on. Back home Lulu and her friends "run bases" between Celeste and me as we toss the ball back and forth. Most days are steamy and humid, so we go to the Cleveland Heights pool, sometimes twice a day. Lulu is a water bug. Between jumping and almost-diving from the board and diving for thrown objects (usually my watch) and improvising chase and capture games in the shallow end of the pool, she is never still. In fact I cannot picture her sitting or standing still when I recall my days with her. I too am expected to be in continual motion, and I am typically exhausted at day's end.

One day between the pool and dinner we drive to the Cineplex to see Maleficent, a new take on the Sleeping Beauty story. In the rather Jungian manner of such entertainments these days, the film seeks to explain and understand what in the old version of the story was simply existential evil. No longer are there purely wicked witches or evil spirits. Evil is now seen always to have a cause; moreover, it is correctible. In this film, which Lulu loves, Maleficent was once sweet and vulnerable, the reigning princess fairy in her own enchanted kingdom, but when she is deceived in love, she becomes a terror. The terror is softened years later by the transformative sweetness of

Sleeping Beauty, to whom Maleficent finds it impossible to be maleficent, and all ends happily. In addition to promoting the deeper "understanding" of wicked people and wicked acts, the film, like so many of the other children's movies Lulu and I have seen over the past few years, no longer sees males as saviors or even problem solvers. As in Frozen, another hit with Lulu, the needed redemptive kiss at the film's conclusion is imparted female to female, the male kiss having failed to make a difference. The message here is of course female empowerment, but one can only wonder if growing girls' expectations are being constellated in a way that makes males at best decorative and, when the chips are down, beside the point. In Lulu's case, I will await developments with interest.

Whatever the trials and the depletion of energy I experience in the course of my Lulu visits, I continue to take deep pleasure in the fact that she is at heart still a child, and a very loving one. She is not too grown up or cool not to creep into my room on first rising and to crawl into my bottom bunk with me. After a consideration of her dreams, we discuss the best possible outcomes for the day ahead. Then she grabs my iPad from the night stand and shows me her favorite videos of kittens and puppies.

In all, a highly satisfactory visit. Twice Celeste and I, having showered away the day's exertions and chlorine, get rather dressed up for a dinner at Nighttown, followed by excellent Jazz, first guitarist Bucky Pizzarelli and then the blind chanteuse Diane Schuur. In the course of our evening outings, I run into a surprising number of people from my headmaster days in Cleveland. The couple seated closely next to us at the Bucky Pizzarelli concert introduced themselves and informed me that I had changed their once wayward son's life and had set him on a course of good writing and good thinking. Panicked that I would not remember their son at all, I was relieved that, with a few clues, I did —and enough details about teaching him and his particular circumstances (twenty years ago?) that I was relieved of having to fake it. The couple in question happen also to be very nice people, and they contributed to an overall pleasant evening.

That night and the subsequent night listening to Diane Schuur, there was an eerie succession of similar encounters, all, thank God, positive and upbeat. While I have not quite submerged my Cleveland life from daily consciousness, I try not to dwell in it, as the drama erupting after my departure— the revelation of my affair with Celeste, the birth of Lulu and what was for a time a whirlwind of gossip and speculation—was something my mental equilibrium required me to let go. In the years since I have been grateful and always a little surprised when former Cleveland acquaintances have digested what happened and manage to reintegrate me into their worlds. I have also resolved not to be surprised or upset by people unable to do this. There are no doubt many Clevelanders in that category, as the school and my role in it were focal for many upper income and otherwise prominent people in the city. Miraculously, I have not yet experienced one snarky snub or charge of moral hypocrisy. I was thoroughly prepared for some journalist to exploit the affair / adultery story for one of the Cleveland papers, papers in which I was frequently featured while at my former post, but that has not happened either. Again, I would not have been surprised by any such slings and arrows, nor do I think they would be undeserved. As it happened, my brief encounters with perhaps a dozen people who seemed eager to resume contact gave me an unexpected lift.

I was gone exactly a week, a week that felt like a month.

June 26, 2014: Back in Ripton. It is raining like stink, and I am huddled indoors trying to restore essential life functions, such as reactivating my various insurance contracts that fell into nonpayment after my credit card was hacked two weeks ago: eternities in the labyrinths of automated phone systems, disconnections, wrong departments. Except for anesthesia, modern life is vastly overrated.

I detect hints of impending dementia and hoarder-ism. Yesterday I decided to clean out my bureaus and rid them of excess. Who, after all, needs 26 black golf shirts? Rummaging through my uncountable pairs of socks in my top drawer I found a series of watches, some of them stopped, others with broken bands, some apparently fine. Finding them aroused dim memories of the cities and circumstances in which I purchased them. But there are TWENTY-TWO of them. Confused about what to do, I took seven of them to a jeweler in Middlebury, and they are now nicely banded and ticking away meaninglessly in a handsome inlaid box on my bureau. The other fifteen await a decision. I have never considered myself a hoarder, but again, why 31 pairs of identical khaki pants? Why 52 pairs of reading glasses? Why, for that matter, 11 guitars? I can see it coming. I will commit myself to an austere religious order and give up all possessions. It can be a religious order that embraces poverty and obedience, but not chastity.

June 28-July 4, 2014: For the twenty-first time I set forth to the annual conference of the International Boys' Schools Coalition, this year hosted by the Montgomery Bell Academy in Nashville. This organization, "founded" tentatively by me in 1994 in the vague realm where whim meets hope, has grown to a robust network of more than three hundred schools from sixteen countries, a development almost beyond my capacity to absorb. This burgeoning is emphatically the work of others, not my own. My contribution this year is to address conferees on how to apply the findings of Michael Reichert's and my relational teaching study, *I Can Learn from You* and to do a talk and a reading from *The Other World*. Neither assignment is taxing, and I look forward to both the place and the company.

As has been the case so often lately when I alight at a scheduled destination, my immediate response is familiarity, as opposed to strangeness or newness. I believe this is my fifth extended stay in Nashville, each of them connected to some scheduled talk or other scholastic business. Almost all of my duties here have been generated or at least hosted by Montgomery Bell Academy, a magisterial and handsomely appointed boys school in the posh suburbs just beyond the city center. My sense that I know this place is informed in part by Peter Taylor's short stories in his collection The Old Forest, stories set in settled, second tier American cities, decidedly southern in temperament: St. Louis, Nashville, Memphis. These cities convey a confident insularity, a sense that they are world enough for those who live there.

It is steamy hot, approaching 100 degrees with smothering humidity. I am lodged at a pricey hotel just across the road from Vanderbilt University. My room is an unnecessarily enormous suite with a kind of parlor and a fully stocked kitchen. As I attend scheduled events, beginning with an elegant dinner for trustees and "founders" like me and feel myself gathered into the collective conviviality of dozens of men and women recalled from past gatherings but utterly out of mind when I am home or elsewhere. A moment of fantasy: say, suddenly it was determined that I had no other home and that this setting and these people were my only world. I believe I could thrive in it. I could make my way. There are men I know who would be my friends and ultimately good friends. There are women who interest me. This city with its rackety musical life and it's almost outlaw ethos exerts a pull. It occurs to me that almost every city I know well exerts a similar yet highly distinctive pull: New York, San Francisco, Chicago, Toronto, Key West. Is this related to my age? That in advanced years I become ever more lightly tethered to something like a home where I belong? I think I may have to go home to answer this.

In the event, my presentations are well attended and go satisfyingly well. I manage to stay conscious of what I am saying in the moment, maintaining eye contact with listeners as I speak and thus avoiding my tendency to rattle on at unnatural speed, reciting rather than conveying. Such nice, responsive people. Despite having presented the relational teaching findings so often to so many audiences, the material seems fresh to this group, composed in good part of international conferees from the UK, South Africa, Australia and New Zealand. They are gratifyingly full of questions and many of them seek me out in the remaining days of the conference for amplification. For good or ill, they request visits and presentations to their schools, a prospect that always seems bright at the moment I agree to it, but then wearying when it comes time to book the travel and prepare.

Even more enjoyable is the reading and discussion of *The Other World*. I introduce the universal tension between spirited boys' early progress through the world and the inevitable suppression of that spirit as they are made to bend their wills and curb their impulses to meet the requirements of school and other cultural conventions. I enjoy stressing that this is not a contemporary problem with an easy institutional remedy. I introduce Shakespeare's image in As You Like It of the "whining school boy" with his "shining morning face" reluctantly dragging his satchel to school. Then the first balcony scene in Romeo and Juliet where, despairing of leaving Juliet's side despite the danger of being discovered by Capulet enemies, Romeo opines that "love goes from love as a schoolboy to his books..." I plant the Jungian notion that boys are spiritually complete and connected at birth, that they do not "grow up" tabula rasa into a succession of adaptive stages, but rather grow down into a world in which their spiritual connectedness is apt to be compromised if not suppressed altogether. I recite the bit from Wordsworth's "Ode on Intimations of Immortality" suggesting that boys enter the world complete, "trailing clouds of glory" before the world's "prison house" begins to close around them. My listeners seem to warm to this, and I read my chapter, "For Love," recounting my hero Jonathan's first gestures at romantic expression in the course of his early school years. The response is heartening and sympathetic, aided by the fact that a number of old friends are in the audience. Better still, the reading motivates listeners to buy copies of *The Other World*, which are on sale at the central gathering place of the conference (thank you, conference organizers), and as I leave, all the books have been sold. My hope is that since the attendees are mostly practicing teachers and school heads, they might, if they like the book, order it in volume for their schools. These days, given the dubious trajectory of most literary fiction, this is about the most promising way for a book like mine to find its way. I depart the session and the conference still buzzing with adrenaline, glad, despite recurring doubts, that I have somehow managed to write books.

Only recently have I seriously questioned the value of having displaced so much waking time writing books, some of which have made very little impact. As a younger man through my middle years, writing always felt a calling, even the highest calling. Questioning it now may, I feel, be an artifact of aging and declining energy. I cannot say for certain. But a comment by my co-author Michael as we were preparing our joint presentation on relational teaching gave me pause. We have published two books together, *Reaching Boys / Teaching Boys* and *I Can Learn from You* as well as several articles and monographs. I have commented in earlier entries my frustration in collaborating. Fairly or not, I was annoyed that I had to do the lion's share of the writing and revising in order to establish a single authorial voice. I endured this because Michael, while not a gifted writer, is a very good man and, since these were his first books to appear in print, I thought he would get a personal lift from being a published author. So I was surprised to hear him tell me that he did not think he wanted to write any more books. He felt the investment of time did not result in sufficient recognition, and compared to the way we are compensated for consulting with schools and addressing conferences, there was not much financial compensation. I would have to consult records to know for sure, but we may have netted $10,000 each from our royalties so far. That does not seem a discouraging sum to me, but apparently Mike had greater expectations. There is apparently little abiding pleasure for him, as there is for me, in Having Written.

And then of course, as I had feared, I find myself stranded in Nashville. In an exact replica of my attempt last year to fly home from the conference in Richmond, I am taxied on a mild, brilliantly sunny afternoon to the airport to find an uneasy stir among those waiting at the gates. Delays, cancellations. Thunderstorms over New York LaGuardia were cited in my case. The posted delay was an hour, then at hour's end another hour, then with a sickening inevitability the cancellation. A hurricane, Arthur, was also moving up the Atlantic coast in the direction of New York and New England, so the prospects of getting out soon were dim, the customer service and gate agents overwhelmed. After the now familiar but still awful tedium of waiting and fussing, it appears that the best bet for a flight back is two days hence, via Detroit. I am assured there are no options. A brief flickering hope is that I might fly to Cleveland and lay over for the Fourth of July and see Lulu march in the neighborhood parade and sing "Fifty Nifty

United States" in the street fair talent show. Hope dashed, all flights already booked, with waiting lists.

Despondent and defeated, I return to the city center, book two more nights at the overly commodious hotel, which has room for me. The conference had been at times exhilarating, and there had been a few nights on the town raucous with country music and satisfying company, but my appetite for more of that is sated, and every last friend had made it out of the city successfully. I resign myself to reading, writing, walking, and solitary meals. The city streets in the neighborhood around Vanderbilt University now seem without interest or charm.

Dining alone in mid-level restaurants was dispiriting, service and food indifferent. I tried to be objective in observing my fellow diners. Imagining their background and "stories" had once been a diversion in my solitary travels, but whether due to insufficient good will or the truth of what I observed, the Nashville folks seated around me looked grim, as if they too were enduring rather than enjoying dining out. It also occurred to me again that the alarming level of American obesity reported in the news is clearly true. Maybe I attend to such assessments more closely since I have recently shed some weight myself, but I feel physically uncomfortable beholding a morbidly obese person or, not infrequently, a morbidly obese family spilling over the restaurant chairs. I seem to feel their discomfort, their effort in movement. But it is mainly the faces of the other diners that hold my attention. They look desolate, beaten. So many of them, even in company, eat in silence. Am I perhaps casting this mood onto a scene that would not be observed by a happy person?

The historian and political pundit John Meacham was a keynote speaker at the conference, and inspired by his excellent address on the virtues of Presidents Jefferson, Jackson, Franklin Roosevelt and of Winston Churchill—respectively embodying curiosity, resilience, charm, and courage—I purchased his biographies of Jefferson and Jackson for my iPad. Beginning the Jackson at once, I am absorbed and relieved. Synchronous too, because Jackson's family residence was The Hermitage just outside of Nashville.

So Nashville will be endured. I note with some wonder that being alone in a distant city I feel, even at my age, insistent but unfocused erotic stirrings. The unexpected confinement somehow frees the libido from familiar restraints. In consequence I feel close even to the erotic pulse of Jackson's life nearly two centuries ago—and this is not a special emphasis in Meacham's book.

July 5, 2014: A refreshingly breezy, sunlit day in Nashville, largely observed through airport glass as I try to divert myself through the long wait for my afternoon flights to Detroit, then Burlington and home. I am conditioned to expect the worst, the DELAY notice flashing onto the Departures monitor, followed by CANCELED. But not this time. Hurricane Arthur seems to have petered out in heavy rains over Long Island Sound and Cape Cod, leaving Vermont untouched. Aboard each flight I try to doze but can't; I have been too idle for sleepiness.

I have had enough of Andrew Jackson's first presidency. I scroll back through my iPad library to Karl Ove Knausgaard's novel / memoir, *My Struggle,* and find it unreadably plodding, a verdict I had reached earlier, disinclining me to finish. The book and its sequels are reportedly such a hit in Norway that I found myself wondering, perhaps ungenerously, how dreary could Norwegian life be for readers to engage in Knausgaard's uncompelling accounts of such trials as failing to win a satisfactory girlfriend in junior high school or his difficulties as a high school boy in securing beer so that he could get drunk at a holiday party. He does recount with an admirable lack of self-pity being very lightly tended by both parents, but he fails to convey why his father's decline into alcoholism and early death moves him so frequently to tears—not that such a father's loss could not be lamented, but Knausgaard, despite a seemingly endless description of settling his father's affairs, is unable to communicate anything that might make a reader feel sad or sympathetic. Inward-looking, self-critical, brooding—perhaps these qualities resonate in a special way with Norwegians and Swedes, and if so, good for them. But in my accrued frustration in the Detroit airport I wrote a curtly dismissive review of *My Struggle* on the Amazon site. It has been a day now and I do not regret it yet.

Both flights arrived and departed on time. The night air in Burlington was refreshingly cool and dry. Not a handful of cars on the hour-long southward drive to Ripton, while stretches of forest between the farms seemed to crowd the road. About midnight I haul my suitcase out of the car under a half moon and stars so bright the lawn and the leaves in the forest across the river look smoky blue. I don't even have to go inside to feel that, yes, this is home.

July 6-11, 2014: M was away from Ripton while I was. She attended a spiritual retreat in upstate New York, then drove down to Marion to settle more estate business. Home now, we both carry a sense of "elsewhere" with us as we move about through our not quite yet familiar routines, an experience at once a little strange and also stimulating.

It relaxes me to realize I have no pressing obligations or deadlines on the near horizon. Three weeks hence M and I will gather with our big girls and their families for a farewell celebration in the big Marion house, but until then the high summer days loom pleasantly. M quickly sets to work embellishing a set of gardens on each side of our side entrance, and they are soon in luxurious bloom. She is trying also to reestablish a regular painting rhythm, though hampered by doctor and dental appointments, bill-paying and other household distractions. I am not obligated enough to be distracted. I find myself welcoming the idlest of errands, a drive down to Middlebury to pick up an item forgotten on M's grocery list or—my favorite—an inquiry into the local hardware stores as to the best Have-a-Heart trap for a chipmunk that M noticed running from kitchen counter to wood stove just as she was leaving for Marion.

We reckon the chipmunk has been living in the house for ten days, with no apparent harm done. If I sit still long enough at my place at the dining table, it will appear from either behind the refrigerator and scamper under the wood stove, or from the wood stove back to the refrigerator. Once or twice it has ventured into the pantry, which is a concern because it contains enough accessible packaged food to sustain the chipmunk for many lifetimes. Thus the trap. I am cautioned by the young woman at the hardware store, herself a veteran of many chipmunk incursions, that the trap may not work, as chipmunks are very clever. They are also Disney cute. Once, when I followed ours into the pantry, it appeared from under a low shelf and regarded me warily. It seemed to have calculated that there was a table and sufficient distance between us and that I posed no immediate threat. I moved a little, and it vanished under the shelf. A few seconds later it was back, this time upright and settled back on his hind legs, rather jaunty. I suppose chipmunks pose the same kind of household problems as mice or rats, but I cannot summon up any antipathy at all for the chipmunk. In fact, I almost like having it in the house. Nonetheless, M baited the trap, and our viewing of the NBC Evening News was interrupted by a clang in the kitchen. There he was, frisking and panicking in his confinement, whiskers globbed with peanut butter. I carried the cage to the margin of the forest at the farthest edge of our lawn and opened the cage door. The chipmunk sped lightly over my foot and disappeared into the foliage.

Two very satisfying rounds of golf this week. The Middlebury course is brilliant yellow-green where the sun hits the fairways, and on these bright, mild mornings the turf under my soles feels springy, inviting exertion. My friend Karl is now back from Africa, and our old Middlebury class of 1967 foursome is reassembled: Karl, Gary, Peter, and I. I play neither well nor badly, but agreeably enough, as I hit strong drives and manage good distance on the fairway shots while botching a number of approaches and easy putts—much preferable, I feel, to striking the ball badly but getting lucky around the green. Together, as I have commented before, we represent a variety of approaches to the game. Karl, once a big hitter and otherwise competitive player, is for the moment rusty and under-confident, with erratic results; Gary, a big man who has come to golf later in life, approaches his shots in a willed, deliberate way, resulting in both good and disastrous holes. Peter, small and muscular, is the least practiced player. He swings mightily and with an athlete's grace, but makes only intermittent contact with the ball. Although we may in the weeks ahead get down to competitive games pitting two of us against the other two, today we mainly whack away, keeping score in our heads. For the present, I am probably scoring best, but Karl could well find his form, and Gary could achieve consistency, and we might find ourselves held in the old competitive grip. For now it feels invigorating to walk the course and to feel the sun on my face. I carry my clubs in a light bag and at the end of a round would happily play another nine, not yet a welcome prospect for the others. After our round we make our way to an eatery in Middlebury, and over beers and light lunch share news and impressions in a languorous way for an hour or so. At meal's end I feel my age, glad for the game, glad for these old friends.

A delightful moment during a late breakfast this morning. M, preparing bowls of fruit at the kitchen counter, makes a startled yip, and says the chipmunk—or a chipmunk—is back. It has boldly darted from behind the refrigerator to behind the wood stove, not two feet from where M is standing. I am certain, for no specific reason, that it must be the same chipmunk, having determined that life was good inside compared to the woody wilds on the hillock next to the house where I released it two days ago. Supporting my feeling that this is "our" chipmunk, it seems a bit bolder as it emerges from under the stove and stops to consider us.

Again we bait the Have-a-Heart trap with peanut butter. From where we sit at the kitchen table we can see him venture to the open end of the trap where he pauses as if considering. A moment later M notices that it is actually in the trap sniffing the tripped plate gobbed with peanut butter. Believing she can close the trap with her foot, M startles the chipmunk and it runs off. Concerned now that the chipmunk has wised up about the trap, we continue our breakfast in silence —then clang! The little bugger is captive again. This time, taking no chances, I place the trap in the passenger seat of my car and drive a mile or so up the Natural Turnpike (rather a grand name for a dirt road) to a small cemetery, where I release the chipmunk to the old stones and cut flowers wilting in the sun. I am cheered on the drive back to see perhaps half a dozen chipmunks scampering across the road in front of me. There will be companions.

So this morning I think: what is this bland cataloguing of golf rounds and chipmunk encounters? One possibility is that at age 69 my perceptions and concerns have thinned to this, that I have floated up from the depths of a fully considered life to whatever strikes me as agreeable on the surface. Are there deeper, more consequential things I should be attending to? I am still reading. There was the unsatisfactory encounter with Karl Ove Knausgaard's dreary *My Struggle* and a continuing immersion in John Meacham's life of Jackson. And last night on a whim I decided to read closely *As You Like It,* and it drew me quickly in. I continue to lose myself playing the piano and guitar for an hour or two a day. I am not fatigued or bored, in fact the opposite. The summer sun illuminating the greens and yellows beyond the windows begs my alertness. No, this spilling up to the surface, my preoccupation with golf, errands, tidying up, cooking is an indication—I feel certain of this—of health. For at the moment absolutely nothing is wrong. Nothing hurts. My appetite is keen—so thank God for golf and exercise. Just below what I hope is abiding good sense and civility, there is an unfocused erotic eagerness. It is simply health, how health manifests itself at 69.

However healthy I am, I am mindful of the fact that this buoyant, invigorating lift that physical wellness provides is temporary, holding me in a pleasing bubble that must inevitably burst. This brilliantly sunny morning, irradiating the greens in the forest across the river, is also a bubble wafting carelessly past yesterday's threatening skies, oblivious of forecast storms. The serenity of this moment in Ripton is most certainly a bubble in a world of troubles that seem one moment near at hand, the next as unreal as something in a child's story book. Yesterday a passenger jet carrying 298 people from Amsterdam to Kuala Lampur was shot down by pro-Russian Ukrainian insurgents in the mistaken belief that it was a military transport, a sad confirmation of the eternal antipathy loveless people are capable of mustering. Such people are at the moment mustering their ill will all the world over. In Syria and Iraq there is a new race for hegemony of Jihadist terrorism.

Al Qaeda, until recently believed to be the agency most willing to do the unthinkably awful in the name of Allah, has now been supplanted by jihadists calling themselves ISIS, while in West Africa armed Islamist thugs calling themselves Boko Haram taunt national governments by such acts as kidnapping hundreds of school girls, with the aim of curtailing their future schooling and converting them to Islam—or perhaps raping them and selling them into sex slavery. Reflexively I ask: am I an old man in decline projecting my decline onto world events? There is no supportable claim that the world in aggregate has grown more calamitous or worse in any sense. I am grateful for Clive James' wise and exhaustive *Cultural Amnesia,* an irrefutable reminder that no historical era yet recorded can rival the mass depravity of the mid twentieth century: the epic assault on life, liberty, and happiness set in motion under Hitler, Stalin, and Mao. From the standpoint of any individual who suffers such depredations, comparing awful eras or awful events is beside the point. Scale matters only to historical reckoning; from the standpoint of a suffering innocent, bad-as-it-gets is a final, incomparable condition, whether in the crossfire of neighborhood gangs in Chicago, heading toward the shower chambers in Auschwitz, frozen stiff in the Siberian Gulag, or blown to bits while shopping for vegetables in Baghdad. Do I step back wisely—in my bubble of safety—and say, ah, Shiva the Destroyer eternally at work maintaining the Grand Design? Instead I muse on, today serene in my bubble.

A postscript about the chipmunks. We are not rid of them. Yesterday marked the fifth chipmunk capture in as many days in the Have-a-Heart trap. The second in the series could have been a return of the first, unwisely released on our own property. Since then I have been driving them farther and farther from the house, depositing them on the Robert Frost Nature Trail a few miles up the road. Last night at a dinner party, a friend cautioned me that small rodents should be released at least five miles from the site of their capture to prevent return. To date I have only released one chipmunk at that distance, and that was in the driveway of the friend who made the recommendation. Now, on day six, the trap stands baited with the apparently irresistible peanut butter. So far my heart has not hardened against chipmunks, as it has over the years against intrusive mice and voles. And so far no harm done, although all the fancy wrapped chocolates have disappeared from their little blue bowls in the red sitting room.

July 26-August 6, 2014: After considerable working out of logistics M and I drive down in separate cars to Marion, where we will convene Claire, Jesse, Kate and their families for a kind of good-bye-to-Marion-as-we-knew-it celebration. We go in two cars because after a week or so, I am scheduled to leave from Marion to celebrate Lulu's ninth birthday in Cleveland and parts west. In addition to the extended family celebration, we will be working to clear out M's parents' house, deciding what we and the other heirs want to keep and to designate the rest of it for sale to antique dealers.

The goal is to have the house empty so that it can be quickly sold in the autumn. Our house in Ripton is already perilously full of furniture and pictures, but it was impossible to resist claiming some of the ancestral pieces in the Marion house, so we are shipping a rather grand and ancient grandfather clock, a fine old desk, some carpets, and several paintings, a few of which were done by distinguished American painters and have substantial cash value. It is hard to say where everything will fit or what will have to go when we cart these new things home.

This kind of reckoning was more fun when I was younger and could imagine what seemed like an eternity of enjoyment in our altered domestic setting. Now each new acquisition or "improvement" to our house evokes intimations of mortality. I find myself musing on exactly how many seasons or years I will still be looking at that picture, sitting in that reconfigured room. I worry too that if we are not careful or lucky, M and I could leave the world with an enormous hodgepodge of possessions that can only be a headache for our children to dispose of. I am reminded of how efficiently my parents shed their household goods before moving to their retirement complex in Los Angeles and how the ease of their passing—my sister and I cleared out their little apartment at the Belmont Village in a single morning and afternoon—contrasts with the enormity of closing down M's parents' house.

M and her brothers and sister have been at work for months trying to catalog and get rid of a rather large household full of stuff. Because, unlike my parents, the Watsons chose to be cared for at home through the end of their lives, their substantial financial holdings—I think between six and seven million dollars—dwindled down to just enough to keep up household payments and annual taxes. When the house is ultimately sold, Molly and her siblings will receive only a modest inheritance, welcome of course, but we will not be steeped in wealth. A good deal of the clearing out work lies ahead of us, but this week we are going to concentrate on enjoying our family.

When you are very fond of the people arriving, the hassle of meeting trains and planes—delays, finding parking, rigging cars up with the legally correct infant car seat—is pleasantly endurable. It is very good to see our girls, Jesse and her brood from Brooklyn by train, Kate and hers from Chicago by plane, Claire and a new beau by car.

All are in cheerful high spirits. The grandchildren Leon (7), Anna Jane (4), Winifred (2) and Alice (1) are eager to move about and soon are out on the lawn running (in Leon's case) and toddling down the grassy slope to the sea wall with its many possibilities of danger. I am reminded of the strain of keeping watch outdoors and of keeping order indoors when the children are afoot. My bouts of solitude in Ripton and in my travels may have made me a little obsessive about domestic tidiness. I worry that following the grandchildren around straightening up their messes might seem a criticism of their parents, so I wait till everyone is off on errands or off to the beach before tidying the rooms. I don't know exactly why ordered spaces in an empty house quiet my mind, but they do, and I make it my self-appointed task after everyone else has retired for the night to tidy up the house, box up the toys and puzzle pieces and colored markers, hang up the towels in the bathroom. Doing this, I reflect with hallucinogenic clarity on our family's long summer residencies in this house when our girls were infants. Even then I was aware of the mounting clutter in the sitting rooms and of the sandy trail we had created between the waterside door to the house and bathrooms and bedrooms—aware but without a thought of cleaning it up, which must have fallen to M's mother and

Edna, the family's devoted housekeeper. No one ever so much as hinted that M and I might offer a hand in clearing up what in our absence was a very presentable house. So maybe beneath my present compulsion to restore order to the house is a deeper drive to atone for being such an oblivious and entitled guest as a young man.

I feel a confused mixture of delight and melancholy in the presence of my grandchildren playing so happily in the sunny rooms of the ancestral house. The delight is in their unguarded expression of who they are and what they want. They are clearly well loved and have been sensibly parented. Already they are able to suspend narcissistic concerns and engage fully in each other. Anna, at four rather a coquette, adores her older cousin Leon, and he, though more otter-like and venturesome, cheerfully reins himself in to play with her. The babies, Winifred and Alice, are unalike physically, Winnie a dark, puckish pixie, Alice a blond Nordic Brunhilde. Paired next to each other in matching highchairs or seated among playthings on the floor, they exchange long, thoughtful looks. Very tentatively they offer each other tiny objects, bits of food. They are taking each other in, and what they take in will be part of an unconscious foundation for a lifelong closeness they will feel, if not quite understand, for the rest of their lives, no matter how far they will one day find themselves from one another. The attraction the children feel for each other is generated in good measure by the close attachment of their mothers, Kate and Jesse. I remember their bond evolving in the course of their own adjacency in identical high chairs and in long peaceful mornings "drawing" on reams of computer paper as they sat on opposite sides of a low coffee table in the sunny sitting room just off the kitchen of our first house in Chagrin Falls, Ohio. The sense of the continuity of family affection overwhelms me, and I find myself trying, not very successfully, to relate this in letters to faraway friends. To my high school friend Lynn in Chicago:

I am still awash, almost literally, in grandbabies here in Marion. There is not a clear square foot of floor, and meal preparation and clean up require every consecutive minute of attention, yet I enjoy the beauties in all of their unguarded actions and utterances. Hats off to Kate and Jesse and their remarkable husbands who are such loving, judicious, relaxed yet attentive parents that their very distinctive children are thriving mightily. I hope I live to observe more of their unfolding.

To my high school friend Laurel in Appleton, Wisconsin:

I am enchanted by Kate's girls for many reasons, but I am fascinated at how they, so eerily like their mother and her sister Jesse who are also two years apart, are so deeply, instinctively connected. That this highly specific relationship could be replicated so exactly a generation apart seems to me evidence of a cosmic design of some kind.

Excessive, perhaps. Certainly overwritten, but what can I do with so much feeling?

And so a week passes in meal preparation and clean up, excursions to Silver Shell, the Marion village beach, slow morning rowboat rides to Meadow Island in the adjacent cove where the children gather shells in the warm sandy shallows. In the afternoon when the wind picks up, groups of four or five board Molly's sister Lea's Herreshoff 12 footer for gentle sails around the outer harbor. Nearly every afternoon I make quiet time to play golf on the eccentric nine hole course laid out along the drive connecting the waterfront houses. There are stone walls four or five feet high encircling several of the greens, providing an element of Druidical novelty. Playing alone is a little melancholy, so I dragoon M's sister Lea, a non-golfer but enough of an athlete to keep up, to join me three or four times. Other afternoons I paddle a kayak along the perimeter of the Marion coves. Most of the shoreline is now protected wetlands where cranes forage in the shallows and ospreys nest in elevated man-made roosts. The paddling is soothingly rhythmic, almost hypnotic, and the sustained solitude proves a restorative respite from child tending.

At week's end when our girls and their families have been deposited at their respective stations, a powerful quiet engulfs the house, in equal measures welcome and saddening. By now, various furnishings—grandfather clocks, desks, bureaus, carpets, paintings—have been carted away by Molly's siblings and their children so the familiar rooms begin to look passed over and forlorn. An uneasy stillness descends at dinner time, and M, Lea and I find it preferable to dine out in the reassuring bustle of other diners.

At week's end I drive west for what is planned as a week-long belated celebration of Lulu's 9th birthday. Interstate 90 is predictably clotted with vacation travelers, but I make excellent time through the Berkshires and the length of New York State. The theme of our time together is supposed to be water parks, still Lulu's favorite outdoors diversion, and we determine that the Finger Lakes region offers an impressive variety. The terrifying roller coaster configuration of the watery chutes Lulu likes best are not something I look forward to, but her enthusiasm is infectious and I am pleased enough to endure our descents in shared inner tubes.

One of the parks we attend, Sea Breeze, just outside of Rochester on the shore of Lake Ontario, has in addition to its water rides actual roller coasters, these, to me, even more forbidding than the water slides. As usual, nobody in the park looks to be within thirty years of my age. Celeste, who has in the past fancied herself as an amusement park daredevil, now demurs boarding any ride that swirls around or swings back and forth, claiming bladder and nausea concerns. Thus it befalls me to accompany Lulu on such rides, which she has determined are her favorites. I strain to consider all of this in some kind of reasonable perspective—very hard to manage when I am actually in motion, being heaved and dropped and yanked at breathtaking speed. But between rides, waiting for my inner ear to reestablish equilibrium so that I am not lurching like a drunk, I determine that the appeal of roller coasters is like that of horror films. There is a kind of catharsis—or at least a system-rousing jolt of adrenaline—in enduring for a few instants unthinkably awful outcomes. In horror films it may be the intimation that some demonic killer will slit your throat; on the roller coasters it is the brief certainty, as your car swings around a curve suspending you out beyond the track, that you are being thrust off the ride into the crowd below. I consent to this so Lulu will not be disappointed, so that, "accompanied by an adult," she is allowed to follow her heart's desire up and down, around and around, that her screams of delight are heard and shared.

And there are compensations, the chief one of which, for me, is leaving the park in anticipation of a nice dinner, preceded by a leisurely cocktail, the three of us perched on a rise above the lovely meandering expanse of Lake Canandaigua. This is I think our third excursion into the Finger Lakes, and I find the region enchanting, not quite like any other terrain I know in the United States. The lakes I know best are Skaneateles, Seneca, and Canandaigua. They are inset deep below rolling green ridges, mostly undeveloped above the shoreline. The roads along the lakes are embedded high up on the ridges, so that as you drive along, there are spectacular prospects of shimmering lake below. In the farm country away from the lakes, the towns are threadbare and forlorn, but the settlements and towns rimming the lake are impressively developed and charming. The Finger Lakes district is also wine country, and Celeste's enthusiasm for wine cannot be overstated, so we stop frequently for tastings, while Lulu forages for, and usually finds, candy. All things considered, we have a rich and full week of adventuring and celebration, and despite the whooshing and shrieking of my days at the amusement parks, my abiding impression is of sitting in lovely declining light on a restaurant terrace high above Lake Canandaigua, sipping a chilled martini and watching Lulu running about exploring the green hillside below us.

August 16-19, 2014: My head busy with bright images of our time together, the drive back home to Ripton passes pleasantly. When I pull into our drive in the early evening, the yellow trim of the house and the garden flowers are ablaze in the low slanting sun. It feels to me like a cry of welcome. M is still in Marion with her sister sorting out file cabinets and clearing closets of her parents' clothes. Despite the impending days of solitude I feel an overwhelming happiness to be home in this luminous place.

Of the many things that might strike a deep esthetic chord, window curtains, I would have thought, would not be one of them. But one lives and learns. The morning after my arrival home a young man from a fabric emporium in Burlington arrives to install thermal curtains in our yellow sitting room. This room is at the back of the house looking out onto river and woods. Three of the walls are banked with windows and there is a glass door opening onto a deck. In winter cold the room loses a great deal of house heat through so much glass, so we ventured to Burlington a few weeks ago to buy thermal curtains. I was not paying much attention in the fabric store as M negotiated construction and installation, but when she came to me in the lobby chair where I was lounging and asked me to have a look at the proposed cloth, I was troubled. She had picked out a neutral beige fabric that the salesclerk said was a standard choice for such curtains, and indeed my sister and others we know have put these up. But I balked. I am spookily fond of the way our yellow room looks now, how the very pale-yellow walls at once soften and brighten everything, bringing up the colors in the oriental carpets and in the framed pictures. While I had given the matter no prior thought, the idea of great slabs of beige voiding the window spaces seemed to cancel out everything I liked about being in the room.

Aware that my qualifications for opining on such matters are poor, I asked the clerk if thermal curtains could be made out of regular fabric, and the answer was yes, since the insulation comes from a kind of batting sewn to the back of the chosen cloth. So, to M's mild annoyance, we meandered the labyrinths of the store's inventory—it is an immense warehouse of a store—until I was arrested by a fat bolt of gorgeous cloth: pale yellow—the yellow of our walls—and soft blue stripes, both colors textured in a kind of damask. From some primitive mental depth arose a strong preference. M was full of doubt, worried that so much striped cloth would make the room visually chaotic, but whether through her natural willingness to consider other points of view or perhaps a germ of actual liking, she conceded to my choice. As it turned out, this was no small concession, as we were both startled by the estimated cost of producing and installing the curtains—about $5,000. We agreed to go ahead, however, and in the busy-ness of our travels and obligations over the weeks following, I think M put the project out of her mind, but for some reason I could not.

In a way that made me feel a little silly and embarrassed, I was full of apprehension the morning the curtain installer arrived. Apprehensive about—*curtains*? The money? Having made a stupid choice? The young man went about his business with a quiet efficiency, and I went upstairs to work on manuscripts. After an hour or so I came down to look, and my heart flew up. He was a little more than halfway finished. Some of the new curtains were bunched above the windows, held fast by their rope pulls; others, the ones he was in the process of installing, were unfurled to the length of the floor-to-ceiling windows. The effect was immediate: something insistently French, confident, elegant. The striped abundance of the cloth pulled the room together, brought out the sheen on wooden surfaces of the grandfather clock, occasional tables, the pianos. To my eye the room was not so much transformed as completed. The finished job confirmed this impression. I took pictures with my iPad and sent them to M in Marion. She reserved an opinion until she could see the room. When she returned home a few days later, she was guardedly appreciative, but with each subsequent day her response grew warmer, to the point that she wants to find or sew new sofa pillows and a more suitable quilt to replace the one over the back of the sofa we like to throw over ourselves when we watch T.V. on cold winter nights.

It has been a week now, and I am drawn to the yellow room in a new way. I go downstairs from my study and refresh myself, registering impressions for stretches of five or ten minutes. As I look around, I cannot stop my thoughts from turning on how many years, if I am given years, I will sit in this room, now enlivened with this fabric, watching television, playing the piano, serving drinks to guests. Will my daughters or whoever else buys or inherits the house feel warmly held in this room? I cannot separate these thoughts from a mounting awareness of my impending death and someone subsequently clearing out, removing the curtains, brightening everything.

August 20, 2014: Today while taking a rare scroll through the dreary postings of Facebook friends, I was brought up short by a remarkable video posted by my sister's good friend Mark Taylor in Los Angeles. As I have written before, Ginny and four of her friends—Mark and Judy Taylor, Jackie St. Marie, and Bill Striglos—have constellated what they call The Core, a relationship in which it is understood that they will be in touch with each other almost always daily, that they will inform one another of personal concerns, that their entertainments will include the others, and that if and when any of them feels a need for company, the others, or at least one or more of them, will come around. Except for Bill, who is ten years older but otherwise in sync, the other four members of The Core have been friends since they met more than forty years ago at Stephens College in Columbia, Missouri. Their friendship coalesced around college theater work. Bill, a graduate of Northwestern University's theater program, was energized by similar enthusiasms. He is now mainly retired, having earned his living on the design side of movie and television productions. These days he conducts occasional tours in Greece and the Aegean islands. Mark and Judy Taylor have made a success in Hollywood, Mark as a character actor in movies and TV, more recently as a film director; Judy as a casting director and now a Disney Vice President in charge of locating and nurturing young talent. Ginny has been a voice over and animation director for four decades, has won four Emmys, and is regarded as perhaps the premier director in her field. Jackie, while she has taken occasional stage roles in Los Angeles, has supported herself for the past thirty years with an office job at Sunkist, a national producer of orange juice and other citrus products. Those identifying details established, it must be said that The Core is unlike any other configuration of friends I have known or heard about.

They are unshakable in their devotion to one another. They celebrate heartily every birthday, holiday and milestone together. When one of them loses a beloved relation or friend, they grieve together as one. When I am at my sister's house, The Core telephones incessantly, providing Ginny, who lives alone (if tending two dachshunds and seven cockatiels can be called living alone), with multiple perspectives on whatever might be interesting her or troubling her at the time. My sister has been married and divorced twice, neither time unhappily but not really satisfactorily. The Core has provided abundantly for her what marriage did not. It has done the same for Jackie and Bill, who have never married and who sometimes partner with each other, more in the manner of brother and sister than lovers. Mark and Judy are happily and devotedly married and parents of two sons, both gay, with whom they are very close. When I am in Los Angeles with my sister I am most days and most evenings with The Core. They strike a celebratory note whenever they are together, and their parties are often augmented by other good friends. Their closeness sets a happy tone. They are enthusiastic drinkers of cocktails, but in dozens of encounters I have never seen one of them the worse for drink. Even as a non-Core member, I feel relaxed and emotionally safe in their company, a sense that I can share anything— and I have—and they with me. When The Core assembles in Ginny's living room where there is a piano, everyone sings. There are obligatory star turns: Bill's hilariously overwrought "Talk of the Town," Jackie's channeling of Judy Garland in "You Made Me Love You," Ginny's over-the-top reprise of "Cabaret" from her long ago role as Sally Bowles in that show. There is a ritual aspect to these recitals, but to me they are enlivening and funny every time.

Mark's Facebook video was a carefully orchestrated tribute to Jackie on the occasion of her retirement after thirty-some years from her job at Sunkist. The nature of her mainly clerical duties at the firm and the corporate nature of Sunkist are such that no vaulting retirement celebration was going to be launched, so The Core, under Mark's skillful direction, created a video in which he, Judy, Bill, and Ginny performed—partly spoke, partly sang—an original composition: "You Won't Bring Us Oranges—Anymore." The video is set in what looks like the nave of some sort of chapel backed by art deco glass panels. A raised table with a large chalice piled high with oranges stands between two formal lecterns behind which Mark and Judy on the left, Bill and Ginny on the right, offer alternate lines of the song supported by unseen piano accompaniment. The song is a musical theater-like ballad, reflective and doleful, hovering between genuine sentiment and kitschy send-up. The lyrics recount Jackie's experiences and duties at the firm, each verse concluding with all four choristers joining the refrain: "And you won't bring us oranges—anymore." At a point near the conclusion of the song, the video shifts to images of the Sunkist flag waving gently in the breeze outside corporate headquarters. This image is followed by a series of shots of various employees at their desks all gesturing farewell with a raised arm. Mark must have somehow made his way into Sunkist, explained his mission and arranged these shots of perhaps two dozen individuals. The effect is to shift the impact from teasingly satirical to touchingly affectionate. Then the camera returns to the chapel / studio where at their respective lecterns The Core have now raised (full) martini glasses to salute Jackie in a final verse, concluding in a line spoken with mock solemnity: "and we don't need your *damned oranges*—anymore."

I don't think anything in the description above can account for the emotional impact this video had on me. It did not reside in the song itself, though it was apposite and funny. Nor did it reside in the concept: the mock formality of the tribute, the chapel-like setting, although those choices were intriguing and visually interesting. After a several viewings—I could not help myself—it finally occurred to me: it was the *care* taken—the production values, the details, the timing and accompanying gestures of the rendered lines, not to mention the logistics of setting everything up, the rehearsals. And underlying the care is the depth of affection The Core so reflexively offers one another year in, year out. Again, I have not seen its like anywhere else.

August 21-25, 2014: M is still in Marion sorting through the remaining household goods and files of her parents' correspondence. I am feeling my solitude in an intense but familiar way. Just as I cannot, when piecing together a new song on the guitar, stop myself from humming along—which interferes annoyingly with my construction efforts—I cannot when I am alone in the house stop consciously *narrating* my every move: *now I will go to the refrigerator to return the mayonnaise; on my way back to the counter I will retrieve a red onion from the sack in the pantry…* I cannot stop doing this and wonder if it is a universal tendency among solitaries. I understand that this ceaseless narrating is a subconscious gesture aiming to provide something like company, if only a voice, when I am alone, but the net effect is to amplify the alone-ness, as might focusing undue attention on the ticking of clocks.

Otherwise I fill time with more extroverted gestures. I invite friends for dinner—or treat them to dinners out—nearly every night I am here by myself. The trick here is not to seem pitiful as I extend the invitations, especially as they are more often than not offered just a day, if not hours, before the proposed meal. Happily I have a number of friends who acknowledge this tic of mine and are now unsurprised to be called by me asking them to dine almost immediately. An additional delicacy in these late-hour invites is that, in addition to longstanding couple-friends, I often invite unattached women M and I know well. This poses no problem if I have known them for a long time and we have shared such dinners repeatedly. This would be the case with my therapist neighbor Carol, who is relaxed about social relations generally and is a bit solitary herself, her company limited, unless I call, to her clients and her three Bernese mountain dogs. M and I often have Carol to tea, and I don't think M is in any way concerned that a dinner with Carol will alienate my affection.

It is a bit more touchy to ask our painter friend Sarah who, while a great but recent friend to both M and me, is presently in a kind of marital / romantic limbo, separated from her husband, Rick, whom M and I also like. When alone for a spell, I have invited Sarah for drinks and a few times to dinner. On the first of these, Sarah showed up and, as we chatted, hesitantly confessed that she felt a little uncomfortable with what (she did not use these words) seemed like a "date" setting. I knew what she meant. At that time we were still getting acquainted. She is younger than I and very attractive, and I was somewhat of an unknown to her, perhaps even a dubious one as she knew my Celeste and Lulu backstory. The last thing I wanted was unease, so on a whim I called M in Marion, told her Sarah was there and would she mind blessing the occasion over the phone. Because this was done in some high spirits and not at all solemnly, Sarah was glad to talk to M and also reassured that no dangerous erotic undercurrents were at work in our dinner together which, in the event, I think we both enjoyed very much and have managed to repeat.

This week, however, Sarah is off sailing with friends, so my impromptu dinner companions have been neighbor Carol, an old Bread Loaf writer chum Sue Ellen and her husband Stuart, vacationing in their Vermont cabin nearby, and Merideth, an old college friend with whom I have recently been reacquainted on Facebook. Merideth lives and works in Montpelier and has a man partner, John, whom I have not met but will soon. Merideth has had an adventurous life, romantically and otherwise, and was untroubled to stop by for a drink and then join me at the inn down the road for an early dinner. I don't think I am quite desperate in arranging these social evenings when I am alone, but the frequency—even adjacency—of these social dinners far exceeds anything M and I arrange when we are home together.

August 26-29, 2014: These late August days have been alternately steamy and brisk, but there has been much welcome sun, the first glimpse of which in the morning triggers the golfing urge. There is a glimmer of summer mornings when I was a little boy, waking to bright sky beyond the window and wanting to get dressed as quickly as possible and outside into the light.

My daily rounds of golf in Marion were satisfying, even when I played by myself. There was nothing effortful in the exertion. Carrying my clubs and walking the course, the forward march after the ball produced an agreeable kind of perspiration that feels as if it is lubricating the joints. I swing and strike the ball and there is an immediate after-sensation of wanting to do it again, and so I strain a little to get to where my ball lies so I can set up and recreate the pleasure. Beginning in Marion after a week or so, my first thoughts on rising are getting out on the course. The Middlebury course is far more extensive and impressively groomed. Most holes present a visual backdrop of cloud dappled mountains. The closely mown fairways feel almost spongy underfoot. My golfing friends Karl, Peter and Gary are inclined to play once or twice a week, but I have cajoled Karl, glad to be back from a trying sabbatical year in Africa, to play more often, and now he too is feeling a renewed urge to play more. Combining these more frequent outings with Karl and rounds with the others, I am able to play nearly every day.

Getting out so often, it is not surprising that I have occasional streaks of inspired play. But in the way of golf, the slightest hubris that my game has reached a new, higher level is met with humiliating failure. I have known this about golf since I started playing as a boy. In Marion and now back home, I have been playing better than I ever have before. In my case this means that I am striking most of my shots well. My successful drives and fairway shots are long enough and accurate enough that I am often at least putting for a par, or more rarely, a birdie. At my very best, I may string a few par holes together in a row. This is when I am tempted to think my game has permanently improved, a condition that seems to release inner demons who let me know my golfing destiny is in their hands, not mine. I will proceed from the green of a hole on which I have, in my view, rather stylishly scored a par to the next tee where the ball shoots off the heel of my driver into the woods twenty yards from where I am standing. I am thus reminded that my game could at any moment fall apart. I could shank the simplest chip shot out of bounds. Anticipating a long fairway shot of, say, a hundred eighty years to the green, I will study my lie, take a determined practice swing, address the ball, and with steely determination swing and nearly miss, the topped ball skittering a few yards to the right or left. When this happens, all previous expectation of hitting the ball solidly dissolves, and I revert to the understanding that the source of good and terrible shots is an utter mystery, to which I must resign myself with gentlemanly cheer. Anything short of this resignation is bad sportsmanship.

While out on the course, striding from shot to shot, I am preoccupied with dread of errors; at home recalling the match in tranquility, I remember only my best shots, long drives, sinking long, tortuous putts. And in that happy state of selective recollection, I cannot wait to get back out on the course. And I think—with reason?— that if I could par that challenging hole, hit those particular shots, isn't it at least possible that I could replicate them? Par that hole again? On one favored day par *every* hole?

This much is true. At present I am playing better and scoring better than at any prior time in my life. At sixty-nine I hit the ball farther than I did when I was twenty-five. This could change, but right now it is objectively, observably true. But as to the vision of combining my best shots— shots I have actually hit and can vividly remember—together into a single exceptional round, that is the Golf Dream at work. Who is to say it won't come true?

October 14, 2014: Once again I am on the southbound train, Rutland to New York City, stalled at the moment for an extended station break in Albany. Soft intermittent sun, mild air for mid October, foliage still holding autumn's reds, russets, and golds.

I have been musing on my reluctance to write in this journal. Over the past weeks there have been many trips, performances, spells of stimulating company, the kinds of occasions that have moved me to record them in previous entries. I think it is just that —what feels like the stale recurrence of past events: talks before school audiences, reading from literary work, drives west to Celeste and Lulu —which disinclines me from registering more of what would be mere log entries. Understanding this has been helpful, clarifying what I have been trying to do in keeping this account, which is to convey what is truest, most urgent in my experience as my days pass, as I age.

There is a quality of desire, or appreciation, in what I want most to record, and that quality —hard to describe in words but clear to me when felt —does not for the time being reside in events or personal exchanges. It registers instead in the apprehension of light, dazzling shafts of late afternoon light brightening only the tops of trees as the sun declines, darkening everything below to a kind of reverent hush. At midday the same bright autumn sunlight intensifies the reds and maroons of the oriental carpets in the sitting rooms. Outside, driving before autumnal expanses of hillocks and the rounded flanks of Green Mountains, I sense the grandness seeming to impart a message, another instance of what I experienced riding the train this past spring westward through the Sierras. My inability to decipher the message with any precision humbles me —appropriately. There is an intimation of greatness in what this light conveys —and in the ease in which it can recede, disappear, so that the merely visible, but not dramatically illuminated, world, whether indoors or out, reminds me of how great the transformation can be when, capriciously, it occurs —and how I long for it. Increasingly these days I long for it.

Not long ago I was struck by a special effect created in the film Winter's Tale, a not very effective rendering of Mark Helprin's strange and wonderful novel. There is a strong metaphysical dimension to the story, including the principal characters' —villains and heroes alike —understanding that all earthly power, all truth resides in knowing how light works, how it defines the relations of things to things. In one brief scene the arch villain of the film played by Russell Crowe illustrates the power of light. By manipulating a crystal, he shows how connecting arrow shafts of light bind all relationships. Again, the film is not overall very good, but in suggesting we are all held fast by bonds of light as atomic particles are held fast in their orbits, I was for a moment transported out of my skin.

So I await further intimations of what light has to say. Maybe I will become better at deciphering the messages, maybe even find words for them. Right now I am rattling along in this coach car. Out the window the Hudson is shimmering like dull foil under a pearly overcast of uneven cloud cover. A greater light seems on the brink of breaking through, and I know it will change that moment's story. I am waiting for it.

October 23, 2014: I am speeding, quite literally—80 m.p.h., 90, more!—in my little Mini across the broad back of New York State on my way to see Celeste and Lulu. All three of us are scheduled to fly to LA to meet my sister and her friends for a long weekend. We have been invited because Ginny, in the largeness of her heart, wants to meet her niece, Lulu. For her part, Lulu is thrilled both at the prospect of meeting her aunt, heretofore known only as the source of birthday and Christmas presents, and seeing California. Celeste is, if anything, even more excited about the trip. Given the dismal condition and permanent antipathy of Celeste's brothers and sister, the prospect of any warm and stimulating "family" encounter is eagerly sought. I suppose I am also looking forward to this presentation of what Ginny calls "my other family" to her Los Angeles set, although there is the possibility of awkwardness, given that group's warm feelings for Molly and our children.

It is a stirringly beautiful autumn day. The rolling undulations of upstate New York are painted with the settled yellows and oranges and reds of late autumn. Intermittent sun dapples sweeping prospects of farmland and meadow before me, and I feel I am being gathered into a profound Afterward.

As I was leaving the house I grabbed, without much thought, the CD of "Les Misérables" off the counter, with the idea that it might ease the monotony of the long drive. Just west of Utica I began to listen. I was rapt from the opening overture, but the second act sent me into the most heightened pitch of feeling I can remember. I know the "Les Misérables" score well, but I was not prepared for this. For perhaps forty-five minutes—from "A Heart Full of Love," the trio sung by the infatuated lovers (Cosette and Marius with each other, Eponine to Marius) to the rousing anthem of the finale, "Tomorrow Come," the muscles behind my eyes and throat were constricted almost painfully in an involuntary effort to hold in tears or whatever it is that wants to combust when there is an intimation of the ultimate.

I am aware that critics tend to pan the musical theater adaptation of "Les Misérables" as trite and overly sentimental, criticism easy for me to ignore, since for me the show is a sequence of irresistible archetypes. American intellectuals are uncomfortable with and reflexively dismiss any robustly Christian cultural offering, but such thoughts were far from my mind as I sped over the velvet smooth macadam of Route 90, head spinning with images and anthems of vaulting love, revolutionary fervor, heroic martyrdom, and final redemption. As Jean Valjean soliloquizes just before the shade of Fantine leads him by the hand into Eternal Life: "to love another person is to see the face of God!" This is sentimental? Overwrought?

Noted, fine, but please bring it on. Not that it needed any urging. There it was, amplified gorgeously in the tiny cab of the Mini, swelling the heart, constricting the throat, driving out all thought, all qualifications. And I realize: this is as much as I have ever felt. There is something in the music continuous with the autumnal Afterward beyond the windshield. There is, I am sure, something in it of being 69 years old, being weary in advance of what Lulu and the California adventure will certainly demand of me, yet gladly willing to do whatever I can to advance everyone's happiness because—I really do love all these people. What could be better, more gratifying than to thrust myself Jean Valjean-like through what remains of my life. On and on I go in my little rocket of a car: Syracuse, Rochester, Buffalo, Erie, Cleveland, Celeste and Lulu.

October 24-27: 2014: Celeste, Lulu, and I rise at six and board an early morning flight from Cleveland to LAX. There is at once a deep certainty that all will be well. The drive to the airport in predawn darkness is swift, quiet. There are no complications getting ticketed and boarding. On the plane Lulu reclines luxuriantly between Celeste and me, her head on my lap, feet on Celeste's. We alternately read, snack, doze, and then we are there. Ginny has arranged a sleek black limo to drive us to her house in Glendale. It is brilliantly sunny mid morning in Los Angeles, and Ginny is uncharacteristically up and out on her lawn to greet us. I am fascinated that there is an instantaneous flash of connection between Lulu and Ginny. My sister, married and divorced twice, childless, is quick to say she is not a "children person," preferring those she is obliged to know when they are well past infancy, able to speak clearly, make appropriate adjustments, behave. Despite these requirements, she has repeatedly told me she wanted to meet Lulu "before she is all grown up" and thus this visit. In my experience, Lulu has always been easy with new people. She is affectionate generally, and adults tend to warm to her. But the bond with Ginny is remarkable and deepens through the long weekend.

As Ginny and Celeste are both tightly wired, in their own ways anxious to control outcomes, I am a little worried that they might not get along. But they seem to. It helps that Ginny, while a bit imperious about what she will tolerate in people's behavior and speech, especially in her house and among her possessions, is clear about what goes and what doesn't. I see that this is easy for Lulu to read and she is not at all resistant when Ginny asks her to clean up after herself or to help her with some minor household task. Celeste, who is genuinely handy and always eager to help out, manages not to trespass on Ginny's routines and is more amused than put out that, once or twice, she is ordered out of the kitchen.

It is cloudlessly sunny outside, dry and hot, temperature in the mid-eighties. I have slept little and risen early for days and it is decided that we—Celeste, Lulu and I, not Ginny—will change into our suits and sit outside by the pool. Ginny's pool is secluded from neighbors by high walls, gorgeous plantings and tall cypress trees. The water is very cold but still inviting given the intense sunlight on the deck. All three of us go in, and the chill of it is bracing. There is a plan to meet Judy Taylor at the Disney studio for a tour, including the sets of some of Lulu's favorite shows. I am glad and relieved when Ginny suggests, with the detectable note of a command, that Celeste and I remain at the poolside and relax while she takes Lulu to the Disney site. Lulu is more than eager, and off they go. Not minutes later, I am, despite blazing sunlight, deeply asleep at the poolside. Celeste may have slept too, although she told me she also took the opportunity to explore the house thoroughly. I was not expecting this: quiet easeful time without Lulu, nothing expected of me, rest.

As usual the interior of Ginny's house is a cacophony of barking dogs and screeching cockatiels. Lulu is entranced by both the birds and the dachshunds, but Jude, the male and alpha dog of the pair, is leery of Lulu—jealous I think—and menacingly snappish. Nevertheless there is a distinctly positive air in the house, and I am happily relieved that everyone is getting along. A dinner has been arranged at The Castaway, a favored restaurant of mine perched high on a mountainside just minutes from Ginny's house. Three of Ginny's "core" friends, Mark and Judy and Jackie, join us. We dine outside in soft air, miles of Los Angeles twinkling below us. Lots of time over drinks, lively talk, and then we are hungry for our food. We leave the restaurant after ten—past one in the morning Cleveland time —and I can see Lulu is groggy with sleepiness, as am I. Back at Ginny's I retire straight to bed and sleep soundly through the night. I cannot remember when I last slept through till morning. Not in years.

We wake to a busy day. After much deliberation it is determined that Lulu, Celeste, and I will spend the day at Universal Studio City instead of Disneyland which, we decide, is too long a drive and where the Halloween week crowds are likely to be unendurable. As it happens Universal City is also teeming with customers when we arrive mid- morning. It is another blazingly sunny day. I buy very expensive VIP passes, which will advance us to the front of the line for all rides, attractions and shows. Given the crowds, this turns out to be a godsend. The Universal facility seems to extend miles in all directions, an amusement park, sound stage, and mall combined: a sixty-foot guitar, an enormous balloon facsimile of King Kong floating over walkways, blinking, beckoning signs to the uncountable shows and shops and rides. Skull-penetrating music, as themes from various Universal films are amplified continuously. The sensory overload disorients me and makes me dim, but Lulu seems to read all the signals, and she guides us through a terrifying and bewildering succession of offerings. We board a floating raft and glide along tortuous streams through a recreation of Jurassic Park where dinosaurs and other prehistoric fauna lunge and swoop into our way. Minutes later we are thrust deep into a virtual reality torture chamber having something to do with the Shrek movies, followed by "rides" derived from other Universal action films that combine elements of roller coasters with virtual reality images, all of them flying at you at great speed. After "rides" through the Despicable Me set and something about Mummies, I am on the verge of vertigo and nausea, so I sit outside while Celeste and Lulu proceed through the Transformers attraction, after which they too are feeling something like sea sickness. There is more of this, which I have mercifully forgotten, though not an elaborate reenactment of the most hair raising stunts from the futuristic movie Waterworld, staged in an enormous amphitheater with acres of constructed sets around a deep pool of water in which crafts of many kind enter and depart, bearing post-apocalypse thugs who battle one another to the death. The Waterworld sequence, enacted before a seated audience of a thousand or more viewers, concludes with an actual plane flying over the ramparts of the set and bursting into flames as it crashes in the water just ten or fifteen yards from where we are seated. Somehow all the wreckage is cleared and the set made ready for another show an hour later.

Leg weary by mid-afternoon, we seek egress through a crowd now milling shoulder to shoulder. On the way to the exit we stop before a live show of the Blues Brothers set in an outdoor plaza. Observable above the heads of the other viewers are exotically attired Asian women on stilts, a giant figure done up to look like Shrek, a vehicle— a burnt out looking combat jeep—bearing on its hood a facsimile of a bloodily broken corpse. I am not sure what Lulu makes of all of it, but I wonder. For me the stimulation drives out all thought but a dull impulse to reach the exit and find a quiet place to sit down and perhaps eat something.

That evening, by delightful contrast, Lulu, Celeste, Ginny, and I repair to her friend Bill's cliffside house where, joined by a few of Ginny's other close friends, we have drinks and a wonderful dinner. The muted lights and quiet chat are a needed antidote to the Normandy landing-like afternoon at Universal City. In a relaxed way, the adults extend themselves generously to Lulu, and even as sleepiness descends, she is warmly affectionate in response.

Sunday, our last full day, Ginny determines that she will squire Lulu around for a long afternoon of projects and errands, to which Lulu cheerfully agrees, as she does not want to go to the Getty Museum, which is Celeste's goal for the day. Celeste frequently takes Lulu to the Cleveland museum to view special exhibits, most of which do not interest her, so a firm resistance has set in. But the certainty that Lulu is going to enjoy herself eases Celeste's mind, and the two of us call for a car and are driven to the Getty, a mountain top aerie designed spectacularly by architect Richard Meier with panoramic views spanning greater Los Angeles and the shimmering Pacific beyond. No setting could contrast more pleasingly with Universal City. The complex of buildings, designed, to my eye, in the mode of I.M. Pei, but without the need to register any attention-getting personal signature, is constructed in massive rectilineal heaps of white stone. Outside, broad expanses of stone terrace bordered by railings invite viewing out over the city below. It is another clear day, a robin's egg blue sky, and moving in and about so much monumental white stone puts me in mind of what it might have been like to walk about the agora of Periclean Athens.

Inside we start viewing the medieval collection: manuscripts, altars, reliquaries, stained glass, then proceed into the renaissance galleries, and I am overwhelmed by the extent and beauty of the pictures. Some faint and fussy impulse from my deep interior wants to disapprove of how this colossal collection was acquired, what churches desecrated, what European cities and households denuded of place-defining masterworks by the lure of Getty's bottomless store of cash. But the impulse peters out, as I am drawn into to complexity and beauty of the work. And, I tell myself, this is *free*. The Getty Museum, including its futuristic tram ride up from sea level to the heights, costs nothing.

Celeste in her way is reverently appreciative of the pictures. Her family and schooling somehow failed to convey any sense of western history or, especially, biblical history, so the themes of most of the paintings— defining incidents in the lives of the Hebrew patriarchs, annunciations, visitations of the magi, flights into Egypt, the martyrdom of apostles and saints—have to be explained to her, which, as a veteran teacher of Western Civilization to ninth graders, I am happy to do. In one gallery Celeste is struck by a painting depicting Christ, the woman taken in adultery, and accusers about to stone her to death in accordance with the law. The adulteress is subtly but persuasively sexy, the accusers menacing, and overall the picture conveys considerable disturbance. Celeste wants to know about it, and I tell her the story, concluding with Christ's shrewd invitation that the man who is without sin should cast the first stone; then after they disperse, Christ's assurance to the adulteress that as the accusers no longer appear to condemn her, neither does he. Celeste responds warmly to this, finds it a beautiful story, and I do not want to spoil her response by adding another word, since, among other family legacies, Celeste was brought up into an atheistic suspicion of all religions, especially Christianity. Neither of us needs to say out loud that the picture has put us in mind of our own adultery and what might, in another context, have been our fate.

After a few hours we are picture-saturated and hungry and have lunch at an elegant and upscale restaurant. The high ceilings and glass walls admit such intense light that the white linen napkins and tablecloths look almost as if they are aflame. I hadn't realized how leg weary I was, and it felt very good to sit and to let the impression of the pictures settle. An agreeable sensation: I knew in advance that our meal would be memorable and delicious, and it was: as pleasing to look at on the gleaming white plate as it was to eat. Wine too, a chilled sauvignon blanc.

After lunch more galleries, as we move, without much interest, through the mannered post-renaissance pictures to the stunning Romantic Era paintings: David, Delacroix. It is in a way too much stimulation, and I feel again the inadequacy of being unable to take in the depth of the messages emanating from the compositions. Maybe it is enough, or at least enough for this afternoon: to be aware that I am in the presence of human understanding and technical mastery. We stroll the maze-like walkways of the outdoor gardens, pause for five and ten minutes at a time to look over the distant prospect of the sprawl of Los Angeles below. When it is time to call for a car to pick us up, there is an insistent little tug to turn back, to stay.

For our last night Ginny has invited the full complement of her friends to her house for drinks, dinner, and music. It is clear when we arrive back at the house that she and Lulu have had a satisfying day together. By the time we clean up and change our clothes the guests are arriving, and in minutes the kitchen and sitting room are noisy with high spirits. Again, generous attention is directed to Lulu, and Celeste marvels at the warmth and ease of Ginny's friends. She tells me later that there was no sense of effort, no perceived resistance in getting to know them. So far as I can see, Celeste is gregarious at the party but not overbearing. In the tradition of such gatherings, everybody sings his and her signature songs, and Celeste is in her element. Except for Ginny, none of the group has heard Celeste sing before, and she is in excellent voice. It is, I am sure, because she is happy and relaxed. I accompany her on a few of our favorites: The Nearness of You, What'll I Do, Black Coffee, and the listeners are impressed, even a little dumbstruck. Lulu is also in top form, belting out "Love Potion Number Nine" and "Doctor Jazz." No little girl shyness, no reticence. Ginny for some reason becomes choked up and teary and is almost unable to finish her usually very funny rendition of Life is a Cabaret. I think it is nostalgic memories of past gatherings and the loved ones no longer offering songs.

A satisfying party—and a late night for Lulu, who is asleep on the living room sofa when the last guests depart. Our car back to the airport is due to arrive early next morning. I am glad and also relieved that this tentative melding of my separate worlds has been possible. I am convinced that personal relations of all kinds proceed best when they are not filtered through preconceptions of what is normal, acceptable, and moral.

We arrive back in Cleveland in the early evening. I determine I am too tired and otherwise spent to drive home to Vermont tomorrow morning. My announcement makes Lulu visibly glad, and that touches me.

October 28, 2014: I wake to overcast skies. Outside the air is damp, and the faint chill, after California, is bracing. Lush shrubs crowding the sidewalks and the towering trees of Cleveland Heights are at their autumnal peak, the leaden gray overhead somehow brightening the yellows and reds. The atmosphere makes me restless to get out and move, so after dropping Lulu off at school, Celeste and I drive with the dog Obie to Lakeview Cemetery for what is always a satisfying hike.

This morning the cemetery seems even more removed from our era than usual. The grounds are impressively vast, descending and ascending to the boundaries of three municipalities: the city of Cleveland, East Cleveland, and Cleveland Heights. The expanse rises behind high stone walls from the city's flat terrain to what is in fact the first gentle escarpment of the Appalachian Mountains. At its highest point, the lawns gather to a crest that overlooks a lovely prospect of the city's north shore and the mass of Lake Erie beyond. Fittingly—or at least emblematic of the gilded American era in which the cemetery was conceived and developed—a towering obelisk commending to eternity the spirit of John D. Rockefeller crowns the crest.

I park the car near the heart of the grounds a few hundred yards below the James A. Garfield Memorial Chapel, an ornate Romanesque structure the interior and windows of which were designed by Louis Tiffany. In its huddled granite and marble bulk the chapel viewed from outside suggests a mighty effort to create Permanence—as do the uncountable lesser monuments—obelisks, Palladian mausoleums, stone angels—surrounding it.

As Celeste, Obie, and I meander up and down the landscaped rises, I feel the familiar elegiac mood rising. I suppose this is inevitable in any cemetery, but especially this one on this day: last vestiges of autumn foliage, lowering skies, varying degrees of effacement and blackening of the monuments, tombs, and inscriptions.

This morning I see all the stone, even the beautifully carved Angels of Death Victorious, as an extended folly, the folly of class and wealth as the memorial chapels and monuments dedicated to the mighty—Rockefellers, Garfields, Hannas, Boltons, Brushes, Criles, Wades—recede to lower ground where the merely prominent are entombed. Down lower still, on the margins of the park, are the tidy rows of headstones of departed working people, set flush to the earth.

Folly or not, there is undeniable majesty in the figures of the stone angels, their serene expressions, elegantly gesturing hands, and spread wings expressing solemn benedictions upon the departed loved ones at their feet. And however wealthy and privileged the angel-blessed, there is a kind of moral corrective in the fact that each of those lovely figures was fashioned by stone masons in the burgeoning slum of Cleveland's Little Italy.

Even while musing on such matters I know I am doing it because I am nearly seventy years old, and while still afoot with some spring in my step, a madly happy Obie bounding in front of me, this city of stone remembrances to my right and left is at once saying "back then" and "coming soon."

November 12, 2014: Back in Ripton. It takes only a day or two and I feel deeply, permanently settled. Brisk windy days followed by rains have sufficiently denuded the trees so that the look is more emerging winter than declining fall. There are still serrations of orange and brown on the flanks of the mountains encircling the Bread Loaf campus where I take my afternoon hikes, but also an unmistakable sense of hunkering down, the near woods hunching its bristly, leafless back against the impending freeze.

The stores in Middlebury are already vulgarly full of Christmas come-ons, but even in the cocooned quiet of my upstairs study, I sense the holiday hurtling toward me with a kind of insistence I cannot understand. I am faintly heartened by the realization that I have not taken down all the light strands from last Christmas, so this winter's efforts will be considerably eased. Christmas! Will the darkening days of the approaching solstice, the glow in the fireplace, the flickering holiday lights and candles once again evoke the sweet ache of holy nativity? I never know. I never quite believe it until I feel it. It is hard to imagine without the sacred music, the choirs of King's or St. John's College, Cambridge, the uninflected treble of the little boys' voices sounding almost frightened in their reverence as they solemnly intone the words of the carols.

November 13, 2014: Last night watching the evening news I was jarred out of dull comfort by an image of death I have been unable to dismiss from visual memory. The report was on the ravages of the Ebola epidemic in Africa, a village in Sierra Leone. The gist of the sequence was that there was no one available to deal with people when they became afflicted. There was a government emergency number to call on the telephone, but no help arrives in consequence of calling in.

The clip showed the heaped figure of a man who had died of the disease. He had been dragged by unknown persons across the road from his dwelling and left at the base of a tree. The untended corpse was less a concern to the agitated villagers than the fact that the men who deposited it across the road were now very likely infected and infectious. Nobody knew who they were or whom they might be contaminating. A hand-held camera shifted to a woman said to be one of the dead man's wives. She was reportedly deathly ill and was lying in a scrubby patch of earth outside the door of her house. No one dared approach her, even to offer life-sustaining water. The woman's arms were extended over her head and she was opening and closing her grip in a way that suggested desperate pain. The image was both upsetting and confusing. The woman lay on her side, a sari-like cloth draped around her waist and bottom. She looked to be very tall and slender, the expanse of her naked back incongruously sensual and lovely—and again, the outstretched arms and the clasping and unclasping of her grip. At the conclusion of the news hour, the network anchorwoman announced that the woman lying on the ground had reportedly died. Like everyone else in the country, I am aware that people are dying of Ebola in West Africa, but the image of this recumbent, still beautiful figure writhing in the dirt recurred in my mind's eye throughout the night and still this morning.

November 14-15, 2014: What the TV weather forecasters call a polar vortex has dropped temperatures across the country to record breaking frigid lows. Here in Ripton it just feels like the winter it almost is, a time for hats and gloves.

There is a light dusting of snow outside and bright sun, which enlivens the house, intensifying colors. I walk through the downstairs rooms with no plan or purpose other than to look around. I take a few steps, pause for a minute or two, taking in what lies before me as if it were a painting. It occurs to me: *Nothing is happening*, or more precisely, *I am making nothing happen.* It is by no means an unpleasant realization. I am beginning to understand that through my youth and middle years, even extending into whatever you call this time of life—my "maturity"—I have been *propelled* through my successive experiences, and I have not been doing the propelling. Aristotle wrote about an immanent force, *physis*, that drives all motion, all development in the world, acorns into oaks, boys into men, clans into villages, villages into polities, etc. And perhaps this *physis* has propelled me through my days, but as it has done so it has necessarily hurtled me past so much peripheral data, excluded so much from vision, contracted my awareness to whatever was directly before my guided path. But increasingly, as today, it's as if the *physis* is petering out, or at least paused. I am simply *here* where I am standing, without task, intention, or a conscious next step. The sunlight is streaming through the window, blanching the lace curtains, and I feel I am, like the furniture and carpets, absorbing it. I do not feel stalled, but stopped. I am at rest, but not "resting up" for subsequent activity. The sensation is at once fleeting and profound, perhaps even a revelation: that at the end of life, one is supposed to feel *arrived* and no longer *on the way*. There is a truth, a completeness in this arrived feeling, for which I am grateful.

More on what solitude has to say: I have been upstairs at my desk in my study for several still, quiet hours. As I did downstairs earlier, I have paused in my chair to take in the room, the complexity of so many framed pictures on the walls and shelves, the milky green light through the stained glass I have fitted into the room's only window. I am not looking for or really at anything, instead trying to take in the whole of it, the feel of it. I begin to muse about the hundreds of quiet afternoons I have climbed the stairs to this garret room, how alike the days have been. Sitting, musing, pecking away at the keyboard, watching the stately Times New Roman letters and words and paragraphs organize the glowing white screen. These sittings are broken up only by visits to the adjacent toilet, which, like my study, is abstracted from the rest of the house, upstairs in a rarely visited guest wing accessed by its own staircase.

Just as I begin to consider the familiar adjacency of study and toilet, a vivid image presents itself from my first year teaching at University School. On the third story of the old school building in Shaker

Heights, there was a former faculty office, for the time being vacant, where I used to sequester myself during my one free period in an otherwise overwrought daily schedule. I was twenty-three, trying very hard to find a sufficiently commanding instructional style, while scrambling to master the American government and ancient history material I was supposed to be imparting to eighth and ninth grade boys. I taught five classes on some days, six on others, in addition to after school coaching and proctoring duties. At the time I was also newly married and enrolled full time in a graduate program at Case Western Reserve University where I arranged to take my required courses in the evening. I do not think there was ever more required of me or scheduled for me than there was that year and the year following.

I remember finding the unoccupied office in the course of an exploratory venture in search of a quiet place to work amidst so much noise and movement in the rest of the school. The third floor extension housed two large rooms that were devoted to orchestral and choral music, and because those ensembles met for only two periods of the school day, the floor was otherwise unoccupied and thus relatively quiet. The unlocked office seemed to me a fated and badly needed blessing. The room itself was disordered. A scratched up, half filled bookcase held collapsed stacks of a departed English department chairman's assigned books, most of them books of or about poetry, many of which I took home to read. There was a battered old desk with most of its drawers locked and a ruined armchair with baseball sized gouges into the upholstery. But behind the closed door of that office I could sit comfortably in that chair, and I could cant my head back and clear my head of all purposeful thought until the bell summoned me back to action. Just beyond the office was a small toilet, so far as I could tell used by no one other than the night custodian. The use of this quiet, secret-seeming toilet seemed to complete the blessing of my discovered sanctuary.

I have not thought about those third floor rooms for nearly fifty years. What they represented to me then—I can feel it now—is a place where I could return to my deepest interior, what felt like my real being, as opposed to the impersonation I was frantically trying to conduct in the lower reaches of the building. An abstracted study and a toilet then; an abstracted study and a toilet now. Both have been blessings, without which I believe my life could have been all propulsion, with no arrival.

December 15, 2014: There has been a flurry of book developments. The small and obscure publisher of my Souls in Boxes book, Robert France of Green Frigate Books, has written to tell me his press is being subsumed into a mostly British publishing house, Libri, which to date has published specialized academic studies but wants to branch out in more general directions. This means that Souls in Boxes will soon be a Libri offering, which required me to sign an elaborate contract with them. Fine, I thought. Then yesterday Robert wrote to me to say that under the new arrangement, he would be able to designate two or three titles a year to be published at Libri—and did I have anything I might want to submit for consideration. No, I thought—and then yes: maybe this very manuscript. While falling under no easy classification, it may, I think, offer something about how we experience aging and impending death. I sent a digital copy of the whole work to date to Robert, warning him of its length (and I am not yet quite out of my sixties). I will be interested to see what the response will be. No one yet has reviewed this work for publication. I was heartened that, in addition to the Libri business, he was forwarding a check for royalties for Souls in Boxes, a sum indicating more sales than I had imagined.

Even better news has been the unexpected acceptance of the second novel of my Jonathan Force series by the Fomite Press in Burlington. I had no idea such a press existed until chatting with my high school friend and lifelong correspondent Lynn Sloan in the course of a trip to Chicago last winter. Over lunch Lynn, an accomplished short story writer, told me she had had her first novel accepted for publication. When I asked who was doing it, she told me Fomite Press—in Vermont, no less. Intrigued, I looked them up on line and saw what seemed an interesting, rather highbrow list of titles. On a whim, I sent the editor / publisher Marc Estrin a proposal for my novel, The Source of Longing. He wrote back an engaging response, saying he didn't like at all the pitch I made for the book, but he liked the excerpt I had included, especially the dialog, and would I send the whole ms. I did, and with surprising speed, he wrote back to say he liked most of it, but had concerns. To my surprise he had done a tentative first edit of the ms. and proposed that we meet. This looked like publication to me, so we met for a pizza supper at his house and he proceeded to tell me very specifically what he did not like about the novel as it was: the intensity of the romance and what he felt was the fairy tale manner in which it was resolved. We agreed that I would try to modify some things in order to meet his objections without sacrificing my intentions, but after some effort in this direction, we both agreed it was not to be. Marc very nicely wrote to me saying he had no doubts about my writing and if and when I had anything else…

A few months later it occurred to me to send him the *Jonathan Force* novel: his education at Yale and coming to full maturity. Once again Marc responded quickly and this time enthusiastically and without qualification. I explained to him that the novel was the middle part of a trilogy, the youthful segment of which had already been published as *The Other World.* Unfazed by this challenge, Marc made some excellent suggestions for how to alter this second volume so that it would more readily stand alone as a novel. His enthusiasm for the project seemed to increase as I made the recommended adjustments—to the point that he has committed to publishing the entire trilogy. This will involve some deft editorial maneuvering, as he will begin publication with what is in effect, volume II, then publish volume III, which he has not yet seen (!), then, finally, re-publish The Other World, currently a cycle of stories, as volume I. When that has all happened, and if we have managed to capture some readers, the trilogy can then be reset in a single volume or perhaps a boxed set. Negotiating our way forward in all of this will require some thought, but so far I have found Marc a stimulating editor. He has strong opinions and preferences, but they are earned by close reading. It helps that he is an accomplished novelist himself, with seven or eight highly regarded, decidedly modernist books behind him. A former Unitarian minister, hippie communard, and social activist, he is, all in all, an interesting fellow. He says he has undertaken publishing as "community service."

Meanwhile, my novel-in-fugue, *Greeves Passing,* is being readied for publication by Battersea Books, a new imprint of Short Story America. My editor there, Tim Johnston says there will be final proofs by January 10, with pre-publication copies ready for reviewers during all of February and early March, then official publication at the end of that month. There will be some launching events, one of them in the South (Beaufort, SC) and one in the North (Cleveland), and then we will see what happens. There is a hope that readers remembering *The Headmaster's Papers* might warm to this new iteration. It is hard to know. I sense my own complicity in creating a preposterous superabundance of books. Nearly every friend of mine writes books, and between the print and on-line reviews I read, it has become almost impossible to keep up with favorite writers, much less identify new ones.

December 16-17, 2014: A strange feeling of being closed in, almost smothered. A freakish storm descended a few days ago, unloading not just a few feet of snow, but snow alternating with rain, the rain then quickly freezing so that it held the snow solidly—and heavily—in place. The visual effect is stunning: every branch, every twig, every fence post, every eave and gable glazed with what looks like a thick coating of powdered sugar. Also coated are the power lines and phone lines, seemingly all of which have collapsed either under the weight of the ice and snow or by bowed and broken branches. Ripton and most of the county has been without power for four days. Owners of a generator, we are able to maintain light and furnace heat, but not hot water. Roads were and still are treacherous, not just because of surface glaze but because tree branches normally twenty feet overhead are bowed down so that twigs scratch at the roof and windshield of the car as I pass below. Every mile or so, a large branch or whole tree has fallen across the road, stopping traffic altogether until the road crews come. So, wisely, we remain indoors in a season already so dark as the solstice approaches. Afternoon light in the morning, dark outside by four.

The closed-in-ness is intensified by a bronchial cold I wanted very badly to avoid. It descended in cadence with the snowfall, trickling and tickling through my nose and throat now down to my lungs where it hovers like a smug enemy. At no time in my life have I ever been more than a few months away from these bronchial bouts. As with the darkening days, this largely endurable malaise—I can go to town for errands, I did an exploratory cross country ski run—carries with it a suggestion of a final closing in, an intimation that it is not temporary, that there will be no relief. And of course, if not this winter, some coming winter that will be the case.

It has been the case with my friend Karl's mother who, at ninety-nine, has just died in her bed at an assisted living facility in Maine. She had not been ill, just a little off her feed. I think of Karl who, like me a year or two ago, has begun sorting through his mother's effects as executor of her affairs, thus closing out the business of the parental generation. I knew his mother a little, Jane Lindholm, a flinty, intellectually sharp New Englander. She had a mordant wit, and in the era when weekly family magazines printed light verses, some of hers were published. She also had a sharp eye for funny printed blunders and would send the best ones she found to The New Yorker where they duly appeared. In an email yesterday, Karl sent me one of her verses—

> One fears this thing called "unisex"
> May well cause massive trauma:
> Alas for future progeny
> Of this strange androgyny—
> Little mixed up Oedipus Rex
> Can't tell Pop from Momma

Not bad. Not bad, too, folding one's long life quietly into the dark of the solstice. Maybe not this year, though not for me to say.

December 25, 2014-January 1, 2015: The holidays loom, arrive. As I begin preparing the house I realize, a little anxiously, that gestures I anticipated in the past with great pleasure—stringing lights, trimming the tree—feel a bit like willed recreations. I want these feelings to dissolve, and they largely do, the passage eased by familiar Christmas music: King's College choir, St. Olaf's Cantus, Pavarotti.

The uncertain arrival of 'the spirit' here in Vermont may be because at the beginning of the month I went by train for a long weekend with Lulu and Celeste, which we consciously structured as a "mini-Christmas," most of it urban, with fancy evening meals out, a jazz concert, a circus, and a Broadway show: a spectacular staging of "Aladdin." There was much shopping, the malls and commercial streets crowded with holiday shoppers, the atmosphere a roar of chatter over amplified carols. Lulu was in elevated spirits, as I had given her two hundred dollars for the gifts she wanted to buy for her mother, brother and sister. Lulu is reliably cheerful company when I visit, and she was an exuberant angel our entire time together. She has a gift, rare in children, of being genuinely, touchingly thankful. I was more torn than usual when I bid her good bye before catching the train back to Vermont. Our time together was suffused with "special occasion" and, perhaps more than I thought then, actual Christmas, and thus perhaps my slowness to reawaken to a second one.

By the evening of our now annual party the day before Christmas Eve, I had managed once again to create a sufficiently twinkling and glowing deep winter ambience in the house, a condition achieved as early as four in the afternoon with the darkening arrival of the solstice. The effect this year was augmented pleasingly by two sets of faux cylindrical candles—fourteen in all—sent from my sister in California. I had admired these vanilla-scented candles at her house when I last visited. They are synthetic and battery-powered but have the waxy appearance of real ones, especially after they are illuminated by either a small switch beneath their base or—thrillingly— a remote control device. When lit, the candles not only emit a lovely glow, shining through much of their milky length, but they also flicker convincingly. Even after repeated lightings and extinguishings, I feel a little god-like as I stand at some distance away flicking them in and out of being with my remote.

Thirty-some friends, old and some new, jollify our rooms in the course of our party, a good party I think, pleasing embraces, lots of laughter. The effort of massing the provisions, laying in firewood, setting up the bar, preparing the food and cleaning up afterward help to prepare me mentally for the succession of visitors to follow. None of our girls are able to manage travel on Christmas Day, and Kate and her family will not be coming at all, as they are moving into their new house, so we invite for Christmas dinner our new friends, the Klein-Wessons: Sarah, a painter and rather a beauty, her amicably estranged husband Rick, Sarah's twin sister Cynthia, and Rick and Sarah's college age son Schuyler. Given their interpersonal dynamics, there was a potential for awkwardness, but the traditional turkey and fixings, preceded by cocktails by the fire, warmed all of us up, and we were able to make fairly merry.

Alone together on Christmas morning, M and I awoke, prepared tea and a few nibbles and opened each other's presents in the red parlor in front of a nice fire. The ritual of our present opening has become something of a joke, as each of us has made it plain—because it is true—that we have an abundance of every material thing we could want or need. Whether outerwear, underwear, reading material, cookery—we are both long habituated to buying whatever we want the minute we are so moved. Our drawers and shelves are full. Our attic is full. Our garage is full. There is no room on any wall to hang a picture. Just two of us occupy the house, but all twenty-six hooks in the mud room are draped with our coats, and there is not an available hanger in the crammed double closet by the door. Nevertheless M and I cannot bring ourselves to offer no gifts, so by mid morning we sit among piled boxes of redundant sweaters, newly released hard-cover books, and gadgets. My most successful gift to M, I think, was two framed watercolors of nasturtiums painted by our friend Sarah. By removing two decorative husks of colored corn from a narrow strip of wall between cupboards in the kitchen, I was able to hang the pictures to pleasing effect. But presents, birthday presents, Christmas presents—it has to stop.

Two days after Christmas the children and their entourage begin to arrive, Claire first with her beau Nick. I am glad to have a day and night with just them because, while I liked Nick when I met him this summer in the course of our ritual farewell to the Marion house, I wanted to get a surer sense of him, as there have been intimations that he might be The One for Claire. It turns out I am not mistaken: the evening of their arrival they informed us over dinner that they plan to get married. They had already announced this intention to Nick's parents at their previous stop in Easton, Massachusetts. They would like to celebrate the wedding hereabouts sometime in early autumn. I sense something deeply right and inevitable in all of this. Nick is a ruggedly good looking, well-spoken, sweet natured young man with a good job in alternative energy engineering. He seems devoted to Claire and she to him. I now feel I can acknowledge fully that I was never very enthusiastic about Claire's previous beau and almost fiancé, who exited their relationship two years ago. Mainly I think: Nick is lucky. It is hard to imagine a more lively, affectionate, effective young woman than Claire. I don't think this assessment is parental over-valuing. Claire has been a consistently bright light since birth. As I proceed through the evening and retire for the night, the prospect of the looming marriage swells and deepens to an indescribable pitch of happiness.

The next day is a series of ebullient arrivals, first Jesse, James, Leon and Alice. Leon, at seven an endearing bean pole, is as talkative and affectionate as ever. Alice, at two, looks like a Nordic cherub drawn by Karl Larsen. This past summer she was, for some reason, cautiously wary of me, but that appears to have dissolved, and she is sweet and funny and a bit of a flirt. It is very good to see Jesse & co. despite their tendency to create a cyclone of mess in the wake of their ceaseless explorations of the house. I am a little concerned about James. He is poised at a highly vulnerable point in his life's path, finishing his doctoral dissertation in a rarified branch of history at NYU while applying for highly competitive teaching posts across the country. He does not know what his work will be for the coming year, or if he will even have work. He and Jesse do not know where they will live, but are desperate to get out of their preposterously small walk-up in Brooklyn. They have no cushion of savings. Their household management has been badly strained by James' having taken a role this past fall in a highly successful off Broadway play, Young Jean Lee's "Straight White Men." The show had opening runs in Salzburg and Paris before a successful six weeks at The Public Theater in New York. Reviews, including reviews of James' performance, were excellent. At another time this would have been a gratifying professional moment for James, but as it happened, his absence from home, even when he was back in New York, put a terrific strain on Jesse and the household. This tension, in addition to the inevitable stress of finishing his doctoral work, teaching, and job-seeking, cannot have been good for James. Added to this was a wrenching decision to decline an offer to play Horatio in a new Broadway production of Hamlet, which will star the movie actors Peter Sarsgaard and Michele Williams as Hamlet and Ophelia. James was offered the part by director Austin Pendleton, one of his co-stars in "Straight White Men." To have taken the role would have been a gratifying and perhaps career advancing—at least stage-career advancing—move, but he knew there was no way that he could make that commitment and still manage his scholastic and domestic responsibilities. In any case, I feel for James as he resigns himself to what he felt he had to do. He is such a good man and such a good father. I wish him some light, some ease, some free, quiet time in the weeks ahead.

Close on the heels of Jesse's brood come four friends of Claire's, two married couples, the females of which were Claire's former housemates in San Francisco. Because we are full up, they are lodging across the street at the inn. Married now and living in Brooklyn, the friends are a mixed lot of school teachers and post-doctoral level academics. We are now enjoying meals for 12, and fortunately it is a compatible, lively lot. There is a cheery cocktail hour and, after Leon and Alice's bed time, meandering chats in front of the fire in the red parlor. To me it is stimulating to be immersed in the company of educated, high spirited people a full generation younger. Comparisons between their generation and mine are inevitable, and I am inclined to weigh in favorably for the younger for what seem to be their more thoughtful acceptance of cultural differences, especially their regard for females, their bone deep commitment to environmental sustainability, the general sense I get that they feel themselves citizens of one world with attendant obligations. There is of course plenty of wit and fun, but these are gentle souls. I wonder more than worry if the very, very, nice males aren't a bit too gentle and accepting for their own good, but that is probably a projection of my own unevolved selfishness. Anyway, very good company, and I am doing my best to keep relatively quiet and to listen for a change.

And so, in a swirl of gathering provisions, preparing meals, washing dishes, burgeoning messes and imperfect efforts to pick up and tidy up, we proceed into the New Year, this time an invigorating passage. Claire's and Nick's impending marriage, Kate's and Shad's new house in Oak Park, the uncertain progression of Jesse and James into whatever and wherever is next combine to raise so many hopes and so many questions, unanswerable questions, the right kinds of questions. And there are Lulu and Celeste in Cleveland Heights, with no means beyond what I am able to provide, but braced against the cold and the dark by big hearts and considerable high hopes. Which is to say no more than that my life goes on, the only difference is that the engine and passenger cars of the train are now chugging and whistling somewhere far out ahead of where I sit, in the caboose, an elderly tag-along musing and pecking away at his keyboard.

January 9, 2015: Cold. Again this year what the television meteorologists are calling a polar vortex is chilling most of the country, from the Canadian border down to Texas and northern Florida. As usual the northeast is especially frigid. It was 21 below zero in Ripton last night, not counting wind chill. The weather advisory is to stay indoors for the coming two days. I have ventured out for groceries and other errands, and the cold does indeed penetrate coat and clothing in what feels a new way. But I am not sure. From my childhood in Chicago I can summon up memories of stunning coldness, a bleary pain in my face as I made my way to and from school. There was less information then—at least in our house—about weather particulars. My mother might say, "bundle up, it's really cold out this morning," before I headed off, but no one ever suggested anything like harm or danger resulted from exposure to the elements, reinforcing in my child's mind that nature, while bracingly dramatic from time to time, knew better than to hurt you. This impression would become a subconscious conviction, and I think it is still at work in my psyche. I have been reluctant to block the sun in high summer or when I vacation in tropical climes. I know people—assignable people, friends, Linda, Celeste, Gary—who have developed melanomas from the sun and then required terrible surgeries, living thereafter under the ominous cloud of a cancerous return. But, again, the sun? Sunlight as danger, as *deadly*?

I remember as a boy reading and being haunted by Jack London's story, "To Build a Fire," in which a solitary arctic dog sledder camping for the night runs out of matches and must resign himself to certain death. It never occurred to me to blame the cold, or even bad planning. It just seemed to me the kind of thing that happens when you are unlucky. I suppose the cold outside my door right now could do me ill or even in, most probably if I drove somewhere off the beaten path and the car broke down, an event so unlikely I cannot work up any concern about it. But it is cold, uncomfortably, almost painfully cold in the course of my short walks from the parking lot to the supermarket, from the house to the post office next door. In these days of extreme, much publicized cold, it takes my Jeep's heater close to 10 minutes to warm up the front seat. Until the car is heated and until I have gained the warmth of my errand destinations, the cold makes me more than uncomfortable. I can't suppress the sense that it is now my enemy and could quickly overwhelm me, to the extent I might not be able to move or breathe. I accelerate the car to hasten my arrival, move from my parking spot to the supermarket hunched over in a half-run. The cold on my face and hands and neck do not concern me; it is the cold in my bones, my ribs, my spine, my knees. Something deep in my interior tells me that the cold is seeking me out, wants *in*, and there is an intimation of what the end could be like: passing entirely into coldness, joining it.

January 24, 2015: Exactly two weeks ago, having carefully checked road conditions between Vermont and Cleveland, I drove west for what was to have been a week of outings, entertainments, and general post-holiday cheer with Lulu and Celeste. Loading the Jeep on the cold but clear morning of my departure I remember being in especially high spirits. I had even packed elaborate evening clothes, including tails and a white tie arrangement, for a night of exaggerated formality out on the town. But as soon as I was on the road, my body began a series of pronouncements, beginning with non-stop sneezing and a ceaselessly runny nose. It seemed inconceivable; I had felt so good, so *especially* good.

I was sniffling but hardly laid low when I arrived in Cleveland at about the dinner hour. Celeste determined that we should go out to dine at a cozy little restaurant in Little Italy. By meal's end I realized that I was impaired and likely to decline. Plying myself with many cups of hot tea and glasses of water fizzing with a cold prevention tablet rumored to work, I retired early, foregoing the music making and storytelling and game playing that usually precedes tucking Lulu in for the night.

The bug, or whatever it was, proceeded depressingly, as it has since its earliest boyhood visitations, into my throat and chest, constricting breathing and raising a harsh, insistent cough. By morning, I was bleary and spent for lack of sleep and too ill to get up and drive Lulu to school. The anticipation of the failure of all the plans she and I had exchanged by email hung miserably in the air. And so it went. In eight days, I failed to rally or recover. By day three both Celeste and Lulu's hacking coughs joined mine from other rooms, the effect like a terrible rebuke. The three of us contracted into survival mode, moving as little as possible and, in my case, saying as little as possible, as generating ordinary conversation, in fact speech of any kind, felt like a terrific effort. The days were cold, and for understandable financial reasons, Celeste prefers to keep the house cold, so I went in and out of spasmodic chills, some nights sleeping in all my clothes under a preposterous pile of quilts. Eight days of this. Not at all feeling up to it, I determined to attempt at least a few outings with Lulu: a film, *Selma* about the historic civil rights march, which I soon realized was too dark and too long for her at nine. With admirable restraint, her complaint was only that "it was too much like school." We also made a trip to the Cleveland Natural History Museum, but had to park so far away that the frigid walk to and fro overwhelmed whatever pleasures we took in the lacquered skeletons of the dinosaurs. Afterward we went to lunch at Lulu's favorite neighborhood eatery, Tommy's. Lulu, anything but a clumsy girl, spilled her milkshake all over the table, twice. I had had no appetite for days, but ordered a bacon, lettuce, and tomato sandwich, which arrived outsized and repellant on the plate. The next day, against all physical inclination and good sense, the three of us went bowling, an exercise Lulu may have enjoyed a little—it was her request—but was an agonizing act of will for me, and I suspect Celeste.

Two more days of bronchial gloom, mine intensified by guilt at having brought the sickness to the house. In an attempt to compensate, I declared that the three of us would dress up and go out to the most elegant restaurant we could find in easy driving range—health and mood be damned. I donned my white tie and tails. Lulu and Celeste also rose to the invitation, Celeste descending the stairs in a get-up that would have made her a credible fixture in a drawing room scene in Downton Abby. Heading out the door, I caught a glimpse of myself in the mirror over Celeste's fireplace: a beaten, sepulchral figure, made emphatically more so by the fancy dress.

Feeling no better, but aware that I could not stay on in failing health indefinitely, I resolved to drive home. The morning of my departure was forecast to be relatively clear of snow along Interstate 90 between Cleveland and Vermont, but when I peeked under the blind upon rising, heavy, wet snow was blanketing my car in the drive and the streets beyond. This put me in a foul mood, recalling prior agonizing, heart-in-mouth eternities over ice-slicked highways, snow limiting the view ahead to ten or twenty yards. Feeling physically compromised and edgy about the coming drive, I snapped unpleasantly at Celeste who was asking perfectly reasonable questions about my preparation to leave. Guilt and shame now in the mix, I attempted to apologize before loading the car, and drove slowly off into the snowy descent.

More numb than concerned, I proceeded at no great speed along the Interstate, and by the time I reached Erie, both the road and sky had cleared, and the rest of the drive east was merely chilly and dull.

It felt wrong to enter the house still gripped with a chest constricting malaise: no appetite, a painful stitch in my back, and a relentless, dry cough. In the two days to follow there was no relief. The discomfort in my back progressed to considerable pain, such that I could not sit or lie down comfortably. I seemed not to sleep at all. In the afternoon of the third day of this, M came up to check on how I was. I had been resistant to her suggestion of seeing my regular physician on the grounds that I knew he had nothing on hand to help me at his office, which was a twenty minute drive from the house, and that he would schedule me for blood work, X-rays, and God knows what at the hospital in Middlebury, all of it entailing more appointments, bundling up, getting into the car and going places—when rising from my chair felt like a titanic effort.

Then it came to me clearly: I had to get up and get treated. I could barely breathe and the discomfort in my back had now effaced all possibility of relaxing, reading and, I am sure, healing. I asked M if she would drive me to the Emergency Room at Porter Hospital in Middlebury. We left the house at once, and I am so glad. I was admitted immediately to care at the hospital. There was a sequence of brief questioning, vital signs taken by a nurse, a consultation and cursory probing of my thoracic region by a young physician, then a chest X-ray. No uncertain waiting, no delays. The X-ray confirmed pneumonia, whether viral or bacterial. I was given the steroid prednisone, prescriptions for a heavy duty antibiotic and a narcotic for pain.

This highly focused and speedy intervention was something of a marvel to me as it was transpiring. The voice within that had so decisively determined to rouse me from my chair and seek medical help did not feel quite my own. Unreasonably, I resist conventional medical advice and treatment, due I think to some deep animal tendency to reduce stress and conserve energy when ill. But this new voice was insistent and clear. I also think I may have been making an unconscious calculation of my steadily declining lung function: a certainty more succinct than anything I could verbalize said, in effect: *if over the next several hours the pain and compression you are feeling in your chest increases as it has for the past four hours, and if your breathing becomes proportionally shallower, you may not be able to breathe at all. Your lungs could be overcome, and you could die.* This impression was then fortified by remembered accounts of people dying just this way. In particular, I recalled the sudden death of the Muppeteer Jim Henson of pneumonia in a London hospital. All of this business arose from an executive agency that seemed to come from somewhere other than my own conscious preferences and thoughts. Yet another indication, as if I needed one, about who and what is really at command central in one's psychic interior.

Today, three and a half days later, the medicines seem to be doing exactly what they are intended to do. Normal breathing has been restored, the back pain and feeling of compression greatly relieved. Better still, I have after more than two weeks regained some appetite for food. Overall, I sense the machinery of a functioning metabolism clunking back into operation. But as in my response to the intense cold temperatures prior to my trip west, there is a new intimation, something close to certainty, that these ambient bugs and viruses that have been hovering about me like bats over the years are, or will be, every bit my match. They are not beaten, but waiting, strong as ever, as I inevitably weaken.

February 22, 2015: My seventieth birthday, February 21, 2015, fell on a Saturday, so it was relatively easy to schedule a little party. I invited a dozen people, my college friends and their wives and a group of relatively new artist friends we have come to like through M's having been invited to join a group of women painters, The Blue Swans. At a prior evening out with some of the Swans and their husbands there was talk of having a Downton Abbey gathering of some kind, the point being to dress in some approximation of the period clothes of that BBC series on public television. The Downton Abbey motif somehow got melded into the party plans, which was agreeable to me, as I still had tails and white tie accessories from some antic impulse back in my Cleveland days when I was performing in clubs, accompanying Celeste.

The plan for the party was that guests would arrive at our house at six for cocktails and hors d'œuvres, then we would drive down the mountain to the Waybury Inn for dinner. We were almost foiled by heavy snow, which began falling without let up from midday on, but in the event everyone braved the elements. I found the women's period apparel—floor length gowns of dark velvet, long gloves, flashing necklaces and earrings, beaded and bejeweled handbags—highly stimulating, even faintly erotic. In my tails and white tie I believe I cut a credible figure as, perhaps, Lord Grantham, or at least the head butler, Carson. The other men did less well approximating aristocratic elegance, most of them wearing what would pass for business dress in Chicago or New York; at any rate they put on coats and ties. In fairness, coats and ties are all but unseen these days in Vermont, so the invited men did take a purposeful step in the direction of formality. My friend Karl and his wife Brett who had spent the past year as visiting scholars in Cameroon, showed up wearing what they explained was the height of formal wear in Yaounde, in Brett's case, a long fitted cotton dress, in Karl's an enormous shirt, both of which were brightly patterned in a way that evoked picnic table cloths—and somehow exactly right for the party. There was soft light from the Tiffany lamps and a substantial blaze in the red room fireplace. In just minutes and only a few sips of our cocktails, we were a noisy with high spirits.

Later at the inn in the course of my welcoming toast, I mentioned half century—and longer—relationships with some of the assembled and, at one point, my perspective as an "old man," which I most certainly am. Sarah, one of the painter friends, and also the youngest and prettiest of the Swans, told me she was genuinely troubled by the "old man" label. She meant I think to flatter me, but there was something else in her concern: that if I am an old man, and this has become her "society," she too is becoming old. This morning I have been poring closely over digital photographs from the party, noting degrees of "oldness" revealed in the images. From my immodest and probably distorted perspective, I appear jaunty in my various poses, mostly partial embraces of the Downton-like ladies. I would assign my age in these pictures as indeterminate. With the exception of Sarah, the other guests looked their ages. It was an unmistakable gathering of the elderly.

But it was a good party, my favorite kind of party. The guests, and I certainly, drank freely. Conversations felt substantial. There was much laughter. Probably because it was such a snowy night, there were few people dining at the Inn when we arrived, and they departed early in the course of our meal, so we had the dining room to ourselves. We were arranged along a single long table in front of the fireplace. Changing seats and seat mates frequently in the course of the meal, desserts, and after dinner drinks, I sensed a reluctance on everybody's part to leave, despite the mounting snow outside.

On the slow and cautious drive back up mountain over an uncertain road surface, we approached a truck, the front end of which was sunk into a ditch. When we stopped, the driver assured us he and his passengers were all right and help was on the way. We crept on, even more slowly, in silence through the snow. Carol, our neighbor, and Sarah were in the back seat. Carol needed to be walked to her door. Sarah, whose car was parked across the street, needed assistance clearing her car of snow. Physical movement, especially walking, seemed reduced to slow motion due to the knee-length depth of the snow, also, probably, to the agreeable anesthesia of a succession of drinks. And I am, I thought to myself as I shuffled through the drifts back to the house, *seventy*.

February 22-March 15, 2015: I enter the decade of my seventies held in a sustained arctic chill. The nightly news is dominated by meteorologists animatedly describing this latest polar vortex which seems to have whisked down the Canadian Pacific coast and wrapped most of the continental United States—including such unlikely chill zones as Texas, Arkansas, and Alabama—in sub-freezing temperatures. Here in Ripton, the contrast is less drastic, varying what is typically experienced as very cold to really cold. There is an unbroken succession of twenty below nights and sub-zero days. Because everything works in the house—lights go on, furnace fires, water runs—there is no sense of impending catastrophe, and should power fail, we have a powerful generator that immediately kicks in. Our larder and refrigerators are well stocked. Gratifying cords of firewood are stacked outdoors. There is absolutely nothing wrong, although the idea of going outdoors to do anything not absolutely necessary is powerfully aversive. South of us, in Boston, and all along the New England Atlantic coast the cold has been accompanied by epic snowfalls. Because their succession has been unbroken by any thawing, snow in and around Boston has overcome the ability to shovel and move it anywhere. Parked cars are buried. Plows cannot gain access to side streets. Many residents cannot open their doors. Roofs that are not steeply inclined are collapsing with the weight. People who are able to get out and try to shovel pathways are soon unable to lift shovels-full to the height of the snow banks their shoveling has created. Schools are closed for a record succession of days. Public transportation is largely incapacitated, unable to meet scheduled arrivals and departures.

For the first two weeks, all of this made sensational news in New England, especially in Boston. Now, extending well into March, the constricting impact of the snow and cold has cast the region into a collective bad mood. Working parents of school children have had to rearrange their lives. All manners of businesses and services— restaurants, shops—have had to close or limit operation, at worrying costs. For urban dwellers any exhilarating trace of novelty has past. For any given mother there is the excruciating and perhaps daily ordeal of bundling herself and her children to face the cold as they clump their way along narrow pathways, some of them barely shoveled and thus impassable for an infant's stroller, in order to reach a market for necessary supplies. Weeks of this.

Here in Ripton there is no hardship whatsoever, at least for M and me, but there is the impression of being stilled in a kind of aspic as an imagined external world goes about its business somewhere far away. *Or,* I let myself wonder, is this hibernated perspective a harbinger of my eighth decade of life? Some days are dazzlingly bright and the house is practically ablaze with sunlight reflected off the snow. Other days are overcast and leaden, creating a monochrome gloom until dark when the houselights offer their small cheer. Except for highly specific drives to the supermarket for groceries and finger numbing runs out to the wood pile for stove wood, I feel sentenced to the quiet of the house. I have forgiven myself the need for any real exercise. I make small, maybe unnecessary edits on my manuscripts, I write and answer emails, feeling a little desperate to hear back from people. I reread, actually savor, *The Forsythe Saga.* I prepare and cook meals a little too elaborately and eat a little too much of them. After dinner, the dishes done, M and I, fire lit, thermal curtains lowered, swaddled in blankets on the sofa, watch episodes of *Mad Men,* and I feel myself dissolve into the characters' mounting unhappiness and degradation. Overall, I cannot escape the impression that I am waiting, not just waiting for this arctic chill to break or for winter to end. I think I am waiting for what being seventy years old has to tell me, if anything, beyond this lingering sameness.

March 16-March 28, 2015: I was hoping this hiatus in Ripton before a flurry of travels in April and May would be restorative and settling for both M and me, but M has been distracted and on edge due to the impending—and literal—demise of her ancestral house in Marion. Now nearly two years since her mother died, M, her sister, and two brothers have deliberated, with what feels to me like excruciating care, about how to dispose of the house which, due to a complicated trust arrangement set up years before their parents' death, is jointly owned by M and her siblings. Unclouded by sentimental associations, my wife's family history, or any searching moral considerations, my own point of view is pretty straightforward. Since none of the heirs can afford either to live in the house (taxes alone are $25,000 a year), which would entail buying the others out (a million to a million and a half dollars), I thought the house would be offered at the handsome market price expected of a prime ocean front property and that each sibling would get his or her share, after which we could all raise a celebratory glass in gratitude and remembrance.

This is not at all how Molly's siblings see it. For some deep and I believe not really examined urging felt by M's sister Lea, it has been determined that the property should be given over to a Wild Lands Trust so that the house can be demolished, and the acreage returned to nature and designated forever undevelopable. On many counts this seems a bizarre response to this particular inheritance. For one thing, although it is a prime seaside property, it is a rather skinny slice of land wedged between two rather grand estates. The razing of the house will not open up an ecologically or esthetically valuable nature preserve. The only actual people to benefit will be the nearest neighbor, a distant cousin who, steeped in wealth, has recently made a ten million dollar renovation of his already fairy tale opulent mansion. He now stands to enjoy a rather larger and more vernal side yard. For this anticipated pleasure he has pledged several hundred thousand dollars to the demolition project, which will go to Molly and her siblings, but which is far short of what the house would have sold for on the real estate market. A rather fuzzy case has been made that the siblings will also gain some future tax breaks because deeding over the property to the Wild Lands trust is a charitable donation. Looked at coldly, as I cannot help doing, it is a bad deal for no positive end. Other families could have lived happily in that house, accruing the same kinds of deep, indelible pleasures that all of us have experienced over the past half century. There could have been teeming new life there. M and I and our children might also have had a bit more cash to secure our futures. Molly's sister's vision, to which her brothers and M have timidly—or is it generously—acquiesced, is, I think, a kind of confused homage to her deceased parents, the loss of which she has not been able to integrate into her life scheme. I wish I could dismiss the whole matter as "their business," but I can't—for both selfish reasons and for what I can only regard as unexamined irrationality on the part of the heirs.

March 19-25, 2015: M and I fly to Chicago for our first visit to Kate and family in their new (old) house in Oak Park. From the airport we taxi under leaden skies through mean streets of strip retail and low slung warehouses giving way, once we enter the western margin of Oak Park, to neighborhoods of closely packed, tidy brick homes.

Kate's house is a bungalow of brick and fieldstone. While not inexpensive—nearly $400,000—it was a sound purchase. Discouraged by their inability to sell it, the prior owners did a massive renovation of essential features, including wiring, plumbing, appliances, bathroom and kitchen fixtures. There are good hardwood floors, and the walls have been freshly painted white. To Kate and family, previously cramped in their upstairs apartment on Chicago's north side, there now is room, even some undesignated, excess room, to move about. In fact, given the prospect of the house from the street, it is deceptively commodious: four bedrooms, three full baths, a substantially large living room / dining room area that might be configured in a number of interesting ways. There are some nice Arts and Crafts touches, heavy oak woodwork and doors, leaded and stained glass windows in the parlor. The basement is enormous, well lighted, and divided into several usable rooms. In all, quite a nice first house and, not incidentally, a short walk to an excellent elementary school and several parks with playgrounds.

Better still, Oak Park is a dimensional and handsome little city, with highly regarded schools and excellent services. Substantial parts of it are affluent, and there remains a clear signature of Frank Lloyd Wright on a long block of houses he designed or enhanced, including his own.

Best, of course, is that Kate and Shad and their girls are infectiously happy in their new home. There is a clear, if not always easy to read, relationship between inner well being and domestic space.

Nearly a week of full days passed as if an instant. There were many excursions, when warm enough, to nearby parks and play stations with the little girls. We spent a satisfying day at the splendid Brookfield Zoo, the zoo of my boyhood. As we strolled about I recalled that once on a family outing with my mother and father when I was either five or six, I wedged by head between the black wrought iron posts separating the zoo walkway from the outdoor lions station. Stuck in that position for some time before zoo workers did something either to my head or to the posts to extricate me, I experienced deep humiliation and considerable fear. Realistically I was in no danger, as the lions huddled among the exhibit's rocks and scrub were separated by a substantial concrete moat from the grassy lawn over which I had inserted my head. It would have taken a mighty leap for one of the lions to reach me, but such a leap was all I could think about as the attendants worked to pry me free. I was periodically revisited by images of that situation throughout my childhood.

When it rained, we headed into Chicago to the Shedd Aquarium and once, without the children, to Shad's very funny Second City comedy show followed by a fairly bibulous night on the town. Unlike our prior visits to Kate's family where it was impossible to bed down comfortably in their little apartment, a commodious bedroom and adjacent bath were available to us, so it was possible to decompress and relax from time to time. My abiding impression of our time at Kate's is of the seemingly weightless, fairy-like movements of grand daughters Anna and Winifred as they moved through the house in the course of the days. While facially quite different from one another, both girls wear bangs resting low on their brow, accenting large, imploring eyes. Because their favored outfits are costume "princess dresses," they seem closer to Lewis Carroll's era than to ours. Anna is nearly five, Winifred two, and their lovely little voices convey their ideas and concerns with surprising clarity. Together and singly they make many surprising utterances, some of which Kate records and posts on Facebook—Winifred's insistence that she has a brother, that his name is Morioni, and that he is a mouse; Anna, when asked what she is doing with Kate's 1998 date book, replies that she is using it as a "guide to paradise." Shortly after our visit Kate reported that Anna had changed her name to Crystal Chandelier and that Winifred was now Bella.

March 30-April 12, 2015: Back in Ripton for only three days before I head west to see Lulu in Cleveland, then to points south where I will work with my Greeves Passing publisher on final proofs and design. Though still bleakly wintery in Vermont, grimy plowed snow still five feet high at the end of our drive, the weather clears on the day of my departure and I have an uncomplicated, thought clearing drive to Cleveland, where I arrive at the dinner hour.

I am gratified that Lulu seems especially happy to see me. It seems an age since my last visit, our time then clouded by my trying not to acknowledge that I was ill. Celeste too is in cheery high spirits, and since there is not a morsel to eat in the house, we make our way to a favorite bistro nestled into the shadows of the Case University campus. Everything about my arrival here is agreeable enough, but perhaps due to my recent adjustments to the circumstances of Kate's world in Oak Park, then Ripton, and now Cleveland in such a compressed sequence of days, I feel again a twinge of uncertainty as to where I really live. In this condition the days—a full two weeks—pass in a blur. There is much dining out, shopping for provisions, long walks in the welcome spring sunshine, and endless fuss about what are now two squirmy little dogs. When I arrive in the South, there is high summer heat, time for long walks on the beach, a general impression of bright sun on vast stretches of aquamarine and profound quiet. The water has warmed to swimming temperature, and one day, when I have swum out to a rock not thirty yards from shore, two meandering manatees surface a few feet in front of me: bulbous mud colored mounds conveying ancient otherness.

In all the time I am away from Ripton, I do not experience a sense of having arrived at another fixed destination, only that I am in flux, registering impressions, adjusting. I muse on whether I could live this way continuously, more or less always on the move, in transition. I believe I could, but I think my sense of both myself and the world would thin airily out. It is hard to feel that I matter much in this condition, a lesson experience is perhaps trying to teach me.

April 2015: M and I drive south to Marion to oversee two kinds of house business. First, we will, with her brothers and sister, observe the demolition of M's ancestral home on the water, the final step in the deeding over the property to the Wild Lands Trust. While we are there we will stay in our own little house in Marion village, preparing it for what we hope is more frequent and enjoyable use by us and our children, now that our nice tenant has departed.

On the way down to the shore, we stop for an afternoon and evening at Roxbury Latin School, where I have agreed to give a talk to the parent body about what it means to "grow up." As we pull into the drive of the school on a bright, crisp, cloudless afternoon, I am struck again by the coherence of the immaculate Charles Bullfinch-inspired buildings that compose the campus—strikingly elevated and removed from the low-slung strip retail and modest working-class residences of surrounding West Roxbury. It occurs to me that I have been coming to Roxbury Latin on one speaking assignment or another for over forty years. The two headmasters who have spanned that time, Tony Jarvis and Kerry Brennan, have become my closest friends. In their fledgling schoolmaster days both were my colleagues at University School in Cleveland before they, serially, answered the call to head Roxbury Latin, not incidentally the scholastically top ranked private school in the United States. It is the country's oldest school in continuous existence, founded in 1645 by the Puritan divine John Eliot, "apostle to the Indians."

As I greet Kerry and his colleagues in preparation for my talk, I am aware of a strange sensation: that I am more at home here, feel more a part of this particular enterprise than I do at University School, the school of my heart for nearly forty years and where I was headmaster for seventeen

Without exactly knowing why, I am relaxed and *happy* as I give this talk. Part of the reason is that the faces of the mothers and fathers seated in front of me are so attentive and warm. I also really like and want to put across what I am telling them: that, despite the educational establishment's tendency to think that boys grow *up* through a sequence of clearly charted "stages," I invite parents to consider that their sons grow *down* from a spiritually connected, finished condition into families, schools, and communities that either welcome what is unfolding before them, or not. I make the case that Wordsworth, Emerson, Hermann Hesse, and certain Jungians like James Hillman make: that boys—children—have destinies. Yes, they grow by increments both physically and intellectually, but as they do that, they are also unfurling in highly specific trajectories that may not match the tempo and requirements that the era and the culture have established for children. For emphasis I read to them a section of Wordsworth's "Ode on Intimations of Mortality." In fact, I read it twice.

> *Our birth is but a sleep and a forgetting:*
> *The Soul that rises with us, our life's Star,*
> *Hath elsewhere for its setting,*
> *And cometh from afar:*
> *Not in entire forgetfulness,*
> *Not in utter nakedness,*
> *But trailing clouds of glory do we come…*
> *Heaven lies about us in our infancy!*
> *Shades of the prison house begin to close*
> *Upon the growing Boy*
> *But he beholds the light and whence it flows,*
> *He sees it in his joy.*

Then I read some sketches of actual boys' lives from my book, *Boys Will Be Men*, closing with the hope that the parents and teachers in attendance will remember to be attentive, caring witnesses to their sons' progress into the world and not mere imposers of get-ahead expectations. I remind them that their son's lives are *stories*, not a series of strategic adjustments on the way to preconceived success. It works. The questions and comments in response are energetic and warm. We go on a bit late, sharing views, but the parents are clearly pleased, Kerry is pleased—a great relief to me. Kerry and a colleague take M and me to a late dinner, and then we are on the road south to Marion and the shore, arriving past midnight.

We wake to bright sun, and as I walk the hundred yards or so from our house to the Marion village General Store for some breakfast provisions, I am stimulated by the crisp morning air and the cheery facades of the stately old homes lining the street. Like ours, most of them are sided with weathered cedar shingles, which gives the street— and indeed the whole village—a pleasing coherence.

It energizes me to think about the tasks that lie ahead for the week. The house is already minimally furnished, but we need a few substantial items, like a dining table and area carpets, and there are not as yet any pictures on the walls. The latter absence is soon corrected, as I forage some beloved but forgotten prints and paintings we had stored in the attic in order to accommodate our tenant's preferences.

And then the much anticipated house demolition begins. All three of M's siblings converge on Marion to witness, Lea in from Santa Cruz, Jacob down from Portland. Doug and his wife live in the village. A week before the bulldozers set to work, a demolition "manager" of sorts was hired to denude the house of anything recyclable and of possible use to others. Doors, windows and screens are removed from the house and donated to building charities. Metal fixtures, right down to door hinges are unscrewed and donated to scrap houses. The empty, doorless, windowless house now stands overlooking the harbor like a gaping corpse.

A meeting is called of the Point Road Driveway Association to consider what "a wilderness site in perpetual conservancy" might actually mean for the adjacent residents. Only three or four people show up, and they are strident in their concern that unwanted visitors—they mention picnickers and youth campers from New Bedford (meaning minority children)—might become destructive nuisances. And who would monitor and control such visitations, should they occur? The wealthy cousin who stood to benefit by the virtual extension of his grounds tried to soothe the questioners by saying there was little chance of such incursion by the public, since while the land in trust was legally open to visitation, there would be no stated indication of this or any clue as to where the property was. Finally, he pointed out with a smile, there was no place to park without trespassing. Not at all persuaded that unwanted public ingress could be prevented, the complainers departed the meeting resigned to the fact that the deal had been done and that it was apparently legal.

On the eve of the final demolition, Lea has an idea. We gather in the drive of the house at sunset, light candles, and make a final tour of all the rooms. Lea encourages us to reminisce as we go. There are a few game attempts to do this as we begin to make our way, but the effect rings a little false, and we proceed in silence. While not inclined myself to make any kind of conversation, the rooms do in fact evoke memories and associations. Our family probably spent the better part of forty summers in that house, including the full span of our daughters' childhood. Windows now open to sky and sea, emptied of all furniture and ornaments, the house looked quite a bit bigger, and I had the impression that in its stripped down state it seemed more a new house about to be finished than an old one about to be destroyed. A lingering sense of *promise* hovered about the place.

When we finished our candle tour, lawn chairs were gathered about an improvised fire pit on the driveway, and there was some desultory chat before we returned to our cars and went out to dine at the single Marion café serving dinner.

The next morning I decided to sleep in and putter around our place in the village, while M met her brothers and sister at the demolition site. Just before noon I drove over there to see for myself. I arrived in time to watch the great claw of a crane bash down the rear end of the house: garages, kitchen, guest room, and upstairs parlor. M, her siblings, and the wealthy neighbor cousin were standing in a cluster down the waterside slope, their phone cameras taking videos of the progressive wreckage. I could not quite read their collective mood, heightened expectation certainly, but also something like false cheer.

Then it hit me: something strong and clear from inner headquarters—I was angry. The whole destruction venture, the pious turning the property over to "conservancy" was irrational, even stupid.

I think Lea and her more passive siblings were aiming at something like an eternal shrine to their departed parents, but for me at that moment it was no shrine at all, but a voiding, a negation of the considerable life that had been generated in that ancestral place. Other families might have been stirred and renewed by the prospect of the broad, spangled ocean past the sentinel islands of the harbor. The racket of the machines and the stink of powdered concrete and flying dirt conveyed to me a great, unnecessary No.

I was glad I had driven over to the site myself, so that I would not have to keep anyone's company for the duration of the demolition. I took a few photos, made my excuses, then drove back to the village house, where I cleared the pictures from the phone.

May 2015: With aggravating slowness, but steadily, trees and shrubs come into bud and then delicately —Blake's "modest tresses bound up for Thee"—into full leaf. My almost daily three-mile circum-ambulation of Ripton is all birdsong and gurgling brooks. It is an inevitable sign of my own season of life, I suppose, that as I walk and absorb, my mind turns on how many more orbits of this regenerative cycle am I likely to witness.

I am alternately rested and restless. Two novel manuscripts are progressing to publication, but at this point require nothing from me. My calendar is dotted in even measure with social engagements and service obligations. The most appealing among the latter is a promise I made to an Elderly Services facility called Project Independence to play the piano for the residents.

Otherwise disinclined to do it, I gave in, because the invitation had been repeatedly made by the very kindest of souls, Betsy, into whose social circle M and I have become embedded since moving to Vermont. A retired special education teacher disinclined to retirement, Betsy is one of the principal administrators of Project Independence, which transports elderly but still functioning men and women from their homes to a large, airy multi-purpose facility where they are engaged all day in mild forms of physical therapy, games, crafts, and other diversions. Now fully subscribed, the facility services more than a hundred people a day.

In the course of my visits to my parents at their retirement home in Burbank, I had gained some sense of the rhythm of collective geriatric life. Moreover, I had regularly volunteered afternoon piano concerts in the Great Room of my parents' facility. As it turned out I was not far off in my assessment of what kind of audience I would find at Project Independence. As it happened, they were an eager and responsive group

When I arrived at the appointed hour after lunch, chairs had been set up in rows, theater-style, facing a stage area with a more than serviceable, in-tune grand piano. Within a few minutes the rows were filled to capacity. A tiny microphone was clipped to my collar, and after a brief introduction by Betsy, I was on my own.

My hunches about how to shape what was to be an hour-long program turned out to be correct. First, I wanted to stick to a repertoire of popular standards and show music dating from the 1930s through the mid-century. Because of my father's dance band years when I was a child, I have stored in permanent memory that chunk of the American song book. So that there would be some interaction and possibly some amusement, I decided to present my play-list as a kind of quiz: who can name this tune? AND what movie / show was it from? What singer made it famous? Success. Hands shot up across the hall. All kinds of answers were offered, from the hilariously off, to close, to correct. I noted a peculiar but also touching cognitive delay in some of the listeners, such that a hand would shoot up, and the volunteer would offer "Tea for Two" from "No, No, Nanette" to a song I had played five minutes earlier. But in all we had a lively time of it, and I found I could make up new challenges as I went along. Particularly popular was a long-ish medley of popular World War I and II songs—"Over There," "Gee, How I Hate to Get Up in the Morning," "Apple Blossom Time," "We'll Meet Again," "Don't Sit Under the Apple Tree," "White Cliffs of Dover"—to which there was considerable singing along.

The Project Independence staff was pleased. They invited me to come back as often as possible and are in the process of compiling a songbook for my next appearance. I left the facility with an unexpected affection for the people I had just entertained, several of whom sought me out afterward to introduce themselves. These feelings in parting contained an element of self-approval for having made the effort, but there was also a strong intimation that in some hard to reckon span of years I will very likely be seated in such an audience, straining to recognize some musical passage from a brighter time in my life.

These soft, blossoming May days pass in a consistent rhythm, strangely suggestive of my prior "working days," before Vermont. There are morning and afternoon sessions at the computer keyboard, editing and proofreading my novel mss., breaks for answering email and hikes around the Ripton loop. Also evoking my prior life, there is now a steady, predictable stream of invitations to friends' homes for dinner, larger social gatherings, gallery openings and the like. We seem to be out for dinner as often as in. There is an overlay of "required" meetings, including my duties as a Middlebury College alumni trustee and sessions at the bank with investment advisors trying to help us make sense of our assets since they were augmented, none too grandly, by M's inheritance.

It occurs to me that I have entered a distinct stage of life: highly functioning Early Old Age. The awareness turns my thoughts to my mother and father at this period of their lives. They were then fully retired to residential life in Walnut Creek, California. Throughout the decade of their seventies they were still, I think, a little dazed at their good fortune to be living in a comfortable, spacious house at the end of a quiet cul-de-sac surrounded by agreeable neighbors in a region where the weather was fair year round. There was considerable travel throughout the western states, tours organized by Elder Hostel. My mother and father were both immersed in the programs of the Presbyterian Church. My mother took Bible study courses and wrote plays for the church's youth pageants. My father sang in the choir and played trumpet several times a week in a quartet who called themselves The Forties Four. He played golf with the same friends two or three times a week. Mother and father both had work to do at their respective desks, and they got together with friends most evenings. I remember thinking of them during these years as living the bright twilight of their adulthood, a condition I have now fully entered.

June 2015: A whole month it seems of impending milestones. The first of these, which I had not expected to be consequential, may prove to be life altering—or, perhaps better, life enlarging. The Event itself was the Middlebury College 50th reunion weekend and memorial service for the departed members of the class of 1965: The men of this class were juniors when I entered Middlebury in 1967: Two of them were my dormitory advisors and served to introduce me not only to college life but to what might be a workable approach to young manhood. I was inducted into a fraternity, Delta Upsilon, composed of these admirable upperclassmen, and by the time they graduated, several of them had become close, formative friends with whom over a half century I never lost touch. For this reason, I was asked to contribute to their reunion memorial service. My job was to accompany the class on the piano as they sang two songs from their undergraduate era, the Beatles' "With A Little Help From My Friends," and the Byrds' "Turn, Turn, Turn," Pete Seeger's setting of passages from Ecclesiastes. In the course of a rehearsal I got to view repeatedly the succession of slides picturing the deceased members of the class. The images were drawn from the college's New Faces publication of 1965 and showed the departed men and women as they looked when they were college freshmen. I was struck by the procession of these youthful faces. There may have been fifty of them, some of them recently and some of them long dead.

I knew I would feel a twinge when the image of familiar friends appeared on the screen, but what I did not expect was the depth of feeling evoked by men and a few women I had known well while at college but had almost forgotten. There was Jeff who edited the college newspaper when I signed up to work for it and who became a helpful mentor of my early journalism and a hilarious raconteur of his raffish life away from campus, vices and thrills then unimaginable to me. There was Karen, an ethereal Nordic beauty, who in manner and bearing, seemed to me a kind of higher being. There was smiley, lanky Tom who unsettled me by falling dramatically in love with my married sister when she came to Vermont for her one and only visit. These memories and associations had lain dormant for fifty years, but stimulated by nothing more than a passing image on the screen, they unloosed a torrent of reveries that continued for days. In all, these friends were a vivid reminder of mortality, both theirs and mine.

Another perspective on reconnecting to persons and settings long past. M's old school, Milton Academy, has invited her and her classmates to celebrate their 50th reunion. While not warmly connected to those classmates, especially the ones who seem to be most involved in designing the gathering, M has decided to attend, and I will go with her. Milton Academy was, in 1965, a well-established Boston boarding school but one whose reputation and well-to-do clientele tended to obscure the fact that the program and faculty were not very strong. When M was there the school was divided into girls' and boys' divisions housed across the street from one another. There were a few joint classes and activities, but M's experience was that of a single sex school operating across the road from another one.

It has been exactly ten years now since I was a headmaster, and although my writing and speaking have kept me somewhat networked into the private school world, I am struck by how that world's centrality has receded with each passing year. Because I did not come from the social or financial background that would have propelled me to a private school myself, I was not, over the four decades of my work at University School, visited by pangs of guilt about the privileges reflected and conferred by the school. I felt we had worked hard to open up the school to all kinds of boys and raised enough financial aid to support even the poorest who applied. I was angry and quick to respond to any charge that the school was "elite," an attribution made reflexively whenever the school was discussed in Cleveland's only daily city-wide paper, *The Plain Dealer*. I was a booster, an advocate, a defender—appropriately, I think, given that I was the school's headmaster.

But since retiring from that post and having quite literally distanced myself from the world of established private schools, I have come to see them in a clearer perspective. Most helpful has been an opportunity to know and observe children who do not and could not conceivably attend schools like University School—one striking example being the primarily Hispanic children daughter Claire teaches in her charter school in Oakland, children whose parents have not attended a college, who do not speak English at home, and whose parents, if employed at all, earn little money. I have also taken note of children who live nearby in Vermont, including Middlebury College faculty children who have come up through the local pubic schools— or for that matter my daughter Lucia, who has advanced up through the fifth grade in the somewhat embattled public schools of Cleveland Heights. It is immediately apparent that these children have the same appeal—*value*—as my students at University School, and while I would never have stated anything to the contrary in my school-mastering days, I had to leave that world in order to experience and *feel* that value.

It is now impossible for me not to acknowledge that well-resourced schools like mine, schools on beautiful, commodious campuses, schools with bright, energetic faculties, schools relatively unencumbered by state mandates to impose a uniform, potentially deadening curriculum on its students, a curriculum driven by standardized tests—that such schools, with their daunting price tags, really do confer advantages that children in other settings do not get. And now as the father of ten-year-old Lucia, a child who, unless my own financial position improves, is not likely to attend a private school, it occurs to me that private schools generally, though some have much to commend them, are rather lucky little worlds, many of them getting luckier as grateful, prosperous graduates help to build monumental endowments.

In any event, this is the perspective that I brought as a "trailing spouse" to the fiftieth reunion festivities of Milton Academy. Having presided over seventeen such reunions over the course of my headmastership in Cleveland, I was curious how Milton might do things —how, in particular, they would navigate the tension between celebrating alma mater and priming the returning alums for cash.

As it happened, the reunion gathering was lifeless. I could sense none of the pleasure in reconnecting after many years—a half century for many of the returnees —that enlivened my own fiftieth high school reunion. M herself, though a high achieving student at Milton— president of her class, a prominent athlete, member of a select choral group—did not have a very satisfying experience at the school. She remembers a number of dull, ineffective teachers. A girl wide open to relationship, M experienced little warmth or interest in her on the part of her teachers.

Her closest student friends chose not to attend the reunion, and a number of the women who did attend spoke mainly in complaint of the tone and quality of the school they remembered. A few of them spoke bitterly about the remembered coldness of the head of the girls' division. So much unexpected negativity may have influenced my physical impressions of the campus. As one might expect of a well established school, there were a number of substantial dormitories and recitation halls of red brick in the Colonial Revival style, a lovely but architecturally unrelated Gothic chapel in gray river stone. The older, more pleasing buildings were concentrated on one side of the street, which had formerly been the boys' division. Across the street was a jarringly incoherent hodgepodge of traditional and modernist buildings. M and I located what had been the main classroom building in her era. I was struck by the worn, shabby look of its corridors and classrooms, peeling paint, scuffed woodwork. I had a strong sense of *school in decline.*

There were talks by the new headmaster and some of the staff about the state of the school. Certain members of the reunion class were invited to reminisce. Spouses were included in a luncheon and a catered dinner preceded by cocktails, the mood faintly melancholic, events straining to cohere.

So it was a relief to me that on the one evening of reunion activities to which spouses were not invited I was able to contact my long-time colleague and friend Tony Jarvis who lives part of the week in Dorchester, just across the river from Milton, where he is one of the rectors of All Saints Ashmont, the Gothic Revival masterpiece of architect Ralph Adams Cram. Tony, as discussed elsewhere, was my early teaching colleague at University School and for thirty years until his retirement headmaster of Boston's Roxbury Latin School, the oldest school in continuous operation in the USA. When he is not in his digs in Dorchester, he is four days a week in New Haven where he directs a program at the Yale Divinity School for those who want to carry out their pastoral callings in schools. I have joined Tony every year since he took the job to teach classes on *The Headmaster's Papers,* which he makes them read.

It is always good to see Tony, as good and deep a friend as I will ever have. Even after not seeing one another for months, we are somehow always able to resume energetic conversation as if no time had passed. The evening of our appointed dinner is clear and mild enough for us to dine on an outdoor veranda of an upscale bistro overlooking the Neponset River. I was very hungry and also a little relieved to be apart from the grim Milton reunion folks. Chilled oysters, a martini—heaven. Because he has been on a grateful upswing from his colon cancer ordeal of two years ago, I asked Tony how he was doing. In a tone bordering on cheerful he knocked me off balance by telling me he was not at all well. Cancer free for over a year, he had gone to a recent checkup and been told that there was now cancer in his lungs, that it was inoperable, and that he was given an estimated year or two to live.

I was almost unable to integrate this news. Something about it would not penetrate the soft air in this lovely setting. Tony was sitting across from me looking as fit and healthy as I have ever seen him, looking, in fact, more like a man in his forties than one well into his seventies. Cancer all over his lungs. A year or two to live. My healthy, moderate friend who had never smoked and who rarely has a drink.

I asked him how he was feeling that very minute. He said he felt wonderful, could not remember feeling better. There was no pain, no discomfort. His appetite was excellent. He seemed surprised that such a grim diagnosis could be true but not in any immediate way *felt.* That he could talk so openly and, again, almost cheerfully about his new condition is a profound reflection, I think, on the conduct of his life. He told me he had no real regrets or fears. While engaged in satisfying work both in the church and at Yale, he had already completed and been much honored for a long and successful headmastership at one of the nation's leading schools. In the past year he celebrated the fiftieth anniversary of his ordination into the priesthood. He had abundantly completed his *career.*

Beloved by his relatives and by hundreds of friends, former students, colleagues and parishioners, he is not desperate for affirmation or companionship. He has traveled the world, including annual visits to the places of his Anglophilic heart. Not at all a materialist, but a lover of beautiful things, he has made something of a miniature museum of his rooms in Dorchester. He has told me repeatedly that he is absurdly comfortable financially, despite having capped his salary at Roxbury Latin at a level below that of many of his teaching colleagues. "I live comfortably on just my Social Security!" he says, as if incredulous that it could be so. I believe Tony has no regrets, no dark road-not-taken recesses in his interior life. While purposeful in his work and always, save for oasis evenings of ease and talk like this one, heavily obligated and busy, he does not feel driven to achieve some next Big Thing on the horizon.

Tony told me that he has been prescribed four rounds of chemotherapy in order to slow, if not arrest, the cancer in his lungs. He said he had not yet decided to follow the prescription. He said he would rather let the lung cancer run its course than experience the abject awfulness he endured while in chemotherapy for his colon cancer. He hoped to complete a final year at the Divinity School and did not want to miss classes because of chemo-related nausea. "I would like to continue on as I have been," he said thoughtfully, "until the darkness falls."

Tony was equally cheerful over breakfast with M and me as we were about to depart for Marion where our plan is to ready our house in the village for what we hope will be more time spent there on our own. My view forward into these preparations is clouded by Tony's news from the night before. I know it will take some time before I am able to reconcile his diagnosis with the man enthusiastically chatting across the table about his coming travels. In a way impossible to describe I am feeling both glad and sad for him.

Arrived now in Marion with the rather pleasant prospect of fixing up our no longer rented house to our liking, there is news that changes our plans. Daughter Jesse and her family are going to move into the house. Throughout the spring they were approaching despair as husband James was working to complete his Ph.D. at NYU with no certain prospects of employment. Even more unsettling, their Brooklyn landlords are selling the building in which Jesse's apartment composed the cramped third floor, so Jesse and co. are going to have to move—somewhere. Without employment and a place to live, a move, probably away from New York, was inevitable, a prospect darkened by the fact that they have no money.

But then the fog began to clear. James successfully defended his thesis and, as Dr. Stanley, was offered a job at, ahem, Harvard. The job was less than full-time, though it carried medical benefits for the family, so it was a lifeline of sorts. Marion, as it happens is within commuting distance to Harvard, so the availability of a serviceable house, in fact a Palace given their prior circumstances, at (M and I decided) next to no rent represented a profound relief. Even better, the elementary school and preschool their children would attend in Marion turn out to be excellent—and just a block away from the house. Prospects improved, Jesse's mood brightens. Moreover, James is encouraged by his colleagues in Harvard's department of history and literature that his appointment may be fleshed out to full-time.

In the meantime, with the help of a friendly property manager, M and I have been busy improving the interior and grounds of the house. As noted earlier, it is a charming, if modest, place, the original schoolhouse of Marion. We think it might be three hundred years old. It is a bungalow with weathered shingles and white trim, three bedrooms, one quite large, and two and a half-bathrooms—again a dream for Jesse and James, who will now enjoy the previously unthinkable luxuries of a washer and dryer, a dishwasher, a full-size refrigerator. But mainly *enough room.*

In a peculiar, irrational way, I find myself unable, or maybe just unwilling, to change the course of my plans to create in the Marion house a comfy little retreat from my Vermont life and travels. At the same time I know Jesse and family will install themselves in the house at the end of the month and that they will remake it into something altogether different, a more durable set up that will weather the children's storms and high velocity play. The paintings I have taken pains to pick out and mount on the Marion house walls, the decidedly antique furniture in the softly lit, faintly formal living room, the oriental carpets, ornaments, knick-knacks—almost all of it will be sensibly stored away by Jesse and James. And though this transformation is impending, I cannot stop myself from visiting my favorite antique emporiums in Marion and New Bedford and acquiring another picture, another urn, another carpet. Not only do I continue to do this almost daily, I find myself *sneaking* out of the house to carry out these errands. M was at first astonished and is now exasperated by my clearly pointless enhancement of the house as it temporarily is.

What am I doing? Though defying sense and actually creating unnecessary work for Jesse and James when they arrive, this desire to realize my dream for the house persists. Taken a bit further this could be mental illness. I am fully aware that what I so fervently do all day will soon be undone. Nor do I resent that this is so. I am at heart tremendously glad that Jesse and her family will ascend out of cramped, teeming Brooklyn into this beloved place, this seaside village. Images of them comfortably ensconced here compose a rival good dream. For now both dreams coexist in my loony reckoning.

For a very pleasant two weeks my house dream prevails, as we entertain Marion friends and then a succession of daughters—Kate, Jesse, Claire and a few of their friends—as they make their way to and from Provincetown, where Claire decided to hold her Bachelorette party. It is prime Marion time, warm, breezy days, stirring salt air on morning walks and outings to Silver Shell Beach. A few blocks from the house I launch my kayak into the harbor and get an invigorating workout paddling against wind and current as I meander in and around

Blankenship and Planting Island coves.

And then it occurs to me what I am probably doing in the course of this uprooted, between-worlds residency in Marion. I am using the house dream and the business of sustaining it to block out a realistic consideration of my impending trip to Cape Town, where at month's end I will be presenting at this year's International Boys' Schools Coalition Conference.

On its face this two-week excursion should be an unbroken pleasure. Traveling for most of it with my great friend Tony Jarvis, we are scheduled to break the long flight from the states to Cape Town with three days in London, where we will visit favored haunts, see some shows and perhaps spend a day at Cambridge where, a half century ago, each of us, though not at the same time, did graduate work at St. John's College. We will then fly together to Cape Town where this year's International Boys' School Coalition sessions will take place. My preliminary researches suggested only positive, beckoning aspects of Cape Town. And as it happens, Tony and I are being honored there as founders of the Coalition, the honor taking the form of a new Hawley Jarvis Prize (cash) to be awarded to someone who has completed some project or research that advances the prospects of school-age boys. This is of course gratifying, as is the Coalition's offer to pay for all of our travels and accommodations. In addition, I have been invited, as its founding president, to give some talks about the history and mission of the Coalition.

Again, all of this should be a bright prospect, but I am aware of a kind of dread, an almost petulant desire to stay put, either in Ripton or in Marion. I experienced some of this a few years back, when Michael Reichert and I flew to Johannesburg in the course of our relational teaching research, a trip that turned out to be deeply satisfying and invigorating. This time the dread is hard to specify, but something about the great distance, all the things that can go wrong these days with air travel, the possibility of getting sick in Africa and unable to get care. And it dawns on me that these are the worries of an old man. Yes. What I really dread is discomfort, the discomfort of long, leg-cramped, sleepless flights, first across the Atlantic, then down the length of Africa. There is a distinct caution, fussiness—*dread*—that would not have occurred to me even ten years ago. At seventy both my confidence and imagination have become contracted. Is this natural, inevitable, right? I don't want to think so.

Impervious to my musing, the days proceed relentlessly toward my departure. The afternoon of my Boston-London flight is oppressively warm, a condition at odds with the kinds of clothes I must pack for Cape Town, where it is winter. This clash of reality and necessity reflects my uneasy feelings about the trip. It feels wrong to be leaving the Marion house. When the car service arrives mid-afternoon to take me to the airport, twelve or thirteen women are chatting amiably in the close air of the living room, a wedding shower for Claire orchestrated by her sisters. I feel awkward making my way through them out of the house and bidding farewells.

Having endured so many air travel annoyances over the past decade, I have taken special care with this ticket, which I booked through a travel agent Tony Jarvis insisted was infallible. I paid $200 extra for a guarantee that the seat I had booked would actually be available to me. This seemingly nonsensical provision, I was assured, would protect me from losing the seat due to the airline's overbooking or some other caprice. Thus it was a jolt to read on the computer monitor at check-in that there was a "problem" with my ticket and I needed to consult an airline official in a far off terminal.

There was of course a long line of other passengers with, I assumed, whatever my problem was. After an hour's idling in line, I learned that the plane scheduled to take me to London had broken down and that the plane chosen to replace it had a different seating arrangement, such that my previous seat did not exist on the substitute plane. I was not a model of patience in response to this, explaining with some force that I had *paid extra* to insure my place and producing the receipt for the additional charge. An apology was offered for my inconvenience, and I was thanked for my nonexistent patience. In what has become a familiar tableau, I studied the troubled countenance of the desk agent as she peered down into her computer screen—for perhaps twenty minutes—her fingers motionless on the keypad.

At length I was given a boarding pass for a similar seat to the one from which I had been displaced. Later, I was able to reconnect with Tony, who had been given a similar run-around, and we boarded the evening flight to London Heathrow.

As I feared—and probably because I feared—I did not sleep at all on the plane and thus moved through customs and the tube ride to St. James Square and our lodgings in a light-headed blur. This was familiar and beloved turf for Tony. He had booked us both rooms at The British East India Club, hushed and sepulchral at this dawn hour. As soon as we deposited our bags at the front desk, he was eager to get out onto the pavement to see things.

As the morning wore on my fatigue progressed into such lightheadedness that I lost all volition. I went where Tony went, ashamed to admit that I wanted only to lie down on a bed. Broad avenues crowded with summer tourists led onto broad avenues: Piccadilly, Trafalgar Square. Spotting a vagrant asleep in an alleyway, I felt only envy. We proceeded through what for a fully functioning person would have been quite a busy day. We toured through the National Portrait Gallery's annual portrait contest where we bought tickets for a coming special exhibit of Audrey Hepburn photos and portraits. Fastidious in his travel preparation and—surprise to me—a member of many clubs, Tony had made a luncheon reservation at the Athenaeum. The day had grown steamy hot, and on a sweltering terrace in our required coats and ties we ate Dover sole on monogrammed plates. By this time I had become almost preverbal with sleepiness, but in exploring the club's stately upper reaches I happened into an empty library lounge where hung a stunning painting of the late Seamus Heaney. I took a picture of the portrait on my phone that somehow made him look eerily alive and present in the room.

A few streets down from the Athenaeum Tony located a building, which from several different windows was brokering current theater tickets. Long lines extended form each window, and while eager to get tickets for a show that evening, Tony wanted to see more sights. Waiting in line seemed closer to the oblivion I craved, so I volunteered to take my place in one of the queues while he went off to visit, I think, churches. An hour and a half of my life utterly vanished. When the energized and perspiring figure of Tony next appeared before me, I had somehow purchased two tickets for a revival of *High Society* at the Old Vic.

By mid afternoon we had zig-zagged through crowded streets back to St. James Square where our rooms were now ready at the British East India Club. Both the lift and the air conditioning were temporarily out of order, and by the time I reached my small, airless room on the fourth floor, I was barely capable of purposeful thought. I pried the ancient window open as far as it would go and fell into the bed.

I came to in early evening, working a bit to establish waking reality from dream. I remembered our tickets and quickly showered and dressed. Tony turned out to be a member of the Garrick Club, where he insisted we go for a drink before the show. It struck me how alike in structure these old clubs were: high ceilings, grand staircases, walls hung with portraits salon style, all of it seeming to insist that we speak in hushed voices. When we took our seat at a table in the bar salon, Tony pointed out that I was sitting beneath a portrait of Noel Coward.

It was a walk of more than a mile to the Old Vic, and we arrived just as the show started. *High Society* was a stirring romp, start to finish. The dancing was acrobatic, the dialog of the patrician send-up was light and clever, and of course the Cole Porter standards were a pleasure. Even more satisfying was my realization during the liveliest stage business that Tony was deeply asleep. And we were in the third row.

I awake to bright sky filling the windows of my tiny room, aware even before I rise that I am now fully back in my body. Coated and tied, Tony and I meet for an enormous English breakfast—eggs, sausage, ham, stewed tomatoes, toast, jam, and pots of tea—in the very formal breakfast parlor of the British East India Club. The plan today is to revisit Cambridge.

The day is again unseasonably warm, in the 90s. We take the fast train from Charing Cross station and arrive in Cambridge mid-morning. Bright sun and cloudless blue sky seem to wash the city with cleansing light. Over the decades since I was a student the colleges and churches have sandblasted and scoured the grime from their walls and spires, creating a strange impression that the ancient place is newly built.

Tourists cram the narrow walks of King's Parade. Tony and I visit the libraries and chapels of Magdelene, Christ's, and Corpus Christi, where I note in a glassed display case a substantial volume written in Martin Luther's hand. At Tony's and my alma mater, St. John's, we enter the dining hall to find a reception for newly admitted students. I suppose we look vaguely don-like as we help ourselves to their lemonade and finger sandwiches.

A curious episode at the Fitzwilliam Museum. I wanted to show Tony a painting that had haunted me since my university days: an Italian Renaissance rendering of St. Julian the Hospitaler. I had difficulty finding it, and the front desk attendant and docents I asked were vague as to its whereabouts. I really hoped it had not been taken down or replaced. The image was firmly fixed in my memory. A figure in armor stands at the center of the composition, and in each corner there is an encircled scene depicting the dramatic moments in Julian's story: his love of the hunt, the near accidental slaying of his mother, his Oedipal crime, his final encounter with Christ. I could picture all of this in detail. I also remembered that the painter was unknown, the picture attributed to some school or other. When I finally located it, I was puzzled to see that my highly specific memory was way off. The Julian figure does indeed stand in the center of the composition. He holds a sword but wears no armor. There are no enclosed scenes in the corners, and the faintly rendered figures in the background do not represent the specific moments I recalled. And the picture is clearly attributed, to Pietro Donzelli. I realize that after nearly half a century I might understandably forget details in a picture, but this was altogether different. I had somehow created and carried with me a highly specific image—if I were a painter I could have painted it— that bore little relationship to the St. Julian in the Fitzwilliam. Where did it come from? I left the museum with a queasy uncertainty about other images and incidents I may have wrongly relayed to others with great confidence.

As we did just a few years back, Tony and I walked for miles under favored archways and along the banks of the Cam. By midafternoon it was bakingly hot, and we stopped into a newly refurbished bistro with a terrace overhanging the Cam. Below us, in slow-motion, comically unskilled punters collided with one another and the concrete banks of the canal. I shed my coat, and there was a welcome breeze. Over a chilled salad and a glass of wine, it occurred to me that I could not possibly feel more content, that perhaps feeling content and at rest had become all the happiness left to me.

Before our evening flight out to Cape Town, we had another marathon day of walking and sightseeing. Again the temperature rose into the 90s, and the throngs of tourists generated an ambient claustrophobia on the streets and parkways surrounding Buckingham Palace. Jam packed and poorly ventilated as it was, the exhibit of images of Audrey Hepburn at the National Portrait Gallery went straight to my heart. I believe I must have a hard-wired genetic response to her face and form—and on the evidence of consecutive sold-out viewings of the exhibit, many others are similarly wired. As with other women I find arrestingly beautiful, it is impossible to specify exactly what feature or set of features transports me. It has something to do with the relation of part to part, the regal extension of her neck and her long legs. By no means conventionally beautiful, the appeal of her face is its suggestion of wistful youthfulness, a promise that was not diminished even in her last years when she was ill. Like so many dancers, she was at once impossibly slender and strong. Each rendering in the exhibit carried me back to my seventeenth year when with a date, probably at the date's suggestion, I went to see *Breakfast at Tiffany's*. From the iconic opening sequence, AH elegantly coiffed in a little black dress, at dawn peering into a display window of Tiffany's on a deserted Fifth Avenue, I realized that she was a kind of message to me, a message telling me that where women, love, and sex were concerned, there was something higher, more rarified than I had ever imagined hovering on the near horizon.

By mid-afternoon we are wilted by the heat and stop into yet another one of Tony's clubs, The Oxford University Club, where we drink lemonade in an airconditioned parlor. Tony is restless and wants to find a post office and buy gifts before we fly out. I have no such desires and we agree to reconnect later at the British East India Club. Alone now in this very formal room, I come agreeably to rest. The deep red walls are hung with portraits of past Oxford luminaries. The air is wonderfully cool, and I have stopped perspiring. Is it my age or a truth my age has allowed me to see that the prospect of nothing whatever to do is such a pleasure?

Checking out of the British East India Club, Tony insists we take the tube instead of an expensive cab to Heathrow. It is nearly an hour ride, each car crammed full, and we stand the whole way in stifling foul air. Despite the daunting prospect of our fifteen-hour flight to Cape Town, I am looking forward to sitting still. I have good books stored on my iPad, journal entries to make, and will welcome sleep if it comes.

But it doesn't. Deep into the night I fall in and out of a restless reverie that skitters on the threshold of sleep, but nothing sustained and restorative. I open my eyes periodically to the video screen built into the seat back in front of me where, on what looks like a map drawn hastily by a child, the trajectory of our flight proceeds in a wavy graphite line over Gibraltar, Tangier, Mali—names as abstracted from my experience as those on the maps of the world hung on the walls of my elementary school. Then the morning flight routines: warm towels to the face, vapid, starchy foods suggesting breakfast, customs forms to fill out. Out the window early morning light irradiates brilliant patches of green below, then a serration of mountains girding a promontory from the sea. We have arrived: Cape Town.

My previous trip to Johannesburg does not prepare me for Cape Town. Lack of sleep feels like extra weight, and I am slow to process the very simple questions asked of me by the customs agent. The airport is clean, bright, not notably crowded, a strong impression of First World. Tony is sharper than I at this hour and seems to know something about a van that the Conference has provided to take us to our hotel. A man with a clipboard is indeed boarding such a van, and although our names are not on his list, he is cheerfully willing to include us. A Cape Town guidebook I consulted said to expect chilliness, rain, and possibly strong winds at this time of year, but it is sunny and mild as we step outside. Good roads, substantial homes and buildings, lush foliage, towering palm trees. The central city sits at the foot of dramatically flat-topped Table Mountain, the steep faces of which visually overwhelm the downtown civic buildings and churches.

Our hotel, a short block inland from the harbor, feels new-ish and substantial. We are greeted with elaborate warmth and courtesy by the uniformed African check-in agents, all of them female, as were the customs agents. Tony and I share a pot of tea in the lounge while we wait for our rooms to be made up. He is anxious to get outside for an exploratory walk, but I decline on the grounds of fatigue. I am longing to lie down on a bed.

Four hours of deep, dark restorative sleep. When I awake it takes me a while to make sense of the view out my hotel room window. There is a curved bend of commercial buildings several stories high lining the harbor against a backdrop of steep mountainside. A few hundred yards above the buildings a bank of white clouds is settled in close around the mountain face. Above the clouds the mountain continues to rise, suggesting a world beyond the world, then sky.

Now I too am eager to get outside and explore. No one has told me explicitly that Cape Town is safer for pedestrians than Johannesburg, but I have already sensed that it is. The short walk to the waterfront reveals a lively festivity. I pause to get my bearings in the shadow of an enormous Ferris wheel. For blocks and blocks adjacent cafés spill out of their respective restaurants onto the promenade. In mid-afternoon they are already doing a brisk business, the amplified music of several live bands combining to a benign cacophony as I walk along. I look for some kind of racial pattern in those seated and strolling, but there is nothing definite, approximately equal numbers of black, white, and brown faces. The overall tone is relaxed, cheerful and, it occurs to me, prosperous. Men and women are stylishly turned out. I ask a passerby for directions to a post office and am sent a block or so farther along the waterfront where rising above the cafés is the entrance to a sizable enclosed mall, the winding corridors of all three of its floors crowded with bag laden shoppers. I find the post office, buy cards and stamps, wander about the mall and then back to the hotel, rightly or not feeling I could be making my way through San Diego or Auckland.

Tony and I intentionally arrived a day before the conference proceedings because we did not want to be jet-lagged. We are thus at leisure to dine out on our own before official business begins in the morning, and so we make our way back to the waterfront for a quiet dinner with another early arrival, Vance Wilson, headmaster of Washington's St. Albans School.

I awake to bright sun, the air outside bracing as we board a bus to Bishops College, the host site of this year's conference. Our party of about 40 consists of Coalition Trustees and special guests. Tony and I are in the latter category, as we are being honored for having "founded" the Coalition twenty summers ago. Bishops lies on an immaculate expanse of greensward surrounded by steeply rising peaks. Founded by Anglicans in the middle of the nineteenth century, the school has prospered impressively. Its scholastic halls, chapels, dormitories and sports facilities are extensive and in gleamingly good repair. Most of the buildings are whitewashed on closely mown greens and stand out brightly against the stark rock face of the mountains.

We are broken up into groups of nine or ten for campus tours, and I feel lucky to be led round by an especially warm and knowledgeable member of the staff. He makes an impressive account of the school's achievements and growth since its founding. Bishops was one of four secondary schools Cecil Rhodes chose in 1901 to guarantee an annual Rhodes Scholarship to Oxford. Now enrolling over a thousand boys from preschool through year twelve, including a sizable contingent of boarders in the upper grades, the school is in extent and architectural coherence reminiscent of a small American liberal arts college like Kenyon or Haverford. Only the next day when the conference formally convened did I realize that our tour guide was Bishops' headmaster, Guy Pearson.

Following our school tour and then an afternoon excursion to the unearthly, prehistoric-looking Kirstenbosch botanical gardens, Tony and I were duly honored at an evening banquet. I improvise a short speech in acknowledgment, sketching the trajectory of the coalition from what began in the US as a rather casual gathering of boys' school heads to talk about what we thought we were doing teaching only boys. An annual cash prize supporting research about boys has been endowed in our name, and the happy first recipient, a British woman who has initiated a number of parallel research projects in schools around the world, is seated to my right at dinner. She is bright and funny, and it is an overall enjoyable evening.

The conference program opens in the steeply vaulted and appealingly austere Bishops College chapel. There are about 700 of us in all. I arrive early and take a seat in the middle of things, but David, the executive director of the Coalition hails me and tells me to change my seat to one on the central aisle, as Bishop Desmond Tutu, the morning's keynote speaker, is planning to shake hands and greet all those sitting on the aisle as he comes in. Pleased by this prospect, I move over, but after some delay in getting started, we are told that Bishop Tutu is not feeling strong this morning. He will make no formal entrance and will speak to us seated behind the pulpit. It is nonetheless moving to watch the frail old gentleman—he is at best five feet tall and 84 years old—make his way gingerly from a back entrance to his place at the pulpit. He addressed us from a prepared script in a thin, slightly halting voice, departing from the text from time to time to make an aside, usually a joke. Apart from the novelty and honor of beholding the great man, a hero of both the Anglican Church and of post-apartheid South Africa, his talk is substantial. In welcoming us to Cape Town, he reminds us that the origin of our species was discovered not far from where we are assembled and that we should acknowledge that we are thus "all Africans." The rest of his address proposed not only the necessity of living for others, but the futility of living any other way. I had an intimation in the course of the sustained ovation at the conclusion of his talk that I was in the presence of a genuinely holy man.

But as it happened, other genuinely holy men were to follow. I had not heard of the next morning's speaker, Edwin Cameron, when he rose to address us. A tall, lean, distinguished looking man in his sixties, he is a longstanding justice of the Constitutional Court of South Africa, the equivalent of the U.S. Supreme Court. Like Bishop Tutu he was one of the public figures in South Africa who helped guide the emerging post-Apartheid state into being, which required a delicate balance between acknowledging past injustices without miring the new order in unmanageable anger and resentment. In other words, Cameron has been an agent of the nation-building and peace-making process Mandela called Truth and Reconciliation.

But apart from decades of humane good work first as a lawyer and then judge, Cameron's personal story is remarkable. Born in 1953 in Pretoria, he was raised in troubled circumstances. His father was jailed for car theft when he was an infant, after which his mother felt she was unable to provide for him. Consigned to an orphanage at age eight, he became an impressively good student and won a place at a competitive boys' school in Pretoria where he continued to excel. He went on to Stellenbosch University near Cape Town where he won a Rhodes Scholarship to Oxford to study law. Back home in Cape Town he represented clients of all kinds who had been oppressed under Apartheid and built up a distinguished, if risky, reputation as a humanitarian liberal.

In the 1980s he came out as a gay man and not long after developed HIV / AIDS. Mortally ill, skeletal from weight loss, with suppurating sores and nearly unable to breathe, Cameron learned that anti-retroviral treatments in the U.S. were showing signs of reversing AIDS symptoms. Tremendously expensive everywhere but ruinously so in South Africa, Cameron managed to arrange the treatments in Cape Town by spending all of his salary and savings. Within months his condition had improved and he was fully functioning. Now a vocal AIDS activist, Cameron took on the official South African policy on AIDS, which was essentially to deny it—at the time the nation's President, Thabo Mbeki had publicly declared that sexual activity did not cause AIDS, blaming instead birth control measures. Cameron's influential book, *Living with AIDS,* did a great deal to clarify and correct the misunderstanding of the disease. In direct response to his activism, the cost of effective treatment in South Africa went from impossibly expensive to universally affordable. In that work alone he has saved tens of thousands of lives.

In sum, Cameron's life has had a Dickensian trajectory, although his brief account of it to us could not have been more measured or modest. There was not a trace of rancor about any of the privations he endured as an orphan, a humane liberal under apartheid, a marginalized gay man, or as an AIDS sufferer. At the heart of his address was a plea to recognize that in adherence to just laws—The South African Constitution after apartheid is in letter, if not yet in practice, the most tolerant and humane national constitution in the world—lies the way to a livable future for everyone. Without rhetorical flourish, Cameron made me want to rise up from my chair and follow him into battle. Without question the most inspiring talk I have ever heard.

Had ever heard. The following morning's speaker was Professor Wilhelm Verwoerd who, like Justice Cameron, is a committed activist who wants to peacefully reconcile the country's apartheid past with a humane, inclusive future. Also like Cameron, Verwoerd began his anti-apartheid activism while the old regime was still in power. What makes his story remarkable is that he is the grandson of none other than Hendrik Verwoerd, the social scientist and later President of South Africa who designed and implemented the apartheid state. Hendrik Verwoerd was stabbed to death by a deranged man on the floor of the South African Parliament in 1966.

Wilhelm Verwoerd talked about his upbringing in well-to-do, privileged white South Africa, including his reflexive acceptance of his family's views about race and class. Against his family's wishes—they were concerned about the influence of liberal viewpoints—he, again like Cameron, went on to study at Oxford University as a Rhodes Scholar. There, as his family feared, he came into contact with strong critics of apartheid, some of them black South Africans. He returned home radically questioning the premises underlying apartheid. Increasingly estranged from his family, he was in effect disowned when he decided to join the ANC, the rising black political movement that would ultimately bring apartheid down. With the ascension of the ANC, Verwoerd worked in various capacities to advance Nelson Mandela's program of Truth and Reconciliation. In that process he embraced what has become his life's work: figuring out ways that former implacable enemies might get to know each other, get past their differences, and live peaceably. Toward this end he has spent more than a decade working with individuals in Northern Ireland to reconcile politically motivated killers and the families of those they killed, a process that begins with the opposed parties sitting down together, hostilities intact, and slowly, guardedly proceeding in the direction of understanding, if not forgiving, one another. Verwoerd believes that this emerging model of reconciliation has shown great promise among the Irish and South African people he has worked with. His program, called Beyond Walls, has begun to work with hostile Palestinians and Israelis.

All of us were moved—I to the very limits of my capacity to feel—by Professor Verwoerd's presentation, but it was not until I proceeded through the rest of the day, took a walk, had some time to reflect on what I had heard, that the full impact of this man's life and work took hold. I am reminded that the impulse to goodness, to do right, does not win you friends or favor, even from family and loved ones. The real thing has nothing to do with any pleasing boy scout-like inclination to do right in the abstract. The real thing arises when there are pressing, daily, real wrongs to be righted. You can ignore them in any number of ways, or you can act. Verwoerd has been rejected and even hated by his family. His father does not speak to him and refers to his son in the press as a "hensopper," an Afrikaner term for coward or traitor.

Verwoerd told a wonderful story about Mandela shortly after his release from prison. Verwoerd had been invited to a political gathering in a large house where the newly liberated Mandela was guest of honor. Fairly well established as a young pro-ANC activist, Verwoerd was hoping to meet the great man, to whom he had sent some letters while Mandela was still in prison. In the course of the gathering the two men had come nearly face to face, but there was no recognition on Mandela's part, no introduction offered. Feeling he had missed his chance, Verwoerd was summoned to a private room where Mandela greeted him warmly. Whatever Verwoerd was saying in his haste to make himself known, Mandela interrupted him to say that he had a question: he had heard that Verwoerd's elderly mother had been ill, and he wanted to know how she was.

My own talk to the conferees was scheduled on the final day. When I first looked over the conference program in the catalog, I was concerned, as I had been in past years, that the speakers were being chosen more for their celebrity than for anything they have said or done that has affected the lives of boys. We are after all an international boys schools coalition, seeking to understand boys better and to improve their schooling. Scanning the names and brief bios of the keynoters—Bishop Tutu, Justice Cameron, Professor Verwoerd—I had thought: fine, right thinking, prominent South Africans, but what do they have to say about the lives and prospects of boys?

By the time I had heard all three addresses, I had no doubts that these men's lives and work have everything to do with boys. For one thing, all three were former boys, all three attended boys' schools, and all three had dedicated themselves to positive social transformation, to healing old wounds, to enlarging the life prospects of others. In their very similar life trajectories, they exemplify what it means to be male and good. Back in the days when anthropologists were struggling to determine what was "essential" about being male or female, a number of generalities were advanced: that men hunt, make war, that from first infancy they thrust themselves out into the world, into frontiers, into trouble, into the unknown, into space; that women tend hearths, nurture children, gather things in, gather other females together in networks. Men at their best, it was proposed, served the polis, defended it with their lives. Our speakers, it occurred to me, had served the polis admirably. Together they compose a coherent lesson for boys everywhere.

In any event I was happy to introduce that notion, a rather last minute adjustment, into my prepared talk, which was about how the Coalition had emerged over the past twenty years in a larger cultural climate in which boys were not generally thriving and in which the meaning and value of being male was at best uncertain. I faulted the male-feminist response to the male "problem" for unhelpfully advocating that males stop behaving as stereotypical males, that is, aggressively, forcefully, fearlessly, confidently; that, in effect, they behave more like stereotypical women: gently, cooperatively, collaboratively. In sum, the tentatively configured "New Age Sensitive Man" was negatively constructed, an accretion of ways not to be, things not to say or do. Whatever the positive intentions of those who would refashion themselves and others along these lines, when these new expectations of males began to be put in effect in school curricula, disciplinary protocols and speech codes, many boys, however outwardly compliant, stopped being able to identify themselves and their like in school. But they were able to find, if not admirable models, at least excitement and life in dark fantasies of mayhem and wildness in the commercial underground of video games and on the forbidden screens and channels of the internet. Far from being tamed and gentled, many boys descended to new levels of misogyny and violence. Good and humane boys' schools, I proposed, are in a good position to restore and offer a better understanding of masculinity. There are good, assignable examples of schools doing this. There are assignable examples of good boys emerging from such schools. And there are, thank God, the examples of Desmond Tutu, Edwin Cameron, and Wilhelm Verwoerd to illustrate what such boys might become.

When I departed for South Africa, I had mainly a tourist's expectation of experiencing new things in a new place. And while those expectations were amply realized in Cape Town and its surrounds, what held me, reorienting my thinking for weeks, was the substance of the conference, the promising but still perilous prospect of South Africa rising out of the divisive, still deadly realities of its past into, well, Truth and Reconciliation. While the sloping mountainside vineyards we visited, the splendid expanses of beach, beckoning even in winter, St. George's Cathedral and the stately civic buildings of downtown Cape Town made a lasting mark, it was the stirring challenges offered by our speakers that defined my time there—and also, in a way much harder to generalize, the distinct sweetness and open heartedness of the men and women who drove our taxis and served our food and managed our lodgings. Several years ago, departing for home from Pietermaritzburg in Zulunatal, I had a strong sensation of not wanting to leave—not wanting to leave the place, not wanting to leave the people. That feeling was evoked strongly again as I flew off from Cape Town.

July 15-August 30, 2015: Before I departed for England and South Africa there had been plenty of signs of summer's arrival, both in Ripton and in Marion. With only modest rainfall, but enough, the Middlebury golf course was luxuriant, gorgeously green, soft underfoot. I again experienced the mysterious emergence of my old golf game, no worse and possibly even a little better for months of dormancy. M's garden bloomed extravagantly, seemingly within days of the plants being put into the ground. M and I lingered over breakfasts on the back deck cheerful with birdsong and the yip and slosh of the river over the rocks.

Yet something in the trip to the southern hemisphere, its geological and floral otherness, the experience of being nationally and racially other, combined to make the reentry to the states feel like summer was starting again. Something in me yearned to stay put, establish household routines, a rhythm of play and work, but that was not to be. I had been longer than usual out of contact with Lulu and Celeste, and after just a few days of restorative rest—I slept no better on the return flights than I had going over—I drove west to Cleveland for the first of three week-long summer visits.

The tempo of life and physical exertion generally pick up when I am with Lulu. If we stay at home in Cleveland Heights, there are daily trips to the pool, yard work, long walks with the dogs. But Lulu and her mother are usually eager to leave home for Lulu's adored water parks and various preserved wildernesses her mother has researched within a half day's drive. Having now explored and become fond of New York state's Finger Lakes, they—especially Lake Canandaigua, with its proximity to *two* substantial water parks—have become a certain destination in the course of my summer trips west. So of course we go. Lulu's sheer otter exuberance in these parks more than compensates for my feeling an ancient oddball as I ascend the many story staircases up to the platform of the water sluices and plummet down through chutes and loops before splashing down, soaked and startled, into the pool at the bottom.

As in summers past, the lakes—this time Seneca as well as Canandaigua—are a balm to my soul. Oblong and slender—like fingers—they extend for miles between rolling green ridges on each side. The country roads run high along the ridges revealing stunning prospects around every dip and curve. What Lulu wants most, apart from the adrenal thrills of the water parks, is to get to the water, whether a suitable pier from which to dive into sections of lake roped off for swimming or, even better, to follow a stream bed up to one of the many tree-canopied waterfalls that spill down the from ridges feeding the lakes. Some of the falls form successive tiers of shallow pools in which it is possible, at least for Lulu, to paddle around and, in the absence of other hikers and bathers, to imagine having entered a prehistoric Eden. I confess to wanting to shed all clothes, even my swimsuit, in such hushed, secluded places, but that is hardly appropriate in the company of my fifth grade daughter.

The other pleasure of these summer traveling days, perhaps more so for Celeste and me than for Lulu, is locating pleasing spots to dine, some of them housed in one of the dozens of wineries dotting the slopes of the lakes. In dazzling mid-day sun (lunch) or at fiery sunset (dinner), we find outdoor bistros perched high over the diamond faceted water, taking our time over invariably delicious, seasonal offerings and, to Celeste's delight, good local wine.

Back home in Ripton, too, it has become a summer of parties. My Middlebury classmate, psychologist, shepherd, and now playwright Peter celebrates his recovery from a broken leg by organizing a party on a high outdoor deck of his farmhouse. The guests are his close college friends, including M and me, who have come to rest in the vicinity of the college. It is a steamy hot evening, but there are saving gusts of breeze as we laugh and competitively reminisce over our half century acquaintance. The acreage beyond the deck spills down a hillside displaying a pleasing rustic hodgepodge: stands of ancient shade trees, a vegetable garden mounded and leafy with kale and basil and squash, some split wood around an orderly stack of firewood in the making, weathered sheds, twenty or thirty of Peter's dusty and matted sheep huddled against the fence of a far meadow. There is a profound peace in our unstated love for one another, a shared awareness, I think, of our advancing age and impermanence against this timeless backdrop of Vermont patchwork.

By contrast, there is another party, this one unexpectedly large, so large that it strains both the outdoor terraces and indoor dining rooms of the Waybury Inn, just down the mountain from our house. The party celebrates multiple milestones in the lives of a musical couple, our friends Diana and Emory Fanning: their 65th and 80th birthdays, respectively, and I believe a wedding anniversary. Although the Fannings have no children of their own, there are a few children racing in and out of the fixed clusters of cocktail drinkers. Most of the guests seem my age and older. It is clearly a substantial affair, a dozen or more "food stations," bedecked with good cuts of meat, varieties of seafood. In addition to two fully stocked bars I passed on my way out of the interior rooms into the gardens, caterers dressed in black and white weave through the crowd offering canapés and refilling glasses. There are at least 200 people in roaring attendance, and I cannot help myself from calculating the cost of everything. An hour or so after our arrival, attention is called to a succession of speeches and offerings of congratulation, moderated by an M.C. and featuring a number of video tributes, including snippets of musical performances.

There were too many people in front of me to allow me to hear or see much of what was presented to the guests of honor, but there was something appealing in Diana's and Emory's faces' as they beamed in acknowledgement of each offering. After a half hour or so of rising on tip toe, straining to hear, I was leg weary, and M and I made our way, I hope unobtrusively, to our car and home. I realized that in the course of about two hours, I had only glancingly greeted my hosts and had otherwise had no sustained, substantial conversation with anybody apart from M. I wondered again, as I have in the past, about the point of big parties, especially "milestone" gatherings like this one in which, unlike Peter's convivial get together on the farm, people our age are put squarely in mind that the milestones are over, and that just beyond the clink and chatter is the end.

My annual calendar will forever follow the cadence of a school year. Just as surely as the opening day of school decrees summer's end, I am invited by my old University School colleague, Doug Lagarde, now headmaster of the Severn School in Annapolis, to address his faculty at the end of August as they gather to begin their work. Doug was a dedicated and admirable colleague in my later Cleveland years. He was an excellent teacher of mathematics and a gifted wrestling coach. While I was headmaster, he also served the school in a number of critical administrative posts, including director of admissions and head of the high school division of the school. He attended boys' schools himself, and taught at a boys' school, the Landon School outside of Washington, before coming to University School at a time when we were becoming very purposefully, and I hope not stridently, a *progressive* school for boys.

Severn School is a coed day school and by all measures rising in the ranks of the region's private schools, but Doug, either wistful for a dose of boy-ness or, as he told me, concerned that his faculty be alert to what may be boys' distinctive learning styles and needs, wanted me to talk to his assembled colleagues. And of course that is just about my favorite subject.

On the very agreeable train ride down to Annapolis—-Rutland to New York Penn Station, then another train down to a stop south of Baltimore—I realized that my sense of Mid-Atlantic geography was sketchy. I have spent a good deal of time in both Washington and Baltimore. They are for me abstracted metropolises, perched uncertainly in a jigsaw puzzle of rivers and estuaries that form my notion of the Chesapeake Bay. I don't know if traveling by train to Annapolis improved my internal geography, but it certainly added vivid images, mainly of water.

Though technically not on the ocean, Annapolis, as I approached it by train and was driven around it by Doug, seemed to be a many-nubbed puzzle piece bounded at every nub by water. This image was not corrected or clarified when I consulted maps, due to a mental deficiency in which I cannot correlate elements in maps to any on-the -ground reality I am experiencing. Yet this much is true: for a good bit of the train ride south of Baltimore, the tracks were bounded by great stretches of water on *both sides*, and since I could not see from my window seat down to the putative rail bed, it seemed as though the train were coursing through open sea.

Annapolis's charming city center, historic and very old by American standards, is a substantial port. The rigging of the yachts moored to the docks suggest old British port cities like Plymouth and Portsmouth, the kind of city that centuries ago used to entice small and not so small boys to want to "go to sea." Being late August, there was a humid heaviness to the air that felt more Deep South than mid-Atlantic. Like Charleston and Savannah, Annapolis's commercial and residential facades are brick and date back to earliest colonial days. My first evening meal in town was taken at the Middleton Tavern, with claims to being the country's oldest inn in continuous operation. The food was what it regionally should have been—crabs, oysters, beer—and the inn's musty, slightly down at heel ambience supported its claims of ancientness. But there was something better than mere ye-olde-ness to the historic part of the city. In the succeeding days I found that many of the eateries were really good. The campuses of the United States Naval Academy and of St. John's College, the "great books" school, add substance and texture to a charming seaside hub not quite like any other place I have been in the United States.

The talks—a full day of them—to the Severn School teachers went well, I think. Less than happy school faculties have a way of conveying their resentments in a distinct collective diffidence when they assemble, while secure and happy ones convey a collective warmth, even a sense of fun. The latter was emphatically the case with the Severn group, who were relaxed, funny, and eager to participate in the sessions offered, which included a good deal of interactivity and shared reflection on their part.

The gist of my presentations was the current scholastic condition of boys and a review of promising ways to better engage them. Like other faculties in coed schools where I have presented, I sensed a real interest, as well as genuine concern, about how boys were progressing at Severn, and absolutely no suspicion or resentment that boys, and not girls, were, for the moment, the subject of analysis. For my part, it was both useful and confirming that the Severn teachers—both men and women—acknowledged without reservation specific types of lessons Michael Reichert and I had identified as especially effective with boys in our *Reaching Boys / Teaching Boys* research project, as well as the relational approaches boys favored with their teachers in our subsequent study, *I Can Learn From You: Boys as Relational Learners*.

My feeling at sessions' end was that I had made a definite connection with the group, to the extent that I think there might a chance that the invitation I extended to look at boys in more nuanced ways might actually alter teaching practice. I was heartened to hear a number of teachers, in their summary comments, pledge to make relationships—that is, consciously creating them, monitoring them and repairing them when broken—more central to their pedagogy.

It is of course always a pleasure—and a relief—to be listened to attentively and responded to warmly, but I left the school with the strongest impression that the Severn teachers' relaxed, receptive good nature was due to their affection and respect for my friend Doug, who in his decade there as headmaster, has succeeded in making them feel that they are supported in their work, that the school's standards are and should be rigorous, and that the boys and girls enrolled matter most. I could feel this in the easy humor in which Doug and his colleagues could banter, in the unguarded warmth of their appreciation of one another. Not yet a famous school, but a very good school.

September 2015: I am pleased to be invited back to Project Independence to play the piano for the elderly whose families sign them up for all-day care at the facility. Since my last visit the staff has assembled a handsomely produced booklet of lyrics to twenty-some tunes I was pretty sure most of them would know: "Shine on Harvest Moon," "Heart of My Heart," "Bye Bye Blackbird," etc. The sing-along was preceded by a few name-that-tune contests I devised: movie themes and show tunes from the 1940s and '50s. I find I have to be careful in my song selection, because my impulse is to choose songs from my parents' generation—which worked well enough when I played for them and fellow their residents at their retirement home in Burbank. I easily forget that my parents would now be nearly a hundred. The sobering fact is that my audience at Project Independence, many of them noticeably infirm, are not much older than I am. I am aware—though I resist the thought—that not far in the future, if I continue to play this gig, I will be offering up the likes of the Beatles in order to kindle a flame of recollection in my listeners. The session proceeds pleasantly enough, and it is good to see the flash of recognition on the peoples' faces when they recognize an old favorite, good to hear the wavering voices join in as I complete the correctly guessed tune. I imagine that from their perspective I am less a piano-playing guest than simply one of them.

Drove to Cleveland for a long weekend with Lulu. I had not seen her since our summer excursions to the water parks and Finger Lakes and wanted to connect with her as she starts her new school year as a fifth grader. The transformation to fall foliage had already begun in Ripton, and though that was less evident on Interstate 90, the drive westward was vernal and restorative, the ten hours seeming more like one. Part of the pleasure is the Mini Cooper, so solid, compact, and close to the road. It exudes something like automotive happiness as it hums along. And while I absolutely, on pain of losing my license, cannot get another speeding ticket on the New York thruway, it is very hard to rein in the Mini to under 80 m.p.h., which I have determined is the speed that motivates the police hovering out of view to turn on their flashers and pursue.

No trouble this time.

Lulu is in high spirits. She has been placed in a "gifted" class of just 15 students. She is enthusiastic about her teacher, whose emphasis is on "project-centered learning," which also happens to be very close to Lulu's heart, since her life unfolds, when she is able to run the show, as an unbroken series of projects, most of them involving putting various materials together to make a product.

Lulu explains to me her research team's most recent assignment, which was to demonstrate that the Vikings settled in North America before Columbus. The facts appear to be on her team's side, and Lulu's personal contribution to the presentation was to write a script for a simulated TV documentary explaining the Viking's conquest of the New World. I am concerned about her unquestioning assumption that various "facts" she accessed on the internet are reliable. She is a little impatient that I am concerned about such things, when for her the fun and the energizing feature of the assignment was producing and performing the documentary. After school on Monday I meet with Lulu's teacher, a relaxed, likable woman with a bad cold, who assures me that Lulu and her classmates will be introduced to challenges of discerning valid evidence as the year progresses. Her unspoken message to me was to relax, which I am certainly willing to do. I have a feeling Lulu is going to have a very good school year, and she will benefit more from my interest in what she actually does than from my fussy concern that she get everything right.

Back home in Ripton, I feel uneasy that in the aftermath of so much out-of-town distraction I am somehow not looking after business. Am I ignoring the house and necessary maintenance? Are my finances in order? Claire's ever expanding and more expensive wedding festivities are looming in less than a month, and it is hard to remember what I have specified we will provide, especially about food and drink, not to mention lodging arrangements for the hundred and fifty or so people coming from out of town. These concerns crowd my thoughts in my insomniac wakefulness most nights.

By light of day, everything seems to be in order. But the suspicion—more a mood—persists that there has to be *something* wrong, and then I remember the dentist—or rather, remember forgetting the dentist. It has been nearly two years since my last check-up. I dimly recall postponing a six-months checkup because I had a conflict with a speaking engagement out of town, then being unresponsive to calls from the dentist's office proposing other dates. There was also some unfinished business about a crown, actually two of them, the dentist claimed were necessary to prevent some very bad oral outcomes due to cracks in some boyhood fillings in the molars on my lower jaw.

I found it hard to share the dentist's concern when he pointed out the problem teeth on a big video screen close to the dental chair. To be honest, I was rather impressed with how clean everything looked. Gums were pink and the teeth mostly white. Even more critical to my assessment, neither of the allegedly endangered teeth hurt or gave me any kind of discomfort. Moreover, each crown, even with insurance, would cost over $1,000, and I did not want to pay it. With a little wheedling on my part, I convinced the dentist to do a stop gap application of some cement-like substance over the cracked part of what he thought was the most at-risk tooth. This might tide me over, he believed, until the crown. The cement improvisation had cost nothing, and now, two years out, neither molar has given me any trouble. But two years without a check-up. Nothing would spoil the coming wedding celebration for me more completely than dental woes: elaborate procedures by specialists in distant cities, wounds, pain, medicine. I called and scheduled a check-up.

On the appointed day, the receptionist was fairly cheery about my delinquency, as was the dental hygienist assigned to clear out the accumulated plaque and otherwise clean me up before the dentist himself would come in and make his summary pronouncements. This hygienist was new to me, a big, athletic-looking young woman with a direct, easy-going manner. I confided to her that in prior appointments the battery powered sonar pick had been unbearably painful, and would she please use only hand instruments. She seemed untroubled by the request and set about her work. I thought it was going all right, at least there was little actual pain, but then, after about forty-five minutes, it occurred to me that there had been a lot of energetic and rather loud picking for an awfully long time. During one of the little breaks when she squirted water in my mouth to rinse out the gravelly bits of plaque that had gathered under my tongue, I asked her if this wasn't an unusually long session, and was she nearly done. A little less pleasantly than earlier, she told me that an awful lot of plaque had accumulated, and there was quite a bit more to do.

Indeed there was, and some of the plaque must have implanted itself very solidly, especially at the base of my lower front teeth, because the hygienist's exertions now required the kind of physical effort and leverage I might have associated with pulling difficult nails out of hardwood with the claw of a hammer. It was an hour and a half before she was finished, the last forty minutes or so grim and wordless, both of my jaws now aching at their hinges from such prolonged, tense opening. She tried not to make a show of the moist cotton pads she used to dab my gum line between applications of the pick, but I could not help noticing they were bloody.

When the dentist finally swept in with his familiar false cheer, there was a dull, throbbing ache all along my gum line, top and bottom. He asked me how I felt the cleaning session had gone. I told him I thought it was very thorough, to which the hygienist added, "He really had a *lot* of plaque." Then the dentist asked me to open up and began lightly probing and tapping with his pick and little mirror. "*Jesus,*" he said, startling me. He told me my gums were really swollen and distressed from the cleaning, but that was somehow a good thing and that the discomfort would subside. He told me to brush gently for a day or so and not to floss until my gums "settled down." The hygienist and I exchanged glances, hers I think a little guilty.

I knew as I departed the office for my car that I was the guilty one. I had let my teeth go for two years, elderly and problematic teeth at that. For my lapse I felt I was duly and rigorously punished, though I took some consolation, after the dentist urged me unctuously to go ahead with the crowns—"yes, I *know* it's a big ticket item"—in refusing to commit to a specific appointment to have the work done. I told him I would think it over, in a tone both of us understood.

Toward the end of the month I make my way down to Beaufort, South Carolina, for a complicated bout of literary promotion. There are two thrusts. First, I am going to "launch" my *Greeves Passing* novel at a kind of party event, which will feature a reading and a signing. The following evening a three-day short story festival commences in which this year's *Short Story America* anthology will be released and distributed. I have been asked by the publisher, my friend Tim Johnston, to give a lecture to the assembled writers and story fans as well as a reading of a story of mine, "A Man Who Prays," which is included in the anthology. I participated in a similar event three years ago and rather look forward to it, but in the way of such things now, the preparation of the material and the travel and lodging arrangements carry a new and slightly aversive weight.

The historic center of Beaufort is a haunting and beautiful place, nestled in what South Carolinians call the Low Country, a region of tidewater estuaries, wide beaches, and miles of shimmering green marsh cut through with channels for the shrimpers and crab fishermen. For me the allure of these southern coastal cities, of which I would include Savannah and Charleston and, now that I've seen it, Annapolis, is an almost creepy sultriness. I liked Savannah so much the last time I would like to spend a night or two there this time, with no duties, nothing in mind but to wander about, get the feel of things, eat the extraordinary food. But while my plane lands in Savannah, I rent a car and steel myself for the hour and a half drive north in hopes of finding Beaufort.

I actually have more confidence these days heading off to cities unknown due to the miracle of Siri who, from either my iPhone or iPad, clearly and melodiously intones directions, while on the device itself, infant-clear renderings and maps indicate exactly where one should turn next. Siri: "In TWO MILES merge right onto Interstate 91…" A minute later: "In ONE MILE merge right onto Interstate 91…" And so on until "MERGE RIGHT onto Interstate 91…" How can you miss? Even I, who have lost my way on every single solo car expedition since I began driving, have come to trust and value Siri and the brilliance of the GPS engineers behind her voice.

Nevertheless, I almost went disastrously off course in my attempt to reach Beaufort. After getting off the plane in Savannah and reaching my rental car, my optimism was shattered when in answer to my vocal prompt to Siri: *Directions. To Beaufort, South Carolina*, there was a confusing response: *Did you mean Beaufort, North Carolina?* My attempts to answer this question, as if I were not talking to a robotic voice, were met by anarchic gibberish from Siri, accompanied by columns of text pouring down my iPad screen indicating hotels and attractions in North Carolina and Georgia. Now soaked with nervous sweat, I idled in the rental car lot, repeatedly trying and failing to make myself understood to Siri.

Then a breakthrough. I noticed that many of the alternative destinations printing themselves onto my iPad were "Bufords," in North Carolina and Georgia. It occurred to me that Siri might be mishearing my pronunciation of Beaufort. Or—*perhaps she did not know the correct one.* I happen to know from my prior dealings with Beaufortians that the correct pronunciation is *Bew*-fort, so I asked for directions again, this time mispronouncing the city as *Bow*-fort—and alas, the correct city in the correct state appeared, along with the name of the inn where I was booked to lodge. Off I drove, with tentative confidence, into the steamy Low Country darkness in the direction of what Siri said was Beaufort, SC.

Sometime between 10 p.m. and midnight I located the historic inn where I was to be lodged, a block inland from the waterfront, in a neighborhood of substantial old residences, their facades under the streetlamps partly voided by thickly hanging Spanish moss. There was not a soul about, and there could not have been a more promising movie set for a sudden, vicious murder. Fortunately, a thoughtful desk clerk, noticing on her guest list that Richard Hawley had not yet arrived at his estimated check-in time, had called me on my cell phone while I was in transit to assure me that she would wait up and be on hand to check me in, a characteristic Beaufort courtesy.

I realized I was starvingly hungry and asked the clerk if any nearby eateries might still be open. So far as she knew, there was only one, which was providentially less than a block down the street, and off I went under the unearthly lamp-lit Spanish moss, hearing my own footsteps clicking on the sidewalk, to a low-slung, dimly lit bistro which, but for a bar tender and waitress, was empty. In ear-ringing silence I drank a chilled martini, followed by oysters and a seafood pasta. Then I made my solitary way back to the inn and through its unpeopled lobby and lounges to my room, all the while entertaining a fantasy that I had arrived in a realm from which all prior residents had been carried off.

My scheduled obligations went well. My only concern about the novel launch was that people would not come. I am still brought low by memories of being invited by bookstores to read and sign books and being progressively deflated as the appointed afternoon or evening wore on that only a dribble of customers—and once, no one—stopped by. I am also aware that *Greeves Passing* is being promoted as "literary fiction," which I hope it is, while grimly aware that very few people read it, much less buy it. This musing over dark possibilities was not helped by a dramatic rainstorm unloosing itself over Beaufort an hour before the scheduled launch party. And it was *Thursday* night. I tried to imagine the kinds and amounts of people in any small southern city who might be moved to leave their homes on a Thursday evening and drive through blinding rain to attend a book event inconveniently close to the dinner hour in order to meet the unfamous author of a new book of literary fiction which, if they only knew, was set in a far away, buttoned up New England, mostly in the closed world of a private boarding school in which all three principal characters were slowly and wordily approaching death.

When I arrived at the venue, a brightly lit and commodious civic Arts Center, I was cheered that my publisher, Tim, had dragooned six or eight people to serve canapés and wine, man the putative book-buying table, and otherwise staff the event—cheered because I knew that in the very worst case I would not spend the evening alone. But as the event commenced—at *six* o'clock, what were we thinking!—people began arriving, first in acceptable numbers, then by gratifying numbers, so I was able to stop counting. Rows of folding chairs were set up in an adjoining room with a stage and a lectern wired for both video and audio recording. The sound technician was a pro, and I began to feel that all would be well, and it was.

Tim introduced me very warmly, and I was glad to see a sprinkling of people I remembered from the last story festival in Beaufort among the gathered audience. I was especially glad to see Margaret Shinn Evans, the editor of an arts mag called *Low Country Weekly*. Margaret has written just about the nicest reviews I have ever had of both *The Other World* and *Greeves Passing*. Seeing her friendly face among a line of other stylishly dressed women in the front row put me at ease— or rather on edge, but in a good way.

I read for about 40 minutes, alternating first person monologues from each of my principals, concluding with three that were very sad, but not quite plot-spoiling. The immediate response was warm. I was surprised, actually thrilled, that Margaret and her decorous seatmates were weeping. Mood elevated, I responded to questions and comments with genuine pleasure.

I treated myself to another nearly solitary, too rich dinner at the same low-slung bistro as the night prior, feeling that nothing could go wrong in the coming presentations, and nothing did. I have always found the close company of other writers and aspiring writers in a conference setting to be a tonic. As we share our work and our intentions with like-minded others, we, or at least most of us, are generous and encouraging, maybe excessively so. The unstated premise is that *in this world, in this company* we matter, and our writing matters. Not a bad condition to enter from time to time.

Perhaps it is my advanced age, but I also find that my energy is drained in these conference sessions, both my own presentations and the ones I attend. Not too long ago I would have been a cheerful player in the after-session parties at designated bars in town, but this time I am happy to slip away quietly to solitary meals and my bed in the ancient inn. The first evening of the conference, after my duties at the Arts Center had been dispatched, I took a stroll through historic Beaufort to work up an appetite and passed the display window of a bookstore. Propped up inside was a poster announcing our conference, and prominently in the middle of it was a photograph of me. Fanned out before the poster like a hand of playing cards was a display of books, *Greeves Passing*, alternating with the new Short Story America anthology, and for a moment my gratitude to Beaufort almost exceeded my capacity to feel.

October 2016: Like the speck of an ocean liner, for hours no more than a dot on the horizon, suddenly and gigantically gliding into port, Claire's wedding day arrived, dwarfing and eclipsing all other domestic business. Claire, beloved third born! And her movie-handsome Nick, with every additional hour passed in his company a miracle of modesty and kindness. The night last December when over the dinner table they announced to M and me that they were going to be married, I snatched up my iPad and took a rapid succession of pictures of the two of them, my finger clicking on the appointed dot as rapidly as I was able to click. The resulting series has the look of a sequence of movie stills, each image only slightly deviating from the one preceding. The sequence captures in both faces first the shy emergence and then the laughing realization of their happiness.

Sisters Kate and Jesse were determined to stage—and 'stage' is the right word—their weddings where they lived, in Chicago and Brooklyn, respectively, because that is where most of their friends lived. Claire's and Nick's friends are so numerous and far-flung that no location would be especially convenient. Thus they decided that since they and a number of friends had attended Middlebury College together, and since we lived there, Vermont would be the site: a stately and commodious old inn, The Lilac Inn, in Brandon, Vermont, a fifteen minute drive from our house and from the village of Middlebury.

Holding the ceremony close to home meant rather more involvement (in addition to merely paying) on M's and my part in the preparations. In the event Claire and her mother looked after almost everything, including such niceties and the kinds of antique jars that would hold the selected Vermont wildflowers on the dining tables. Not that paying was in any way a small matter, my own chief contribution may have been to specify how much of and what kinds of alcoholic beverages would be available to all at various points in the celebration. Since so many invitees would be coming from out of town, advising about and arranging lodging became a challenge, as the wedding day, October 10, fell in the heart of Vermont's "leaf season," which has become a booming tourist draw, which means that many hotels,

B&Bs, and inns were already booked.

In any wedding the commingling of brides' and grooms' families can be an occasion for awkwardness and tension, if not outright hilarity. M and I had previously managed to host Nick's parents, the Benjamins, for dinner and an overnight stay at our house and subsequently went to dinner at their house, and to our great relief found we like them very much. It had been determined that they would host and arrange a sizable rehearsal dinner, and we would assume all the responsibilities and costs of the wedding itself. Energetic, and attentive to detail, the Benjamins were a pleasure to work with and, not incidentally, succeeded in looking after and lodging their extensive clan. So, unless I missed something, our families have more coalesced than collided.

It was clear from the guests' arrival at the rehearsal dinner through the farewell breakfast under the wedding tent that a robust—and bibulous—party atmosphere would prevail. The rehearsal dinner at a restaurant venue in downtown Middlebury was happy-noisy. By the time our hosts and designated friends of the groom rose to give toasts, there was no question that multiple cocktails had been downed. I feel uneasy listening to celebratory toasts, because too often, even without the disinhibiting effect of alcohol, the person offering the toast has not thought things through, relying on warm sentiment to carry the message. The more rambling and ineloquent the toast, the more reluctant is the toaster to relinquish the microphone and sit down. And so there were some patience-testing moments both at the rehearsal dinner and the wedding itself, though, again, no bad will.

One of the wedding toasts will not, I believe, be forgotten by anyone in attendance. It was offered by one of Nick's college room-mates who seized the microphone and, after an extended caesura in which he dramatically fortified himself for something he felt was of special consequence, unleashed a highly personal confession of his mounting and at times unrequited affection for Nick, beginning from the moment they met. He spoke for fifteen or twenty minutes, but it seemed much longer. The account was broken up by uncomfortable pauses, and for much of the narrative he gave the unsettling impression that, impervious to the occasion and those seated before him, he was talking to himself, working out deep personal business. Nobody I talk-ed to afterward failed to remark on the toast, the consensus being that it was an attempt to come to terms with years of closeted romantic longing. Sometimes, but only sometimes in my experience, a ritual ceremony like a wedding actually becomes a ritual. You know it when it happens, because there is an unmistakable feeling of being drawn up into it, passing what the Greeks called *chronos* into *kairos,* a condition somehow rapt and out of time. Claire's and Nick's wedding was such a ritual. Despite its decidedly secular liturgy, a sense of sacred solemnity descended from the moment Claire joined M and me for our rehearsed walk between the seated rows of guests to the improvised altar set back in the inn's gardens.

Not because I wanted to respect traditional taboos on observing the bride before she is ready to be presented to the groom, but because I had been otherwise distracted, checking various arrangements inside the inn, under the vast tent that the staff were struggling to heat adequately, and out on the lawn where the guests were assembling for the ceremony, I did not catch a glimpse of Claire until she appeared before M and me to take our part in the processional. Claire by any reckoning is a pretty girl, petite, elfin with bright eyes and a quick smile, but she was something more indelible than pretty as she stood before us in her wedding dress. M had no doubt consulted with Claire about the dress and other matters of turnout, but I had no prior expectations. Her dress was simple and fit closely to her slender form. Because there was an autumn chill in the air outside, she had draped a sheer lacey shawl over her shoulders. More than anything else her broad smile expressed an uncontainable happiness. I know parents symbolically "give away" their daughters to their fiancés at the end of the bride's processional, but the thought of giving Claire away— giving her *up*—actually occurred to me as we processed, and I knew that, except to the degree time and circumstance had already made it happen, I was incapable of giving up that girl.

The ceremony itself played out with the heightened vividness of a dream. The procession of events did not seem to succeed one another in chronological time. Instead, they combined to what felt to me like a single moment, *kairos*, a sustained timelessness capturing the feeling of what had transpired. Contributing to this other-worldly impression was the intense late-afternoon sunlight. The weather forecast for the day had been discouraging: unseasonably chilly, clouds, and intermittent rain. That morning when we assembled at the inn's garden to rehearse the wedding sequence, the sky overhead was grimly overcast, and it was so cold those who had them showed up in winter coats. It seemed obvious to me that unless we moved the ceremony indoors, we would all be needlessly uncomfortable. Earlier Claire had made it plain that Nick was committed to holding the ceremony outdoors, so I drew him aside to make the case for moving inside. I thought that since I was shivering with cold as I made the proposal, I could persuade him to reconsider. But he was cheerfully unmovable.

As the day wore on, the clouds overhead occasionally broke apart and it warmed up, but only a little. About fifteen minutes before the ceremony commenced, the clouds dispersed altogether, and shafts of late sun irradiated the garden, intensifying the color of everything. Guests' overcoats were shed, and just before stepping out into the light, Claire discarded the shawl she had planned to warm her shoulders.

Claire and Nick had requested two musical offerings for the service. The first, a Beatles ballad, "I Will," was sung by Jesse, accompanied by James on the guitar and Leon on the violin. It's a simple, lovely melody, and Jesse rendered it as purely as if it were a hymn. The three of them made a pleasing picture, Leon's intense concentration over his bowing—he had chosen to wear a top hat and tails—just short of comical. The second number was the love song, "Till There Was You," from *The Music Man*, sung by Piper, one of Claire's teaching colleagues from San Francisco. I was to accompany her on the piano, though all I knew of her until the wedding rehearsal was that Claire thought she was an accomplished singer, a judgment I was inclined to trust, Claire being a fine singer herself. A week before the wedding, Piper had sent me a recording of the song performed by the Broadway soprano Kristin Cheneweth, Piper noting that she liked the key and the tempo. I agreed and was relieved she had not sent me a score to struggle with. On the eve of the wedding, after the rehearsal dinner, Piper found me and we made our way to a piano where I sat down, chorded a little introduction, and Piper sang through the song with great feeling and confidence. I could tell she sensed what I was doing in support, and it was easy to find the right fills. At its best, accompanying a singer is like carrying out a highly nuanced conversation. The trick is not to double the melody line. One more time, and we had it to our mutual liking, a rendition we managed to duplicate exactly the following afternoon.

There was, as I said, a dreamy rightness to everything that unfolded in the course of the ceremony. Two days earlier Claire and Nick had dedicated an entire afternoon upstairs in our house to composing their marital vows. At the celebrant's invitation they stood facing each other in front of the altar of flowers. Nick was to go first. He extracted his typewritten text from the jacket of his coat, fixed Claire with a stare, and tried to speak but could not. He took a series of deep breaths, opened his mouth to begin, but could voice no words. For what felt like a very long time, he stood there, looking into Claire's eyes, unable to speak. Tears coursed down his cheeks. A by no means disagreeable tension mounted among the seated guests. Then Nick was at last able to speak. He said—loudly, his voice breaking—"Claire!" One of the groomsmen made a funny crack, the tension dissolved. Then Nick, still in tears, found his voice and read his loving and lovely vows. Nothing could have been more moving, more affectionate, more revealing of his good nature. Vows exchanged, the ceremony concluded briskly and joyfully. Not five minutes after Claire and Nick, man and wife, recessed arm in arm along the garden path, the sun sank below the tree line, and we were no longer held in its urgent, warming light.

The ensuing "reception" included quite a long cocktail hour accommodating the necessary commingling, a satisfying dinner punctuated by mostly appropriate toasts, and then a whirl of dancing and more drinking into the small hours. Inevitably, M's and my friends—and most of the others within ten years of our age—paid their respects and parted before ten, while a hundred or so peers of Claire and Nick accelerated the pace, inhibitions shed. Clapping circles were formed around certain dancers deemed to be especially athletic, exotic or funny. At one point Claire was hoisted up by her bridesmaids so that she was lying flat in their arms and then tossed in the air to the beat of the tune. By midnight, the proceedings had become a blur. I somehow settled up with the innkeepers, tipped all the people I could find to tip. I do not remember driving home. Very deepest sleep.

Reflecting in bed the following morning, I tried to recreate the wedding's sequence of events, but could only manage a bright, pulsing composite in which all the elements were fused into a single picture. I summoned up images of Kate's and Jesse's weddings. Each was distinctive and memorable. I could recall being lost in and, in a way hard to describe, being personally effaced by each of them. But this morning I could not shake the feeling that Claire's wedding carried its own significance for me. And then I had it: this would be my *final* wedding. Realistically, it is unlikely that I will live to celebrate Lulu's. Like so many other, lesser events these days, Claire's wedding was deepened by and inseparable from my impending death.

The wedding also took an unexpected physical toll. Upstairs getting dressed for the ceremony, I was overcome for a minute or so with a sneezing fit. I did not, at the moment, feel ill, but something familiar in that kind of sneezing put me on edge. I was not surprised to feel diminished and depleted the morning after the wedding. There was still a lot to do. Our house was full of lodgers, including both Kate's and Jesse's families. Claire and Nick, who decided to postpone their honeymoon until Claire's Christmas break from school, were also on hand. My sister and two of her friends were lodging at the inn across the street and expected company and amusement. As the wedding approached, I had not considered, though I probably should have, that our house would be a kind of gathering place for those arriving from out of town. A number of Claire's friends assumed this would be the case, including a few who lodged with us. As a result, for a few days both before and after the wedding, our first floor rooms were filled to capacity with lively visitors eager for food and drink. Taken together they were pleasant enough, but I could not get used to how readily they assumed the house was open to them and that they would be fed and entertained. In this response I suspect I am again showing my age.

I really wanted quiet, rest, and restoration after the wedding, but it was not to be. In a festive mood Claire suggested that a group of those staying on—about fourteen—drive down the mountain to the Waybury Inn for a convivial post-wedding dinner. She did not have to tell me that she assumed I would pay for it. By this time I knew that yesterday's sneezing had heralded a genuine malaise, and it was working its way into my respiratory system. The realization put me in a foul mood, which I tried mightily to suppress, or at least disguise. Over drinks in our red parlor before heading off to the Waybury, Ginny, my sister, gave me a long look and said, "you look like something is wrong." I did my best to explain there had been a lot of events in a row requiring special energy, and mine was running low. This seemed to puzzle her.

I endured the dinner, and I endured the next few days of good-byes and then a massive clean-up, and now I was thoroughly sick with a raw throat, cough, and, if I bothered to take my temperature, a fever. Darkening the picture, I had an especially demanding succession of obligations coming up on the weekend: a day and a half of Middlebury College alumni board meetings followed on Sunday by a reading and launch party for *Greeves Passing.*

As I feared, the all-day board meetings were nearly unendurable, partly due to a thin, padded agenda and partly due to what had become an insistent, impossible to suppress cough. Toward the end of the first day's program, I had to step out into a corridor twice for sustained spells of hacking, embarrassing for me and I am sure unpleasant for and possibly resented by my fellow board members. The other-regarding, sensible thing to do would have been to plead illness and stay home. But the board only meets twice a year, and all of us are urged warmly, even sternly, to attend all sessions. The following morning, coughing only moderately, I managed to sit through an hour of Middlebury's new president Laurie Patton's initial impressions of the college and its prospects, but by midmorning break I was hacking again and had to offer my apologies and depart. Had I been well, I would not have looked forward to the scheduled fund-raising and reunion-planning meetings, but I cannot shake the guilt of being a weak contributor to business I had signed on to do.

I was no better Sunday morning, but I could not think of a possible way to cancel the launch party for my novel. It had been planned for some time. I had sent out personal invitations to dozens of literary and other friends, some of them from out of state, and most were coming. The event was to take place at the Chipman Inn across the road, and I had asked the innkeeper, Chris, to prepare highly specific hors d'œuvres and to stock in special wine. I had also been looking forward to it very much. These are people I really like, and I had little of the usual apprehension I feel before I read. This time it would be a close version of what I had done for the Beaufort launch, which had gone well. And frankly, I don't feel much apprehension about *Greeves Passing*. It is grim in parts, sad in others, understandably not everyone's kind of book, but for those for whom it is, it usually hits a mark.

By drinking lots of hot tea, I found I could dissolve the gravel out of my speaking voice. My other worry was the cough, which was still rumbling and insistent, but would abate for an hour or so. Every few hours, I coated my throat and digestive tract with swigs of this or that over-the-counter cold medicine the pharmacist assures me is worthless. Just before party time I changed into my black good-luck reading clothes and looked into the mirror. A pretty good facsimile of an aging, tubercular writer.

Sometimes you just go ahead, and this time it worked out. I got a positive lift from greeting the arriving friends, some of whom I had not seen for years. The innkeepers had made the interior rooms welcome-ing, and there was a blaze in the ancient fireplace. By the time people had had a glass of wine or two, I knew everything would be fine. The room designated for the reading was a mix of chairs placed around tables and chairs in rows. The arrangement was a little cramped, but a too-small room with people standing is preferable to a great hall only lightly sprinkled with listeners. We had planned exactly right. Every chair was filled, no one had to stand, and the preliminary chatter was cheery and welcoming.

I had worried, despite its agreeable reception in Beaufort, that the reading might, at forty-five minutes, be too long. For my part, I can remember only being relieved that my voice was close to normal, and there was no cough tickle. The introductory remarks came easily, and then, feeling pretty much on autopilot, I read. I was able to establish enough eye contact to note that the group seemed to be attentive. There were lively questions afterward, and that there were any at all touched and flattered me, so I believe I was "on." But it was a terrific relief to finish. By now it was early evening and dark. A dozen or so of us decided to drive down the mountain to the Waybury Inn, which since the wedding was coming to feel like an extension of our kitchen at home. We dined in good cheer; many drinks. Back home, I got into bed glad I had gone ahead with everything. The company had been stimulating, the meal satisfying, but I knew in every cell that my malaise had not receded, just paused.

Three days running of worsening cough, relieved a little by the fact I was not obligated to do anything outside the house. What had begun as a little ache under my arm and behind my shoulder blade became an insistent pain whenever I coughed, which was practically all the time. By the end of the third day it was almost impossible to sleep. M drove down to Boston for a spiritual retreat, and I thought lying low in solitude might hasten my recovery, but the pain did not abate, and nothing in the medicine chest—ibuprofen, aspirin, Tylenol—helped at all. Feeling more defeated than frightened, I drove myself to the Porter Hospital emergency ward, remembering the sign at the reception desk indicating that anyone with breathing difficulties or chest pain would be streamlined into immediate care.

Qualifying on both counts, I was in minutes gowned, vital signs taken, and hooked up with wires to an ECG machine so they could determine if I was having a heart attack. That possibility ruled out, I was wheeled down the corridor for chest x-rays. If anyone told me why I was also hooked up to an intravenous drip, I forgot. Since my arrival I had been attended by a confusing whirl of nurses, doctors, and technicians. Then I was left alone for what felt like a couple of hours.

A thin hospital blanket had been offered but I was still very cold. At last a doctor came in and said the x-rays indicated both pneumonia and an inflammation—pleurisy—in the lining of the lung, the location of which indicated why I had been in pain. The prescription was a powerful antibiotic, a narcotic for the pain, and lots of rest. It was suggested I would feel much better in a week to ten days.

There was a bizarre and slightly comical incident before I left the hospital. After the doctor's explanation of my illness and its remedy, a nurse popped in and said I could get dressed and depart. Another nurse was due in to detach the ECG leads and the IV from the crook of my arm, but I was not told this and proceeded to free myself of the devices myself.

The ECG leads were no problem; I just pulled the little suction cups away from my skin and left them dangling. I was uncertain about the IV. I have had a few of them inserted in the past but did not recall ever having to detach one myself. The needle going into my vein looked substantial, and it was held in place by sturdy overlays of tape. I would have liked some counsel at this point. I waited for a few minutes, even called out for assistance, but no one came. All right, I figured, I had been told to get dressed, and there was no getting dressed without pulling the IV out of my arm, so I ripped off the tape and yanked the needle from the vein, which resulted in an alarming spout of blood several inches in the air. I had clearly done something wrong. Reflexively I looked for some kind of cloth to press down into the spout, but I could find nothing in the room. So I unfastened my hospital gown, wedged it into a ball and pressed it down into the little bleeding hole and held it fast. This was probably the right thing to do, but it took a few minutes for the bleeding to subside. When I determined that it had, the gown had been nearly blackened by my blood. Glad that the crisis had passed, I quickly got dressed. Then a nurse came in, probably the one who had been assigned to take out the IV, and expressed astonishment that I had proceeded without her. I explained the situation, but she was upset, especially, I could not help noticing, taking in the bloody gown I had left on the examining table. Either of us could have reasonably assigned fault, but I was overall glad to depart the emergency wing with medicines in hand and a promised recovery.

But there was an abiding uneasiness. The doctor who explained the pneumonia and pleurisy had said it was lucky I had come in when I did. He said the progression of the pneumonia could have been very bad. He didn't have to say life-threatening. I was also mindful of the fact that only months ago I had been treated in the same emergency room for the same emergency. Was every cold now going to progress to a bronchial crisis? Is this how I will go?

M returned from Boston more concerned about my condition than was necessary. In just a day or two the medicines seemed to be easing both the pain and my cough, and I was able to sleep. In a week I was up and about, feeling normal. This was encouraging because a trip I had scheduled to visit Lulu and Celeste in Cleveland was fast approaching. I have in the past kept my commitments to visit Cleveland when I was not feeling well, only to decline further on arrival. This time Celeste made it clear: *don't come* if you are sick. This perfectly sensible instruction gave me pause: I have now apparently registered with Celeste as someone who is sick often—annoyingly often—and in that condition I am unwelcome, perhaps even dreaded. It does not stretch imagination to calculate that illness aside, *other* aspects of my septuagenarian condition—more lines in the face, a greater inclination to be sitting than moving, a lack of enthusiasm for the household's favored films and pop music—could well be dampening what had previously seemed a gratifying eagerness to see me. The prospect of Daddy coming could be giving way to The Old Guy is coming.

November 2016: In the event both health and energy stood up in the course of my week in Cleveland. There was a succession of dress-up evenings out, reliably stimulating for Lulu who gives a lot of thought to turning herself out elaborately, even exotically, for special occasions. Cleveland's economy and collective morale are on the rebound these days, not entirely because the city's almost homegrown (he was reared in Akron) NBA superstar LeBron James has returned to the

Cleveland Cavaliers after having defected for four years to play for the more high-flying Miami Heat. Public Square, the heart of downtown, is being massively renovated, including new high-end residences, hotels, and restaurants. The theme of this particular visit is to explore downtown, sampling some of the favorably reviewed eateries. It is always energizing for me, but especially so after my close quarters convalescence in Ripton, to live it up in an urban way. In a week we dined in only twice, and that was in order to try new cooking ideas stimulated by happy discoveries in the restaurants we frequented.

Reconnecting with Lulu is once again a pleasure. Since I last saw her, she has managed to hound her mother into repainting and, with Celeste's help and guidance, otherwise reconfiguring her room. I should say "rooms." There are two chambers to Lulu's bedroom, separated by a wide archway. In the earlier arrangement, the nearer chamber was set up as a sleeping room, dominated by a canopy bed, bureau, and bookshelves. Through the arch were a work desk, bins of toys, mounds of stuffed animals, etc.—a playroom. In the new set-up the former bedroom is a rather formal, child-scale "sitting room," an arrangement of upholstered chairs, a Victorian love seat, a coffee table and standing lamps. The archway, now hung with gauzy curtains, opens into the new sleeping quarters, featuring a sizable double bed, a small desk, and bureaus and hutches for Lulu's burgeoning wardrobe. Somehow it all coheres to a complete, well-appointed little world. I am impressed by, among other things, how the outcome reflects both Lulu's fierce, insistent preferences as well as her mother's guiding hand. I also reflect on how, given the restraints of having so little money, Celeste has managed, through thrift shop foraging and garage sale bargaining, to create such seemingly opulent quarters for Lulu— such a seemingly opulent household, for that matter. I summon up a picture of my own boyhood bedroom: always the smallest, most out-of-the way bedroom in our modest houses' second floor: a single bed, a bureau, sometimes a desk or table to write on.

It is a good week, as these visits go. It falls to me to oversee Lulu's rising for school. I drop her off in the morning and pick her up in the afternoon, reviving acquaintance with a few of her classmates' mothers as I wait outside for the bell ending the school day. During school hours, I work a little on manuscripts, answer emails, go with Celeste to various food stores to stock her larder, take the dogs for long, unhurried walks.

I am a little preoccupied by a *Greeves Passing* launch party and reading scheduled mid-week at a Cleveland bookstore called Loganberry Books. It is a wonderful store, situated midway along an inviting string of antique shops and restaurants in the Larchmere section of Cleveland, just off once posh Shaker Square. The previous summer I had wandered in out of curiosity and was taken by the beauty of the place. Nothing about its anonymous façade or modest display in the window suggests the majesty of the place inside. The first room you enter is vast: high ceilings, oriental carpets on the hardwood floors. Dark oaken book shelves rise from floor to ceiling, with sliding ladders on wheels accessing the volumes on the shelves beyond standing reach. There are occasional tables and seating for those who want to lounge and read. This room alone makes Loganberry's the most welcoming and certainly the most handsome book store I know of in the city. But there is surprisingly more of it. At the far end of the room doors open up to a variety of other large rooms, dedicated to children's fare, rare books, used books, special collections. Wondering, I introduced myself to the clerk behind the main desk and asked her to tell me something about the store. To my surprise she said she knew who I was—and that they had "all my books" in stock. I doubted the woman knew of the extreme obscurity of some of my publishers and jokingly bet her they did not. Rising to the challenge, she led me in and out of the nether rooms and showed me six or seven of my old titles, multiple copies of a few of them. I told her how glad and grateful I was that they had stocked so many of my books but confided that there were indeed many more and she should not be concerned that they had escaped her notice.

In the course of our chat she led me to the store's owner, Harriett Logan, who asked me what I was working on, and I did my best to describe *Jonathan Force*, which was under consideration by Fomite Press, and *Greeves Passing* due out later in the year. Harriett offered to host a reading when JF appeared, and I could think of nothing nicer. Leaving the store felt a little like leaving Shangri-La or Brigadoon. I had lived in Cleveland for 40 years, returning about once a month since moving to Ripton. In all of that time I had fancied myself in the know about the city's book world. I had, for that matter, reviewed books for *The Cleveland Plain Dealer* for over twenty years. How could I have missed this vast, gorgeous book sanctuary?

In the event the reading went about as well as I had hoped. Enough people dropped by, including some of my beloved former colleagues at University School, two of them writers themselves, but I had the bad luck of my reading being scheduled the same night the newly appointed headmaster of University School was addressing the school's trustees, alumni and parents downtown. Those people would have been my principal audience. Nonetheless a sufficient number wandered into Loganberry's to fill the designated room. I was touched that Lulu who, at ten was unlikely to warm to a dark novel about a family facing mortal illness, alienation, and despair, wanted to go and got rather impressively dressed up.

As in the prior *Greeves Passing* readings in Beaufort and Ripton, this one I believe hit its mark, and subsequent discussion was lively. Chit chat over wine and cheese renewed some old relationships, and nearly everyone who showed up bought a book. Afterward and a little spent, I took Celeste and Lulu to a favored little Bistro called Gigi's for a late supper. I praised Lulu warmly for her patience and gracious interactions with a long succession of strangers. She insisted that she enjoyed it. Sweet, generous girl.

The ten-hour drive home to Ripton seemed more restful than taxing. The weather was faintly overcast and mild, so the usually stormy stretch of Interstate 90 along the lakes was benign. The passage was also lightened considerably by listening to hours of William Manchester's audio book about Churchill, *The Last Lion*

World figures aside, It was a satisfying visit to Cleveland, and as always it was a little wrenching to say good-bye to Lulu. It looks, though, like barely a month until I will see her again in early December. I think we both enjoyed plotting out what we were calling our "mini-Christmas."

Back in Ripton and a run of solitary, seemingly identical days at my keypad in the murk of my upstairs study—murk because the only light is cast by the low glass globe of my desk lamp and what little daylight filters through the small, eastward facing window fitted with a panel of mostly green stained glass. By afternoon the room has the feel of late night. Although I work in absolute quiet in this room with the door closed to the passage outside, there is a strange sensation of being watched over my shoulder by the figure of Lady Godiva who, when I very occasionally turn to *look* over my shoulder, hovers there gorgeous and naked in the outsized framed reproduction I bought a few years ago of John Collier's famous painting.

These writing days are saved from monotony by the occasional errand in Middlebury, my favorite of which is playing the piano for the elderly men and women who attend an adult day care facility called Project Independence. It is a bit of a challenge to structure these sessions, which run for about an hour. The setting is a large sitting room with about forty chairs set up in rows facing the grand piano. The listeners range in age from mid-seventies through their nineties. Most of them are attentive, some of them musically alert. This time I began with a few minutes on the elements of music—tempo, pitch, harmony, major / minor—and how varying them affects the way we experience the composition, then about twenty minutes of contests— what is the name of this song? from what musical or movie?—and finally a sing-along of about twenty old standards I submitted a few weeks ago for which the Project Independent staff has collated the lyrics into little booklets they hand out to the participants. As before, this session goes smoothly, most of the group responsive, three or four staring ahead glassy eyed, as if in troubled reverie. I know I bring a boy scout-ish sense of community service to these outings, but there is also a measure of genuine satisfaction in it. I drive away this time aware that I have been perspiring from the tension of the effort.

It is decided that we spend Thanksgiving at our Marion house with Jesse and her family. This will be the first time we are "entertained" in the recently renovated house since Jesse, James, and their children took up residence. As mentioned earlier, my feelings about turning over the house to them while James found his feet as a beginning instructor at Harvard were a little mixed: of course very glad that the family could begin this new phase of their lives without financial strain, but also a little wistful that the comfortable and charming—but delicate—arrangement of the rooms we had established over the summer would be broken up, perhaps even literally, by the needs and exertions of two physically active and uninhibited children. For that matter, even acknowledging the impossibility of keeping tidy quarters in the preposterously too-small apartment they lived in in Brooklyn, Jesse and James, perhaps owing to their artist temperaments, have not yet shown any inclination to keep what most people would consider "up for show." The best response I could manage was to imagine the worst case and let it go at that.

But no, to my glad surprise, the place looked not only pulled together but inviting when we arrived. The main sitting room retained some of the charm of our earlier arrangement, with mostly different pictures on the walls, some new shelves and cabinets for necessary storage and, most impressively, a new, sturdier dining table built from salvaged timber by James. Even the former guest bedroom upstairs, now a jam-packed studio for Jesse's painting and illustration projects, was tidy enough to accommodate our sleeping up there. Best of all, there was for the first time in the children's lives, a spacious, comfortable place for them to sleep and play, with plenty of room for toys and construction of their many projects. I was especially taken with grandson Leon's "office," consisting of an old family desk flanked by bookshelves where he is able to store his supplies and drawings for a series of "books" he has published under the heading Flairy Productions, as the stories recount the adventures of two principal characters, Fred and Larry. In addition to writing and illustrating the Flairy volumes, Leon has recruited a (paid!) staff of assistants from his new schoolmates at the Sippican Elementary School down the street. I asked him what the staff did for their pay. Leon told me "shipping and handling."

Marion was unseasonably mild, enabling us to walk the streets of the village in just sweaters. The gabled masses of the Gatsby era palaces along the water seem uncomfortably exposed in the absence of foliage, not just unoccupied but abandoned, the inner harbor glassy and benign without the summer's forest of masts.

Thanksgiving day was a little jarring in its succession of scheduled events. The morning walk to Silver Shell Beach was bracing and welcome, soft sea air and pearly light over the broad expanse of Buzzard's Bay. But then, problematically, there was a gathering of M's cousins and assorted others at the Saltonstall cousins' house in the village center, just a block from our house—problematic in that by noon, we had become a rather awkward party. At three, granddaughter Alice is unpredictable in her movements and preferences, not a good candidate to sit or stand still while the adults chat over wine and nibbles, even less so during the "traditional" Thanksgiving readings, reflections, and hymn singing that has characterized these gatherings in the past.

Besides the challenge of engaging, or more likely suppressing, Alice for an hour or so in close, unfamiliar quarters, we had now been joined by James' mother Vivien, and stepfather Jerry. The problem was not that they would be unknown to the Saltonstall cousins and unfamiliar with the rituals associated with their Thanksgiving observance; nobody would be more reliably gracious to unknown visitors than the Saltonstalls. The problem was that Gerry, whom I have only seen a couple of times since Jesse and James' wedding, has now begun the journey into dementia—not, as Jesse put it, "completely around the bend," but unpredictable in what he might say from moment to moment, a tendency to make sudden pronouncements unrelated to anything previously uttered, his answers impossible to connect to questions asked. Truth be told, even apart from my concerns about how to integrate Alice and Gerry into the Saltonstalls' gathering, I had been looking for an honorable excuse—I would watch Alice, I would stay behind to look after the turkey in the oven and other simmering preparations—not to attend. But I had agreed to play the piano for the hymn sing, so there was no way out.

In the event, Alice was, though squirmy, more endearing than annoying. Harder to integrate into this mostly familiar configuration of company was Gerry who, while wonderfully cheerful, was bafflingly incoherent with every person who attempted to engage him in conversation. I could not help straining to listen in as his hosts, the senior Saltonstalls, tried to determine some basic things from Gerry, such as how was the drive in from Connecticut and how long would he be staying in town. Gerry's genial response veered into a hot air balloon adventure he had participated in years ago over Sydney, Australia, the account melding seamlessly into difficulties he had run into importing vintage wall posters from Europe.

I think the Saltonstalls were relieved—I was certainly relieved—to call a halt to the casual chit chat and to begin the planned program. This consisted of the eldest male Saltonstall, Bill, reading excerpts from William Bradford's log of the Mayflower's new world landfall, first at an unwelcoming Provincetown, then in Plymouth. When he had finished the Bradford account, Bill chose to amplify the passages with some personal impressions of old Plymouth. To just about everybody's astonishment, these were interrupted by a series of pointed corrections offered up energetically by my grandson Leon, nine, who had just visited Plymouth historical sites on a school field trip. Without references to hand, it was impossible to tell if Leon was correct on all counts, but in my experience he has been remarkably retentive of facts, and he was outwardly more confident than Bill. The result was an uneasy collective mood: murmurs of surprise and approval at Leon's apparent precocity but also a sense of inappropriate and uninvited intrusion into Bill's presentation, certainly an awareness of competing claims to mastery of the material.

This uneasiness was in turn relieved by the invitation to begin the hymn sing. A stapled packet containing the lyrics of the hymns was distributed to all, and for a half hour or so the stern Protestant stand-bys were delivered with a force approaching ferocity, which I attributed to the relief everybody felt that we did not have to do anything else. That relief, combined with the relief of having to part, put us all in appropriately festive spirits as we thanked our hosts and headed home to our respective feasts.

Touchingly, James had taken pains to prepare an exact replica of the traditional Thanksgiving meal I had enjoyed throughout my childhood, a feast perfected first by my British grandmother, savored by our extended family every Thanksgiving and Christmas until my grandmother grew too old to do it, but continued faithfully by my mother and now M, when we are home: roast turkey, sage dressing, cranberry sauce, mashed potatoes and gravy, creamed onions, green beans, with apple and pumpkin pies for dessert. By dinner's end I was overcome by sleepiness and, just as I did when I was a boy, went directly upstairs to my bed and dissolved into deepest sleep.

December 2015: December proceeded strangely this year, not as a succession of distinct days, but as a seamless procession of gestures attempting to express Christmas. Perhaps my age is at work in this, a heightened awareness that the number of future Christmases cannot be great—five, ten, fifteen? Whatever the reason, this year's gestures felt consciously effortful, but no less necessary for that.

Early in the month, December 4th, I drive to Cleveland for a week with Lulu and Celeste to simulate what Lulu and I have decided to call our "mini" Christmas. The drive west was blessedly easy, as there was no snow and nothing more forbidding along the way than brief showers. In an attempt to break the ten hour monotony of the drive, I brought with me out a thick box of CDs containing the rest of William Manchester's life of Churchill, *The Last Lion*, read by a British actor unknown to me. Within minutes of inserting a random disc into the Jeep's CD player, I was lost in what seemed a minute-by-minute account of Churchill's colossal attempts in the late 1930s to persuade the timid Chamberlain government that the Germans were preparing for a new massive war. For years at University School I had taught the world wars to my ninth grade Western Civilization students. My colleagues and I had taken pains to emphasize the remarkable vision and heroism of Churchill in narrowly guiding the allies to victory over the Nazis. We watched grainy movie documentaries of the great man striding through the ruins of London during the Blitz. We listened to recordings of his BBC radio speeches—"What General Weygand has called the Battle of France is over…the Battle of Britain is about to begin…" Extra credit was offered and enthusiastically won by students willing to memorize those speeches. But listening now to Manchester's account of Churchill's daily ministrations in all their depth and detail brought me near tears of gratitude for such a life.

My days with Lulu passed in a blur of shopping excursions, fancy restaurant meals, and a few evening entertainments, two of which have stayed with me. The first was a Broadway musical review performed by an ensemble of about twenty musical theater students from Baldwin Wallace College, which is something of a hotbed for theater talent. Familiar show-stopper numbers were brought brightly to life by very attractive performers, young enough to carry the promise of youth, mature enough to embody the roles they sang. I found myself at once moved to a pitch of feeling I experienced when my older daughters performed the female leads in University School's uncommonly good stage productions. Near tears again, my age no doubt again a factor. I was also very happy to see Lulu's clear engagement in the show.

The second performance was quite a Cleveland Event. I managed to get, at daunting cost, tickets for the annual Christmas Concert performed by the Cleveland Orchestra and Chorus. I had attended several of these in my University School days and suspected Lulu would be impressed by the spectacle. There is a credible claim that the Cleveland Orchestra, dating from George Szell's reign as conductor, is the best symphony orchestra in the world. Severance Hall, a Palladian jewel box in Cleveland's University Circle, has been recently renovated, partly to enhance the interior décor, mainly to augment acoustics to world-class standards. It is elevating to enter Severance Hall from street level on any occasion, but softly lit and bedecked with seasonal glitter, it seemed to gather us up into an enchanted world. Lulu, in her fanciest velvet dress, seemed rapt. Of course all of the offerings, except a medieval carol or two, were familiar to her, but the musicianship and the power of the singing was not lost on her. All along a rather long walk from the concert hall to the restaurant in Little Italy where we dined, Lulu was humming and striding in cadence to Handel's Hallelujah Chorus.

I had planned to drive home to Ripton on Sunday but decided to stay an extra day, as Lulu and I could spend that no-school day together, and while we made an energetic and enjoyable day of it, including an excellent evening meal at home and a raucous round of poker afterwards, extending the visit added, for me, a measure of sadness. This visit had been in every way I could devise lively and enjoyable, but it was nonetheless just a visit. Lulu would proceed into the holidays without me and I without her. There was no thought, uttered or unuttered, of circumstances being otherwise, but I could not hold back doubts and regret about the extent of the fatherhood I am able to offer Lu. Such are our respective lives. I am grateful that to date she is such a lovely and loveable person.

Back home, I set myself to the usual Christmas preparations, putting up the trees, hanging wreaths, reconfiguring the ornamental lights—'reconfiguring' because I left quite a few strands in place from last year, an indication not so much of age-related laziness on my part as age-related reluctance to put Christmas behind me, to relegate it to a mere season. So out came the Victorian angels, the CDs of carols and sacred music sung by St. John's and King's College choirs, by St. Olaf's Cantus, by The Cleveland Orchestra chorus. A month's worth of firewood is hauled in and stacked on its iron rack.

This year we will have only a family-stranded friend or two for our Christmas feast. Our far-flung daughters and their families will join us for New Year's week instead, due to the expense and stress of trying to book flights and drive over icy highways for Christmas day. M and I are thus alone through a succession of mostly solitary, seemingly identical winter days. It is easy to feel stranded and isolated in our tiny hamlet on the eastern end of our time zone. The days approaching the solstice grow dark a little after four in the afternoon. That is when I clump downstairs from my study, light the Christmas lights in every room, turn up the sacred music, by turns mournful and joyful, light a blaze in the fireplace. I set the table, get dinner started, pour out two cocktails, and wait for M to come over the shoveled path from her studio to join me for our evening ritual of news watching, unhurried dining, and easy talk. Sometimes I walk outside after dark with no other purpose but to look into the windows of the house. Softly lit by globed lamps and the sparkle of Christmas lights, the interior rooms emit a muted glow, like the light from a fire nearly out.

The New Year: January through March 2016: A significant gap in the narration, or at least in the narration of daily events. I have let this happen once or twice before, when the close adjacency of practical obligations, travel, and book-related business has left me with too little time to sit down and take a reliable measure of what is occurring. "Too little time" is not quite right. I have been far from beleaguered all day every day to the extent that I could not sit down at my computer and enter a passing reflection or two. The issue is less time than inclination. It has felt distinctly *aversive* to continue this narrative. The aversion did not extend to other writing. Over the past few months I think I have been a more active correspondent, email and otherwise, than at any other time in my life. I have made considerable revisions in what now looks to be the final version of *The Three Lives of Jonathan Force,* due out this June. I have worked hard on talks already delivered at various schools and on others scheduled for this spring and summer. So I am not experiencing writer's block. The aversion has been only to this.

I have not for a second considered giving it up. Among other things, perhaps morbidly, I want to see how it ends. Having had so much time to reflect, it is clear now that two things were at work in staying my hand on this project. The first is the eerie *sameness* to the most focal events that have transpired since my Christmas entry. There was a highly satisfying Christmas day gathering and feast with, as mentioned previously, some Ripton friends who for various reasons found themselves unable to visit or be visited by extended family. I could easily have registered my impressions of our time together, which was, as Anthony Powell might have put it, "not without all interest." But however interesting, the gathering, the setting, our talk proceeded nearly exactly as it had the year prior when in more or less the same company we said and did more or less the same things. Similarly, the arrival of our daughters and their families the following week passed agreeably, everyone, especially the grandchildren, in suitably high spirits. But no surprising announcement, no last minute excursion, in fact nothing whatsoever distinguished this lively, house-crowded episode from any previous visit. In itself, the sameness was not at all unpleasant. I enjoyed myself throughout, but the feelings evoked, the qualities observed in my children and grandchildren have been amply noted in previous entries. To have written about it, to have documented the sameness would have depressed me. There is something insistent, even ornery, in my impulse to record the essence of these latter years. The impulse is also saying something like: *don't keep going to the same places.* But doesn't being who I am and who I have been require going to the same places? Is acknowledging the sameness of the central rituals in my present life an admission of the narrowness of my existence, yet another feature of aging?

And then there was, on February 21st, my 71st birthday. Its arrival signaled neither the passing nor the arrival of a milestone year. 71 suggests a certain degree of oldness, though in light of average longevity and the frequency of people living on in their nineties and beyond, 71 is hardly venerable. I think if I read an obituary of someone today in *The Times* who had died at 71, I would not consider that an especially early exit. News of friends my age dying reaches me, if not daily, regularly.

The most touching instance occurred two days ago when the web site established by my high school graduation class—the class of 1963 —on the occasion of our fiftieth reunion reported the death of my steady high school girlfriend, Jan. I have mentioned Jan in previous entries, as we have corresponded over the years in some depth. She was a significant figure in my adolescence, to the extent that I have drawn on my experiences of her to convey aspects of certain girls and women in my poems, stories, and novels. Jan had written to me a year or so ago to tell me of her very discouraging diagnosis of stage four lung cancer. She had already lost mobility and function and was not given very much longer to live. Hearing this was a jolt, because Jan had, among many other admirable qualities, projected robustly good health. So far as I could tell she was moderate in all her appetites, perhaps even rigidly so. She had never smoked a cigarette.

The blunt fact of her passing, posted tersely but touchingly by her second husband, also a classmate, triggered hours of reminiscence on my part, affectionate and only a little sad. Whether or not it should have, it did not occur to me that Jan had been taken too soon. I regretted what I know must have been her suffering at the end, struggling for breath. I knew she had found peace and comfort with her adoring second husband, an outcome that seemed to me thoroughly deserved, her first husband having been hurtfully unfaithful and otherwise hard company. But again, there was nothing in this reckoning with my old girlfriend's mortality that felt untimely, that she was "taken too soon." Nor honestly do I think, were I stricken this minute with a fatal heart attack, would anything like *not now* or *too soon* register in the promised instant in which "my whole life flashes before me." If I am indeed granted such a flash, I am pretty sure it will be something like: *Oh—it's like this.*

As it happened, there was no real celebration of my 71st birthday, not just because the number 71 evokes so little interest or feeling, but because I was away from home on the designated day. Tony Jarvis had once again invited me to address his Yale Divinity School class, this time not necessarily about any of my books, although he did make them read *I Can Learn From You: Boys as Relational Learners*. Tony is a meticulous organizer of his courses and has in past years been very prescriptive with me about what he wants me to cover with his students, so I was touched when he told me to do anything I liked. I think this gesture was in recognition that, given his diagnosis, this would be the last time we would work together at Yale and he wanted to honor me with some latitude.

Because no train from Rutland could connect me to New Haven on the weekend, I took a Friday train to the New York, so that I could see a show and then spend a few extra days with Tony. I am always treated like visiting royalty on these visits, lodging in well- appointed rooms set aside for Divinity School guest lecturers. We dine at splendid restaurants, including, always, the Union Club and Maury's. I can't think of another friend with whom talk comes more easily— including animated arguments, always about politics. Though ordained an Episcopalian, he is sentimentally Roman Catholic, and it is his Catholic ardor that seems to fuel his, to me, incomprehensible abhorrence of abortion. He is temperamentally inclined to politically conservative issues generally, although, like other educated Americans, he cannot locate actual practicing conservative political figures that he can bear. He wants conservatives—Republicans—to conform to impressions he formed in childhood of statesmen long past, especially Churchill. But as there is little Churchillian in the likes of the Bushes, Mitt Romney, John McCain, or—horribly—the likes of Donald Trump or Ted Cruz, it is hard for him to carry the day in making what he would like to be partisan points. He has not a kind word to say about President Obama, whom I revere and admire, but he felt, given the dreadful alternatives, conscience-bound to vote for him.

But our talk and our communion generally are not dominated by politics. We reminisce. We gossip. We are at heart schoolteachers and headmasters. Decades ago we learned how to teach in the same school. University School was a crucible for both of us, and we have been comparing notes ever since. He has been a celibate priest, and I have been an ardent husband and lover of women. He represents a fascinating Other to me in that regard, and I think I represent that to him. Tony seems stimulated and at ease among colleagues and friends who share his ecclesiastical and anglophile references, people who know who the Anglican and Episcopal bishops are, people who have read Evelyn Waugh, Nancy Mitford, Cyril Connolly, Anthony Powell, Harold Nicholson.

Tony is learned in a non-showy way. His art and especially his architectural history are solid, and some of his best teaching has been introducing medieval and renaissance art to very young and soon very appreciative boys. He is passionate about his convictions, which can make him sometimes brittle, but there is something childlike in his enthusiasms and allegiances that I find touching even when I do not agree with him at all.

He is not subtle. He doesn't withhold judgments and impressions. He is wonderful company because he lets you know how much he likes the concert, the company, the meal. He laughs, jokes, and teases a lot, but in an obvious way that would be hard to take for anything critical or dismissive. He conveys overall a sense of being well worked out, happy but not self-satisfied. You find yourself wanting to please him, which has been crucial to his success as a teacher and a pastor. I find myself not wanting to think about the world without Tony in it, but when that is the case, I will do my best to summon up that sense of his that rightness and goodness are, with a little effort, at hand.

As I taught what would be my final class to his Yale divinity students, I felt driven by my affection for Tony to make it substantial, to raise questions and problems I knew the young men and women would take to heart. Once again—for the seventh straight year—they were an attentive, thoughtful, responsive group to teach, ethnically diverse, an equal number of men and women. I did not give a systematic account of how I came to see the educational power of relationship, but I stressed relationship above all other elements of teaching, concluding with an account from *Souls in Boxes* of an episode from my early teaching days when, in the company of the young friends and colleagues at University School, I experienced something like ecstatic happiness after an especially rich and exhausting school day. Tony was an unnamed figure in the narrative. As I read through the familiar passage evoking that tender and formative time in our lives, I became involuntarily choked up. So did Tony. It was as if for a few moments we were inhabiting the same being.

My unacknowledged seventy-first birthday passed in New Haven. That evening, Sunday, Tony and I dined at the decorous Union Club downtown where, preceded by a chilled martini, I feasted on oysters, roasted chicken and crème brulée. A delicious meal shared animatedly with a beloved old friend, lodging in comfortable rooms right across Prospect Avenue from the Divinity School. I could not have been more replete or more at peace: an excellent condition in which to review my state of being on entering my seventy-second year of life.

I am fairly healthy. I am fully ambulatory and all systems are functioning properly. There are perhaps three or four gout twinges a year, but they are eased by a few prescription anti-inflammatory pills. I require no regular medication, but take a daily multi-vitamin designed for people over 50. When I fail to take the vitamin, which I tend to do when traveling, I can tell no difference in how I feel. I have an excellent appetite for all three meals, and need to restrain myself a bit, especially when home and feeling in the mood to cook. I am savvy enough about nutrition to know what is likely to add pounds and to diminish energy, but I give myself generous leeway in the amount I eat and drink, especially when any kind of company or entertaining is involved. I think I have a natural tropism for celebration, so that limiting the pleasurable intake of anything while entertaining or being entertained feels puritanical and anti-life.

This approach to food and drink, while making me overall happy, leads me frequently to put on ten to fifteen pounds more than is right for me. When formerly comfortable slacks feel tight in the belly, when certain shirts cling too tightly to my torso, I know I am overdoing it. M is always happy to step in at his point and set up a very astringent vegan sort of diet which, after two or three weeks, gets me back to reasonable trimness, but also back to my celebratory inclinations.

I exercise with some regularity, but I tend now to go very easy on myself in the winter months, where the options are long walks and crosscountry skiing. This past winter there has been so little snow I only went skiing three times. At best I hike three or four miles three or four times a week, but this winter I have let that slide. I have not had a bad respiratory bout since just after Claire's wedding, though I fear one always lies waiting.

There are small things that concern me. I sit a lot. I sit for hours at a stretch at my keyboard when I am writing. I sit while doing on-line crossword puzzles and Scrabble games. M and I sit watching an episode of some television series or mystery nearly every night after dinner. I sit for an hour or more when playing the piano. Each time I rise to my feet, there is an effortful ache in my knees, and until I have taken a few steps, my ankle and knee joints feel almost fused. I picture the scene in *The Wizard of Oz* where the rusty Tin Woodsman pleads for an oil can. This leg stiffness is even more pronounced on my long drives to Cleveland and back. I tend to go for four-hour stretches before stopping to refuel and relieve myself. Immediately on stepping out of the car, I cannot walk properly. Feet, ankles, knees—everything hurts until I have walked thirty or forty yards. While not really debilitating, this new aching and seizing up of the legs bothers me. It is a relatively new development, and I am certain it is only going to get more pronounced as time passes. I don't like the idea of being in any way infirm on my feet. I remember noting warily in Anthony Powell's diaries that when he was in his eighties, he would recount motoring to luncheons in nearby towns. Feeling increasingly unsteady on his feet as he walked to and from the appointed restaurant, he had to rely on a cane. After one especially discouraging luncheon outing he wrote, "I was *doddering*." I can picture myself doddering.

I am also aware that I tend to think I am in better physical shape than is probably the case. This unwarranted optimism is at least partly driven by a dread of life constricting measures that would be imposed if a really serious symptom were identified. So if I have a gout flare up in a foot, knee or wrist, I tend not to acknowledge it at all or to minimize the discomfort to M, who invariably notices when I am in any kind of discomfort. More seriously, I think, I do not let on to anybody when, say, driving to town or in the midst of a sustained bout of writing at my desk, there is an uncomfortable feeling of compression in my chest, not so intense that I cannot breathe, but mounting sometimes to a distinct burn. I want to think that these episodes are digestive in some way, instances of what the TV ads call "heart burn," a temporary discomfort quickly relieved by a fizzy antacid tablet one can buy over the counter at the drug store. I do not buy or take any such tablets, but I like thinking that there is a quick, easily obtainable remedy. Each of these periodic episodes over the past few years has passed without consequence. But while in the midst of one, I let myself wonder if something is going wrong with my heart. In the course of my last very casual medical check-up, my physician, Dr. Barrett, a profoundly unhurried and unexcitable man, told be that my blood pressure had gotten higher, hovering near the level where a prescribed medicine, a statin of some kind, might be necessary. I didn't like hearing this. He said that before he would prescribe anything, I might try lowering my salt intake. For several weeks I have attempted to do this. I would also like to lose ten pounds as quickly as I can. I have resolved for the time being to drink alcohol only when entertaining or being entertained. I have so far maintained this resolve, although we entertain and are entertained several days a week. Of course it is perfectly possible that I may just have a touch of heartburn, and not heart trouble. But my thoughts stray to my University School trustee friend Jack who, before he underwent multiple bypass heart surgery, was concerned about tightness in the area of his heart. He told me that as he was leaving the arena one night after a Cleveland Cavaliers basketball game, the burn around his heart had mounted ominously. He reckoned that either he had a serious heart condition or he didn't. He tested the proposition by running as fast as he could to where his car was parked, the unexamined assumption being that if he could do that and his heart was still functioning, he was probably all right; if not—he was unable to go there. He made it back to his car. His heart did not fail him, but he was by no means all right and shortly after received confirmation of serious heart disease. For the time being I am pretty much in the run-as-fast-as-I-can-to the car mode. But I will continue to self-monitor. I find the idea of undergoing surgical heart repairs dreary beyond imagining. And dreary is the right word. I am not really *afraid* of such a major violation of my physical integrity: submission to the ordeal, the horrible, faintly septic atmosphere of hospitals, being diminished, "recovering," the tentative, cautious regime prescribed for life–after-medical-interventions—utterly dreary. I might add that my last two bouts of heart-area constriction were relieved by tall glasses of water.

Then there are lesser matters. It saddens me that over the past months a kind of arthritis in the little finger of my left hand has left me unable to bend it at the joint. There is no pain, and the condition would be only a minor distraction, but that finger is critical to chording the guitar. For that reason, and because of an increasing stiffness in the wrist of my chording hand, I am less inclined to pick up the guitar to play. As recently as a year ago I was apt to play daily, sometimes for hours. With some effort and concentration, I can work my left hand around the frets to create music, but it takes ten or fifteen minutes of warming up before I can competently play anything more demanding than blues runs. I haven't quite resigned myself to guitar-less days, but I now go a week now without playing one or even thinking about it.

By way of compensation, I am playing the piano quite a bit more. There are likely to be two or three half-hour sit-downs in the course of the daylight hours, and sometimes a longer session just before I retire upstairs to bed. In consequence, I am playing pretty well. With daily repetition, tricky fast riffs come easily —it seems to me more easily than any other time I can remember. Is it possible that I am *improving?* It is still deeply pleasurable to play, no audience required. It almost makes me laugh to be filling the silence of the house with lickety-split renditions of Fats Waller and Gershwin. The unbending digit does not seem to affect my piano fingering, and I suppose my happy hours at the instrument are a kind of compensation for the receding guitar. I do not want to think about losing the ability to play the piano, whether due to a hearing loss, loss of dexterity or something neurological. In his early eighties my father, an excellent trumpet player, gave up the instrument when by some cruel neural failing, he could no longer hear true pitch. A true third or fifth or octave sounded dissonant. Not only was he no longer able to hear truly what he and others were playing, all music sounded gratingly out of key to him, to the point that he could not bear to have recorded music playing in the room. I dread being diminished in that way, but I can imagine it happening.

General appearance. It is increasingly difficult to say with certainty what I look like. It took entry into Old Age to realize that the image staring back at me in the mirror is more or less distorted by psychic projections. Probably the most telling of these reflections is my first glimpse of myself in the morning as I am brushing my teeth: a comically haggard old gent, half me, half my father. If I am just out of bed, there will be what M once termed "bags under my bags." Registering this, I tell myself I will look better when showered and dressed, an impression confirmed in subsequent viewings during the day—but, as I said, an impression formed after the corrective projections have been imposed. Nor are photographs much help. In this era of non-stop cell phone photography, I am presented with a continuous stream of images of myself. Given the different camera angles, proximity to the camera, and available light, the images vary crazily, to the extent that, taken together, they do not, to me, portray the same person. I look pleasingly presentable, not assignably "old" in some of the pictures, beaten, distracted and a bit too heavy (for my taste) in others. In any event it is a wonder that I still *care* about my appearance. I do not believe conventional vanity is at work. Most days I don't see anyone socially. There is nobody to register, admire, approve or disapprove of what I look like. Something in me wants to be inherently, unwaveringly presentable.

March 2016: An intense response to a Sunday afternoon piano concert at the college. Over the past few years I have frequently, through mutual friends, come into the orbit of Diana Fanning who, on the evidence of the publicity I have read, is a distinguished classical pianist. She has played with many orchestras in the US and in Europe and is much recorded. Though I had not yet heard her play, I had come to like her in the course of social outings and a few dinners. She attended Middlebury a few years after I graduated, apparently already an accomplished player. She studied with a Middlebury music professor, Emory Fanning, and, despite a significant gap in their ages, fell in love with and married him. I have come to like Emory as well. Though classically oriented, he is very good conversation on the kinds of jazz I like, and he has had generous things to say about my own playing. Emory is in his early eighties, still flies a plane, and, unlike nearly everyone else we socialize with now, enjoys a few drinks.

I had been feeling guilty about being out of town for a number of Diana's concerts, of which she kept me informed by email. This particular performance had been scheduled for the college's new concert hall months in advance, and I took some care to honor the date, a Sunday afternoon while students were on spring break. In truth, I went mostly out of friendliness and courtesy. I am capable of being unmoved by much of the classical piano repertoire, especially busy pieces which feel to me as if they are composed mainly to reveal the virtuosity of the composer. But Diana is a warm, attractive, rather stately presence, and I thought it would be pleasant enough just to watch her.

The program included lesser known works of Beethoven, Brahms, and Debussy. A few seconds into each piece I was carried away: a strange synthesis of her bearing—leaning into, intently listening to her own playing, almost in an attitude of conversation—and her exquisite playing. She was disciplined to the extent that I could hear each distinct, delicate key stroke, even in speed of light grace note trills. Given that I decided to attend in the spirit of doing Diana a favor, it was an emotional come-uppance to realize that M and I were lucky to find a seat. The auditorium was packed to standing-room capacity. Audience attention was intense. Applause was thunderous. Diana clearly has fans! And, as I had predicted, she was a pleasure just to watch. She greeted the audience warmly on taking the stage and she preceded each selection with brief but interesting background notes on the place of the piece in the composer's oeuvre. I had a strong intimation of how, decades earlier, Emory had fallen in love with her.

I can't remember enjoying a piano concert more. There was a life-enlarging concert by Oscar Peterson years ago at Severance Hall in Cleveland, but it was music from a different universe. I was uncharacteristically almost speechless when I greeted Diana at the post-concert reception. It was M who succeeded in finding the right words. She said: after a few minutes Diana wasn't even there —there was just the music.

Diana's concert has stayed with me. It makes me reflect on my own work and, uncomfortably, to wonder if I have achieved—or, more importantly, if I am still working toward—Diana's level of command in what I am attempting to do. This reckoning comes at just the right time. For the past year or so my work has consisted of presenting material here and there from previously published books, shepherding my new novel / trilogy *The Three Lives of Jonathan Force* (publication date June 15) into print, and intermittently working on this manuscript, whatever it is. Because I am satisfied with my already published work and because I am deeply invested in *Three Lives*, my self esteem has not been troubled. I have been feeling sufficiently productive, enough like a writer. But Diana's concert gave me a jolt. Am I working that hard, that intensely on *my* art? Truth is, I don't feel I am *working* at all, much less working hard. What in my routine would be the equivalent of the *practicing* Diana must do to retain her touch and to master such a repertoire? I do nothing of the kind.

I am not only easy on myself, but lazy. I alternate a paragraph or two on a manuscript with sustained bouts of crossword solving or on-line scrabble. The edges of my email screen peek out from behind the manuscript screen I am working on, so that whenever the arrival of a new email dings into view, I attend to it immediately, relieved to be free of the concentration required to create what I am trying to create. I console myself, or try to, by acknowledging that the bits of *Three Lives* I proofread or otherwise correct every day seem really good, that very possibly something might happen with this book. But Diana's acuity at the piano undercuts this tendency to self-congratulation.

It doesn't help that at the moment I am reading a big novel by Ethan Canin, *The Doubter's Almanac*. It was recommended to me by my nice publicist, Caitlin, who thinks Canin's book has tonal and structural similarities to *Three Lives* and, because it got respectful reviews from major critics, she would like to pitch *Three Lives* as a comparable work. As it happens, I was quickly absorbed by *Doubter's Almanac*. It's a multigenerational saga mainly focused on the life and work of a mathematical savant who has a difficult time, even a tortured time, negotiating his way through ordinary life. Canin is good. Characters are sharply drawn. The dialogue is fresh, real, wonderful. Even more impressive, Canin, like Diana, seems masterfully accomplished. Among other things, the book is dazzlingly good about the theoretical frontiers of mathematics and physics—moreover, it is *readable* about those things. Canin's research feels to me like Diana's practicing. When have I done anything like that? I had not previously known much about Canin, but I looked him up and, sure enough, he was a kind of scholar prodigy before becoming a writer. He was an undergraduate at Stanford and later became an M.D. at Harvard, but he does not practice medicine, instead teaching and writing at the University of Iowa Writers program. He is fifteen years younger than

I am. He is clearly working *hard*. Have I ever worked hard?

April 24-May 7, 2016: A weeklong, complicated trip to California — the emotional effects of which I am trying to sort out. There were two reasons to go. The combined public schools of Orange County had invited me to do a series of presentations on contemporary boys. The talks would draw on Michael's and my studies of effective teaching and of teacher-boy relationships, plus some of my recent musings about how boys unfold more than they are shaped and molded. The second reason is that having enjoyed themselves tremendously in the course of their prior visit, Celeste and Lulu were eager to see my sister again in Glendale. As it happened, Ginny was agreeable, so I was able to stitch the two events together. In all, it was a rather expensive prospect, but the pay from the Orange County people was generous.

I had prepared the presentations well in advance and was confident enough in the appeal of the material that I was rather looking forward to presenting it. Most of my talks have been to private school people, mostly in boys' schools, so I figured the public school teachers and principals and school board members would be something new. There are more than 500,000 school children in Orange County, and I was interested to know their teachers' concerns about the boys. But despite agreeable expectations, the trip did not begin well.

For years I have experienced a recurring dream—very anxious, just short of a nightmare—that I have a speaking obligation in a distant city and I cannot get there. The cities can be anywhere in the US or Europe. Travel plans are complicated. I have to transfer from plane to train to car. In some of the dreams I am in a cab very close to my appointed destination and realize the text of my talk is back at my hotel. Returning to retrieve it, the cab becomes gridlocked in traffic, or the cab takes me to the wrong hotel, or we have mistakenly driven to the wrong venue, the wrong city. In these dreams I am closely aware of the clock, the number of minutes left before I have to perform. As the dream progresses, it is increasingly impossible that I will be able to make my scheduled appearance. Without exaggeration, there have been hundreds of variations of this dream. When I awake there can be a full minute or two in which I am certain the events in the dream have occurred, that I have failed to keep my commitment.

I was scheduled to speak on Wednesday afternoon in Orange County. My flight to Los Angeles departed from Vermont a little after noon on Tuesday. This flight would take me to Chicago where after an hour layover I would change planes for LAX. It had been a mild spring, but I awoke Tuesday morning to a heavy snowfall. Ever wary, I left home for the airport hours early in my snow-tested Jeep. The rural roads between my house and the Burlington airport were slick with mounting slushy snow, to the point that about halfway along what is normally an hour's drive, cars started sliding off the road into ditches. I was soon in a closely spaced line of cars and trucks crawling along at about twenty miles per hour. There was a ding on my cell phone with a message telling me my flight out of Burlington would be delayed by an hour and a half. I was going to miss my Chicago connection. A minute or two later as I approached a sharp bend in the road, traffic halted. Five minutes passed, ten. I considered pulling out of line, reversing direction and figuring out an alternative route, but there were deep ravines on either side of the road making such a maneuver impossible. At length a man behind me got out of his truck and walked up ahead to see what was blocking us. On his way back, he told me two cars, one on each side of the road, had gone off into their respective ditches and a tow truck was at work hauling them out. A half hour passed idling in the snow, and I realized that I had achieved the exact level of anxiety of my recurring dream. It was now conceivable that I would miss all possible connections to Los Angeles and that however rescheduled, I would not arrive in Orange County in time to keep my commitment. Moreover, I was not going to wake up from the situation.

When I arrived at the airport, having missed even my delayed flight out, I was rebooked on a later flight to Chicago and a still later flight to LA. I would miss a dinner party my sister had arranged to celebrate my arrival, but I would be on hand to be picked up the following morning for my Orange County talks, a satisfying enough resolution. I was nonetheless fascinated that for several hours actual circumstances had propelled me into the misery of my dream.

I got out of the cab at my sister's just after eleven. Her dinner guests had all departed for home. I had telephoned ahead about the delays, but I could tell she was disappointed that the dinner plan had not worked out. I think I disappointed her further by being poor conversation, but it was three in the morning by my body's clock, and it was all I could do to unpack the next day's clothes, brush my teeth, and collapse into bed.

The talks went down well enough, though my venues were farther from my sister's house in Glendale than I thought—about 90 minutes, most of it stopping and starting along LA's clotted six lane freeways. In the afternoon I conducted a long workshop with principals and teachers who, though weary after their full school days, were attentive and responsive. From there I was driven to a towering glass Hyatt Hotel where I addressed two groups of school board people, the first before dinner, the second after. Seated for dinner at the head table with the higher-ups in the Orange County Department of Education, I sensed a group rather distanced from actual children and classrooms. They were agreeable enough and praised my remarks in a general way, but it was hard for me to tell if anyone was moved to reconsider anything that might improve the lot of boys in their schools. I am pretty sure that in big public school systems, it falls to committed teachers and principals to be change-makers.

Celeste and Lulu arrived at Ginny's midmorning the next day in brilliant sunlight. Rested, my duties behind me, I felt ready to celebrate, amuse Lulu, and see some sights. I rented a car, and off we drove, first to my favorite dining spot in California, The Castaway, perched high on a mountain ridge overlooking miles of the LA sprawl below. Relaxing on the outdoor terrace under bright sun, all the anxieties about my travel connections and speeches dissolved. It was impossible not to be happy. Celeste and Lulu were both eager to see things, so we drove into the heart of Hollywood and meandered a mile or so up and down the Walk of Fame, pausing to photograph Lulu crouching over Elmo's, Julie Andrews' and Harrison Ford's stars. I don't think it troubled Lulu that the walkway was mainly lined with down-at-heel souvenir shops and tattoo parlors. Had we lingered any longer the ambient dinginess of a long passed over "Hollywood" and the saddening presence of the empty-eyed homeless would have brought us low.

We drove on to Venice Beach, which I had never seen. It was refreshing to take in a broad expanse of beach and breaking surf, but I expected more eccentricity and charm from what I had read and heard about Venice. A paved walkway lined with abutting surf shops and head shops and piercing parlors extends for miles along the beach front. There are very few eateries and cafés along the way and so far as I could tell only one full menu restaurant. The atmosphere is suffused with leftover hippiedom. Many sun-leathered, no-longer-young faces, frizzed hair of both men and women banded back into ponytails, tattooed expanses of arm, neck and calf. I have an impression of preoccupied, almost angry looking faces, nose, eyebrow, and lip piercings glinting in the bright sun. The temperature is a little chilly still, high 60s, so there are only a few sun bathers on the vast beach. I note the women are topless. A hundred yards off shore a few surfers lie prone on their boards, gently paddling, eyeing approaching swells.

We stop for a mid-afternoon meal at the one substantial restaurant and nearly leave because a street musician who has somehow unloaded a battered grand piano onto the walkway is making a punishing racket. The pianist looks to me a ruined figure. Dressed in a black tee shirt, black trousers and barefoot, he inclines forward over the keyboard, his face nearly touching the keys. His playing is unvarying: incessant pounding, fragments of what once might have been a showy repertoire of light classics, memorable movie themes and musical comedy hits, now mashed together a-rhythmically with missed trills and runs: a bit of Chopin's *Polanaise*, the themes from *The Godfather,* from *Dr. Zhivago*. The piano is metallic sounding and slightly out of tune, piercingly amplified. Just as we agree to get up and leave, he stops. The atmosphere instantly calms. Ordering our food, we avert our eyes from the pianist who has moved to the half fence separating the restaurant from the concourse and is hectoring the seated diners for tips. I look up and briefly meet his eyes. His face is boiled red, whether from exposure to the sun or from substances consumed. He is drunk or high, raving and apparently angry, but like so many street inebriates, conveying little sense that he could do anyone harm. It is a relief when he wanders off.

We finish our snack and determine that Venice beach does not bear further exploration. The scene seems to have made Lulu pensive. She pauses to consider a heavy set young woman half-reclining on a blanket alongside the concourse. She has scrawled a sign on cardboard saying "HOMELESS, NEED MONEY FOR CHEESEBURGER AND WEED."

The following day is better, as we drive to the Santa Monica pier. It is warmer, again bright sun and cloudless sky. After Venice, Santa Monica is reassuring in its prosperous solidity. The ocean front is lined with high end hotels, restaurants, and boutiques. The pier itself is swarming with families and tourists, festive but not oppressive. To Lulu's delight the pier houses a small amusement park, including an impressively grand Ferris wheel, a sufficiently terrifying roller coaster, and a half dozen or so moderately nauseating rides. We ride the roller coaster—twice—and stop at the photo booth at ride's end to purchase a color print of the three of us making the coaster's final descent. Lulu and I share a double seat. Celeste is seated behind us, holding up her phone as she films us. In the photograph Lulu is smiling broadly, and I am agape, my hair blown back, apparently screaming in either mock or actual terror. Celeste is leery of joining Lulu on a banana-shaped ride that see-saws its riders along an inverted arc. So Lulu and I board the apparatus, and after a minute or so of being sloshed back and forth, up and down, I am aware of a distinct nausea, not so severe as to make me productively sick, but enough to unsettle me for an hour or so. We take a restorative meal at a rather nice open air Mexican restaurant at the end of the pier, looking out over dazzling expanses of ocean and breaking surf. Some desultory shopping in which Lulu finds a fetching little dress she plans to wear for her fifth grade graduation ceremony, then back to my sister's in Glendale just ahead of what was starting to be demoralizing rush hour traffic on the freeways.

My sister has arranged dinner gatherings of one kind or another every evening of our stay. One of them, as a kind of nostalgic nod to the evening parties she hosted when our parents were alive, features musical offerings to my piano accompaniment from each of the guests. This goes down well, as both Celeste and Lulu are eager to perform, Celeste some torchy ballads from our playing-out days, Lulu a perky rendition of "Love Potion Number Nine."

The following morning when we are momentarily by ourselves on the deck of Ginny's pool, Celeste confides to me the discomfort she feels when my sister dismisses her contributions to the conversation. She recounts—and I have noted it too—how in the course of a discussion of some show or some actor's performance, Celeste offers something to the effect that "I am crazy about that show / person," and Ginny will respond abruptly with "I *hate* it," or "She's the worst actress in the business." Almost everyone in attendance is a longstanding friend of my sister's, used to her signature brashness, a feature all acknowledge as inherent to my sister's approach to life and to her sense of humor, but for Celeste who has no such footing or comfort in that company, the dismissals are jarring. "What am I supposed to say when she does that?" Celeste asks me. "It says to me I have no taste or maybe no right to have an opinion." She has a point, and I have little helpful to say in consolation. It is hard for me to imagine my sister being otherwise. The idea of calmly raising the concern with her at an opportune moment is, given my sister's temperament, unthinkable. There would be a six-month rift in speaking relations. As she likes to put it these days, "I'm not Gandhi." Her e-mail sign-offs are followed by the printed slogan "know me at your own risk." While I sympathize with Celeste's reasonably expressed concern, I am aware that her own effusiveness, especially when trying to please new company, can put up walls to certain listeners' receptivity. I do my best to acknowledge Celeste's concerns and point out, not very helpfully, that, yes, that is my sister.

When Celeste and Lulu and I have said our farewells at the airport before boarding our respective flights home, I realize that a certain weight of tension begins to dissolve, the tension of possible crossed transactions between my sister and Celeste. I know there is little I can do about it, that both my sister and Celeste have evolved, probably unalterably, into the people they are. They may interact a little or a lot in the future, but how that goes must be their responsibility. For a self-congratulatory moment I tell myself that I have reached a new, wiser perspective. A moment later it is clear: I have reached no disinterested turf beyond the fray; I simply have less energy for it. I'm just older.

My return flights to Vermont began with a red-eye to Washington Dulles, then a regional jet up to Burlington. It is now clear that I must not book another all-night flight. Hunched this way and that in my cramped window seat, I did not sleep at all, not even a momentary doze. Disembarking at dawn, I strode as if mentally impaired the full length of Dulles Airport to the vicinity of the gate for my connecting flight. I was grateful to find a full menu restaurant open that early and tried to normalize myself with a breakfast of eggs, sausages, and potatoes. The restaurant was all but empty, and few travelers passed by on the concourse. For an hour and a half I sat there, sipping coffee, occasionally clicking on my iPad, but I could summon up no motivation to read anything, attempt a crossword, make a Scrabble move. I had too little energy for thought. At length I rose stiffly from my chair and wandered off in the direction of my flight gate, resigned to sit there for what I believed would be another hour's wait before take-off. It was lucky that I did, because I had mistakenly transposed a "30" for an "03" on my boarding pass and very nearly missed the plane. In the air for less than an hour between D.C. and Burlington, I managed to fall asleep briefly, which bought me just enough energy to retrieve my car and drive home, though in something like zombie-mode.

May 13-15, 2016: I was probably in my late forties or early fifties when the realization struck me: I should never join anything. I had long been aware of a roiling, non-specific aversion to looming organizational meetings of one kind or another, but it did not occur to me that non-joining was a practical possibility. Two very different writers helped to make the possibility seem real for me. One was Robert Johnson, a Jungian analyst and writer I admire, who in his memoir *Balancing Heaven and Earth* recounted sharing a dream with Jung in the course of his, Johnson's, analytic training in Zurich. The details of the dream were not revealed, but Jung's response was unambiguous: he told Johnson he must never get married or join any organizations. Johnson said he subsequently did his best to follow the advice, and on the few occasions when he faltered and joined something, disaster ensued. The other categorical non-joiner was Nabokov, who, so far as I know, never veered from his commitment.

Now that I think back, I might have been a temperamental non-joiner as early as my undergraduate days. I remember feeling a powerful but un-nameable pressure not to be bothered, to be free of commitments, to stay in bed longer. Going to classes was onerous enough, and I skipped as many as I could. But there was a warring impulse to get into the swim, to matter in the larger world. I had always liked writing, and journalism appealed to me, so I steeled myself as a freshman to join the Middlebury Campus newspaper staff as a reporter. I did not mind composing assigned articles and the occasional light feature, but I hated going to the required staff meetings. Over the next three years my involvement with the paper increased, as did my ambivalence: I liked composing articles and appearing in print; I did not like showing up at assigned places at assigned times. My senior year I was named Editor-in-Chief, now *in charge* of all the meetings and assignments and deadlines. I did not "get over" my organizational aversion. I just learned to live with it, because, being now in charge, it would be embarrassing to let the larger enterprise disintegrate.

Since then the pattern—joining something with misgivings, then, as if in punishment, having to be in charge—has repeated itself with eerie consistency. In order to support myself and M after I rather swashbucklingly proposed marriage, I realized I needed a paying job. So I joined the faculty of University School, which could not have been a more demanding employer of young teachers: *six* classes, lunch table supervision, after school sports, individual student advising, departmental and all-faculty meetings. For my first three years at the school, I was also a "full-time" graduate student, completing both Masters and Ph.D degrees. I was committed to organizational requirements to the extent I nearly lost touch with my inner self—what I now call my soul—altogether. And as with the college newspaper, I was put in charge of the organization, as Headmaster of the school, halfway through my career there. And as with the college newspaper, I learned to live with the simultaneous, irreconcilable urges to chuck it all and to carry on mightily. I do not believe it was apparent to others that I was living for so long in this divided way, but it took a toll. I think it inclined me to drink more than was good for me, and it inclined me to take more than a few sensational personal risks, including my affair with Celeste which resulted in Lulu. God moves in mysterious ways his wonders to perform.

I would like to think that there is some ennobling element, like honor, at work in my sticking with and even presiding over organizational commitments that I at least half-dread, but I am afraid that element is more vanity than honor. There is status in being in charge. There is also loss of status in being a bad leader.

My ambivalence about organizational participation came into high relief this past weekend when I fulfilled my two-day round of meetings with Middlebury College's Alumni Council, a position I agreed to take—after too little deliberation—four years ago. As board commitments go, this one is not very demanding: weekend meetings twice a year, and an understanding that one will look in on college events from time to time. Since the principal reason—if not the stated reason—for this board is to stimulate annual cash gifts from graduates, it is understandable that the college's money-raising staff plans the meetings and drives most of the activity. Knowing these things from my own days as a school head and strongly averse to asking people for money, why on earth did I join the alumni council? There may have been a twinge of duty: my undergraduate experience was important and formative, and I feel a boyish urge to return the favor. But there was also vanity. I was flattered to be asked. There were no other board members within 15 years of my age, and I thought it might be fun to mix it up with younger people.

And there was the college itself in all of its complexity. Each round of meetings included debriefings from the college president, students, selected faculty and staff. I was genuinely curious about how the place operated, what the leaders thought they were doing. I was also hoping to sound out some of my emerging views on higher education and Middlebury College in particular: how preposterously expensive private colleges have become, resulting in, among other things, a generation of college graduates shackled to life-diminishing debt; the arrogant inclination on the part of some faculty to minimize student contact, often under the pretense of deepening their immersion in their respective fields; the exponential and expensive growth of staff, especially fundraisers.

The agenda this time was pretty thin, always aggravating for me because meeting attenders fill in the dead space with empty, no-forward-motion talk. Such talk comes compulsively to certain people. It was informative, though, to hear from the new college president, Laurie Patton, very bright and very tightly wound. Over what was supposed to be a chatty luncheon, she talked in an earnest way about the difficulty of getting a perspective on, much less controlling and directing, the complexity of an organization like Middlebury, with its new west coast campus, its dozens of schools and programs abroad. Alumni like me want to think of Middlebury concretely, as the gray cluster of limestone buildings on the hill above the town, but in operating fact it is a hodgepodge of scattered centers, many sharing little common purpose or quality other than enrolling, for money, people into various pursuits. I sense Laurie Patton trying to like Middlebury— she readily admits liking it better than Duke, where she came from. Trying to summarize the college's current condition, initiatives and challenges is an assignment too big for her allotted hour, and she talked in a torrent, not pausing even to take a bite of the little sandwich she had picked out from the buffet. Like a small monument to the hopelessness of a single person running a college, the sandwich sat there untouched next to a plastic cup of water for the duration of her presentation.

Next up was Gregory Buckles, director of admissions, who summarized this year's applications and the students yielded. I had heard Buckles earlier in the year, and he was once again confidently analytic, comfortable in his command of admissions complexities. As in recent years, about 9000 students applied for 750 places. Nearly all the applicants were qualified to be admitted. Middlebury now crosses applications with the very strongest small colleges and with the Ivies. Most of these very able students are declined, and Middlebury thus remains "highly selective," though there is mounting doubt, even from people speaking up at Harvard and Yale and Stanford, that this selectivity, which on one hand casts a sheen of superiority on the highly sought after schools, but which on the other raises the specter of very prosperous, well-established institutions further grooming thoroughbreds to assume various kinds of elite status, as the educational picture for the vast majority of Americans continues to dim.

A number of my fellow alumni board members volunteer to interview students applying to the college, and they convey to Buckles their frustration that none of the students who impress them seem to get in. Not at all defensively, but in a measured, practiced manner, Buckles recounts the obstacles to admitting even very able, likable high school seniors. It is not as if there are 750 wide open, beckoning spaces to be filled. Each varsity coach of men's and women's interscholastic teams—twenty-seven of them—are given a quota of applicants they may designate as preferred. Slightly less formally, the same kind of consideration is given to students indicated as especially desirable by directors of programs in music, theater and the arts. A desired quota of international students is specified each year, and the college's much heralded commitment to racial and economic diversity means that minority students, especially African Americans, are given special consideration. More recently, in an effort to reach out to students who are not culturally or economically positioned to know about strong private colleges, Middlebury has made a priority of admitting students who are the first in their families to apply to college. Sixteen per cent of this year's entering freshman class fall into this category. Finally, "legacies"—children of alumni—continue to be two and a half times more likely to be admitted than non-legacies.

It takes Buckles quite a while to summarize and clarify these admissions constraints, but when he is finished it is clear to all of us that for an able and willing white boy or girl who is not a coach-preferred athlete, not a foreign national, not a first generation college applicant, and not the son or daughter of an alumnus, the gateway into Middlebury College is dauntingly narrow. That established, nearly all of us in the room—including most certainly me—muse on the fact that we, at eighteen, would not have been admitted to Middlebury today.

A peculiar surprise at the alumni board's dinner banquet that evening. Various retiring college officials are toasted and given a small gift as a token of appreciation on behalf of the Alumni Council. Then, to my utter surprise, I am called to the group's attention, given a modest tribute and a small framed photograph of a college prospect in recognition of my two terms of service. It reveals something of the shallowness of my commitment to the board that I did not know I had completed my second and final two-year term or, for that matter, how long a term was and how many I had served.

My surprise was mixed with conflicting emotions: relief, certainly, that I was now free of any subsequent day-long meetings, but also an undeniable pang of shame that I had not engaged in the board's business more enthusiastically. But I honestly never felt I could. Both as headmaster of University School as it grew in extent and prospered, and as a fairly close observer of Middlebury's ever more commodious facilities and expanding programs, I have been concerned about what seems to me growth without vision: additions and expansions, whatever their internal justifications, accompanied my steeply rising costs. In University School's case, should a year of albeit spiffy kindergarten cost 25,000 after tax dollars? In Middle-bury's, should a year (actually seven months) of residence cost $62,000? In light of what most American families earn and have, the answer is a clear no. My discomfort with these costs and a realistic reckoning of my own none too booming financial reserves have caused me to reduce my own annual gifts to the college. In fact I am a little ashamed that I give anything at all, aware that my children at this point in their lives need the money more. That I give any money to Middlebury is due strictly to the shame I would feel—as a grateful graduate, a recipient of an Alumni Achievement Award, and, until a few days ago, a member of the Alumni Council board—in not doing so. Conflicting emotions indeed, also the whisper of a conviction that this is how old people feel about institutions they loved when they were still in the vital swim of things.

May 18, 2016: I am invited again to play the piano for the elderly participants in Project Independence, the adult day care facility in the heart of Middlebury. As before, the directors have set aside an hour after lunch which I am to fill by structuring a number of name-this-tune type of contests—songs spanning the World Wars, songs from films, songs from shows—and concluding with a sing-along from a booklet the directors and I have compiled containing a few dozen popular standards. This is I think my fourth appearance, and while the previous three have gone quite smoothly, this one feels rather a strain, which I am pretty sure is my fault.

As I peer out over the length of the grand piano, more faces than usual seem to be distracted, some of them in apparent discomfort. Three or four of the fifty people in attendance tend to name all the songs. I grow edgy as I note that the various contests take quite a bit less time than I had estimated. As we move into the sing-along, there is still a half hour to go. Because I am looking at the lyrics in the song book as I sing along, I can only intermittently look out at the audience, and I sense that fewer listeners than usual are singing along. Even before I finish playing I begin to conclude that this session is flatter, less diverting than my prior ones. When we finish the last number in the song book, only forty-five minutes have passed.

I ask Betsy, the very sweet director who has been helping to lead the singers, if the group has had enough, hoping she will agree. I can see from her expression that she would like more. Perhaps the facility's afternoon schedule depends on the participants being engaged for a full hour in this room. So we repeat some of the sing-alongs. I dredge up tunes I knew to be hits in the 1940s and '50s and ask if anyone remembers them. The same alert three or four people do. I am on edge and strangely exhausted when the hour is up. I walk to my car feeling that while not an abject failure, this session was far

from a success. It is not a particularly warm afternoon, but I realize I
am perspiring uncomfortably

May 25, 2016: After a good deal of thoughtful prior arranging on their
part, Les And Debbie Nash, M's and my old friends from Cleveland,
come to visit us in Ripton. Decades ago, they enrolled their son Doug
in University School, and I became his teacher and faculty advisor.
While physically hearty and youthful in outlook, the Nashes have both
entered their eighties. Les until his retirement was a leading orthopedic
surgeon in Cleveland, Debbie a college guidance counselor at
Cleveland's Hathaway Brown School, a girls' school more or less
partnered to University School. For a decade before her retirement she
came to University School to work in our admissions office. Together
Debbie and Les were engaged parents and cheerful contributors to
various boards and civic organizations in the city. Prosperous,
outgoing, and intellectually curious, they were and are easy to like.

The plan was to meet at our house for cocktails, then drive down
the mountain for dinner at the inn where they were lodging for the
night. As in our past social outings with them, events proceed with a
seemingly scripted ease. The air was mild but crisp, late sun streaming
through the windows of the house when they arrived. We had drinks
and nibbles on the deck, the river gently sloshing over the rocks.
Unlike so many of our Vermont friends, Les and Debbie are no enemy
of spirits, vodka and scotch respectively. Our talk was lively and
uninhibited, each of us anxious to catch up.

Drinks proceeded to dinner down the mountain with no let up in
our chatter and what I realized unmistakably was depth of affection I
had not anticipated. Throughout what must have been six or seven
continuous hours of chat, I felt insistent eruptions of *gratitude* roiling
up from my deep interior, gratitude for such a long, unbroken
relationship with these generous and kind people.

At one point M was engaged in an intense discussion of something
or other with Debbie, and I decided to ask Les how he settled on
medicine as a vocation. I wanted him to tell me how he came to be
able and even eager to spend grueling days cutting into the bodies of

his patients. I did not expect what he told me in response. I had only heard him referred to in the most glowing and admiring terms by other physicians well placed in Cleveland's medical complex: with respect to spines, hips and other joints, Les Nash was "the best." Les told me that as a boy he had been pretty confident in himself socially and athletically, but at Amherst College he did not feel especially competent at anything. He felt no special leaning toward the sciences, in which he had shown little academic promise, and certainly not medicine. He believed he was pretty good at practical tasks, at figuring out directions, fixing things and making things. He was good with his hands.

With little conviction he signed on to work in business—I think one of the steel companies—which he hated and quit as soon as he could. After peacetime military service abroad, more because friends had entered medical school than any vocational inspiration, he began his medical studies. What he remembers most about medical school is close fellowship with a group of bright and likable fellow students, some of whom I would come to know in Cleveland. He was self-aware enough to know that he tended more to action than to analysis, so sawing and rearranging bones became a clear choice of specialty. He thrived as an orthopedic surgeon, advancing steadily to national prominence.

A nice story, a success story, a story told with such directness and modesty that I felt a renewed surge of fondness and admiration for him. More than fondness: a realization that while he and Debbie are enduring friends, they are not really close friends, though it is hard for me to imagine feeling any closer to them as we draw out our talk over dessert and coffee. Like the burst of appreciation I experience when I am reunited years later with all but forgotten school colleagues, my feeling this evening for Debbie and Les is part of a summary reckoning of the substance and value of my life: that in addition to family and other intimates, relationships with beloved people a remove or two away from my "real" life have not been just adornments or a pleasing value-added; those relationships, if not centrally positioned, are nonetheless essential to how well or badly I have made my way. They have not just pleased, served or amused me; they have helped to *compose* me. I do not exist, have not existed, apart from them. Fondness, gratitude, and love are the tones in which this realization arrives.

May 31, 2016: I decide to celebrate M's 69th birthday on the actual day, and though it fell on a Tuesday, a putative working day, enough of our friends are retired and not tethered to conventional work that I knew we would have a festive gathering, and we do. Because the days now are reliably fair, we come together in M's gallery and on its screened porch overlooking the river. The party consists of cocktails and ample hors d'œuvres, to be followed by dinner down the mountain at the Waybury Inn for those able to extend the evening. M and I are also interested in our guests' responses to M's new paintings that have just been hung in the gallery.

Everyone who was invited, three dozen or so, showed up, and it was at once a spirited and bibulous affair, the guests gratifyingly appreciative of M's work, including a few sales. I had forgotten to mention in the invitation not to bring gifts, and everybody did, an unexpected bounty when M unwrapped them at breakfast the following morning.

In the days leading up to the party my friend Karl joked with me about whether I would be picking up the tab for everybody's dinner at the Inn, something that, stimulated by an admixture of good will and several cocktails, I had done at a few similarly structured parties over the years. I told him emphatically that I would not, although I was pretty sure I would, and in the event did.

While the good will and the love for M expressed at the party were genuine, there was something else at work, something harder to express—a distinct *presence* among us—as we chatted, ate, and drank. Again, the party was very similar in structure and setting to past gatherings and included many of the same guests, some of them friends who go back with us a half century. Outwardly we were honoring M on her birthday, but there was a deeper sense of participating in a ritual reenactment, the ritual serving as a kind of mirror confirming how we are now situated in life: as older, established people, held fast in our material conditions, our mannerisms, our personal histories. Together at this party we politely, if not quite consciously, acknowledge the arrival of our more or less final condition, before the impending insult of decline and death.

Elderly people celebrating birthdays, holidays, anniversaries—in equal measures sweet and sad, the Present feeling already like Afterward.

June 3-10, 2016: A week in Cleveland, the central purpose being to celebrate Lulu's graduation from the Roxboro Elementary School. The drive west this time—in under nine hours, a personal record—seems to take no time at all, as I fall into a kind of agreeable trance once I turn onto Interstate 90 in Albany. I am aware that my judgment must be impaired, because while fully conscious that I must not get another speeding ticket at any point along the 350 mile stretch of New York State lest I lose my license, I allow the Mini to cruise for miles-long stretches at 90 m.p.h. and above. The little car is so quick and quiet and surely fixed to the road. I take pains to peer ahead to the no-U-turn ramps where the police cruisers lurk, while frequently checking my rear view mirror for any vehicles mounted with what could be flashing lights. What is this practical, possibly even moral, weakness? There is nothing to be gained by appearing at Celeste's house earlier than expected.

On arrival I learn that I have been scheduled for several shopping outings in addition to Lulu's end-of-school-year festivities. The shopping assignments indicate to me that Celeste is operating close to the margin financially and needs help. This periodic need is never discussed openly. There is no formal or even tacit understanding that I will pay for whatever household goods and groceries are purchased in the course of my visits, but I have done so reliably, and what might once have been a hope on Celeste's part has now become an assumption. I do not begrudge her these outlays, which mount to hundreds of dollars in the course of my stays, because I am better fixed than she is and for the time being able to do it. But lately I have been concerned about the steady shrinkage of the corpus of my retirement holdings and know that if I live for ten years or longer, I am not going to be able to manage as I have been.

The closing school days of Lulu's fifth grade year are unclouded by anything like schoolwork. There is a "field" day of races, games, and improvised competitions on the playground. There is a class trip to a nearby amusement park. There is a class picnic and a dance. Celeste has volunteered me to help preside over the field day. She, another willing mom, and I are assigned to preside over an exercise in which each elementary school class manipulates a circular cloth tarp of about 30 feet in diameter so that it balloons up into a kind of canopy under which the children take turns running, executing an assigned move, then dashing back to the perimeter before the suspended canopy collapses over them. It takes a good bit of rigorous flapping on the part of all of the children and the three adults to raise the tarp into a sufficient dome. A dozen different classes appear at fifteen-minute intervals to participate in the tarp event, with no rest time between sessions for the adult flappers. After an hour I can feel the strain in my upper arms and shoulders, but as our team's only adult male, I feel pride bound not to complain or, I hope, show any sign of distress. We continue flapping and calling out commands to the shrieking children for another two hours, in the course of which Celeste and the other mom drop out of action periodically to rest, drink water, and relieve themselves. I flap on manfully alone. When the last class has passed through and the adults are blessedly free to be mere observers of the concluding event, a series of very funny class vs. class tug-of-wars, I am seriously arm-weary, and Celeste is in pain, a condition that will persist throughout my visit.

My exertions aside, I leave the field day playground full of appreciation of what seemed to me unusually cheerful and well-behaved children, demonstrably affectionate with one another and clearly having fun. One might think that having encountered every single child in the school over the course of several hours, I would have observed at least one clear basket case, but I did not. I was also impressed with the principal and physical education head, both hulking athletic types, who led the games with a sure, cheerful sense of command. It was clear that the children—and Lulu certainly—are respectfully fond of both men. I especially liked that they had no qualms about larking around a bit, as when they mock-sneaked into this or that tug-of-war team's lineup and changed what had looked like a certain defeat into a raucously contested victory. In all, the field day evoked the strongest impressions of Good School.

I am mainly pleased that for six consecutive years, kindergarten through grade five, Lulu has thrived in this school. Her home room teachers have been quite different from one another—men, women, older, younger, introvert, extrovert—but each one has been highly competent, respected by colleagues and children alike, and from what I have observed highly appreciative of Lulu's gifts and quirks. For her part, Lulu has been easy to like. She is a quick study, does her work, collaborates and participates enthusiastically in classroom business. She has a raft of friends and, so far, no apparent enemies. Each year teachers have commented on her originality and creativity, her commitment to making things.

Without having to be told, Lulu approached the graduation ceremony itself with a touching solemnity. In the course of our final outing in Santa Monica while visiting my sister, she and her mother spent, for me, two excruciating hours picking out a dress she would wear at her graduation. In the event a satisfactory choice: a cheerful pattern of red cherries against a dark background. For two full days prior to the ceremony at school Lulu cut out, decorated and inscribed lengthy notes of appreciation to all of her teachers from kindergarten onward. No one asked or expected her to do this. It is not a tradition at the school and none of her friends thought to do it. It is the kind of sweet, feeling gesture she likes to make. I don't think that at her age she could know what those notes will mean to the teachers, but I know what I and what every one of my University School colleagues would feel if we received one.

The ceremony itself takes place mid-morning in the school's central auditorium. The rest of the student body is seated before the graduating fifth graders, suitably dressed up, file in by pairs and take their places front and center. A few selected boys and girls speak fondly of their time at the school, and a few teachers speak fondly of the fifth grade, and then a number of student awards are conferred, ranging from subject matter distinction to notable improvement. Celeste has been informed that Lulu will receive an award, but we do not know what it is. It turns out to be the music award, fitting, as midway through the program and at its close she leads her class in song. The principal's and other adult talks from the stage are heartfelt and mercifully brief, so that in less than an hour we follow the giddy fifth graders out of the assembly into the crowded library where families and other well-wishers are offered sweet rolls and undrinkable sugary juice. Every teacher who greets us praises Lulu extravagantly. Several of them tell us they thought Lulu deserved all of the awards.

In all, the ceremony moved me to my core, and I cannot find words for why. It was sweet and orderly, but it was also completely ordinary. And perhaps that is it: its very ordinariness was so welcome, so fine, a gratifying assurance of something no less profound than the national civic life progressing as it should —and that there is every reason to expect the best of these beautiful and affectionate children.

June 14, 2016: I read from *The Three Lives of Jonathan Force* at the Vermont Book Shop in Middlebury. As the day approached, I was more anxious than I ought to have been because my relationship to the current store owner had become strained. Two years prior when I asked after a possible reading and signing for *The Other World*, I was told curtly no, that recent readings and signings had not gone well. Before I could offer assurance that I thought there would be a decent turnout, she looked me in the eye and said, "Nobody comes." I left the store and vowed to buy no future books there—and I had been a pretty good customer, especially around the holidays.

Caitlin, the book's publicist, made a good case for a local reading and managed to schedule one at the store on the eve of the official publication date. In the ensuing arrangements I neither saw nor spoke to the owner, nor did she attend, but other staff were cheerful and helpful, taking what I thought were impressive pains to publicize the event in advance. Nonetheless, I was worried that not enough people would attend, and that the owner's discouraging prediction would hold.

The event was scheduled for 7:00 to 8:30 in the evening, and by the time I showed up a half hour early to be sure all was properly set up, there were a dozen or so attendees waiting to be seated, including my favorite undergraduate professor, the political philosopher Paul Nelson. By seven, most of my Middlebury friends and plenty of others arrived, causing the store staff to retrieve extra folding chairs from the cellar. Confident now that the event would not be a commercial disappointment to the owner, I was relaxed and in the high spirits. I welcomed the attendees and made a brief account of the book's intentions before reading a bit from Book II, about Jonathan's reuniting with Elizabeth at Yale and their foreshadowed life partnership. Aware that Paul Nelson was in the audience, I felt a twinge of regret that I had not chosen a more introspective and philosophical excerpt—they abound in the Yale sequence—but it seemed too risky to improvise on the spot.

Though reading aloud from my own work invariably puts me into a kind of trance, I was aware enough of the seated listeners to know that, if not raising deep questions as to life's meaning, the passages I chose were reasonably interesting and amusing. My friends commented with predictable generosity. The question and discussion period that followed was warm. I was surprised to behold among the seated latecomers one of my former University School students and now a father of a Middlebury undergraduate. He asked a number of good questions about the relationship between personal recollection and created episode. I was also struck by the enthusiastic responses of a beefy young man sitting in the front row. Later, when he appeared at the signing table, it occurred to me that I had seen him somewhere before, and then he told me. Weeks prior when M and I were dining out with my writing friend Phoebe Stone and her husband, we had exchanged banter with our extroverted waiter, who announced that he too was a writer. Phoebe told him that I would be reading in Middlebury and that he should make an effort to attend. "Absolutely! I'll be there!" our waiter responded with jovial bluster—but he remembered and came. And bought a book.

June 20-July 5, 2016: A jarring succession of travels. Even as I made the arrangements, I knew the events I had committed myself to for June and July were not going to cohere. My departure in June overlapped and to some extent interfered with promotional events Caitlin, the new novel's publicist, was trying to arrange. Since I would be headed to the west coast, first to see daughter Claire and her husband Nick in Oakland, then to address the International Boys' Schools Coalition in Vancouver, Caitlin thought it would be a good idea to arrange a reading / signing event either in Los Angeles or Santa Barbara. An agreeable event in LA turned out to be difficult to schedule, so we opted for Santa Barbara, a city I had long wanted to see and where E, an old college love lives. Having rekindled our friendship at her 50th Middlebury reunion the year prior, I hoped we could reconnect. E has been in treatment for the past several years with a rare blood cancer which has been arrested somewhat by experimental drugs. She was decidedly unimpaired when I last saw her and she is reliably lively in email exchanges, but I did not know how I would find her.

I was thus very glad to see that she was up and about and willing to meet when I arrived in Santa Barbara. As it happened I was awkwardly delayed as my connecting flight from LA was cancelled due to bad air conditions caused by raging fires along the flight path. A very slow, traffic-snarled bus ride north put me in mind again of how I could never live anywhere near a major city in California. At one point about 20 miles north of Los Angeles, stopped still, bumper to bumper, I noted that our bus was held fast within six lanes of northbound traffic and six lanes of southbound traffic. It was possible to imagine passing out of this life in an eternal, insoluble gridlock.

As we approached Santa Barbara and drew closer to the Pacific, the horizon opened up, and a combination of declining sunlight and the smoke from the fires turned the entire sky a sulfurous yellow-grey: an impression of end-of-the world ugliness.

In the two days that followed, however, Santa Barbara proved a delight: invigorating walks along deserted beaches and along the city's

216 •• RICHARD HAWLEY

bustling waterfront. E did her heroic best to be a lively civic guide, but she could not help being preoccupied with a new swelling under one arm and accompanying malaise, all requiring doctor consultations, preparation for biopsy and possible surgery. I departed the city with a lingering impression that I had not so much visited a new city, but a new country, the arched and cobbled byways and orange tiled roofs suggesting an opulent metropolis in Spain or Mexico.

Flew north to Oakland from Santa Barbara's small but country club-opulent airport to see daughter Claire and Nick. Claire has not been reluctant to remind me that I haven't visited her since she and Nick moved to Oakland. And it occurs to me that, despite dozens of trips to San Francisco over the past four decades, I have never been to Oakland and harbor a blurred image of it as a battered, troubled non-San Francisco. Claire, however, has reported only positive things, not just its relative affordability—cosmopolitan friends tell me Oakland is now San Francisco's Brooklyn—but also its neighborhood charms.

My initial impressions are encouraging. Claire and Nick's apartment is a two-story, nicely appointed partition of what was once a sprawling mansion. The building has a vaguely Victorian look, as do the abutting houses on either side. Dark heavy woodwork and high ceilings suggest a prior era, but while worn, the place is far from run down. The rooms are comfortably furnished, the kitchen well stocked, the baby's room readied for its arrival in September.

Claire and Nick are both at work when I taxi in from the airport, but they have placed a key under the mat on their front porch, and I let myself in. Because Claire and Nick have a cat to which I am strongly allergic, I will not stay overnight in the house, Claire having rented a small apartment for me through Air B&B a block or so away. Because the cat is immediately fond of me, I decide to leave the house and explore the neighborhood, with an eye to finding an agreeable place to have lunch.

The network of streets surrounding the apartment is hard to categorize: a hodgepodge of single family residences, converted mansions, and newer apartment buildings huddled closely together. Like San Francisco, many of the streets are steeply inclined, so that walking uphill for a block or two I find myself leg weary and perspiring; walking downhill I have to plant my lead foot deliberately to avoid breaking into an involuntary trot.

At length I make my way out of residential neighborhoods onto a pleasantly teeming commercial street, Piedmont, lined with interesting shops, coffee houses, and eateries. I dine undisturbed—it is mid-afternoon—at a brew pub, read the NYT and answer emails on my iPad. Walking up and down the steep inclines on the way back to the apartment feels energizing, and I am aware I am going to feel at home here.

When Claire returns home from school, she walks me to the apartment she has picked out for me. It is on the top floor of a four-story building, comfortably furnished, with a balcony view of Oakland harbor. We make a dinner plan, and Claire leaves me for an hour's rest.

Claire and Nick have decided on a favored restaurant, a short walk from their apartment. I do not find it a short walk—a mile plus—but Claire, now grandly pregnant, cheerfully strides out ahead, up and down the steep inclines. The café selected is crowded and noisy when we arrive, but we have a reservation, and it is a relief to be seated in the din. It is a Friday night, and I try to take the measure of the other diners. Apart from Claire and Nick they are not notably young, but they are dressed as youth might dress: blue jeans, hooded jerseys, complicated-looking athletic shoes, a determined dressing down. The restaurant is expensive, so this must be for the diners an "evening out," but the urban mood today, whether Chicago's Lincoln Park, Brooklyn, LA, or—clearly—Oakland, is aggressively anti-formal.

Though I have been on the west coast for days, I am still not fully adjusted to the time change, so that while it is dinner time, I feel it is much later. I am very hungry and even more eager for a cocktail. When at last asked, I tell our waitress I would like a Tanqueray martini, up with an olive. She tells me they do not stock Tanqueray gin, which puzzles me. So I say Beefeaters gin, also not stocked. Ditto Bombay gin. I am taken aback, and the waitress hands me a menu of the spirits available in the café. There are thirteen "artisanal" gins listed, with names like Oxley, DSP.7, RHok. All of them are expensive, but trusting they approximate what I know as gin, I order a martini made with one. When it arrives, I note the glass, a small, round bottomed tumbler, is also apparently artisanal, as are the dark olives. I am startled by the taste: a strong impression of an industrial solvent, awful, undrinkable. Despite Claire and Nick's upbeat, agreeable banter, I begin to lose enthusiasm for the meal to follow.

There are seemingly hundreds of complicated offerings on the menu. Claire explains that this is a "small plates" restaurant, and the plan is to order perhaps five or six of the offerings and to share them. I do not want to sour the proceedings by admitting how much I would like to have a substantial steak and potatoes, all to myself. As it happens, there is a steak offering, albeit small plate and complicatedly artisanal, and we include it in our order.

The small plates begin to arrive. I have replaced my gin martini with a glass of potable wine and am starting to relax, catching up on various developments in Nick's and Claire's lives. Most of the food is unrecognizable to me, either by taste or appearance. I think root vegetables figure prominently under various murky sauces. The steak, when at last it appears, is the size of a slice of tomato. In the spirit of the café, we share it. Despite my inner conviction of Never Again to the café and its like, I have enjoyed myself, as it would be hard not to in Claire's and Nick's high spirited, funny, affectionate company. Appropriately, it falls to me to pay the check and, despite protests, do. It was, with tip, nearly $300. The steak, I noted, was $60.

It is good to catch up with Claire and to get a sense of where and how she lives. I like the warmth and easy humor she and Nick share and their enlivening anticipation of the baby's imminent arrival. Back in my rental apartment, my thoughts necessarily turn to the Vancouver conference and the presentation I am scheduled to make.

At the San Francisco airport I am at first flummoxed and then impressed by the new high tech arrangements for checking in to my scheduled flight. Because it is an international flight, the monitor and keyboard I am clicking through and typing into includes a crude schematic diagram instructing users how to insert their passports so that they can be photographed. In many tries I cannot get it right. Is it face up? Face down? I know the device needs to photograph my passport picture, but the directions instruct me to do it in a way that puts my picture out of range of the camera. I ask a woman using the adjacent machine for help, but she gives me an irritated look and declines.

An alternative would be to enter one of the lines of passengers waiting to be checked in by living airline employees, but the lines are hundreds of yards long, and no one seems to advance in the time I have been fumbling with the automated check-in apparatus. In fairness to the automated system, I am bad at interpreting instructional diagrams. Even simpler schematics, such as the ones ATM machines and gas pumps use to indicate how to slide one's credit card along a track in order to begin service, baffle me, suggesting the very opposite of what the machine says it wants. The problem is probably lodged deep in my nervous system, failed neural connections in the part of the brain in charge of interpreting visual symbols. I remember as a young driver realizing that the many green signs overhanging interstate highways conveyed too much information too quickly—exit / entrance, merge left / merge right, north / south, this road / that road—for me to draw any useful conclusions, reducing all interstate driving decisions to guesses. Even more primitive is my occasional inability, especially when I am in a hurry, to interpret the crude human figures used to indicate which gender is welcome in which bathroom. The triangular skirt intended to indicate *women* doesn't register to me as a skirt; the figure seems no more than a generic person with a triangular bottom. Nor do the rectangular pant legs of the putative male figure register to me as particularly male. In fact, I reflexively associate the pant-leg figure with Hillary Clinton.

In any event, I finally succeed in inserting my passport correctly— I had been putting it in the wrong enclosure—and, almost tearfully grateful, gather up my printed boarding passes and proceed with minimal interference to my gate and plane.

My realization that I am now making my way through the modern world as an impaired person deepens when I arrive in Vancouver. Relieved to pass quickly through customs, I get into a cab and tell the turbaned driver to take me to the Fairmount Hotel where I have booked a room for the duration of the conference. He asks me which one. Which *one?* I have no idea and ask him which one is likely to host the attendees of a large conference. He tells me both of them could do that. I propose that we try one, and if it is the wrong one, we drive to the other. He assures me that we can do that, but the afternoon traffic is now heavy, and the two Fairmounts are quite a distance apart. How far apart, I ask. It could be an hour's drive in this traffic, he tells me. This won't do because I have a late afternoon meeting I must attend and a formal dinner to follow. I am at a loss, and so is the driver who awaits clarifying instructions as we make our way over high bridges to Vancouver proper.

Then it occurs to me to call one of the hotels on my cell phone. If it is the conference-designated Fairmount, we will proceed to it; if not, to the other one. But my cell phone does not access service of any kind, which I realize is because I am no longer in the USA. Now entering a bad-dream state of mind, I ask the driver to pull over to the curb, while I deliberate on what might be a promising next step. In a flash I remember that there is a number—611—I can dial on my phone that offers all kinds of customer service. After a maddening string of automated prompts I am relieved to reach a live agent, though quickly frustrated that I can't make out half of what he says in what sounds to me like an Indian accent. I ask him to slow down, speak louder, which he tries to do, I am pretty sure the apology preceding each of his answers to my requests is a scripted protocol. At length I make it clear that I want to extend my service to Vancouver, Canada, and I am momentarily cheered to hear the agent tell me no problem, it can be done. But in order to buy a one-week phone plan for Canadian service, I am asked to supply my cell phone account password or the social security number associated with the account. I have been stalled at this roadblock before when dealing with cell phone issues. Annoyingly, our cell phone contract was established by M, and I do not know the password or her social security number, but maybe…maybe…I wrote it down on a scrap of paper and inserted it in some crowded compartment of my wallet. I ask the Indian agent to hold the line while I look.

As I do my phone gives out a beep and a buzz, then a screen indicating "low battery." I am perspiring. My fingers are fumbling like an aged person's through dozens of small scraps of paper on which I have scrawled names and long-forgotten phone numbers, which I can barely read without my glasses, which are in my suitcase, which is in the trunk of the cab. Miraculously I find the scrap with M's social security number, which I practically shout into the phone. The agent proceeds to install the plan but, maddeningly, is required by company policy to read me all of its many terms at the conclusion of which I must orally agree. I plead with him to skip this, but, while elaborately apologetic, he refuses. When at last we are finished, I thank him and dial information—411—to get the listing for one of the Vancouver Fairmount hotels. I hear the familiar "you have reached Verizon 411 information search. What listing, please?" And then the phone goes dead, the battery having lost its charge. A moment or so of no useful cognitive activity. An urge to curse, to kick the vinyl back of the driver's seat. I note that the driver is talking on his cell phone, and I ask him if he could possibly call one of the Fairmount hotels to check if it is associated with my conference. He kindly agrees. The first Fairmount he reaches is not the one. The second one is. We pull away from the curb, into bumper-to-bumper rush hour traffic. Forty five minutes later, I gather my bags, thank the very kind and patient driver. A beaten, diminished figure, expecting the worst, I begin my work in Vancouver.

Five interchangeable days of bright sun and mild air in a metropolis that, like Capetown, feels at once maritime and alpine. My only prior visit was more than a decade ago when my assignment was to interest a wealthy University School trustee in supporting student scholarships. My impression then was of a slightly more rugged San Francisco. As my trustee friend toured me around, he said the city was in rapid transition. Rich Chinese, uncertain about the mainland government's plans for them, were buying up residential real estate, enrolling their children in local schools, and otherwise setting up for potential expatriation. From what I could see now, a good bit of this has come to pass. The old city is ringed with new identical-looking high rise apartment buildings, starkly rectilineal, faced with glass on all sides, so that the waterfront façade of downtown looks like a vast cosmetics counter.

The conference is hosted by a prosperous suburban Vancouver boys' school, St. George's. One of the school's trustees has invited the Boys' Schools Coalition leadership, including me in a kind of honorary capacity, to a pre-conference outdoor banquet on the grounds of his manicured estate on the residential outskirts of the city. Fifty or sixty of us make our way there by on a chartered bus. Though a private residence, the buildings and grounds feel rather like a country club. Lawns are manicured to a golf green texture. Linen draped dining tables have been set up under a massive tent. Two fully stocked bars have been set up at pool's edge, and for an hour or so before we dine, uniformed caterers ply us with fancy nibbles. I look around for our host, because I want to meet him and thank him. A friend points him out to me, and I do not at first believe him. The owner of this grand estate appears to be a teenage Chinese boy, but apparently his appearance is deceptive, as is the appearance of his wife, who could pass for twelve. A short line has formed to greet the couple, who are smiling broadly and making little nervous bows. As I join the line, my friend advises me to keep my greetings brief, because neither husband or wife speak any English, although their eleven-year-old son, a student at St. George's, is standing a few feet apart from them and translates some phrases of the guests' good wishes to his parents. I am curious about how this particular family volunteered—or were they dragooned?—to host this rather expensive and, for them, by no means socially comfortable outing. A St. George's staff member tells me the Changs (or Yangs?) value education highly. In the course of the meal to follow, the son who, like his parents, looks years younger than his actual age, greets each of us individually and hands us a gift bag containing stationery, a fancy pen, candy, and assorted toiletries. He is a pleasing, comfortable presence, and his answers to our questions are generous, even witty. He and his family may have been what my trustee friend was describing on my prior visit. It was not hard to imagine the future of Vancouver belonging to the Changs / Yangs.

It is a large conference this year, about seven hundred people representing schools from twenty different countries. When we convene for our first general session, the St. George's headmaster greets us and introduces a native American woman representing British Columbia's First Nations tribe who offers various blessings and good wishes. I try to fathom the point our hosts want to stress in orienting us in this way to a conference dedicated to school boys and their prospects. My curiosity deepens as our first keynote speaker, Amanda Lindhout, is introduced. She is a tall, slender young woman, elegantly dressed and strikingly pretty. The program notes indicate that she is a rising print journalist who had a formative experience in Somalia, where she was taken hostage for more than a year before being released. A Canadian film is in the works about her ordeal.

She has a fascinating manner of speaking: extremely careful articulation of syllables, a slow, measured cadence suggesting a willed effort to control her tone. Her language is direct, unadorned, with no literary flourishes as she recounts her personal background. She grew up in a small town in rural Alberta in a working class, single parent household. After high school she became a waitress, saving money until she could afford a bout of world travel. On one of her trips she made the acquaintance of an itinerant photographer who supported himself by selling pictures of trouble spots and war zones to newspapers and wire services. The idea of actually earning a living while traveling the world inspired her, and on her return to Canada she took some journalism courses and then set out to do her own freelance work abroad. After some initial success in the Middle East, she got an assignment from one of the wire services to cover Somalian war refugee camps, their condition at that time a humanitarian crisis. Once arrived in Somalia, the plan was for her and a photographer to be escorted to the camps in a chartered vehicle complete with armed guards to protect them. At some point on a desolate desert road, a truckload of armed Somalian rebels overtook the journalists' vehicle and chased off their armed protectors.

The Somalis—teenage boys with AK 47s—made their intentions clear. They wanted Amanda and her photographer friend to give them their family contact information at home, so they could demand a ransom, a million dollars for each of them. The captors made their initial demand on the spot, using the captives' cell phones. Since such money was not available, Amanda and the photographer, never named in her talk, were taken to an abandoned building where they were closely guarded and intermittently fed. Something about Amanda's measured way of describing these experiences conveyed their sheer awfulness.

As it happened, it was a long story, as both Amanda and her friend were held, in steadily worsening circumstances for eighteen months. In part because of her controlled calm, she was able to convey the depth of horror she experienced. The all-being fear, the isolation from any possible source of relief or rescue, the physical deprivations, the repeated threat of her impending execution turned out not to be the worst of it.

Months into their captivity, a stroke of ingenuity enabled Amanda and her friend to escape through a bathroom window. They made their way overland to a nearby mosque where a prayer service was in session. As they attempted to convey their situation to the worshippers, their captors broke in brandishing their weapons. They seized Amanda and her friend and secreted them away to another, cruder dwelling where, shackled, Amanda was kept in a room sealed in complete darkness. This, she said, is when she experienced the worst: doubts about whether her life, or anybody's life, mattered, a sickening fear that she was losing her mind. She was raped and otherwise abused daily. Her teeth were knocked out. Earlier in her captivity, she had made an attempt to get to know her captors and learned enough to know that the boys were orphans, some of them survivors of their parents' murders by Somalian forces. There would be no empathy from the boys, who were sustained solely by possibility that ransom money would somehow be provided. One of them shared with Amanda his hope that he might emigrate to the west and sacrifice himself in the killing of many people in a store or a theater.

Miraculously, it seems to me, Amanda was spared. Her working class mother and estranged father somehow over the 18 months managed to crowd source the necessary ransom, and she was airlifted out of Somalia and eventually home to Canada. In the four years since, she has dedicated herself to working with rape and other trauma victims to support their recovery. When she was finished speaking, she thanked us fervently for having invited her and for listening to her because, she said, telling her story was still an essential part of her own continuing struggle to recover.

I was full of questions after her talk, but she was whisked away immediately. It was explained at the reception following that she is too emotional after these presentations to socialize comfortably. I understood this. She had conveyed an almost unbearable sense of being hurt past recovery—damaged. In the course of the reception all of us wanted to talk about what we had heard. The women in attendance were especially animated, some of them upset and critical of the conference planners for having struck such a jarring note at the outset of a conference dedicated to best practices for nurturing boys. I too had wondered about the thinking behind such an invitation, but after an hour or so decided Amanda's presence before us, preceded as it was by the First Nation woman's appeal to our spiritual connectedness, made profound sense. All the while she was relating her abuse at the hands of her boy captors, I was thinking about the boys: what particular circumstances, what absence of nurture, love, and warmth could enable them—daily for weeks, months—to inflict pain and degradation on another human being, an innocent woman, a noncombatant, a beauty. I believe those boys may have been hurt as badly as they hurt Amanda.

One of the things I wanted to know was how, after her near fatal malnutrition, loss of her teeth and most of her hair, multiple internal and skeletal injuries, she could appear so well turned out and lovely. My curiosity in this regard was not to be satisfied, although some women conferees sitting closer to the stage than I said that Amanda's knees and calves, visible below the hem of her dress, were badly scarred.

Over the four days of the conference there were some other engaging keynoters and one or two very bad ones, but none approached the existential depths of Amanda Lindhout's presentation. I once again let a wave or two of pride—but mostly gladness—wash over me in the realization that the Coalition a few of us founded so tentatively a quarter century ago has become so robust and, in its many workshops and special sessions, so clearly doing better by boys in dozens of highly specific ways.

I wanted my own talk to be good. It was an extended version of ideas I have offered in other conferences: that we do better by boys as attentive witnesses and supporters of their individual unfolding than by trying to bend them to "stage of life" or grade-level expectations established by dubious child development theories. In the event, I had the impression I engaged my listeners. There seemed to me good eye contact throughout and lively, substantial questions afterward. But my old friend Tony Jarvis, who has listened to me speak for decades and who has read practically every published word of mine, told me he thought I tried to cram too much into my allotted 90 minutes. He did not dismiss anything I said as beside my point, but he felt there was too much to integrate, that less would have struck home with more force. Because I know Tony only wishes me well, I suspect he is right. No, I know he is right. My own personal take on even the best presentations I hear is usually, like Tony's: give me less, make it clearer, make it shine.

In the course of conference socializing, my understanding of the national political scene is corrected. I had felt certain that the bubble of Donald Trump's unchecked progress through the Republican Party's primary process would soon burst. I did not find it surprising that in a divided field of 13 very peculiar candidates someone as preposterous as Trump could surge ahead of the others. But that a majority of Republicans—much less a majority of American voters— would take such a person seriously seemed impossible. The pundits early on predicted the inevitable ascendency of Jeb Bush, and it was hard to believe otherwise given what to me appeared the feast of fools running in opposition: Chris Christie? Ben Carson? Ted Cruz? *Donald Trump*? But Bush's very normality served to cast him into the shadows in the course of "debates" in which so much acrid name-calling and insult prevailed.

With Trump cruising very plausibly to the Republican Party nomination, I had adjusted my assumptions to a stock line. Reasoning that since most Republicans do not like him and virtually all Democrats do not like him, he would be massively defeated. "He will lose every state," I said confidently in the course of conference dinner conversations." "He won't lose Tennessee," answered my friends from the Montgomery Bell Academy in Nashville, to which a chorus of other southerners, all more politically attentive and better informed than I, assured me that the South and much of the West was solidly in support of Trump. I looked at them closely to see if they were kidding, or at least exaggerating. They were not, and a chilling realization of what was now for me an unrecognizable American political landscape has hastened a resolve to better understand my countrymen.

I do not know a single person who takes Donald Trump seriously as a person, much less as a political leader. But why on earth have I assumed my own views were so widely shared, that I was anything like normative? It is clear that I am the one in a bubble, though now anxious to get out of it and to understand what is going on. Trump, it seems to me, is a consistent representation of what he has always been: a me-first, deal-making, self-promoting blowhard, an espouser of not merely bad proposals, but of proposals so muddy and unworkable that they cannot be taken seriously by any reasonably educated person. But if Trump is what he has always been, there are now apparently legions of people who, for reasons not yet known to me, would like to see a person like him lead the nation. The origins and views of these people are what I need to understand. I need to put aside qualifications like "reasonably well educated." I need to know about the Trump supporters who dismiss clear evidence that he is often wildly mistaken as to facts and that he outright lies. Far from being concerned about his misogynist and bigoted statements, Trump's "base" is positively energized by them. Are there really *millions* of American people in this "base?"

Understanding who composes this base, how they came to be, what they want, and what they really need has to be the most urgent issue in this darkening era.

After four days, somewhat to my surprise, I find I am tired of Vancouver, notwithstanding its bright heights, its urban piles spilling down to panoramas of sparkling sea. I am tired of the opulent and unnecessary comforts of my hotel room, the too much-ness of every meal, of my own lack of discipline and laziness in having reclined into so much ease. A few times I tried to purge my feelings of post-conference indolence by striking out on urban walks, following my nose, but the exertion failed to satisfy. There was only city, stacked residences, hotels, restaurants, stores: T. J Maxx, The Gap, Banana Republic, a gaudy new Trump Tower. Nothing to differentiate Vancouver from Toronto, Chicago, San Francisco, Auckland. Much of this can be attributed to my own restlessness to get out.

I realize I am travel weary, the clothes in my overstuffed suitcase badly in need of laundering. Nevertheless, I am glad I scheduled a Cleveland stop before returning to Vermont. I have been missing Lulu and look forward to spending the Fourth of July with her. As it happens, the Fourth is a rather big deal on Somerton Road, Celeste's street in Cleveland Heights. The full three blocks of the street are closed to traffic for the day, and the residents have scheduled a series of games, contests, and diversions, including a short parade consisting of the costumed neighbors, adults and children alike, most of them walking their pets, to the cadence of an improvised oom-pah band.

Celeste has been assigned to host the neighborhood breakfast, which involves hauling various kinds of seating and makeshift tables into the back yard. The morning is mild but overcast, a sense of drizzle or rain hovering but not quite descending. With some borrowed items from neighbors, we establish a makeshift dining area for about three dozen people. In the event many more than this show up, bearing coffee cakes, egg dishes, fruit bowls. We have arranged to brew coffee, and for the better part of two hours I enjoy convivial exchanges with people of all ages and types and largely unknown to me. I am still sleep deprived from my flight in, feeling dull witted but amicable. It strikes me that gathering neighbors and deepening acquaintance is a very good thing, and for the first time in a long while the Fourth of July seems to cohere into something commanding and purposeful.

It is enough just to behold Lulu at play. She has decorated her bicycle, weaving red, white and blue crepe paper through the spokes of the wheels. For the parade she and neighborhood girlfriends arrange flower garlands in their hair, don pale pink frocks and circle a designated Queen of the May as she marches the length of Somerton Road. After the parade, adults conduct a series of games and competitions for the children: tossing balls through hoops, egg tosses, three-legged races. There are also adult competitions: a game called Corn Hole, in which teams of two compete to toss bean bags into a hole cut into the inclined top of a wooden box. There is a round-robin three-on-three basketball tournament dominated, to the embarrassment of several paunchy male teams, by an excellent team of women, some of whom were stars of their college teams. In and about all of it Lulu flits like a butterfly, somehow managing to be everywhere, competing, racing about in her gaggle of friends, but never far from my gaze.

At mid-afternoon I am sitting, half reclined, on the wicker sofa on Celeste's front porch, conserving if not restoring my energy. Celeste's older daughter Francesca, newly admitted to a Ph.D. program at the University of North Carolina where she will study colonial history, seeks me out to talk. She is not one to engage in the neighborhood festivities, preferring serious chat about politics and history—or even better, from her perspective, exploring arcane aspects of the Star Wars films, to which she has been devoted for years. I am in a way touched that Francesca likes to talk to me, as she can be reserved and even prickly in company she finds intellectually shallow. I tell her again that I somehow missed the entire Star Wars phenomenon when the films first appeared and—because I know she will be energized—ask if there is a compelling reason for me to reconsider. She has just launched into what she calls the "metaphysics" of the Star Wars narrative when an adult neighbor and friend of Celeste's, Pav, joins us on the porch and sits down to talk. As it turns out Pav is the older brother of one of my former students, Andre, a gentle, agreeable boy who was a gifted cellist. Pav caught me up on his brother's circumstances, effectively silencing Francesca, who I could tell was anxious to get back to Star Wars, a signal Pav missed completely. Instead he launched into a long and excruciatingly detailed report of his recent heart by-pass surgery. He kept looping back to how, had he not gone to the doctor for a routine physical, the damage to his heart would have gone undetected and that he would certainly have had a heart attack and died. He spoke with an urgency that made me—and I am sure Francesca—wonder why he was confiding this experience at such length to strangers who had not inquired about it. I thought that, having now made a full account of his procedure and recovery to us, he might continue down the street, but he made no move to leave. Then Celeste joined us on the porch, and he seized the opportunity to recount his ordeal to her, although she reminded him several times that they had already had this conversation. I was at this point longing for him to go away. Francesca's eyes were fixed on the porch floor, her expression ominous. Pav regarded her closely and said, "*You* should get a check-up." Then, for emphasis, Pav unbuttoned his shirt and exposed the red surgical scar running the length of his sternum. I told him I bet he was glad all of that was behind him, and in the course of his protracted response, Francesca got up from the porch and went into the house, and with that I was aware that, for me, the Fourth of July festivities had come to an end, as had my visit to Cleveland and the entire journey west.

July 15, 2016: I am back home just long enough to feel again that it *is* home, the colors, the carpets, the arrangements of the pictures in all the rooms reestablishing their pleasing patterns.

I am glad to see an email invitation to dinner at the O'Briens. Although my prior impressions of them could not have been more positive, Dennis and Judith O'Brien were not people I expected to befriend when we moved to Vermont. In the course of a number of interactions with Dennis when I was an undergraduate and he was Dean of Students, I felt he was somehow interested in me. He wanted me to expand on whatever problematic view or utterance had come under review. He is a philosopher and asked me good, interesting questions. These days when we are together talk comes easily: political developments, arts, music, our children. Like M and me, the

O'Briens have three daughters, like ours immersed in the arts and social service. And in the event, it is yet another convivial, satisfying evening. Judith has taken care to cook a curried dish, because she knows I am mad for Indian food. Dennis has baked an enormous rhubarb and strawberry pie. We talk and talk, drink more wine than I am sure either of them is used to. M marvels again at their extraordinary collection of sculptures and paintings, each object beautifully lit, everything in the house just so. As are the O'Briens: just so. And I muse driving home how, while on balance satisfying to me, my life and circumstances are anything but just so. I also resolve to tell Dennis and Judith about Lulu and Celeste. Perhaps they know already, as it is hardly a secret among our shared acquaintance, but we have never discussed it, and it is starting to feel like a willed deception on my part not to disclose so central an element in my life. I don't believe it will end or strain our friendship, but you never know.

July 20-23, 2016: I fly into Chicago for a *Jonathan Force* reading and signing event hosted by a bookstore, The Book Cellar, said by Chicago friends to be something special. Spooked now by past travel snafus, I decide to fly in a day early against the possibility of flight cancellations, delays, what-not.

And sure enough. The regional United Airlines jet scheduled to take me from Burlington VT to Chicago at midday does not arrive from its prior stop. A phone text from the ticketing agency tells me the delay will be two hours. The TV monitor above the check-in counter indicates the delay will be one hour. Panicked travelers stream to the ticketing desks on floor below to see what can be done about their missed connecting flights out of Chicago. Throughout the afternoon the airport TV monitors and phone texts post updated, contradictory delay estimates. As evening approaches, I begin to panic myself, even though I have a full day's cushion, wondering whether the delays will proceed into tomorrow when I will begin to enter the mental territory of my dreams.

Around dinner time, it is established that the delayed plane is indeed en route and will arrive within minutes. The gate agent announces that the flight is oversold, and the standard incentives for surrendering one's seat are offered. My boarding pass indicates my seat has been assigned, which should assure me I will not be bumped, and I am not. The little plane—two seats on one side of the aisle, one seat on the other—makes its buzzing, malodorous way to Chicago's O'Hare airport. It is oppressively hot and humid in Chicago as I wait for a cab to take me to the little hotel I have booked in Lincoln Park, not far from the lake.

Checking into the hotel, I realize I have made a logistical mistake. The venue of my reading—The Book Cellar—is in Lincoln Square, which I mistakenly believed would be in the heart of Lincoln Park, a neighborhood of Chicago's near north side I know pretty well. The desk clerk informs me that Lincoln Square is not in Lincoln Park and is miles to the north. I had pictured myself walking to and from the book store, but no—it would be a twenty minute cab ride in light traffic. I decide to go to there right away. I want to get a feel for the place. Daughter Kate had told me Lincoln Square was "fun," a hodgepodge of with-it shops, bars and restaurants, one of which I had called earlier to book a late meal after the reading for whatever people known to me showed up. As it happened traffic was clotted as the cab made its way north. The Chicago Cubs, now leading the national league, were playing at home, and tens of thousands of people were making their way to Wrigley Field, which stands midway between Lincoln Park and Lincoln Square. So it took a half hour or so, mainly crawling along side streets to reach The Book Cellar.

It was muggy and hot—mid-nineties—as I stepped out of the cab. I walked only a block or so to reach the store, but I was perspiring uncomfortably as I made my way inside. Posters and fliers announcing new books and coming events were taped over the glass walls of the vestibule, and I stopped to see if a *Jonathan Force* poster was on view. I didn't see one and felt a wave of unease as I proceeded inside.

I was encouraged that in the early evening on a weekday The Book Cellar seemed alive with customers and staff. Floor-to-ceiling stacks and service counters surround a café and wine bar. I introduced myself to a pair of young, owlish clerks behind a counter, and they confirmed that my books had arrived and that tomorrow's reading was all set. They introduced me to the store owner and manager, Suzy, who was working through a stack of papers at a table in the café. She explained that the café tables and chairs would be rearranged in a way that would provide focus for tomorrow's reading. It occurred to me that I hadn't eaten since early morning, so I ordered a sandwich and a glass of wine. I wanted to settle myself after what I realized now was a jarring day of travel. I was touched that the young man at the café counter refused to take my money for the meal.

Back in my hotel room sleep would not come. Then I was visited by an especially disturbing can't-reach-my-destination travel dream, this one involving missing trains from my boyhood home in Arlington Heights, Illinois, into downtown Chicago. Awake in the small hours, I tried to picture who might show up at the reading, alert to the possibility that no one would. What had I been thinking accepting this invitation to come to Chicago, to a bookstore unknown to me, in a location unfamiliar to me and to the few scattered people I knew in the city? My reading / signing was scheduled from 6:00 p.m. to 8:00. Anyone driving there would have to fight Chicago's awful rush hour traffic. The people who still might remember me from my school days live in the northwest suburbs, an hour's drive or more, and I cannot imagine any urgency on their part that would impel them to make such an effort. My niece Kim, who lives with her family in Arlington, would be a certain attendee, but she had emailed a few days earlier to say she was performing in a community theater musical the week of my Book Cellar event. Daughter Kate would certainly come in from Oak Park, but without her husband, unless a baby sitter can be found. I could not rid my head of an image in which I am standing next to a table stacked with *The Three Lives of Jonathan Force* in The Book Cellar café, its tables and chairs empty save for the one in which Kate is sitting, her discomfort and embarrassment magnifying my own.

In the morning I stride out into the already sweltering city to find a promising place to eat breakfast and settle my thoughts. Over eggs and toast I check emails on my iPad and immediately sense an omen. A Chicago friend of my sister's who had heard about the reading wrote to say she was planning to come but had forgotten that it conflicted with her husband's art opening, so she wished me well...And then I remembered that my novelist friend Lynn who lives in Evanston had written to me a week prior saying she broke her foot on a hike and would try to come, but could not promise. I could not finish my breakfast. I took a long walk in punishing heat in the direction of the lake, sat for as long as I could bear it on a stone wall overlooking a torpid marina, then made my way back to my hotel, my clothes soaked through with perspiration.

Then in the early afternoon a better omen. My high school best friend Gary, who still lives in Arlington Heights, said he would be at The Book Cellar at least an hour early and was hoping for a chance to chat. I leave my hotel with plenty of time to spare, a good guess because it is another stop-and-wait crawl to Lincoln Square. I enter the bookstore to find not just Gary seated at a café table but his wife and an elderly couple I do not recognize. As I move to greet them I realize that it is Jack Martin, my high school English teacher of more than a half century ago, and his wife Helen. Gary has taken pains to drive them from their home in Arlington to Lincoln Square. They have ordered a chilled bottle of champagne, and an oppressive weight lifts from my midsection. In minutes we are cheerfully reacquainted. Jack —I have to will myself not to call him "Mr. Martin"—reminds me of a book report on *The Catcher in the Rye* I handed in to him when I was sixteen. Reading *Catcher* and composing that book report (in Holden's voice) were formative moments in my writing life, and I interrupt Jack to quote the report's opening line. I begin, "What I really mean is..." —and Jack interrupts me. "No," he said, "you wrote 'If you want to know the truth...' and finished the sentence. This after 55 years.

As six o'clock approached, the store staff began arranging the tables and chairs into a kind of bowl around a table stacked with my books and a space where I was to address the listeners. Then in close succession people started to arrive: another beloved friend, Greg, from even earlier school days and his wife, Diane. My foot-broken friend

Lynn hobbled into the café on crutches, trailed by her husband and a writing friend of hers. They had driven in through heavy traffic from Evanston. Then daughter Kate, looking beautiful, if flustered, as traffic had been heavy coming into the city from Oak Park. I was struck and pleased at Kate's easy presence among these figures from my boyhood. At one point she remarked of Jack Martin, "You can't have been my dad's high school teacher. You aren't old enough. In fact," she told the others, "none of you are old enough." Meanwhile, people unknown to me had slipped into the café and filled the available seats. Some had already purchased books. This was now beyond satisfactory. It was, I felt, going to be a pleasure.

And it was. The presence of these ancient friends plus the relief that we had assembled a respectable crowd gave me an adrenal boost that made it easy to talk about the book's origins and intentions. The passage I chose to read was from Book One of the trilogy, in which the elementary school-aged Jonathan recounts a series of romantic attachments to girls in his classes. I had read this passage before and was sure it contained enough humor and narrative tension to engage. I think I guessed right. There was the right kind of laughter and appreciative hums. When I was finished, I invited questions and comments, which were interesting to me and easy to respond to. I was especially gratified by the interest shown by listeners unknown to me. For the last twenty minutes or so, I signed books and chatted with the people who bought them.

About a dozen of us then proceeded down the street to a restaurant / pub where I had reserved a long table where we dined together. I felt an intense sweetness reminiscing and catching up with the Martins and my childhood friends. Gratitude cannot describe the feeling. At about eleven it began to rain hard, lightning and thunder rattling the windows of the pub. During a brief let-up my friends departed for their cars. Kate had parked some distance away, and though I had no umbrella, I walked her to her car and saw her safely off, then, sheltered in a doorway, called an Uber car to take me back to my hotel in Lincoln Park, where I arrived, for the second time that day, soaked to the skin.

July 25-August 1, 2016: Most of a week with Lulu and Celeste in Cleveland. We will celebrate Lulu's eleventh birthday. She is a little blue that there is no plan to return to the New York state finger lakes and the water parks she loves so much.

Instead, Celeste, with my blessing, has booked tickets to two productions in this summer's Niagara-on-the-Lake Shaw festival. Niagara-on-the-Lake is in southernmost Ontario a few miles over bridge from Buffalo, NY. I had hoped driving in and out would be painless, but it was not, especially exiting Canada for the States: hours of stalled lines waiting to go through customs, the questions from the agents extensive, conveying unnecessary unpleasantness. I think, as I have in the past: uniformed authority so often brings out the worst in people—but I also wonder if there are national security concerns or U.S.-Canada tensions I am unaware of.

In any event, traveling to Niagara-on the-Lake, slowed by border crossing, made for both long days and, at least for me, a feeling of being held captive in a setting at once charming and cloying. Niagara-on the-Lake's commercial center has been elaborately restored to a period suggesting the early twentieth century. Store and restaurant facades are so manicured, so pristine that the main thoroughfare, Queen Street, looks like a movie set for one of the '30s MGM musicals starring Judy Garland and Mickey Rooney. The town center gives way in all directions to shaded residential streets lined with immaculately restored Victorian houses, most of them displaying well-tended gardens, everything in opulent bloom on the cloudlessly sunny days we are there.

With a day in between, we see two shows, a matinee of a new treatment of *Alice in Wonderland* and a revival of Stephen Sondheim's *Sweeney Todd,* good choices, I think, for Lulu. I had heard from friends that the production values of Shaw Festival shows were very high, but I was not prepared for the dazzling stagecraft of Alice in Wonderland. I knew from the recent Broadway and national touring company shows I have seen that, with enough money and technical savvy, previously unimaginable visual effects could be created on stage—but I had never before seen the likes of this Alice in

Wonderland. In fact, as the reviewers noted, stagecraft overpowered the labored and overwrought script. In the opening scene a youthful Charles Dodgson / Lewis Carroll is rowing about in a lily-padded pond with the Liddell family, including the eponymous Alice. The dialog establishing the various characters and their relationship was lost to me because I was fascinated that the boat appeared to be rowing through real water enclosed by a benign jungle of greenery, swooping birds, and dragon flies. In a subsequent scene, not just Alice but we in the audience descended, as if riding a roller coaster, down the rabbit hole. True to the original text, Alice became too big and too small, the effect achieved as believably as in a film. But while Wonderland's fantastical characters—Mad Hatter, Cheshire Cat, Queen of Hearts— were stunningly costumed, the succession of visual images could not carry the ploddingly discursive lines the characters speak. At two and a half hours, the production was an hour too long. I can tell Lulu experienced the show as I did, her expression brightening with each special effect but going slack as the plot attempted to proceed. We leave the theater, stepping out into bright daylight, and I am aware of being awash in glittering, pleasing images but with no sense whatsoever that a story had been told.

The production of *Sweeney Todd* was also brilliantly mounted. I had seen a competent production years earlier in Cleveland which left an overall negative impression, due mainly to the wretched story line: a previously wronged ruffian escapes captivity and returns to the Victorian era London slums of his origin, where he establishes himself as a barber and, motivated vaguely by revenge, slits the throats of selected customers, their bodies descending by a specially designed passage into a cellar where they are butchered into material for meat pies sold in an attached eatery. Since the story first surfaced as a macabre penny dreadful in the 1840s under the title, "The String of Pearls," there have been many iterations prior to the Stephen Sondheim / Hugh Wheeler hit musical in 1979.

When I first saw it, I wondered why it was a hit. In the course of a protracted score—the show is more opera than musical comedy— there are only a few memorable musical phrases. Even with excellent enunciation on the part of the singers, Hugh Wheeler's sung dialog is too complex and meandering to be heard and understood. Despite those, to me, considerable limitations, the Shaw Festival production was impressive. The gruesome progression of events carried enough narrative tension to engage Lulu, for which I was grateful, especially since Alice and Wonderland had been so unsatisfying. The set was well conceived: a kind of industrial ruin lit in a gloomy palette of grays and urine yellows. There was a credible, hellish representation of the lower reaches of the barber shop, to which the bodies of murdered patrons would descend for butchering and incineration. And while the players admirably rose—or descended—to the expectations of their roles, a "successful" production of Sweeny Todd is a dubious achievement. Because there is nothing admirable or even very interesting about the Sweeny Todd's character that might mitigate his repulsive aims and conduct, the narrative engages solely in its portrayal of gruesome events. Unlike Victor Hugo's Jean Valjean, another unjustly imprisoned convict, no submerged inner decency impels Sweeney Todd in his impostor's return to liberty. So again, stepping back, even the most fully realized production of Sweeny Todd can only be—robust performances and inspired stagecraft notwithstanding—awful people doing a succession of awful things to no redemptive end. To "enjoy" Sweeney Todd is to submit oneself to a kind of unsavory voyeurism.

Back in Cleveland, Celeste and I decide to celebrate Lulu's eleventh birthday by booking passage for her and seven of her friends on a dinner cruise aboard the *Nautica Queen*. The *Nautica Queen* is a commodious motorized ferry fitted out to provide an elegant sit-down dinner and lounging space on two levels for about 150 passengers. The ship is docked on a siding of the Cuyahoga River in the industrial flats just west of the city center. Passengers board at six p.m., and shortly after the *Queen* clunks into gear and motors slowly around a serpentine bend of the river and out into Lake Erie. For three hours the ship traverses back and forth along the Cleveland waterfront as passengers drink, dine, dance, or lounge against the deck rails watching the lights of the city blink into being against the darkening sky.

I remember highly satisfying summer evenings in the company of friends aboard the *Nautica Queen* when I lived in Cleveland. As it turned out, the outing was a distinct hit with Lulu and her friends. Per Lulu's instructions the girlfriends all showed up in their fanciest dresses, their combined turnout creating an impression of fetching sophistication, though in their banter and exuberance they were still pre-teen, pre-sexual little girls. I was grateful that our group, composed of the eight girls, Celeste, and me, were so safely and conveniently contained in the confines of the boat. Our dining table served as a home base, but the girls could wander freely between decks, indoors or in the open air, without concern on my part that they would be lost or unsafe. After our dessert course, a disc jockey invited diners to take the floor and called out instructions to various line dances. The girls responded at once, most of them dancing without a pause until the ship returned to its mooring. Except for one or two lap-held infants, the girls were the only children aboard. High spirited but admirably well behaved, they charmed the other passengers in their dressed up, smartly coifed beauty. As all of us gathered to disembark, Celeste and I received effusive compliments on "our children." An older gentleman took me aside and confided that as their father I must have my hands full with such a spirited brood. But while not my brood, Lulu's friends were indeed spirited, an unbroken pleasure to be with, mannerly from their arrival to their effusive thanks on parting. My many iPhone and iPad photographs of the voyage confirm that they are, singly and together, lovely girls.

August 2-9, 2016: I drive directly from Cleveland to Marion—680 miles at high speed in the Mini, and I arrive in just nine and a half hours. The idea is that we Hawleys, or as many of us as can arrange it, will reconvene in the seaside town where the girls spent their childhood summers. Jesse and family are living in our village house. Kate and her girls will fly in from Chicago. Claire is too pregnant to manage the crosscountry flight from Oakland. With some bedroom doubling up, Jesse can accommodate Kate's family. M and I have arranged to lodge in the empty house of a cousin, Philip Dean, across the harbor from the village.

Though our Marion house—temporarily Jesse's—is cosy and situated at the heart of an almost too charming village center, there is for me a ghostly quality to Marion since M's parents died and the family house across the water was demolished, the property given over to conservancy. As I have reflected before, M's parents' house was probably the least grand in the line of gabled mansions fronting a grassy rise at the far side of Sippican Harbor. It had been a summertime paradise for me for forty years and for Kate, Jesse, and Claire since they were born. While M's parents were alive, the grounds of their property spilled into that of their adjacent cousins, The Saltonstalls and the Piersons, creating the effect of a single shared estate, the rolling lawns, waterfront bath houses, stables, tennis courts, docks and boats available to all at all times. When M's parents died, their property reverted to wild land. The Saltonstall and Pierson mansions were sold. Boundaries were restored, and with them a gated quiet descended.

The Dean cousins dwelled a mile or so down the coastal road and were integral to our Marion summer life. Hope Dean was M's mother's sister. She and her husband Phil, a wealthy Boston investor, summered in Marion and lived the rest of the year in a grand house in Brookline. The five Dean children—M's cousins— were frequent but not constant presences in our summer lives. Their property was its own self-contained estate, a walled-in, Spanish tiled complex including a main residence, a cottage, stables, boat house, and dock. Philip, the youngest of the cousins, has inherited the main house, while his older brother Peter, a designer of art furniture, inherited the stable complex, which he has renovated into a stunningly graceful residence.

Neither M nor I know Philip well, but the family ties have always been cordial, so it was not uncomfortable to ask if we could stay in his Marion house if it was vacant. As it happened, it was, and as we would soon see, understandably so.

Beginning in my early twenties, I spent quite a few of my summer days at the Deans' estate. They had an excellent, always available tennis court, and through my fifties I played a lot of tennis, as did M and her many cousins. The court's outer fence was surrounded by aromatic pines and shrubbery, but there was a sense of bracing salt air, as the waterfront and dock were just down the path. Our tennis outings consisted of many sets, followed invariably by a swim in the harbor or a chilled gin and tonic provided by M's Aunt Hope and Uncle Phil in the airy living room of the main house.

There was no trace of that airiness—or of anything else to summon up those past summers—in the Dean's house when we made our way inside. Outside, the grass had been recently mown, but the gardens were untended and the shrubbery so overgrown around the front entrance that we had to push through it get to the door. Inside the still air held the musty, faintly sour smell of neglect. The rooms were minimally furnished, and a bed had been made up in the master bedroom, but my immediate impression was of forlorn incoherence. Nothing in the sitting rooms invited one to sit down. It was airless and oppressively warm inside, so we attempted to open windows and sliding glass doors, but whether warped or rusted, they scraped in their tracks and resisted our efforts. As we settled in for the week, it became clear that any pleasures to be experienced in the course of our week in Marion were going to take place outside this house. There were no pleasing interior touches, no pictures on the wall or family photographs or knickknacks to suggest the imposition of anybody's taste or care. There were adequate furnishings—beds, tables, chairs. There was silverware, cookware, glasses and plates. Taps squeaked and, like the window sashes, resisted movement. There was a dark scar of rotted wood lining the kitchen sink. But these minor infelicities were not the cause of the strong aversion I felt. Objectively, a large, commodious house and grounds—a waterfront estate—had been provided to us at no cost. That it had been neglected, had literally seen better days, was not really a concern of M or of mine or of M's sister Lea who would join us for part of the week. It was something more subtle and deeper: a sense of lingering *death*, of the purpose of the place, of my belonging there, being profoundly over.

Out of the house, we passed a pleasant week, soporific days at Silver Shell beach searching for crabs with the grandchildren, intermittent dips in the August-soupy water of Buzzard's Bay, solitary

Kayak outings into Hammet's Cove, hikes around the perimeter of the village, chaotic evening meals cheerfully prepared by a rotation of talented cooks. It is good for me to see Kate and Jesse so fond of each other and of each other's children. It occurs to me that we may be making our own kind of generational mark in this ancient seaside place, the daily impressions, sights and sounds, imprinted more vividly in the minds of Leon, Alice, Anna, and Winifred than I could ever imagine.

August 17, 2016: My old University School student (class of '81) and now friend Michael Ruhlman reenters my life.

Mike has been much on my mind this year. At University School I taught him Western Civilization when he was a ninth grader. As he progressed through the school he determined he wanted to be a writer, and we arranged a year-long "fellowship" which allowed him to work with me one-on-one as he developed a collection of short stories. I was impressed with his earnestness as he approached his assignments, and it was clear that had the talent, the eye, and the drive to be a writer. He went on to Duke where he established a mentoring relationship under Reynolds Price, followed by a year with the New York Times, then other journalism stints before he got a book contract from Henry Holt to do a year-long chronicle of boys' experience in a boys' school— University School, of which I was then headmaster. I agreed to let Mike have open access to classes, activities, and, to the degree they were comfortable with it, the boys and faculty in their free time. In the course of that year, Mike attended my senior philosophy course every day, as well as an Advanced Placement senior English class and a ninth grade Western Civilization class. To his credit, he managed to establish himself as a serious, likable, and unintrusive presence among us as he went about his work.

I probably should have given more thought to what kind of book Mike might write about me and the school and what kinds of consequences it would have for my work. I liked Mike and trusted him. I think he liked me as well, although I sensed he wanted to grow past the student-teacher, child-adult aspect of our relationship. Before he took on the book project, he was doing magazine work in Cleveland and solicited a number of articles from me, mainly commentary on books and films. In the course of editing those pieces, he seemed to me energized by the structural role reversal. He had also remained close friends with a number of classmates who, under my headmastership, had been disciplined or otherwise annoyed by me, and he did not hesitate to let me know of their abiding hard feelings. So there might have been some murky oedipal dynamics at work as Mike composed what would become his book, *Boys Themselves.*

As it happened, the school year Mike chronicled, 1993-4, was fairly dramatic, in that it included more disciplinary crises and faculty concerns than usual. Because Mike had won the confidence of many older students, including those who had been disciplined, he was able to narrate their experiences from a close and—I felt—awfully sympathetic point of view. But otherwise, especially in his extensive and meticulous recreating of what actually transpired in classrooms, I thought his account of the year was impressive, even ground-breaking.

The book was not easy for me to read. Mike sent me a copy of the prepublication galleys, asking for impressions and corrections as to matters of fact. He also advised me "sit down" when I read it (as if I would read it standing up?), as there were likely to be passages that "upset me." The galleys arrived on a summer afternoon when school was not in session. I sat down to read at about four in the afternoon. I must have eaten dinner, though I cannot remember doing so, and otherwise read straight through until I finished at three in the morning. Nothing in what I could see was going to be a substantial book "upset" me, in the sense of being wildly inaccurate, unfair, or unkind, but the text did deliver a number of jolts.

My overriding response was *good work.* Reading the book brought back emotional currents from that school year which I had mostly suppressed, causing me, literally, to live those experiences again, including a few tense and even terrible moments. I had only one complaint. In an account of disciplinary measures I had taken with a boy who had savaged one of his teachers in a written document, Mike concluded with what I thought was too dark an assessment of the student body's reaction. In my recollection, the boys' resentment had gradually mellowed, as had the animus of the boy who was punished. Mike rejected my proposal that he reconsider. He accepted other, minor suggestions and corrections, including his considerable under-estimation of my church attendance.

My impression that Mike had written a substantial book was confirmed by a strong positive review in the *New York Times* Sunday Book Review. In the review, my work at the school was for the most part treated favorably by the reviewer, Beth Gutcheon, although I was struck by being termed "the iconoclastic Headmaster" of University School. In another passage, she wrote that in the course of the year "Hawley did not always cover himself in glory." Not for her treatment of me in the review, but for an unrelated personal reason, I found Beth Gutcheon's mailing address and wrote her a letter. In it I shared my responses, mostly praise, of her treatment of Mike's book, but also took the occasion to ask her a personal question I had wanted to ask her ever since I read her school novel, *Saying Grace*. I enjoyed the novel very much, a story set in a small, California independent school. In the course of a single, harrowing school year, the headmistress of the school goes through a series of agonizing crises and personal losses, ultimately reconfiguring her life. Not long into the book, it dawned on me that the story line was remarkably close to that of my first novel, *The Headmaster's Papers*. This conviction was strengthen-ed when I learned that Beth was married to Robin Clements, headmaster of a school much like the one evoked in *Saying Grace*. Looking back through my book correspondence, I found that Robin had written me a feeling letter about *The Headmaster's Papers*. What I wanted to know, but had previously been uncomfortable asking, was whether Beth had read *Headmaster's Papers* prior to writing her novel and—still more awkward to ask—had it been an influence. Beth wrote cheerfully back to say, yes, she had read *Headmaster's Papers*, that it had moved her profoundly—and that she would never tell me if it influenced her novel. She also indicated in her letter that she had personal ties in Cleveland, including people close to me and University School and proposed that we get together when she was next in town. We did, and have remained friends, have read each other's subsequent books in manuscript and, once, co-taught a summer writing workshop for teachers with writing ambitions—to which we invited Mike Ruhlman to make a guest presentation.

Mike has gone on to a considerable career as a writer. He followed *Boys Themselves* with *Making of a Chef*, a similar year-in-the-life treatment of The Culinary Institute of America in Poughkeepsie NY. This nicely observed study of cooking was especially close to Mike's heart, as he had become in his twenties an accomplished and adventurous cook himself. Over the years M and I have been appreciative guests at a number of *haute cuisine* dinners prepared by Mike. Sales of the first two books were sufficient to win Mike contracts for three successive books in the literary non-fiction genre. Inspired by the likes of John McPhee and Tracy Kidder, he wrote *Wooden Boats,* about the receding craft of building wooden sailboats. His next book, *House,* chronicled his purchase and restoration of a dilapidated but worthy old residence in Cleveland Heights. Perhaps his most ambitious undertaking, was *Walk on Water*, a study of infant heart surgery, an art so exacting that only a few people can do it, in effect creating a climate in which only a small number of the babies who need it can benefit. This was a hard book for Mike to write because it took him so far from anything like familiar turf. The book was respectfully reviewed both by critics and practitioners, but it did not sell well, possibly because general readers do not have the stomach for close observation of babies' open heart procedures.

Despite what looked to me like so much literary success, Mike, now with a young family, was in need of money. A relative sure thing, he found, was writing about cooking: the mastery of specific chefs, techniques, recipes. Both his journalism and subsequent cooking-related books have been widely praised and reliable money makers. Mike's cooking writing has enabled him to travel extensively on expense accounts and to network with culinary high rollers across the country and abroad. Mike's rangy, movie-star good looks have made him an appealing presence on camera, and with the rise of "foodie" culture in America, he has appeared on a number of TV cooking shows, most notably as one of the three judges of PBS's "Cooking Under Fire."

As Mike has come into his own as a writer, we have met periodically for lunches, cocktails, and dinners, enabling me to come to know his wife, Donna, and to follow the trajectories of their children, a daughter Addison, and a son James. Once, when Lulu was two or three, I was reclined on the floor with her in the Children's Books reading room of The Cleveland Heights Public Library when Mike, on some errand to do with his own children, was startled to see me. I had not seen him since the arrival of Lulu and moving to Vermont. I had not had occasion to discuss my affair with Celeste and the subsequent arrival of Lulu. I had assumed—correctly—that he had been a party to all the gossip surrounding that revelation in the University School world, but I had not thought to wonder what his own reaction was.

But when our eyes met in the library, I realized I should have been in better touch. Seeing me there with Lulu seemed to upset him, or at least confuse him. He had indeed heard about my situation—in fact, wildly inaccurate things about it. I think what unsettled him was what unsettled most younger people I knew, including my own children, as they tried to integrate what I had done. If, like Mike, they were creating a family life of their own and had believed, for good reason, that mine had been satisfying and exemplary, my straying from convention—an affair! a child!—could knock them off emotional balance. In ways they might not want to articulate, my behavior represented a kind of betrayal. There was certainly a sense of that in Mike's surprise at seeing me in the library and in the fumbling conversation that followed. He could not seem to take his eyes off Lulu who, happily immersed in a heap of picture books and toys, was a vision of contentment.

One thing Mike made clear that morning: he thought Lulu was "beautiful." In the clarifying, situation up-dating emails that followed, Mike repeated his impression that Lulu was a beautiful child, as in "and now you have this beautiful child."

Mike and I have kept in fairly regular touch since. About a year ago he made me aware that his marriage was collapsing. For years his daughter, a precocious beauty, had been disaffected and rebellious. Hints of relational tensions with his wife Donna had been dropped over the years. I remember Donna telling me and M in the course of before-dinner cocktails that it was hard being married to a man more beautiful than she was. It was a self-effacing joke, but there was little levity in the telling. As Mike made his way in the publishing and TV world, away from home often, in stimulating company and exotic places, I wondered how this played out at home. When he told me he and Donna were separated and proceeding to divorce, he registered the same kind of discomfort I sensed in the library with Lulu.

Even as Mike assured me there would be no repair, that he and Donna were finished, he seemed painfully uncomfortable. His mother and father divorced when he was a junior at University School. The foundation of our continuing relationship may have been our talks in my office as his family was breaking apart. As a boy Mike had been forthright and, to me, inspiring in declaring he wanted to fall in love and have a terrific family. He had asked me once how did you know when a girl was *the one.*

Mike confessed that he initiated the divorce. He had had an affair with a new love while staying in the New York condominium he and Donna had bought and fixed up as a *pied-a-terre.* According to Mike, Donna was furious and inconsolable. He acknowledged the guilt and shame he felt. He was anxious, but helplessly so, that his daughter and son were processing his departure through the filter of his furious wife. He assured me he was in love and that, for the time being, he had best not reveal with whom. My immediate speculation was that it must be someone famous.

In confiding all of this, he was physically agitated, radiating discomfort. Meeting for lunch or just for drinks, he drank more and faster than at any prior time we were together. I was worried about him, and given my own experience of marital dislocation and extra-marital passion, I wanted to be a helpful presence. In the course of a sequence of sessions with a psychologist I had consulted when I was first involved with Celeste, she, the therapist, told me, "You need to *unpack"*—meaning that I needed to set out in words what was happening in my troubled interior. Mike clearly needed to unpack, and I felt I could best serve as a non-judgmental, attentive witness to whatever he had to tell me about his evolving situation. I also sensed, given his agitated state, that it might be helpful to remind him of the importance of taking care of himself in very concrete ways: eating properly, drinking moderately, getting enough sleep, enough rest, enough quiet.

I shared with Mike the darkest moment of my own troubled past: driving down the mountain from Ripton to Middlebury on a brilliantly sunny day a few weeks after moving to Vermont. Lulu was newly born. M and I were raw in our struggles to integrate what had happened into our lives. Celeste was in panicked despair, feeling unsupported by anybody, cast off from her family, not knowing how she was going to sustain herself materially or otherwise. All of it was my fault. I remember registering the beauty of the morning, the spectacular dappled sunlight on the road and on rocks lining the mountain stream below me—and feeling: *this beauty no longer touches me* and that I would never be happy again. In time, as I have written previously, I lived through, grew through that condition into a saner, better one. I have since experienced more than a little happiness. I wanted Mike to know this was possible. He wanted to know how. I told him not to worry about having all the answers as he moved through his days. I told him what worked for me was "loving all the people" in my personal constellation, especially the ones who were hurting the most. A bromide certainly, but what I believed.

In the months following this conversation, Mike and I exchanged a few emails but we did not meet. His first published fiction, three novellas under one cover, titled *Short Measures*, had just appeared, and he had been invited to be a Fiction Fellow at this summer's Bread Loaf Writer's Conference, the campus of which is just a mile up the road from my house. When he got the news, he wrote asking if we could get together for a drink or a meal during the course of the conference. We settled on late afternoon cocktails at the house. A few days prior to that M and I went up to Bread Loaf to listen to Mike read from the new book. When I entered the auditorium, Mike was seated in the front row bent over his book, preparing his presentation. I tapped him on the head and said, "Hey—you better be good." Startled, it took him a moment to see that I was joking. He was as nervous as I had ever seen him. He was also uncomfortably nervous as he read, though he got through the excerpt he chose passably well. After the reading, he told me his "beloved" was coming up to join him at the conference and asked if she could join us for our scheduled cocktail.

In the intervening days M and I speculated at length as to whom the "beloved" might be. I had by now read Mike's *Short Measures* and had earlier read some of the material in manuscript. A good deal of all three stories involved a narrator rather like Mike coming to terms with old loves, loves that had come awkwardly to bear on the narrator's marriage. I knew enough about Mike's early lovers to suspect that one of them would soon to show up on his arm. It was also possible, I thought, given Mike's dashing good looks and eminence in the publishing / entertainment world, that he would bring some known celebrity, possibly a runway model. I imagined, in any event, a younger woman, someone decidedly un-wifely, un-Donna.

And so I was more than surprised—stunned—to see Mike moving across our lawn hand and hand with my old writing friend and former Bread Loaf colleague Ann Hood. *Ann Hood.* I have known Ann for thirty years. We first met at the Bread Loaf Writers Conference when I was invited there as a fiction fellow after the publication of *The Headmaster's Papers.* Ann had just published her debut novel, *Somewhere Off the Coast of Maine* and was, like me, on the junior rung of the Bread Loaf teaching staff. Though newly published and new staffer at Bread Loaf, Ann loomed large there from the outset. Blond, beautiful, extroverted, and drop dead sexy, she conveyed a misleading ditziness. Before she decided to dedicate herself to writing, she had been an airline stewardess, which was both easy and stimulating to imagine. Nothing about her in those first summers we were together at Bread Loaf suggested *writer,* though in truth the same could be said of quite a few of the writers I go to know there, which says something about what I knew about practicing writers.

Ann was fun, a pleasure to talk and joke with over drinks at Treman House, the staff lounge. I was under the impression that she was married, or at least partnered, to another Bread Loaf writer, Bob Reiss, but I was not sure. After a year or so of hearing her read from her work at Bread Loaf, I began reading her and was impressed by her ability to bring her characters to life, especially through their dialog. Toward the end of our time together at Bread Loaf we were paired together in an afternoon staff reading, which I think we both enjoyed. I remember giving her some story manuscripts I was working on and being impressed by what she saw and recommended. Beyond Bread Loaf we have managed not to lose touch. I have let her know when I like her new books, which I think have progressed from amusing to wrenchingly good. In 2013 she contributed a kind and helpful blurb to the back cover of my story cycle, *The Other World.*

I didn't know much about Ann's personal life, apart from widely known details, such as the devastating loss of her eleven-year-old daughter who was carried off in just a few days by a virus. I was dimly aware of failed marriages and believed, on the strength of a Bread Loaf reading she gave a few years back—"I married a Republican"—that she had settled down in Providence, Rhode Island, with a reliable husband. Ann's presence in my life—a daily presence, as it happens—is in the form of on-line scrabble ("Words With Friends"). We have sometimes a dozen games going at a time, and we exchange moves regularly throughout the day.

All that aside, Ann is the last person I expected to see walking hand-in-hand across my lawn with my former student Michael Ruhlman. Ann tells us a story: she has been invited to a small literary conference in Chagrin Falls, Ohio, where M and I used to live. Mike has also been invited. They had previously spoken just once, glancingly, at Bread Loaf when Mike was a scholarship student and Ann was senior staff. Mike had asked her a question, and she had answered as they passed on a walkway. Years later, in Chagrin Falls, Mike takes the podium to address the conferees. He sees Ann seated in the audience and says, "And there is Ann Hood, a woman I have been in love with for twenty years." Ann is giddily pleased at this remembrance. As I return to the sitting room having refreshed their gin-and-tonics, I admit I have forgotten whose is whose. Ann, again giddily, says "It's not as if we haven't exchanged fluids." I joke, "Too much information!" We all laugh, but it is.

Because Ann and I began at Bread Loaf together at the same point in our writing lives, I had assumed we were roughly the same age, but when I google into her biography, I see she is only 60, born in 1956, and thus only seven years older than Mike. I have been trying to let impressions settle.

August 31, 2016: Memory. At noon Karl and I are sitting opposite one another in a booth at Rosie's Restaurant just outside of Middlebury. Our waitress stops by to ask if we are ready to order. Karl is in the middle of a complicated story about his relatives in Maine. I am pretty sure I have heard it before, but decide not to let on. I tell the waiter we will need a few minutes. Karl tries to resume, but he has lost the thread. "What was I saying?" he asks. I tell him, "Maine relatives." He looks troubled, anxious. "I've lost it," he said, "Can't think what it was." A pause, then, "Why was I talking about my relatives?" I laughed and said I couldn't help him with that one. The waitress returns, asks what we would like. Karl starts to order but stops. He can't remember the name of the sandwich he usually orders. As he considers, I order my food. Karl then orders a tuna melt.

Later, at home at my desk, I muse on memory lapses, in particular my increasing inability to call to mind a person's name or a book title or an author well known to me. Usually the names will come back to me, as if floating up to the surface of a black, murky pool, but the delay could be a minute or more, thus taking the intended reference out of the conversation or stream of thought.

A week ago M and I were walking the Ripton Loop, a hike of about three miles, talking politics as we strode along. I was holding forth on Dick Cheney and how his financial interests had benefited obscenely from the Iraq war. I had reached a point in a sentence that required the name of the engineering firm Cheney had headed before becoming Vice President. Like Karl trying to summon up the name of the sandwich he wanted, I could not locate the word. I tried to be humorous about it, but I was annoyed. I kept saying, "It will come," but it didn't. I could not let it go. I said out loud: "*Sounds* like…" and uttered a bunch of words that did not help. More frustrated than I let on, I finished my thought about war profiteering and changed the subject. We walked on for about a half mile and were nearing home when, with no reflection, I blurted out *Halliburton.*

M and I now call all such cognitive blanks Halliburtons, which has provided a peculiar kind of relief. I told the Halliburton story to Karl, who has embraced the practice of labeling his lapses Halliburtons. Conversation with both M and Karl are now full of Halliburtons.

September 11-18, 2016: Back to Cleveland for a week, principally to see how Lulu is faring as a new sixth grader and Middle Schooler. The Roxboro Middle School stands only a few hundred yards adjacent to the Elementary School, where Lulu thrived in the care of six consecutive excellent teachers. The Middle School's reputation among parents is not strong. Both of Celeste's older children had unsatisfactory experiences at the school: theft of their belongings, the distraction of problematic children acting out, the inattention and ineffectiveness to some of their teachers.

Visiting the school and meeting with each of Lulu's teachers, my concerns are somewhat allayed. I am grateful that each of them set aside time to meet with me, as I had missed the school's Open House for parents, and they have next to no free time. My general impression was that her teachers are distinctive, likeable, experienced and committed to their work. In only a few weeks each of them seems to have gotten to know Lulu and to appreciate her quirks and enthusiasms. I was also reassured that the sixth graders are instructed in a contained section of the building and thus buffered, at least for a year, from the more clamorous ambience of the larger school. Lulu's test scores continue to qualify her for the school's Gifted program, which places her in advanced levels of some classes as well as in non-graded, Gifted-specific classes called Creative Thinking and Problem-

Solving.

If Lulu had not herself given me a very positive account of beginning this new school year, I think I would have been alarmed. Dropping her off in the morning and picking her up in the afternoon is sharply different than it was at the elementary School. Lulu at 11 is a slender four feet ten inches tall. She seems tiny as she emerges from the building, a little white mouse making her way among throngs of adult-sized, mostly black children. This is not an illusion or a projection on my part. The school is indeed mostly black, due to many white families, including those who professed to be pleased with the diversity of the Elementary School, enrolling their children in private and parochial schools for what they imagine to be their more consequential school years. Fortunately for Lulu, most of her friends continued with her into the Middle School. Only one, Willa, left to attend Hathaway Brown, one of University School's sister schools. Willa, as it happens, is the daughter of one of my former students, J.D., with whom I have established a cordial relationship since being unexpectedly reunited in the paternity of friends.

The fact is that Lulu, if she continues through the Middle School and High School, will do so as one of a minority of whites. There will be positive features to this experience. The school district's upper level instruction is still considered excellent and challenging. Contending and adjusting as a white student in a predominantly black school will, I think, prepare her to make her way in any and all future community environments. And there are negative features. Her present school building, Roxboro Middle School, though a rather handsome brick structure, is tired and shabby. Hallway carpets are soiled and stained. Ceiling tiles are missing or smudged with age. Painted surfaces need paint, wood-work generally nicked and chipped. Out of view, plumbing, wiring, and heating systems need to be replaced or repaired. Recognizing this, the district will next year take the school off-line for two years, so that Lulu and her schoolmates will attended classes on the site of another, already brim-filled Middle School to which scores of temporary classrooms—trailers—will be attached. At this point, even Lulu's teachers cannot say with certainty how the two schools' programs will meld over the two-year period while Roxboro is renovated.

In the course of the week, Celeste and I drive by new Middle School several times. It is just off a commercial highway, Cedar Road, a miles-long expanse of malls and strip retail. The temporary classroom units are already in place, appearing to me, yes, like a trailer park. Doubt and worry descend. I cannot possibly afford a private school tuition should the reality of Lulu's schooling become unacceptable. My mind begins to turn on improbable late-life money making prospects. At home, after school, Lulu cheers me up. She and her friends have heard the temporary classrooms are nice. She thinks the new arrangement might be fun. An adventure.

Wednesday evening I do a *Jonathan Force* reading and signing event at Longanberry Books. It has been less than a year since I read and signed books there for *Greeves Passing*. The close adjacency of these events is a little odd from a publishing standpoint, and I feel uneasy asking the Cleveland people I know to come again so soon. But as it happens, it was another satisfying outing. Part of the pleasure for me is that, as I have stated in previous entries, the store is spectacular. Its deceptively modest façade from the street gives no indication that it opens up to high ceilinged chamber after chamber of floor-to ceiling books: rare books, used books, new books. The innermost room, where I read, is set up in a comfortable arrangement of armchairs, sofas, and end tables. Wine and nibbles are on hand *gratis* before and after the reading.

I was surprised but not really disappointed that many of my old Cleveland acquaintances who attended the prior reading did not show up for this one, but in their place were a number of unexpected faces, including quite a contingent of University School people, including a former trustee, some teaching colleagues, school parents, and a number of former students. In all a good, receptive group. I was interested in the questions asked afterwards and because they made me think, I enjoyed answering them. The signing business lasted about forty-five minutes, which allowed for extended exchanges with some of my former students, two or three of whom, in their girth and receding hairlines, seemed impossibly old.

Celeste and Lulu attended, as the plan was to go out afterward to a festive meal, school night be damned. I was touched that Lulu stayed close by my side as I signed books and chatted with people. She wanted to know who these former figures in my life were, what they were like. Earlier in the week, Debbie and Les, a former colleague and her husband emailed me to tell me they were coming and would like to dine with me afterward. When I wrote back to say that would be fine and did they mind if Lulu and her mother joined us, they demurred, saying it might be better to get together for a drink at their house later in the week. I felt a little sting, but understood: for years in Cleveland they had been close friends of both M and me, and the still jarring fact of my affair with Celeste and the appearance of Lulu, although we have talked about it extensively since, made the prospect of dining with me in a new configuration uncomfortable for them. They did, however, greet me warmly at the pre-rereading reception. While we spoke, Lulu joined us from across the room and introduced herself charmingly. She was stylishly dressed up, and I could see that Debbie was taken with her, especially as Lulu told her, "I really like your scarf."

Free of my duties, Celeste, Lulu and I had a terrific meal at Mia Bella in Little Italy, each of us in high spirits. And, I might add, a gratifying number of books were sold, including quite a few old titles. Hail Loganberry Books.

September 22-24, 2016: Fifteen or twenty of my class of 1967 Middlebury classmates convene for a long weekend to prepare for what will be our fiftieth college reunion celebration this coming June. Our class's business is scheduled in concert with a homecoming of all of Middlebury's alumni, so that in addition to my classmates' planning sessions, there are massive gatherings of alums who hear from the college president, various administrators, and faculty about the state of the college, these sessions wrapped around a long Saturday afternoon of soccer and football games. With somewhat mixed feelings I participate in all of it, including restaurant dinners in town just for our class.

My feelings are mixed because while I am curious and for the most part eager to catch up with most of my classmates who are attending, I know from decades' experience in my own school and recent service on the college's Alumni Board, that the driving force of "reunion planning" is the college's anticipation that the reunion classes—especially the 50th year classes—will combine for an impressive gift.

Two women employed by the alumni office are assigned to guide us through our planning. One of them oversees what will be the "program" when we assemble in June. This will include a memorial service for the departed, various personal presentations and panels reflecting on what some of us have done with our lives, and a "yearbook" containing then and now photographs and biographical entries of those of us still living. The other alumni office staffer guides us through the process of "gift planning." This part of the business is unavoidably delicate and a little tense. Its major assumption is not stated outright: that we are, all of us, expected to give money, and as much as possible. This expectation necessarily raises the also unstated and uncomfortable issue of how much money each of us has, the shame of having less than others, the guilt of having more, the certain prospect that either our poverty or lack of generosity will be glaringly plain when it is time to declare what each of us is willing to give. All of the rhetoric on the college's part is about our having a wonderful time in June, but the energy driving the process is the college's determination to maximize the size of the class gift. The actual theater of this business as it is worked out in our dinners and meetings tends to make my skin crawl.

Our closing dinner is held in two elegant adjoining rooms of the Swift House Inn, an upscale lodging house and eatery in the heart of Middlebury. Outwardly we are celebrating the good work we have accomplished setting up our various committees and establishing "goals" for the gathering in June. We are called to attention after a liberal round of cocktails by the tinkling of a glass held by the classmate who has agreed to chair the Gift Committee. In the very words I heard for seventeen consecutive years in the course of presiding, as Headmaster, over similar dinners for fiftieth reunion classmates of University School, my classmate, eyes downcast in an awkward simulation of modesty, announces that an "anonymous donor" among us has issued a "challenge" such that if we collectively pledge a sum (I have forgotten, but I think several hundred thousand dollars), he or she will *match* it.

The expected gasp of surprise and appreciation is not heard. Undaunted, the Gift Committee Chairman announced that in response to the generous anonymous offer, he and five other classmates seated at his table were getting the challenge rolling by pledging ten thousand dollars. An uncomfortable moment of silence, then a tepid smattering of applause. Part of the reason for the silence and thinly offered applause may have been that the tables in the room where I was sitting were distanced by French doors from the Gift Chairman's room, so that we had to strain to hear what he was saying. The servers had also just refreshed our cocktails, and there was a related reluctance for us to mute what had been an amiable roar of cross table chat. But when we did quiet down enough to get the gist of what had been announced, I sat waiting with the rest of the group for the other hoped for foot to fall: the spontaneous rising of others to announce something like, "I'm in."

Apart from the five individuals previously announced, nobody else was, for the moment, in. The rooms quieted to silence. Then the alumni staffer assigned to Gifts, a diminutive, serious woman in her early thirties, rose and in a quiet, sad-sounding voice thanked all of us for the exciting development of the matching challenge and for our terrific start in meeting it. I could not help feeling very bad for her. Nothing had gone seriously amiss, but I knew she and the office must have had higher hopes. Her work was cut out for her.

For me, the real pleasure of the weekend was taking in what had become of the young men and women I had known, in various depths, a half century ago. As I experienced three years prior at my 50th high school reunion in Arlington Heights, Illinois, there was a dramatic variance in how attendees had aged. The Middlebury classmates assembled this weekend ranged in age from 70 to 73. Some had gained so much weight, skin so fallen from the former structure of their faces that I could not associate them with their earlier selves, even with the aid of name tags. It gave me a tinge of sadness to see one classmate, whom I remember for his very ruddy cheeks and impatient, driven approach to undergraduate business, doddering into our meetings with Parkinson's tremors, able to speak only with difficulty. He had been, like me, a school headmaster, and over the years we had exchanged a few letters and emails to do with school business. By contrast, certain others seemed to me miraculously unchanged, if anything improved. One of them, C, who was throughout my four years at Middlebury a good friend, though never, despite a "date" or two, an amorous one, appeared to be exactly the girl I had known. Dark, trim, and by all other measures attractive, she was a lively, amusing presence through all of our planning sessions. I was struck that she aroused in me a distinctly erotic response.

In fact, I experienced a stimulating lift as I felt myself regress with a number of the returnees, including some I had not seen or thought of in the fifty years since we graduated. Because I live locally, the house just off the road linking Middlebury's Bread Loaf and town campuses where our meetings were held, it was convenient for some of us to gather at my house for after-session drinks and chat. The weather had turned autumn-brisk, and it felt good to light a fire, drink, and reminisce. As in my response to C, I found myself helplessly falling into a mode of banter and kidding with the men seated around me as if they were still my dormitory mates and fraternity brothers. Even as we spoke, I felt in the presence of who they had so vividly been, not the gray and balding figures they have become. The lift of experiencing them this way confirms a conviction I formed years ago and which I believe may be really true: that the formative periods of our lives do not dim and die, supplanted by a succession of new ones; rather, I think, those conditions live on, interior shafts of an internal cable which over time become surrounded by new shafts of subsequent adaptations, the newest, most external of which shape our present consciousness. But triggered by the right memories or reacquaintance, the interior shaft is switched on, comes to life with the full range of original feeling. Renewing, thrilling when it happens.

September 25, 2016: On Sunday following our reunion business I am invited by the college to participate on a panel of writers to discuss before an audience of returning alumni the practical aspects of the writing life. The convener's prompts asked five of us to share how we sustain ourselves financially and otherwise if we are exclusively writers or, if we have day jobs, how do we find time to write. A faculty member moderated the session, but the event was conceived and hosted by the editorial staff of the college newspaper, *The Campus*. We panelists had been selected because we had as undergraduates worked on *The Campus*, some, like me, as Editor-in-Chief (1966-67), others as sub-editors. Two of the others chosen were investigative journalists five or ten years younger than I am, one a Vermonter writing for local papers, the other from Oakland CA, both of them left-leaning in their concerns. Seated next to me was a pleasant woman a few years behind me at the college. She had been a business writer but was now at work on a fantasy saga for young readers. The other panelist was a young man just two years out of Middlebury who was making his way as a sports journalist in New York.

I had no idea what this event would be like before I showed up, but it turned out to be lively. Entering the designated lecture hall, I was greeted by a tall, poised young woman who introduced herself as the present Editor-in Chief of *The Campus*. I joked with her about having held the post a half century prior. She was both composed and responsive as I, genuinely curious, asked her questions about how the paper, now a daily, was set up. The *Campus* staff, she said, now numbers sixty or more, and there are a dozen editors—more than the entire *Campus* staff in 1967:

As we got started, it was clear that my job was to discuss the challenge of working writing into the constraints of a day job, as the other four were more or less full-time writers. As they discussed the life style compromises they felt they had made—none of them was at all well off—I felt an unexpected pang of sympathy for them, along with unease about the comparatively safe and financially secure path I have taken. I had not expected the depth of these feelings. At one point, one of the investigative journalists was asked, in effect, how *do* you make a reasonable living as a serious free-lance writer? Is a livable income possible? Health insurance? Anything like a retirement pension? The writer paused to consider, then said bluntly, "Don't have children." There were some oohs and ahs at this and some laughter, but the writer went on to amplify. He had determined early on that he could not afford children on his earnings, nor would he have had the flexibility and mobility to do his work. I did not want to let this gloomy formula stand, so I said that as a former child, I hoped the audience might at least keep an open mind. Much laughter, including, thank God, from the childless journalist.

There may have been fifty or sixty in the audience, mixed ages but mostly, I would guess, men and women in their twenties and thirties. When we had formally finished, many of them stayed to ask individual questions or just to chat. I was touched by the courtesy and the intelligence of the young men and women who sought me out, reminding me again that I need to check my mounting crankiness about the college's new opulence and extent—at my snarkiest I have been calling it a spa. Because in every single encounter I have with current or recently graduated Middlebury students, I am struck by their open-ness, intelligence, and good will. Daughter Claire and her Middlebury friends are such people, people so well suited to and desperately needed in the world they are entering.

October, November 2016: There is a disquieting sameness to the days and weeks at home here in Ripton. The autumnal mood lingers into November, the foliage so vivid it draws me unexpectedly up and into it as I drive down the mountain into Middlebury or take my daily hikes. Walking the perimeter of the Bread Loaf campus I cannot resist trying to capture on my phone camera some semblance of what I am beholding. Though each picture fails to convey the depth and intensity of what is before me, I proceed only a few yards before another panorama impels me to try again. From an exercise standpoint, these walks have been ruined, but such is the beckoning power of the blaze of yellows and reds blanketing the huddled mountains, a message I cannot quite translate, a kind of enchantment.

The beyond calendar-pretty New England backdrop and the sameness of my days combine to give this passage a post-Real Life feeling. I continue to shop, to cook, to walk, to play the piano, to read. M and I meet at the same time, to the minute, for each meal, our talk turning almost entirely to the sickening prominence of Donald Trump in the printed and televised news. I try too hard to make each evening meal extraordinary, almost idiotically blocking what should by now be an obvious acknowledgement that M prefers an astringent diet of fresh produce, not my elaborately sauced and seasoned pastas and curries.

What were once refreshing breaks from routine—weekly lunches with Karl in Middlebury, working up songs to play for the old folks at Project Independence—have now become themselves routine. As I have noted periodically before, nearly everything I do each day feels like a pale *recurrence*. Even my week-long trips away to Cleveland to see Lulu and Celeste, while in atmosphere and rhythm clear breaks from my Vermont life, have become their own invariable routine: long mornings in the same stores, restocking provisions to Celeste's refrigerator and shelves, walking dogs up and down the same streets, the same meals out at the same restaurants, the same too long cocktail hour. Celeste and I both acknowledge that the steady rhythm of our time together is a healing antidote to the storms of our affair and its breakup, but like my weeks at home, the weeks in Cleveland are becoming sheer recurrence.

I find myself longing to reenter moments of my earlier life, to feel more of the arousal I experienced fleetingly in my encounters with my undergraduate classmates in the course of our reunion meetings. I am increasingly drawn to old photographs. Out of the blue, my high school friend Gary emailed me to tell me he had recently heard from Annabelle H., my late sister Binky's best friend growing up. Annabel and Binky were four classes ahead of me in school, so that when I was a high school freshman, Annabel was a senior. Almost a fixture in our house in those days, she was warm and receptive to me. She was also very beautiful in an unembellished way. I remember the sheen of her brown hair, which in the style of the day she wore in a pony tail. I think I always had a submerged crush on Annabel—to the point that, homesick and lonely in my first weeks at Middlebury College, I telephoned her in Arlington Heights from a pay phone in the village. She had gone on to work as a secretary in a brokerage firm in downtown Chicago, very much, it seemed to me, a grown woman. I remember stammering through what little I had to say. I don't think I made myself clear, but I wanted to ask her if she would consider a visit to Vermont.

This was not Gary's first mention of Annabel to me. I have not seen her since my sister's wedding in 1965, but knew she had married and shortly after contracted muscular sclerosis, becoming progressively diminished and then housebound. Gary would occasionally see her at a restaurant and stop to chat. In his email he told me he had seen her recently and that she wanted to hear from me. Sensing an urgency, I did call, but the phone rang on and on until the connection was lost. I wrote to tell Gary this, and he said she was probably alone when I called and was unable to pick up the phone. Before I could call again, my house phone rang and, not recognizing the number, I let it ring through our voice message prompt. We were eating dinner, and I suspected the call was some kind of solicitation. Then a female voice mentioning my name could be heard in the voice message, and I picked up the phone. It was Annabel. I felt something like an electric current and may have spoken a moment or two of gibberish. I was struck by her voice—wonderfully clear and familiar. I tried to picture her in her bed or wheelchair but could not do it. I did manage to say how glad I was to hear her voice. She asked about my life, how I was situated, and I briefly described my family, my children's whereabouts. We spoke for no more than ten minutes, during which I was so over-stimulated I realized I was almost shouting into the phone. M, who could not help overhearing from the dinner table, was alarmed when I returned. It took me minutes to settle down. It was, I think, an instance of the experience I have tried to describe in previous entries: that switching on of dormant shafts of prior life. On the phone with Annabel I had been overcome with too many sensations to carry on sensibly. The fact of her calling—her *wanting* to call. Her bell-clear voice unloosed a torrent of past sensations: the gloss of her lipstick, her dizzying, sweet scent, her pink cashmere sweater exposing at the neck the prim white scallops of a collar. My heightened awareness of her in my sister's room, a floor above me in our old house on 45 South Ridge, Arlington Heights, Illinois. The time I heard her ask my sister about a filthy joke she had heard at school but did not understand. For ten minutes on the telephone I was held in a cartoon-like bubble with Annabel, in 1959, as real and beautiful as she had been then.

And on go the sameness of my days. I feel very much the Grandpa as we drive to Marion for a long weekend with Jesse and family in the Marion House. Grandson Leon at nine is making his stage debut as one of the street urchins in the town production of *Oliver!* He and the show are surprisingly polished. M and I do a night of babysitting while Jesse and James attend a theatre production in Boston. Granddaughter Alice resists going to bed and wants only to talk and talk. I try not to let on, but I feel bone tired almost every minute I am in the house. I feel far from my familiar rooms, my slow, easy quiet routines. I feel—*old*, perhaps what 71 is supposed to feel like, but unsettling nonetheless.

November 9, 2016: M and I began watching the election returns on PBS after dinner. Based on what the major papers and polls had reported, I was confident that Hillary Clinton would defeat Trump and hoped that the victory margin would be significantly more decisive than the pundits had predicted. At no point over the ensuing six hours were my confidence or hopes affirmed, as "battleground state" after battleground state—Florida, Michigan, Wisconsin, Ohio—fell to Trump. M went to sleep on the sofa and up to bed some time after eleven, just after Trump was projected to win. I retired at about two a.m. when it appeared likely that even Pennsylvania, where for hours Clinton showed a narrow but promising lead, had gone for Trump, but I did not sleep. More than disbelief and disappointment were at work. The frustration—I might have called it outrage then—I had felt when George W. Bush was elected and then *re*-elected, was of an altogether different order from my gut reaction to the prospect of a President Trump. A transparently *awful man*, loathsome in his personal manner, spoken utterances, and in the conduct of his life had won the votes and allegiance of millions of Americans, enough to insure an electoral college victory. Donald Trump is by any standard I can recognize the ugliest possible American. At the most charitable, he is a cautionary tale about living in service of the wrong things, a figure of fun—and on track to become President of the United States.

Sometime between a brightening in the bedroom windows and 7 a.m. I dozed off. I awoke and, sickeningly, remembered. My first impulse was to open my iPad and scan the New York Times headlines for a signal that in the small hours some irregularity, some projection-defying tabulating error on behalf of the television networks had reversed the outcome, but no. I felt and still feel a sinking, all-body unease. Sneering, blustering, self-adoring images of Trump over the course of his campaign rise up like gaudy cartoons before the mind's eye. My thoughts turn to Trump's "base." I was aware that throughout the election cycle I had arrogantly and mistakenly underestimated the numbers and the determination of Trump supporters. Much of my discomfort, I can now see, is with my own failure to see what so many people liked about Trump and what so many people disliked about President Obama and Hillary Clinton. Today I can get no further than to conclude that I have badly misjudged the character of what looks to be at least half and may even be a majority of my countrymen. I do not for a minute believe I am mistaken in my certainty of Trump's awfulness, nor of the grace and intelligence of the departing Obamas. But feeling and thinking as I do in the face of this new *evidence* is quite literally sickening. Its immediate effect is to spin me apart from an unexamined sense of one-ness I felt for my fellow Americans, whoever they were, whatever their ethnicity, station, or type. On waking this morning I feel I must now proceed tentatively through a culture I do not really know or trust. I regress emotionally and fantasize: *Canada*, just an hour's drive to the north. I think *Vermont*, my tiny beloved republic, so many of us shot through with affection for our Bernie Sanders. So odd to feel like this after a long lifetime of feeling nothing like it. The way forward is clearly to act, to learn what I have obviously failed to see in the course of Trump's rise. And then, who knows, to man some kind of barricade. I haven't been out and about much yet, but I have checked in with startled, tearful daughters and other loved ones, and whether sustainable of not, I am feeling some comfort in not being alone in this new condition.

November 16, 2016: My old University School friend Keith writes to say he wants to meet for lunch in Hanover, New Hampshire, which is roughly midway between Ripton and Portland ME where he lives. We have done this several times. A few running hours of chaotic, rambling conversation gives both us a lift. Keith is British and confidently unconventional. Very bright with a good ear for languages and music, he attended King Edward's, a top British Grammar School, and Trinity Hall, Cambridge, a few years before I was at St. John's. He now lives like a hermit in a rental outbuilding on some kind of estate just outside of Portland. He spends his waking hours reading and watching obscure YouTube videos to do with Bing Crosby, British comics like Tony Hancock, and the Nazis. Now sober for years, he was a problematic alcoholic who could go months without drinking and then go on a tear, sometimes getting DUIs and into other kinds of trouble. He is a terrific mimic and has the quick wit and comic genius of Peter Cook and John Cleese. He was not always a manageable colleague at school, where he taught French and German, but over the years we grew close enough that he knew he could reveal his inner conflicts to me without censure on my part. At any rate, it is always good to see him.

Our rendezvous point was the lobby of the Hanover Inn, just across a green from the campus of Dartmouth College. I arrived first and was struck as I watched Keith get out of his car and make his way into the building that he had aged considerably in the year or so since I had seen him last. He had put on weight and with a monk's fringe of hair surrounding his baldness, his face looked a bit puffy. Somewhat stooped over, his head canted forward on his neck, there was an immediate impression of Churchill and of the actor Robert Morley. Once again, over the course of maybe three hours, we had a satisfying reconnection, with a lot of laughter and personal disclosure on Keith's part. He seemed to want to confess his late life conviction that he has not lived well. He has determined that he was unkind to many of his teaching colleagues and that his wit and sarcasm had served mainly to put them on edge and to diminish them. I considered this and told him honestly that I thought he was being overly hard on himself, that the colleagues he named as the objects of his derision mostly liked him and appreciated his eccentricity and humor. This was no mere mollification on my part. Keith's uninhibited, anarchic response to the things so many of us were concerned and worried about served to lighten the larger enterprise in what I think was a saving way. Nonetheless, I sensed his need to make an apologetic reckoning which, while unnecessary as far as I am concerned, was touching. I drove home to Ripton full of affection for him.

November 25-27, 2016: M and I decide to spend Thanksgiving day together with no guests or other outside diversions, a quiet pleasure which includes a salute to my grandmother's annual Thanksgiving meal: roast turkey, sage dressing, cranberry sauce, mashed potatoes, creamed onions, green beans, and for dessert a freshly baked apple pie.

Friday morning Jesse, James and their children arrive for the weekend, the inevitable improvisations and clatter an agreeable counterpoint to the order of our invariable daily routines. The weather turns warm and wet, making mush of what had been a lovely first snowfall. For a few Saturday afternoon hours the mush is a perfect medium for snowman construction, and we complete a satisfyingly eccentric pair, facial features composed of kitchen vegetables and flowers. Four-year-old Alice has arrived with a runny nose and croupy cough but is full of enthusiasm for all projects outdoors and in. As we put the finishing touches on the snow people it occurs to me that I am suddenly tired in an unfamiliar way, more a descending heaviness than fatigue. Then a too familiar scratchiness at the back of my throat. I do my best to remain cheerful, but I am on edge. I don't want a bout of bronchial malaise.

November 29, 2016: Urged by my sports entranced friend Karl, I leave my dinner table early and drive down to Middlebury to watch a basketball game. What would once have seemed a harmless and possibly even engaging diversion from my daily routines this time feels strange. I cannot place the outcome of the game—the importance of Middlebury's winning or losing—in any kind of relationship to other elements that now compose my life. I sense the possibility that if, as in previous seasons, I watch a sufficient number of games, I will become familiar with the look and then the names of the best Middlebury players, admire their skills, become reflexively partisan, want them to win. Or just as easily not.

As I watch the game, a Middlebury victory over Rensselaer Polytechnic Institute, I am aware that, except for the half-time pause, time passes agreeably enough. The Middlebury basketball program has been steadily rising for a decade, now vying annually for conference championships against other similar small colleges in New England. The level and the furious pace of play are impressive. Karl marvels at the difference in the present team's ability and that of the teams he played for a half century ago, teams whose chronically losing seasons may represent the nadir of the sport at Middlebury. For me the rise of basketball and of athletics generally at the college seem continuous with the mounting opulence of the place and with the gleaming extent of its facilities.

It is not effortful to maintain interest in the progress of the game, although I find myself stirred more by the prospect of a drink afterward with Karl in town. The gently nagging possibility that I might be merely filling time is due I think to the prominence that sitting at my desk writing has assumed in my life. Apart from anything that might become of it, my writing is now the core of my daily existence, without entirely eclipsing relationships to loved ones and the shifting calculus of managing my material circumstances. I spend most of my waking hours at my desk when I am home, and when diverted from steady bouts of writing by travel and other commitments, I begin to feel anxious and insubstantial.

I do not yet know what public value or interest anything I am writing, including this meandering reflection, may contain. I am confident, however, that in the time left to me I will be able to determine if anything in my new work is worth sharing / publishing. What impels me forward day to day is an unbidden urge to register what seizes my attention, what seems to matter. If there is some transpersonal aspect to any of it, I think, in time, I will recognize it. And it may take the mild diversion of a Division III college basketball game to remember that.

December 1-8, 2016: I drive west to celebrate a "Christmas Week" with Lulu and Celeste. Over the past month we have made elaborate plans for this visit, and I am looking forward to it, though concerned that what has become a runny nose and light but insistent cough might, as on more than a few past visits, spoil everything. The roads are relatively clear for most of the drive, light flurries and a few bouts of heavy rain. It was a pleasure and relief to give myself over to an audio broadcast of Graham Greene's *The End of the Affair,* read beautifully by Colin Firth.

Weeks earlier Lulu had surprised me by asking if we might get tickets to one of the holiday shows at downtown Cleveland's Playhouse Square: "Alan Cumming Sings Sappy Songs." I admire Cumming from what I have seen of his screen performances and stage work. He was much celebrated for his ghoulishly androgynous portrayal of the master of ceremonies in a recent Broadway revival of *Cabaret.* There is a sinister cast to the roles I had seen him in, but I wonder what possible appeal he might offer a sunny eleven-year-old girl. And what was with "singing sappy songs?" Apparently Lulu and Celeste had watched a good deal of the TV series *The Good Wife* in which Cumming played a Chicago political deal maker, and Lulu was fascinated by his character.

So following a fancy, rushed, and rather too expensive dinner downtown, we proceeded to the Palace Theater for what was, except for three accompanying musicians, Cumming's one-man show. I probably should have done some preliminary research, for as it happened the show, while at times touching and generally very funny, was not at all pitched to children. Unknown to me, Cumming can really sing, and the "sappy songs" were in fact show tunes and pop ballads that clearly moved him. In films and on television, I had seen him play various British and American characters with accents so flawlessly authentic that it did not occur to me that he is a Scot with an appealing but pronounced native burr. He is a wonderful raconteur, but the personal anecdotes he related were by turns wrenching and sexually explicit, not at all appropriate for Lulu. Cumming recounted his startling discovery in mid-life that the man he believed to be his cruelly abusive father was in fact not, causing Cumming to reconfigure everything he had assumed to be his nature. He talked at length about his fortunes as a gay lover, at one time summoning to the stage a former partner who had broken up with him, painfully, after a passionate interlude in New York while he was playing the lead in a revival of *Three Penny Opera*. The lover was / is not only a Clevelander but happened to be in town, so, a little awkwardly, he made his way from the audience up to the stage, embraced Cumming, waved, and returned to his seat.

I was by turns riveted and amused by Cumming's anecdotes and impressed by the power of his singing, but I am not sure what Lulu made of the evening. When asked, she said she "liked it," but she was hard to read, and she did not amplify the remark on the ride home or afterward. I think she was moved by the spectacle of the beautifully refurbished Palace Theater and the thrum of its enthusiastic sold-out crowd, but as we made our way haltingly to the exits, I did not see one other child.

Lulu's enthusiasm for a full weekend of Christmas shopping was by contrast unambiguous. Like Celeste, she has become a thoughtful gift-giver and card-sender. She had saved some money, and I gave her a bit more, so she had close to $200 to spend on gifts for her mother, siblings, and about a half dozen friends. She had given her projected gifts a good deal of thought and had written down a list designating recipients, intended gift, and the store where each gift was most likely to be found. Most of the stores were in the massive Beechwood Mall, a twenty minute drive east from Cleveland Heights. It being a weekend with Christmas looming, I should have realized that the mall would be teeming. Milling about shoulder to shoulder along the glittering corridors and store aisles, dulled by the punishing repetition of amplified carols and seasonal novelty songs, I descended at once into a state of mall stupefaction my years in Vermont had allowed me to forget.

I am touched that Lulu, at eleven, does not feel too old or too self-conscious to take my hand when we are out together in public. Given my tendency in malls to lose my physical bearings and to sink into a fuzzed, reptilian level of awareness, I would have been literally without direction had Lulu not confidently tugged me along from store to store, floor level to floor level, as we sought out the exact small stuffed animal or the precise scent of the bath oil Willa or Ella would treasure.

It occurred to me that Lulu had acquired the signature shopping habits of her mother. She compares potential purchases rigorously with all conceivable options. Final decisions entail handling and considering every alternative item on display. If she was seeking a particular glittery hair clip, each clip in the bin had to be regarded from all angles, held up to the light to assure its rightness. I might have known this would be the case when on previous trips to the grocery store, she would not approve my purchase of a carton of eggs until she had removed each egg from its indented housing and inspected it for possible cracks.

Also like her mother, Lulu is prone to tortured second guessing. It did not trouble her, as it did me, to stand in line for a quarter of an hour, intended purchase in hand, waiting to pay, and then to decide firmly that one of the *pastel* glittery hair clips would be better for Willa. No amount of phone message checking on my part or willed reveries of happier times in other settings succeeded in filling the time Lulu would spend selecting the more satisfactory clip before resuming our place at the back of the now longer line. Sometimes the need to replace or improve Lulu's gift selection would occur to her after we had left the store or even the mall, and there was for her no cheapening of the mission by settling for less, so back we go.

I love Lulu, and the emotional agony I feel even to be in a mall, much less retracing endless steps in one, gives way without much resistance to Lulu's genuine good will and good cheer. She is even *funny* in parrying my complaints. But I am tested by our several visits to the American Candle store.

Observing, correctly, that her mother takes great pleasure, especially in winter, lighting her sitting room and dining room with candles in the evening, Lulu resolves to buy her mother a large, aromatic, cylindrical many-wick candle, the likes of which she has seen her mother buy enthusiastically in the course of her many outings to thrift shops and garage sales. American Candle candles, Lulu has heard her mother say, are best quality. When at length we locate the store, it is almost impossible to enter because every aisle is chock-a-block with shoppers, but Lulu insists we wedge ourselves into the throng. Even unlit, the candles heaped in stacks on the shelves emit a confusing musk of vanilla, cinnamon, rose, lemon, chocolate cherry. After ten or fifteen minutes of shuffling through this atmosphere, nudging and prodding past overcoated strangers, I persuade Lulu that it is too unbearably crowded, and that we might have better luck if we returned later. Surprisingly she agrees, but we get no farther than the store entrance when she sees behind glass the *exact* candle her mother would want. It is a bright red cylinder the size of a coffee can. Arranged on top in a triangle are three black wicks. Lulu makes her way back into store, picks up the candle and sniffs—wonderful smile. This is the one!

I try to reenter the store myself, but the crowd of candle shoppers has grown to the point that they seem to be lining up outside the door waiting to get in. Lulu, candle in hand, finds me, takes my hand. She tells me it costs $40, but she thinks she has it. I ask the gentleman in front of me if he is in line to get into the store. No, he tells me with a defeated look, this is the line to pay the cashier. They only have one, he adds. I stand on my toes, crane my neck, jump a little in an attempt to see how far away the cashier's desk might be. I can't locate anything like a cashier, but I can see the line winding about the store for thirty or forty yards. I say, I hope not audibly, *for fucking candles?* I invite Lulu to consider the line. Isn't it ridiculous? Shouldn't we come back later—or better, find another store that has candles like that. I suggest that non-mall stores like T.J. Maxx and Marshalls will have those very candles, and for a lot less than $40. Lulu squeezes my hand. This is the right one, she tells me. We can wait. And we do. And her good-hearted, quiet determination to do exactly as she planned is irresistible, is admirable to me. Two full days of this.

The Friday night before I depart, Lulu has been invited to a friend's party, so Celeste and I attend a play, *Meeting Mr. Green*, staged by a community theater in Chagrin Falls and directed by my University School friend Carol Pribble. At school Carol had exhibited a positive genius for eliciting extraordinary performances from school age boys and girls. She had told me how much she liked this particular play, a two-man show about how a succession of encounters between a curmudgeonly old shut-in and a court-mandated social worker improbably change each of their lives

If not exactly eager, I was curious to return to Chagrin Falls where I had lived for fourteen years before becoming headmaster of University School. M and I chose the town for its charming separateness from the look and feel of Greater Cleveland and as a safe and pleasant setting to raise our children. While just a ten minute drive from the school's high school campus where I worked, the town, while functionally an outer suburb, was bounded by enough parkland and even some farmland to retain a charming semi-rural appearance. It was an easy enough commute to downtown so that Cleveland-based professionals and other well-to-do people with a taste for exurban living were able to support the town's shops and restaurants.

The town center is laid out on the pattern of New England villages, northeast Ohio having been the Western Reserve of colonial Massachusetts and Connecticut. The Chagrin River bisects the village center, its waterfall a pedestrian attraction in all weathers. A triangular village green with a band stand is surrounded by well-maintained nineteenth century facades of banks, shops, and eateries. Around one corner, adjacent to the little theater where we will see our play, is a rambling yellow clapboard inn, once operated by the parents of the poet Hart Crane, who as a boy worked at the popcorn shop, which still stands next to the bridge overlooking the falls. The streets leading into the village center are lined with well-maintained older homes, many of them Victorian with filigree woodwork adorning their porches and upstairs gables. The streets beyond "the historic district," including Orchard Street where we lived, were more varied and less grand, some of the residences and outbuildings down-at-heel remnants from the town's rural beginnings. For me and I think for our daughters when young, the town held a hint of the sweetness Norman Rockwell conveyed in his paintings of American town life.

The play, as I anticipated, was very good, both the elderly and youthful leads knowing exactly what the play wanted to achieve, a signature of Carol's directing. After the play, I stayed on to congratulate the actors, one of whom turned out to be a University School Spanish teacher. Some of his colleagues, including a few from my era, also gathered afterward, and briefly catching up with them on school matters was an unexpected pleasure.

Making my way to dinner at an upscale restaurant housed in the inn the Hart Crane family had once managed, it occurred to me that the town had been transformed in the decade I had been away. Spaces between and behind buildings in the commercial district had been filled in with new construction. Some of the buildings had added upper stories. I was told when I ordered tickets for the play that parking might be a problem, and though I arrived a half hour before curtain, it was a problem. Though a chilly evening, sidewalks were swarming with people, lines of them waiting to be admitted to familiar and unfamiliar restaurants, an unpleasant pitch to the noise inside, like barking. When we were seated at our table, I asked Celeste if she noticed anything distinctive about our fellow diners. She looked around and said, "Yes, a lot of money and they are all white." She might have added that most of them were also corpulent. I don't know if I projected onto them a pleased-with-themselves demeanor, but I had that impression, possibly carried over from my discussion with Carol and her colleagues after the play when they told me that in the school's mock presidential election, Trump had won by about the same margin—five or six per cent—that he had carried the state of Ohio. The news upset me, as I could not imagine any of the student bodies in my time at the school crediting the candidacy of someone like Trump. Like me, the teachers seemed discouraged by the student vote, which they attributed to the influence of the boys' parents. That too gave me pause. Would the majority of the parents I knew, even the wealthiest, have supported Trump? I wanted to think not, but as I scanned the faces of my fellow diners, something, if not outright smug, unmistakably *comfortable* suggested that the burgers of Chagrin Falls and the parents of boys able to afford to send their sons to University School might well be feeling great again.

While in Cleveland, the shallow cough that had set in the week prior persisted. It was not annoying enough to take me out of action, but I could tell Celeste was aware that I was not in top form. I drank lots of water and juice, washing down over-the-counter vitamin C tablets, but to little effect. On the drive east to Ripton, free of the effort to restrain the tickle and hack, I realized the old bronchial crud was upon me.

December 21-January 4, 2017: Cheerfully but insistently, daughter Claire has made it plain that M and I attend to her and visit her less often than we do her sisters. The "attend to" claim is unsupportable in that either M or I talk to Claire at some length *daily* on the telephone. It is true that since she has lived in the SF bay area, we tend to see her less often than we do her more proximate sisters. Claire's complaint comes appropriately leavened by her practicality and sense of humor, but it moved me sufficiently to surprise her by booking not just a visit but a *two-week* residence in her neighborhood over the Christmas holidays.

Securing a rental house a block away from Claire and Nick's Oakland apartment plus coast-to-coast plane tickets at holiday rates strained finances a bit, but the prospect of spending more time with Claire and getting more than a photographic sense of baby Levi elevated my mood—until the possibility and then certainty that I would show up sick, possibly even very sick, brought me down.

I did my best in the interval between my return from Cleveland and departure to Oakland to rest and eat sensibly. I don't think I had a fever, and there was nothing remotely painful, like a sore throat. Each night on retiring I swigged over-the-counter cough medicine to ease the cough tickle and aid sleep, but the cough persisted, more a hacking, honking embarrassment than anything debilitating. As always, M thought I should see a doctor. As always, I could not imagine what a doctor could do.

As our departure loomed I determined that, Claire's expectations being what they were, my condition did not warrant aborting the trip. My immediate dread was the long flight. I knew that even with the aid of cough syrup and lozenges, I would cough on the plane. Vivid images of past flights in a similar condition surfaced: rightly resentful seatmates contorting themselves to distance their faces from my steady eruptions. And in the event, the flight went exactly as I thought, adjacent passengers resentful and tense as I coughed and coughed. Because of runway delays and heavy head winds, what is usually a five hour flight from Boston to San Francisco took nearly seven.

Our rental house when we arrived was substantial and commodious but furnished with peculiar dark heavy pieces. There was a huge mirror framed by four rough bundles of sticks tied together at right angles with rope. Primitive nonrepresentational paintings rendered in angry looking slashes made me reflexively avert my eyes. When we entered the house the air was dank and musty from lack of ventilation. M and I were both baffled by a complicated thermostat that involved concentric circles of dials that had to be depressed to specific depths in order to activate fans and regulate the temperature. Table lamps of very low wattage cast a gloom over the place, although in fairness my travel fatigue and hacking cough may have inclined me to gloom had I made my way into a luxury suite at The Four Seasons.

It further weighed on me that I would not be able to put myself in any kind of convalescent mode. Our stay in Oakland had been conceived as a Claire-centered lark, but it had grown complicated. My sister Ginny, who as a single woman living alone tends to dread all holidays, decided at Claire's urging to join us, and she would be arriving the following day. Then M's sister Lea, also a single woman living alone, wondered if she too could stay with us for Christmas week. When Ginny announced her willingness to come, there were a number of conditions she insisted be met, including that her room have its own bath and that there would be no other guests. I gingerly floated the possible exception of Lea to Ginny, and to our relief she said that would be fine, as she rather likes Lea. Ginny however let us know she would not be fine sharing lodgings with Nick's parents, who planned to come to Oakland over New Year's and hoped to stay with us. The awkwardness created by this clash of expectations was averted when Ginny made it clear she would be flying home before Nick's parents arrive. Had I been in robust good health, the prospect of a full, albeit eccentric, house would have been a positive prospect, but in my diminished condition I could foresee only not enough quiet, not enough rest, and a lot of coughing behind closed doors.

In all it was a strange but deepening experience to feel so completely abstracted from anything familiar. I never got used to the house, which while certainly roomy enough and sufficiently stocked with everything necessary for cooking and bathing, was grotesquely furnished. None of the several, oddly configured seating areas was comfortable. The *objets d'art* atop ledges and end tables seemed to have been chosen to confound. There were glassed in terrarium-like boxes filled with only dirt and stones. Large ugly terra cotta vases held stalks of long dead fronds. The building itself was, like others on the steeply inclined street, solidly built, probably a century old. High ceilings, dark woodwork, and the size of the sitting rooms suggested prior, grander days. Since we could never to manage to prevent the temperature inside from feeling too warm or too cold, my reflexive impulse from waking onward was to get outside, cough notwithstanding.

After a day or two making my way to and from Claire and Nick's apartment and after a few exploratory walks, I was able to orient myself in what the locals call the Piedmont section of Oakland. Except to drive through it on my way to somewhere else, I had no fixed impression of Oakland, despite having been to San Francisco dozens of times over the past half century. In my imagination Oakland stood in relation to San Francisco as Brooklyn stood to Manhattan: a less substantial but habitable adjacency. It should have occurred to me that being only a bridge span's distance from San Francisco, it would share its dramatic volcanic terrain. Walking to and from Claire's apartment, walking to the shops along Piedmont Avenue, walking anywhere in Oakland meant steep inclines and descents. Despite my bronchial troubles I did quite a bit of walking over the course of my stay. Claire's apartment is too small for all of us to assemble at the same time, so most meals and all evening meals were taken at our house, necessitating for me many trips, on foot, to the supermarket, two and sometimes even three per day. And while I was mainly glad for the exercise and pleased with myself for preparing what I thought were quite a few satisfying dinners, it also occurred to me that, between groceries and cocktail provisions, I was spending a lot of money.

I enjoyed preparing the evening meal. The prospect of extended "company" carried the invigorating anticipation of pleasing them. Our cocktail hour before dinner was reliably satisfying. Nibbling good cheeses, sipping our drinks and generally coming to rest and into collective focus reassured me every evening that it was right to have left home and to come here. Everybody got on well, had ample opportunity to adore the baby, did his and her best to pitch in. My poor sister showed up with the first stages of what turned out to be a miserable bug: chills and fever and a cough deeper than mine. She did her best to rally, but despite long silent bouts in her room under heavy blankets she was seriously unwell. More I think for psychosomatic reasons than any actual transmission of germs, my condition deteriorated with my sister's arrival. Several nights running I awoke with a burning cough, sweated through the bedding. I did not take my temperature but I knew I had one. Even after Ginny returned home to Glendale, I stayed inside to rest while the others went on hikes and excursions.

Not for a day in the course of the fifteen we spent in Oakland did my cough abate. Over the New Year's weekend, when Nick's parents, the Benjamins, were houseguests, I went along with the group to the de Young museum but could not enjoy it for my bronchial discomfort. Two or three times I had to exit the building or find a quiet place apart to relieve a coughing fit. That afternoon the temperature rose into the 70s, so we decided to walk the botanical gardens surrounding the museum. Not wanting to call attention to my cough, I strode out ahead on the garden trail and did not realize until I had circled back to the museum entrance that I had lost contact with the others. When M finally located me, she was upset and uncharacteristically angry, confirming what I am sure was the overall awfulness of my company.

A few days before our flight home, I determined, with no high hopes, to see a doctor. I located an urgent care center across the city, and they agreed to see me right away. I took a cab alone to the facility, an anonymous storefront on a desolate block of mostly boarded up concerns. Inside, a narrow lobby with a few metal chairs was separated from whatever medical business was taking place by a counter with glass windows through which those seeking care presented their circumstances and proof of insurance to receptionists. A few minutes after signing in, I was escorted behind the counter to a cubicle and instructed to wait. I waited for about a half hour, and then a young Asian woman greeted me and introduced herself and her position, which went by me in a blur. I heard nothing like "doctor." She regarded me cautiously but seemed to register my concern about the duration of my cough. It was probably clarifying that I coughed a good deal while explaining. She left me in the cubicle for fifteen minutes or so, then returned wheeling in an apparatus containing a mask which, when I strapped it on over my mouth and nose, emitted a mist she said would open my bronchial passages. She examined my mouth and throat and listened through a stethoscope to my breathing from a number of different points on my chest and back. Because she heard what she said was a "crackle" at the base of one of my lungs, she set up an ex-ray in a chamber down the corridor. After another solitary spell in the first cubicle inhaling mist, the young woman returned and told me that while my breathing "efficiency" was excellent, my blood pressure was fine, and that I had no fever, there was visible congestion in my lungs and that she was prescribing a cough suppressant, an inhaler, and a course of antibiotics. I left the facility with a distinct feeling that, while there had been nothing warm or effusive in the young Asian woman's manner, I had been looked after attentively—cared for.

I filled the prescription at a pharmacy near the house, and set about taking the medicines as instructed. And while I did not feel detectably different or cough less during my remaining days in Oakland, my spirits brightened considerably, and I began almost to enjoy myself. I had not been acknowledging that just below surface consciousness I had been reckoning with the possibility that my condition was serious, even mortal.

January 6-12, 2017: As always, good to be home in Ripton, good to be solitary in quiet, familiar rooms, good to work through the correspondence and other obligations piled on my desk. Though relieved of the strain of trying to conceal or make light of my cough in the company of others, the cough has not gone away. Since I have taken the full course of the antibiotic prescribed in Oakland, I make an appointment to see my primary care doctor, a new one assigned to me when the wonderfully unexcitable William Barrett, my doctor of several years, retired. The new doctor, Dr. Beauregard, is a big, rangy, extroverted man in his forties. He seems likable enough, but he cannot seem to sit still or to stop moving while on his feet. I tell him my problem: a cough that has persisted for over a month. To my surprise, he has a transcript of my exam at the Oakland urgent care center, the results of which he summarizes impressively. He listens through his stethoscope to my lungs from six or seven places on my back and chest. A nurse has already taken my temperature and blood pressure. He hears a faint rattling in the same place the Asian woman in Oakland did. Otherwise, he determines, I seem to be breathing pretty well. He asks me what antibiotics I am allergic to, and I tell him penicillin. He asks how bad my reaction to it is. I tell him very bad: hives, liver and kidneys shut down, I pass blood. Good to know, he says, and prescribes a structurally different antibiotic, which he is confident will work. He does not seem at all concerned that there is something badly wrong with me, which lifts my spirits. Driving off to fill my prescription, I decide I like Dr. Beauregard. My appointment has taken eight minutes.

January 13, 2016: This time the prescribed antibiotic did the trick, and by week's end in a genuinely celebratory mood I accompanied M to the opening of a month-long show of her paintings at the Middlebury Town Hall Gallery. Earlier in the week I had helped haul her paintings to the gallery and, with the gallery director, determine which picture went where. M's paintings have been hung in group exhibits in past years, but this was her first solo show there. When finally arranged and lighted, the work looked impressive to me. Having seen the pictures often in the course of their creation, I was surprised at the drama they conveyed when viewed from farther off than I was able to stand in M's studio. There were about three dozen images in all, Vermont and Cape Cod landscapes and a few portraits. It had been determined that I would play ambient piano music for the two-hour duration of the show, after which with selected friends, we would go out for dinner in town.

In the event, I was glad to be playing the piano—Gershwin, Porter, slightly jazzy American song book standards —which gave me something to do over the two-hour course of the opening other than drink the tangy white wine being passed around and chat for longer than I wanted to with the people who turned up. M was pleased that there was an appreciative turnout—and at least one buyer. My happiest moment occurred when my distinguished musical friends, the Fannings—Diana, a world class concert pianist and Emory, an organ scholar and for decades chairman of Middlebury College's music department—*both* confided to me that they thought my playing was really good. An additional delight: Emory, who at 80 has an impish side, made it known to me that he had a pocketful of tiny gin bottles, should I care to approximate a martini instead of the awful wine. Preferring to keep a level head and not wanting to risk sloppy playing, I thanked him but declined.

From the opening ten of us proceeded across town to Fire and Ice Restaurant where I had reserved a table. High spirits were established at the outset, much of the talk in deserved praise of M's work. We were seated around a large round table, and it occurred to me that I genuinely liked everybody in the group. Our great friend Sarah, also a painter and a distinct beauty, sat on my right. She is not much of a drinker, rarely able to finish a glass of wine, but she seemed especially exuberant, every now and then taking a forkful of boiled potatoes from my plate, laughing each time at the impertinence. I was stimulated by this little flirtation. At one point I asked if she would like the *rest* of my potatoes. *Our* potatoes, she said. An excellent evening.

January 16-23, 2017: Marc Estrin, my Vermont publisher, has written to his Fomite Press authors soliciting essays in response to the calamitous national political picture as Trump prepares to take office. A godsend, because without quite realizing it I have been spinning mental wheels for weeks, constructing Trump-related complaints and arguments, often in the sleepless small hours of the morning. To write something down should be clarifying. There are three arguments I want to make.

I was slow to acknowledge there is a base composed of *millions* who support Trump, I want to identify their several motivations— specifically, who feels so marginalized, so resentful of the prevailing neoliberal political order that they are able to filter out Trump's transparent narcissism, childish mendacity, mental vacuity, and overall personal awfulness in order to advance—what? The right to keep and use assault weapons. That no one may have an abortion. That Muslims and Mexicans will be kept out. That obsolete and unnecessary jobs will be restored, jobs like tightening bolts on assembly lines and mining coal. Uneducated, unneeded white males apparently require no awfulness filter. They actually like and admire Trump: all that money, his name in gold on huge shiny buildings, unapologetic sexual aggression, a man who says, tweets whatever comes into his head, tells is like it is (in that head).

So: millions of dim white males have lost scholastic and economic ground, lost it to more resilient females, to bewildering technology, to robots, to menial jobs shipped abroad. Dim white males have become *losers* with an unarticulated dream of becoming great again. *Again.* Then there are the women held in sway of such men. Also factored in is the unacknowledged but mightily present racism that wants to obliterate the fact that Obama rose to the presidency, resentment that he did not fail, that he and his wife were even *impressive* in their respective roles, that the Obama *name* was on things, like the national health care system. To those so driven, Trump is nothing short of vindication. Factored in, too, is antipathy for Hillary Clinton, fed by several streams: outright misogyny and dread of a confident, capable woman in charge; contempt for an educated, wealthy neoliberal white woman offering herself as a champion of labor, minorities, and the poor; and finally, an elusive, unconvincing aspect of her public persona, a strange, warring combination of entitlement and lack of confidence. This latter impression could be fueled by my own unacknowledged misogyny, but I hope not. Once Bernie Sanders conceded the Democratic nomination to H, I was mad gung-ho for her to prevail over Trump, especially after she managed with impressive grace three excruciating, seemingly endless televised debates with Trump at his most reptilian.

And though they could not have carried the day by themselves, the Wealthy, ranging from the comfortable to the billionaire moguls, did their part, often cynically, to advance Trump, along with mainstream Republicans willing to endure a measure of Trump awfulness in order to secure and enlarge their holdings.

Essay Number One will consider Trump's emergence as a consequence of stalled, if not outright failed, masculinity.

I also want to get below the distracting surface of the crazy-making emergence of outright lying as an intentional, unapologetic political tactic on the part of Trump and his 'team.' Between the preposterous, provably false assertions—"thousands and thousands of Muslims were cheering triumphantly on the streets of Jersey City after the Twin Towers fell on 9/11"—and belligerent denial of established facts, there is a real possibility of what some pundits are calling a "post-truth" culture. Post-*truth*. As if there are no clear cautionary lessons at hand? Goebbels / Hitler, Stalin, Mao? How prophetic the dying Clive James' big book, *Cultural Amnesia*—the very idea that in less than a century we could forget who, how many, and *what* was lost to no-truth totalitarianism.

When I am finished with that, I want to explore how the daily awfulness of Trump has created a cultural climate that not only feels like, but maybe is, a genuine pathology: that a sick president and a sick regime are making citizens physically and mentally ill. That proposition can be supported by Plato's and Aristotle's notion that the citizen is developmentally *completed* by the polis of which he is a member: a just, functional polis enables citizens to cooperate and thrive; an unjust dysfunctional polis makes citizens antagonistic and sick.

We will see.

January 25, 2016: I am summoned, along with a Middlebury classmate, Margaret, to a meeting at the college alumni office to plan the memorial service for departed members of our class. The service will be the centerpiece of our 50th reunion weekend in June. I agreed to help plan the ceremony—occasional music, what will be said, who will say it—because I was moved by the service held for the class of 1965 two years ago to which I contributed some piano accompaniment. In advance of our meeting, I wrote up a sequence of presenters we might invite to reflect and some suggested musical offerings. Lyn, the alumni staffer responsible for shepherding us through the reunion weekend, and Margaret were excessively grateful for this not very demanding gesture on my part. In the decade since leaving University School I had forgotten that planning any kind of formal occasion is for many people, especially nice, gentle people, daunting. Such people are easily overwhelmed by concerns that their ideas might exclude, offend, or otherwise not measure up to somebody's expectations. Mired in such concerns, planners resist closure, explore every imaginable alternative, and generate maddening complexity. A firm, clear proposal spared us hours of deliberating over what should we do and who should do it, leaving only the easily dispatched job of contacting the presenters to confirm their participation. That matter quickly settled, we fell into a relieved, almost jubilant mood and departed well ahead of the hour Lyn had proposed our meeting would adjourn. Driving home to Ripton I could not quiet swirling memories of endless, airless University School afternoons and evenings in which I presided over colleagues, trustees, and parents attempting to plan something.

February 3, 2017: From out of nowhere, C, a former student I had not seen or thought about for forty years, sought me out on Facebook, first asking to be a "friend," then sending me a series of personal messages asking me if I had kept up with various of his classmates and teachers and would I please share what I knew. His messages to me were intelligent and well written, and there was something insistent in their tone.

I have mixed feelings about Facebook generally and have learned to be cautious about "friending" people not well known to me, due to the tedium of reading what are so often deadening posts about meals enjoyed, eccentric pets, vacation travels. But despite the dimness of my recollection —when he first contacted me, I could not confidently place C within a decade of his time at University School—he had been a distinctive presence in the school. I could picture him, remember him. He was a wiry, muscular boy who sat and stood erect. His facial features had a bulldog aspect, an expression of determination bordering on combativeness. I remember him as bright and well spoken, a fixture in his class's brainy set. He would remind me that I had directed him in a production of "Beyond the Fringe," the satirical review that introduced the youthful Dudley Moore, Peter Cook, Jonathan Miller and Alan Bennett first to London and then New York audiences. My abiding mental image of C is as a distance runner on the school's track and crosscountry teams. He was a strong runner, the best of his year. The force of his stride and agonized facial contortions as he ran conveyed that the exertion, however awful, was necessary for him.

Through a series of Facebook messages and emails, we located each other geographically, C in a suburb north of Boston, I in Ripton. He alluded to a wife who was a Canadian citizen and told me he frequently drove through Vermont on his way to and from Quebec, and did I want to meet for lunch one day. His persistence, first in making contact and now wanting to meet face to face, suggested that something might be troubling him, that he might be seeking help.

This turned out to be correct. I proposed lunch at a restaurant easy to find on the traffic circle in the center of Middlebury. I arrived first and from my window table kept an eye out for a man in his fifties who might bear a fleeting resemblance to the earnest distance runner he had been forty years ago. As it happened, I recognized him immediately as he drove past in search of a place to park. The bulldog visage, an expression of troubled concentration.

He strode into the restaurant, and we shook hands. He was still rangy but now with a bit of a paunch. He registered no special pleasure in greeting me. He seemed on edge. I asked him to catch me up, tell me what he did for work. He described a series of jobs, something to do with managing accounts at a Boston bank, a succession of computer tech jobs evaluating new software. I got the sense that he had been let go from some of the prior positions. There had been spells of unemployment. I had not known his family well when he was in school, but I had the impression that his parents, like most who sent boys to University School, were comfortably well off. C did not look prosperous.

I asked him if he was still a runner. He told me no, he was no longer strong enough and went on to explain that he was in poor health, the extent of which took a long time to explain. As a young man, possibly beginning in college, he had a series of mental breakdowns for which the only effective medicine was librium, which he took in heavy doses for more than a decade. The librium destroyed one of his kidneys altogether and damaged the other to the extent that he is on a waiting list for a kidney transplant. While he waits, his blood is cleansed nightly by a dialysis apparatus set up in his home. He explained that his frequent trips to Quebec were due to his plans to set up residence there, something he is able to do because he is married to a Canadian citizen. Canada's health care will apparently enable him to afford the kidney transplant, the procedure apparently out of the financial question in the US. C was direct and reasonably composed telling me this. Nothing about him suggested weakness or illness. He ordered and ate a fairly heavy meal.

I expressed concern. Were there (considering his lunch, which I doubted I could comfortably digest) dietary restrictions? Could he sleep? How was he able to work? Late in his life he had fathered his first child. How was that going? He seemed glad to be asked. There were problems on all fronts, and sleep was indeed an issue, since he suffered from sleep apnea but could not wear the prescribed nocturnal mask, which opens breathing passages by forcing oxygen generated by a bedside pump into mouth and nose. C found that when connected to both the dialysis and breathing machines he was unable change his position in bed, so he has abandoned the apnea device and tries to keep breathing by sleeping on his side. Diagnosed with sleep apnea myself and unable to sleep without a jaw-protruding mouth guard, I asked C if sleeping on his side worked. He said not very well, that he was now prone to daytime narcolepsy, which worried him when driving any distance.

The amount and severity of his various troubles startled me. C did not complain about his condition, but he did not need to. When he told me about prescribed librium destroying his kidneys, I asked if there was any kind of actionable malpractice. He said he had explored the possibility with a lawyer, but suing would cost money he did not have. His doctor told him that, whatever the devastating side effects, librium had been the only drug that relieved his condition. I asked C to describe his condition, and he told me he was bipolar and that before librium he had wanted to kill himself.

C asked me if I was aware that there were multiple suicides and much mental illness in his extended family and that his father had died when C was eight from acute alcoholism. I did not know, had not known. For me C had been a dogged, competent scholar, rather blunt in manner, a driven long distance runner, a boy easier to respect than to warm to.

Now, at the restaurant, I felt that C wanted something from me, and I did my best to be a sympathetic witness. He wanted to know my recollections and impressions of several of his classmates. He was especially interested in what I had thought of two very bright and eccentric boys who, like C, had been in my senior philosophy class. The first boy he named was K. C wanted to know if I remembered K getting up onto the seminar table and reciting "The Wasteland." I did not remember, and I am almost certain it did not happen. In my memory K was a shy, chubby, awkward boy who scored brilliantly on standardized tests but who found it painfully difficult to speak up in class. K had been admitted to Harvard. C said he visited him there and that K clutched his physics textbook to his chest the entire time they were together. On their last evening, C said, K passed out in his room after drinking most of a bottle of bourbon while still clutching his textbook. C also asked me about T, another bright, troubled classmate, also a member of our philosophy class and one of my student advisees. I did not think it was appropriate to be too disclosing about T, as I had worked closely with him and his parents, both psychiatrists, to ease him through alternating bouts of debilitating anxiety and depression.

It occurred to me to ask C *his* impressions of K and T How were they doing? Had he kept up? Apparently not at all. Moreover, as far as I could tell C maintained neither past nor present friendships. He wanted to hear my impressions of my lifelong friend Tony Jarvis, in C's day a popular history teacher and a prominent figure in the school. C was unaware that Tony had gone on to become the headmaster of Boston's Roxbury Latin School where over the course of thirty years he had made a great success of it. "Jarvis *hated* me," C said. I chose not to question or challenge this, although I could not imagine any such response on Tony's part. C recounted two instances when Tony had upbraided him for speaking critically of something or other. "I did not like Jarvis," he said again. "He *hated* me."

We were at the table for nearly two hours before C had to get on his way. As he rose to leave he asked if we could meet again for lunch, and I assured him that we could. That evening he posted a flurry of Facebook messages to me. He asked me if I could remember any additional details about K and T. He recalled that when Tony Jarvis had dressed him down there had been a red throbbing vein on Tony's forehead.

At this point it is hard to tell what C hopes to gain by reconnecting to me, but it is clear that he is eager to disclose things about his life and wants me to corroborate incidents and impressions from his schooldays. As a result I have been revisiting C's time at the school, the middle 1970s. I try to summon up images of K and T and our philosophy classes, but am unable to recall much more than I told C over lunch. To his message about Tony Jarvis' throbbing forehead vein, I replied that I have never known Tony to be especially angry in his dealing with students and that I could not imagine Tony hating him.

This sudden emergence of C has struck something deep in me. In addition to a concern about his health and viability, there is a nagging feeling that I was inadequate in my responses to him when he was my student. He has not made that claim, but when he informed me of his family's psychological problems and his father's early death, I wondered how I could have been unaware of such troubling features of one my student's home life. The fact of the matter is that I had not been aware of anything to do with C's life outside the school—or of countless other boys' home lives. As I have said, I saw C as a scholastically able boy, a reliable contributor to his teams and, though I had forgotten it until he told me, an actor in a sophisticated review I had directed. I therefore saw C in multiple settings in and after school. To the degree I thought about his viability after University School, I am sure I would have said he was a good bet for success. At a deeper level, I am disturbed by how easily I imagine not just my former students but most of the company I have kept over the course of my lifetime proceeding through their circumstances more or less as I do: relatively healthy, satisfyingly attached to loved ones, overall glad to be carrying on. This visitation from C is a concrete, credible, across-the-table instance of life going wrong, of doubting, of existential unease. Message: wake up, feel, relate, take in everything. Swim out of my sweet drowsy bubble of comfort.

February 6, 2017: Dennis O'Brien has invited me to his house for lunch because he has read my *Three Lives of Jonathan Force* and wants to talk about it. This pleased me on many counts. Dennis has an impressive—and to some people daunting—intellect. Retired now from academic life, he is still an active Catholic philosopher. As I have written earlier, he was my dean at Middlebury College and after that president of Bucknell and Rochester Universities. He has read several of my books since we became reacquainted after I moved to Vermont, but I was uneasy about how he would respond to *Jonathan Force*, especially Book III in which Jonathan abandons his former life as an intellectual pundit and becomes a kind of hermit in Key West, not incidentally visiting a Gentleman's Club nearly every day and finding meaning there. It was not impossible to imagine Dennis dismissing this material as frivolous, if not offensive. Whatever his response, I was touched that he read the book and wanted to talk.

It was a long lunch and a wonderful talk. Far from disapproving of anything in Book III or otherwise, Dennis was full of questions. I could tell he was concerned about and also fascinated by Jonathan's forsaking (transcending?) the life of the mind in order to become an uncritical witness to experience. Dennis said he has been working on a personal memoir, inspired by the writing of the late Catholic philosopher John Dunne, who maintains that we find ultimate meaning not through abstract thinking but by locating ourselves in meaningful stories. Like other accomplished older men I have known, Dennis seems to be reckoning whether his accomplishments *are* his story and whether believing that is an obstacle to realizing himself fully. The last thing I wanted to do was to suggest that I might clarify the meaning of his life. I told him what I thought I was doing in *Jonathan Force*.

Years ago I read the Jungian writer Robert Johnson's *Transformations*, about the development of the male psyche, and was thereafter transformed myself. Johnson sees the male life cycle proceeding through a sequence of three archetypal stories. In youth we are spirited fools. In mid-life (if we able to grow past our foolishness) we become discerning—literally disillusioned. We are capable of seeing through everything but in consequence become jaded and miserable. If we proceed through this dark night of the soul, we may reach a satisfying acceptance of our presence in the world. Johnson illustrated the progression of these three successive stages with readings of *Don Quixote, Hamlet, and* (Goethe's) *Faust*. Each successive life transformation requires the loss of one's prior certainties and defining features. Quixote was delusional, but his delusions inspired him.

Hamlet's disillusionment is profound. He is the smartest person in the play, but suicidal for being so. Faust is a scientist and philosopher, the wisest of men, but he has to forsake all that he has been. He must embrace the vulgar, the irrational, the sinful, the sensual—the devil himself—in order to complete himself. I thought—still think— Johnson's thesis is compelling, and I wanted to embody it in a single contemporary character, Jonathan Force, and thus the novel.

Revealing the book's substructure interested Dennis. He said several times in the course of our discussion: your book engaged me philosophically but my real interest is personal—it's made me ask myself all kinds of questions. No response could have made me happier. On arrival, pulling into Dennis's driveway, I had been thinking: does he really want to talk about *Jonathan Force*? I wonder if he knows it is hardly selling any copies. When I left his house two hours later, I did not just feel, I *knew*, I was right to have written that book. In telling me the novel raised personal questions for him I felt he was consciously adjusting our relationship. I had up to this point quite rightly regarded him as older, more intellectually accomplished and—now that I think about it—more morally upstanding than I was: that in our late life reunion we had resumed a more informed version of the mentor-pupil postures we had established when I was an undergraduate. Now there was a liberating sense of parity.

In the course of our luncheon in a bright alcove in the elegant house he had designed, my eye was diverted to a number of striking small sculptures he had placed atop cabinets and shelves. I noticed that the facings of the cabinet doors along one wall were hand painted as a continuous landscape—his work. I had marveled on prior visits at the gallery-like—if not museum-like—quality of the house's central rooms. Bright sunlight was now irradiating all of it, and as I looked across the table at Dennis, now in his mid-eighties, he was animated and *happy* to be asking and holding forth. He seemed a very young man, a boy.

February 14, 2017: Valentine's Day and I am invited back to Project Independence in Middlebury to play the piano and talk about love songs to a gathering of the elderly. I selected a half dozen love ballads from the last century's Broadway musicals and interspersed these with twenty or so popular standards which we sang together. I have now done enough of these sessions that I have become a familiar presence to the group. I can tell from their faces this time that they are, both men and women, in a receptive mood. The love song theme was not my idea, but it was an inspired one. The group sang along like a gathering of appealing children; no trace of reserve or inhibition. I liked the glad flash of recognition in their various faces when they realized they *knew* the song I had begun to play—"My Funny Valentine," "Let Me Call You Sweetheart," "If You Were the Only Girl in the World and I Was the Only Boy."

Without prior reflection I shared an anecdote before we began "I Left My Heart in San Francisco." A former student of mine, Andy, grew suddenly ill at the end of one school day and was rushed to the hospital where it was determined that his heart had become dangerously enlarged. He hovered close to death for a day before he was flown to a Stanford University hospital for a heart transplant, at that time a novel and rare procedure. Andy and his family flew together to the west coast, where the transplant was performed successfully. In the course of his recovery, Andy was temporarily enrolled in a new school, from which he wrote a series of letters back to us that were printed in the student newspaper. Andy had been a great wit, and he titled his first letter "I left my heart in San Francisco." As I recounted this, my audience greeted each turn with gasps of concern, then laughter and something like a cheer at the heartening (!) outcome. Valentine's Day. Love songs. My most satisfying outing to date at Project Independence.

February 28, 2017: A midmorning dental check-up. Once again, I managed to miss and then fail to reschedule an earlier appointment, so it has been a year.

I enter the facility with two mild dreads. I don't want to be told that I must have a crown put over the gap where a few years ago a childhood filling fell out. Seeing this, the dentist had said I should schedule an appointment for the crown right away. But he also expressed surprise that what had become only a partial tooth when the filling fell away was "so clean"—cavity free. Since the crown was going to be annoyingly expensive—more than a thousand dollars after insurance—I asked if the procedure was urgent. He hedged and said not really urgent, but prudent. I asked him if he could improvise something in the meantime, some kind of protective covering over the jagged fragment. To my surprise, he said he thought he could, and in no more than a few minutes mixed up some kind of cement, worked it over the partial tooth, let it dry, smoothed it off, and I was able to leave the chair. He told me the cement should last for a few months. It has lasted now for more than two years, and I am afraid I will be told that the crown is now urgently needed.

My second dread was that the hygienist would hurt me as she removes the past year's accumulated plaque. When I showed up a year ago, having missed several six-month cleanings, the plaque removal was deservedly excruciating. Not this time. In the course of 45 minutes of metallic prying and scraping, she finished, assuring me that teeth and gums "look good." When the dentist came in for the ritual closure, he raised the subject, as I knew he would, of the needed crown. This time he added a new caution: that there was some distancing between the cement patch and the tooth beneath, and thus an entry point for decay. I asked him if he could see any decay. He admitted he could not, in a defeated tone. I left the office once again merely advised but not commanded to install the crown.

As I drove off I reflected on my cagey aversion to getting the crown. I would very much like to avoid serious dental troubles, and I can afford to pay for the procedure. Then it was clear: I was putting off the crown due to the same subterranean pool of reckoning that inclines me to put off getting rid of my Jeep, which no longer reliably gets me to and from Cleveland without breaking down. Not quite consciously I have been calculating that by easing my demands on the Jeep, using it only for local errands, it might become —my *last car*. Until now, I had not let myself register that, with continued dental luck, my temporary crown may also function until I die. And while I have no immediate reason to think death is imminent, it would not amaze anyone if, at 72, I suddenly bowed to one of the standard life-enders—heart attack, stroke, pancreatic cancer. Winding my way up Rte. 125 to Ripton I laughed out loud: with mortality looming I am *economizing.*

March 2-4, 2017: I knew right away when I finished my Fomite Press essay on failed males' role in the emergence of Trump I was not finished. I think the published piece made its point, and comments back so far have been positive, but every day something I read or hear about Trump and his people cries out to be refuted and debunked. Not that there is any lack such outcrying. The mainstream commercial press—the TV Networks, CNN, The *Washington Post, NY Times*—now devote most of their news and editorial attention to Trump's utterances and deeds, the tone more straightforwardly dismissive and critical than anything I have seen in my lifetime. Other prominent politicians have been famously at odds with the press—Nixon!—but there has been nothing like the vituperation of Trump's and Bannon's responses. Trump: the establishment press includes "the most dishonest people on earth." Bannon: "The establishment press was humiliated by Trump's surprise election—and *should keep its mouth shut.*"

I have taken pains to sample daily papers—*The Chicago Tribune, The Des Moines Register, The Houston Chronicle, The Indianapolis Star*—outside the coastal cities maligned as "liberal" and "establishment" and "elite" by the Right, and while there is notably less stridency in Trump coverage from the heartland, it is clear that papers everywhere are paying a new amount and a new quality of attention to Trump-related matters. Energizing the attention is a dizzying notion that the new President may not only be a sensational liar—"thousands and thousands of Muslims were cheering on the streets of Jersey City after 9/11," etc.—but an unashamed, unapologetic liar: that there might be some real possibility of a "post-truth" era.

The time may be right for unapologetic public liars. Outside the bubble of earnestly well-intentioned fact-based journalism, the atmosphere buzzes with assertions begging for credulity. Thanks to the internet and the blessing of instantaneous digital sharing, anybody is a click away from bloggers, hackers, leakers, "alt."-something news sources, conspiracy theorists, hobbyist dissemblers, and proudly confessed purveyors of intentionally faked "news." Far from clarifying the distinction between what is true and false, what is substantial and what is nonsense, the proliferation of purported "information" tends to democratize all claims, such that one man's Breitbart News is another man's *New York Times*.

So I am going to write a second essay on "post-truth." I don't want to get bogged down in the presidential lie of the moment, because that will both date the piece and lock attention onto an instance of the problem instead of the problem itself, which is the ascendancy of power over truth.

I think I know how to proceed. I will start with a brief summary of Trump's well known unsupportable claims, just enough to raise the possibility of disestablishing truth as reliably knowable. Once that question is posed, I can go to systematic considerations of lying—Augustine's *Confessions*, Sissela Bok's *On Lying*—to build a case that anything other than a truth-expecting social fabric is disastrous. And if I can do it in a non-pedantic, non-plodding way, I want to include Socrates' case in *The Apology* and *Crito* for the primacy of truth.

Feels right. Feels good. Hard to believe I have Trump to thank for a surge of energy.

March 1, 2017: I think I may have begun my gradual withdrawal from the larger world. Or maybe I am just accelerating the withdrawal begun when, at sixty, I left my post as headmaster and moved to Vermont. At the time, I was not consciously withdrawing from anything. I thought I was reorienting myself to the world as a writer. I wasn't going to be doing less, I told myself, I was going to be doing different things, writing.

But beginning this fall I began to think differently. I knew that when winter descended, I didn't want to fight it in airports or on icy highways. I didn't want any more heart-in-my-mouth tension of wondering if I were going to make it to the event I had committed to, wondering if I would measure up to what was expected. In truth I wanted more than to avoid winter hassle. I wanted to sit still, gather my thoughts, watch. I am only just now reckoning the formative impact of my father's telling me when I was a boy—of ten? twelve?— *"Rich, there are the people up on the stage and there are the people in the audience watching them. Who do you want to be?"* This was a rhetorical question. My father wanted to be and *was* on the stage. He did not want anything less from me. But I can still remember, even as my father was laying out the alternatives, half *wanting* the perspective and safety of the audience.

Having mentally kicked myself in recent years for accepting speaking gigs that were really not that appealing, but which assured me I was still in the professional swim, this fall I decided I could resist. I said no to the Yale Divinity session I had enjoyed so much when my friend Tony Jarvis was in charge. In that case I realized that the pleasure was all bound up with spending stimulating time with Tony; the idea of making my way to New Haven, lodging there, and performing for its own sake had no appeal at all. I also declined attending the annual Headmasters Association conference in February, where good company, including Tony's, was assured. In this case, the deciding factor *was* winter travel dread. The Headmasters used to assemble in Princeton, then to a similar venue in Philadelphia, both easily accessible by train from Vermont, but when the meetings were moved to Durham, NC, attending would mean multiple flight stops in chancy weather, for which I no longer have the heart.

Today I telephoned to cancel my participation in an Ohio-wide book fair in Columbus. The event was scheduled for a mid-April weekend and would have featured my novel *Jonathan Force*. The roads would certainly be passable. I could attach the Columbus stay to a visit to Celeste and Lulu in Cleveland. I know *Jonathan Force* needs every boost it can get if is going to reach any kind of readership. But I just do not want to go. I don't want to negotiate my way through anything unfamiliar or complex. The organizers in Columbus have been courteous and enthusiastic throughout, but nothing—not guilt, not the urge to self-promotion, not curiosity about new faces in a new setting —-stirs me to proceed. There is not enough fuel in the tank. I wrote to the host organization, and they graciously accepted my grounds for declining—"personal developments"—and told me they would invite me next year. The indication that I have indeed reached a new level of detachment is that I feel no twinge of regret in declining to participate, only relief that I will be spared the exertion. Old. This is being old.

March 9-13, 2017: I drive west to Cleveland in blessedly benign weather for a long weekend. I have two reasons to go. I want to see Lulu perform—in the *lead,* no less—in her school production of "Fame." Weeks ago, when I dropped her off for her early morning audition, I was delighted by her pluck. She is a lowly sixth grader in a 6th-8th grade junior high school, but she had prepared herself impressively—and she sang her audition number charmingly. The second reason is to make up for my flat, no-fun prior visit when poor Lulu was miserably ill.

The show runs two nights, and I arrive in Cleveland Heights just minutes before curtain on a rainy, blustery Thursday evening. I am relieved to be done driving and I am full of anticipation for whatever transpires. I remind myself that this is junior high school and that it has been years since I have attended a performance of school children. I feel surprisingly *happy*, and I am prepared to be tolerant.

The director, a likable, lanky, sloppily dressed young man, took the stage and thanked us for coming. He praised the hard work of the cast and crew and explained that players on the right side of the stage may appear to be in shadow as two of the stage lights had blown early in the week and had not been replaced. The curtain opened, up went the show's recorded soundtrack, and out into the (working) lights stepped Lulu. She was phenomenal! From the opening all-cast number, through her solos and closing bows, she was a smiling, expressive marvel. Her big number, "Let's Play a Love Scene," was a show-stopper. She has the musical theater touch: strong, tuneful voice enlivened by a slight vibrato. She already has the knack for both acting and singing a song, aware of what is touching or funny and able to bring it across. I felt as though I were being lifted out of my chair— bringing back the exact sensations I experienced years ago watching Kate sing "Tomorrow Belongs to Me" in *Cabaret*, Jesse singing "Joshua Novick Kissed Me Today" in a University School summer stock revue, and Claire singing "Maybe" in the Heights Youth Theater production of "Annie." And I am reminded again of the greatest blessing of parenthood: to observe, unnoticed, a child performing or competing or contending well in a world apart from you— aware that she is launched, effective, *out there.*

We manage to have a good, jokey, upbeat time the entire weekend. We dine out nearly every night, including two celebratory post-show dinners, for which Lulu changes into fancy clothes. The temperature in Cleveland Heights is so unseasonably summery that lawns grow and daffodils and crocuses appear a month ahead of regional schedule. It is too warm outdoors even for a sweater, and we improvise summertime chores like washing the cars and tending the lawns. Because she has birthday parties to attend, I let Lulu persuade me over my exaggerated objections to go mall shopping for presents. As I have explained in prior entries, enclosed shopping malls, unless I am guided hand in hand by my daughter, are a vivid preview of purgatory. Mainly, I am reassured that Lulu is healthy and herself again.

Celeste mildly annoys me by announcing that she is taking Lulu for a week in Tulum, Mexico, at the end of the month. I am surprised because she floated this prospect about a month ago and then decided against it. I am annoyed, as I was a month ago, that the expense of such a trip, even with extreme economizing, would seem to me unaffordable, given Celeste's limited means, provided almost exclusively by me. I can certainly understand the desire to seek the sun after a Cleveland winter, but Celeste sought it for almost two weeks in Jamaica in December. And—she tells me—there will be a trip to see friends in Palo Alto in May. I explain to Celeste that *I* cannot afford a tropical vacation in the foreseeable future and am thus surprised that she can. But by some means or other she has booked flights and lodg-ing, and that is that. She disarms me a little by urging me to come along.

Apart from the flight, she tells me, there would be practically no extra expense: a week of beach, whooshing surf, soft air, fresh fruit. I think she knows, money aside, it would be too awkward for me to propose such a trip to M, who is still not quite resigned to my times away in Cleveland. I am certain Celeste's pleasure in my company would be enhanced by her relief that I would be on hand to pick up tabs.

Celeste accepts, and I think respects, my position on her impending trip, but she is determined to go. Her drive to get away, especially to parts south, is almost impervious to reasoned deliberation. It is like her drive to acquire clothes and furniture at bargain rates. While I do not share either drive, Celeste is impressive in her resolve to carry them out.

April 6, 2017: Another hour-long piano gig for the old folks at Project Independence. I have not worried about preparation. I offer a few benign listening quizzes: what *place* does this song refer to? ("I left My Heart in San Francisco," "I Love Paris," "We'll Take Manhattan," etc.) What *person* is addressed in this song? ("Whatever Lola Wants," "My Gal Sal," "Lulu's Back in Town," etc.) We talk a little about what makes music "classical," and I play bits that I think illustrate people's points. Then we sing along from the songbook of old favorites. For some reason this is an extra warm session, big smiles and lots of eye contact from the seated singers. We are having a nice time. It helps, I think, that we are becoming familiar with each other. Nothing feels effortful. I realize that I like doing this. I like these people.

April 15-22, 2017: I feel myself drawn into the swarming hive of Middlebury College. Faculty insiders and various older alums have let me know their respective frustrations related to a now notorious reception given to political scientist Charles Murray last month when he was invited to speak. Murray is to me a disagreeable character who in the mid '90s published a controversial and now campus-unmentionable study of race and intelligence, *The Bell Curve*. The book made a case for genetically determined variances in cognitive ability of Asians, Whites, Blacks, and Hispanics. The science drawn on for support was more than questionable, and some of the policy recommendations offended minorities and their campus champions. But to give Murray some credit, he makes hypotheses and offers theoretical and empirical support for them; however questionable his findings, he operates within the protocols of social science. Predictably, *The Bell Curve* made Murray a darling of Bush era conservatives, and he has been an employable presence on college faculties and right wing think tanks.

The Bell Curve legacy was the cause of Murray's hostile reception at Middlebury, though he had been invited to speak about his new book, *Coming Apart*, which analyzes the appeal of Donald Trump to unhappy white Americans. This would seem to me a compelling topic, inviting all kinds of responses from students and faculty, but Murray never got a chance to contend. With considerable advance planning, the two hundred or so students who were first to arrive at the designated lecture hall turned their backs on Murray and drowned out his attempts to speak with chanted slogans. The political science faculty members, themselves no fans of Murray's work, who at conservative students' request had invited him, determined that, one way or another, Murray would be heard and questioned.

They accompanied Murray to a different building where his presentation could be recorded on video, along with questions and responses offered by selected faculty. This improvisation also met with resistance on behalf of the protesters who gained access to the recording session and shouted that down as well. Then, as the national press reported at length, the protesters followed Murray and his faculty hosts to their car, and as they attempted to drive off, were physically threatened. Protesters leapt onto the hood of the car and shouted abuse. In the course of the fracas faculty member Allison Stanger's hair was pulled, and she received a mild concussion, for which she was treated at a nearby hospital. A scene, a mess, and a continuing embarrassment to the college.

There is much to object to in this matter, from both left and right perspectives. I am interested and also annoyed that a very righteous-sounding body of younger alums stood and still stands stridently by the obstructive students. Prior to Murray's arrival they complained that, given his *The Bell Curve*, he had no business being invited on campus. They derided Murray and his book as racist, but held up no specific propositions from his published work, apparently convinced that because the Southern Poverty Law Center and other left-leaning organizations had condemned him as racist, he deserved condemnation. A vocal cohort of college faculty, if not a majority, also took this position, some of whom openly admitting they had not read *The Bell Curve*, nor would they ever read it. Other faculty and many older alumni, including some of my classmates, objected passionately to silencing Murray. Some of them have withheld their annual gifts to the college. Some have decided not to attend our fiftieth reunion in June because their values and opinions would not be respected on campus.

These antipathies seem to me a miniature footnote to the nation's overall political dividedness. The college's president Laurie Patton and her colleagues in the alumni and development offices have wrung their hands past all wringing. This is not, President Patton has pronounced, Middlebury at its best. To date there is little sign that scores have been settled, wounds healed. The college has imposed what they are calling "sanctions" on a few dozen of the identified protesters. The sanction amounts to an account of the incident on the students' official college transcript. None of students involved has been removed from the campus or otherwise disciplined. To a student convinced that he or she was right to have silenced and harassed Murray, the transcript "sanction" is probably a badge of honor—and an unlikely impediment to admission to graduate schools or to employment in the larger world. But the fact that any discipline, however mild and symbolic, was imposed has been greeted as an intolerable injustice on the part of the faculty, students, and alums holding a moral ground high above what they believe to be the rhetorical sophistry of "free speech."

And where am I in all of this? I am, like everyone else in this little world, upset. I am disappointed in the students who would not listen to Murray and with the alumni and faculty who support them. The incident has driven me to review *The Bell Curve* and to learn as much about Murray as I can. As a result, I have found him a repellant, self-absorbed figure. I think his political thinking serves an unexamined ideology on his part. I don't believe he is seeking any kind of truth; he is seeking self-validation. I wish he had had his say on campus. I wish I had been there. I would have liked to hear bright Middlebury students jump all over his arguments instead his car.

April 27, 2017: Claire and Nick and baby Levi arrive for a four-day stay. Having determined to leave the west coast and relocate in Vermont, they have made bold moves. Claire announced her departure from her Oakland charter school and then was promptly hired to teach first grade at the elementary school in Wallingford, Vermont, a charming little town about ten miles south of Rutland and 40 miles south of us. Nick's environmental engineering firm is willing for him to continue his work from Vermont. They must value him because not only are they letting him work far from corporate headquarters, they have just given him a whopping bonus. Claire and Nick have become in their middle thirties financially comfortable, certainly more so than I was at their ages.

Their plan was to look at a variety of houses in the vicinity of Middlebury, Rutland, and Wallingford, but the one they chose is in Wallingford, close to Claire's new school. A week or so ago M and I drove southward to look at the Rutland and Wallingford properties Claire had highlighted. We determined that an old restored farm house in Wallingford was by far the most appealing. It is a charming yellow frame house, mostly modernized, with plenty of room and ready for occupancy. It is situated in meadowlands at the floor of a sprawling valley with mountain views. There are kitchen gardens and charming outbuildings, in all a very right-feeling place. Claire and Nick bought it for what I think is a bargain price, $240,000.

I am of course happy to have Claire and Co. within easy visiting orbit, which will alter, I suspect agreeably, the rhythm of M's and my days here. Plans are already in the works for a set day of the week, Thursday, in which we will babysit Levi for most of the day, and the pattern of future holiday meals and gatherings is becoming clear. Now that Jesse and her family are only a few hours drive away in Marion, only Kate and her brood in Chicago remain geographically hard to reach.

These new family circumstances feel to me an invigorating shake up of established routines. At the heart of it is the realization that I *like* Claire's and Nick's company. I like their conversation, eating and drinking with them. And baby Levi is a cheerful love. But more profoundly, this geographic rearrangement deepens my sense of being no longer central, but peripheral, to the developments bearing on my life. **May 2-7, 2017:** My friend and Middlebury classmate Karl is mad for baseball, if anything even more so than we first got to know each other fifty years ago as fellow pitchers on Middlebury College's baseball team. Encyclopedic about the game even then, he has gone on to study baseball. He wrote his doctoral dissertation on baseball as an expression of the American pastoral dream. He *played* baseball—hardball baseball—in a senior league up into his fifties. Since returning to Middlebury to serve as dean of this and that, he has introduced a semester-long course on Negro League baseball. He has written a number of scholarly articles about the Negro leagues and presents regularly at an annual conference devoted to Negro league history and lore. He writes a sports column for the local paper, often about baseball. Not surprisingly, the college has named him faculty advisor to the baseball team.

In the spring Karl attends almost all of Middlebury's games, even away games, including spring training games in the southwest. He often invites me to join him for home games, at which he fills me in on details about the players' pasts and their various potential, so that within an hour or so I feel like a savvy insider. I also realize that after so many years I can still warm to the rhythm and drama of a baseball game. It helps that Middlebury' team, unlike the teams of my era, is now competitive in what has become a very good small college conference. The quality of the ballpark, of the coaching, and of the players' abilities so far exceed what I remember of Middlebury baseball as to seem discontinuous. It is like so much else about the college today: less an improvement than a complete makeover, streamlined, burgeoning, state-of-the-art.

Karl, who has experienced the college intimately as a teacher and dean for the past three decades, sees this differently. For him the college is indeed bigger and better, improved, yes, but bearing the essence of what we knew and felt as undergraduates. His is surely the better earned perspective. But whether he and I state it openly or not, I think we share a considered conviction that the boys we were would be unlikely candidates to be admitted to Middlebury today. Nonetheless, it is hard not to admire the intensity and quality of the baseball team's play.

This week I had a parallel experience, also in Karl's company, of the scholastic side of the college. Probably because I have recently served on the alumni board, I was invited to attend what the college calls its spring Symposium, a full morning of presentations by graduating seniors in which, for fifteen minutes or so, they summarize their researches and special projects. As there were hundreds of these, tightly scheduled in various rooms of the college's enormous new Bicentennial Hall, I had to pick and choose. In the course of the morning I heard mostly from humanities students interpreting literary texts, sorting out theological concepts, demonstrating mastery of the classics.

It was explained to me late in the morning that these were not required recitals. They were not graded or otherwise assessed. The students volunteered to share their interests and views, apparently honored to be invited to do so. I was engaged and impressed by every presenter I heard, stimulated to ask many questions. The only presentation to which I had any objection was from an English major who had applied a kind of post-modern consideration of gender to a series of poems which were hardly illuminated by the analysis. But while my honest response was what a waste of this bright young man's time and energy to cast a jargon-ridden blanket over what the texts were otherwise so clearly saying, I also felt an admiration for his determination to master the daunting protocols of the dreadful critical theory, no doubt commended to him by one of his professors held in its thrall.

But in all, a morning alive with the voices and ideas of eager, winsome, eloquent young men and woman I was sure I would find easy to like and glad to know. It is comforting for me to think of a civic future under the watch of such people. So hats off to Middlebury College. That it would not admit the likes of me today is probably all to the public good.

May 26-28, 2017: A confluence of events featuring M's painting, including a Vermont Open Studio weekend in which her studio and gallery will be open for viewing and her pictures for sale. As in the past we have decided to launch the weekend with a Friday evening cocktail party in the gallery. No doubt because we invited the same people for the same fare, this gathering was just about exactly the same: bibulous, cheery, celebratory. It was no small factor that M's new paintings compelled attention—dark, almost forbidding Ripton winter landscapes made subtly luminous with patches of captured afternoon light. She calls these The Winter of Trump.

There was a gratifying stream of visitors over the course of the weekend and some sales, but I think both of us sensed that the preparation for the weekend and the event itself represented something of a milestone in M's artistic life. Among other things, it was a kind of prelude to M's 70th birthday on the 31st. I sensed that for M arrival at 70 was potent. Never inclined to call attention to her birthday, she had remarked on this one with a notable intensity. I don't think it was due to anything she said, but I found her gathered and closely hung paintings powerfully engaging, the newer work for me the best and most dramatic since she began painting seriously.

Monday morning following the Open Studio I was sitting in the yellow parlor at the back of the house finishing my breakfast tea and glanced up at the staircase to our bedroom where an ascending series of large pastel pictures M had done decades earlier are hung. They are gorgeous in their rich reds, suggesting, together, something of a medieval tapestry. It occurred to me that the pictures were more than accomplished; they are *great*, part of a significant body of work, but also part of my daily life. I will find a way to tell her this.

June 5-6, 2017: I am invited to St. John's High School in Shrewsbury, Massachusetts, to talk to their faculty about our research findings for successfully teaching boys. St. John's is a Catholic school of about a thousand boys. It was formerly affiliated with the Xavierian order but is now run and taught by laymen, most of them Catholic. My preliminary talks with the new headmaster encouraged me that the school might be an unentitled, forward-looking place.

Because they wanted me to address the assembled faculty in the morning, I drove down the night prior and was lodged comfortably near the school. I arrived a half hour or so before I was due to present and was interested that the faculty meetings began with prayers. These set a suitable tone —between cheery and reverent—for the business to follow, including mine. In the event they were a warm and responsive audience. I divided my remarks between findings about the kinds of lessons boys best respond to and findings about the kinds of relationships boys value. Though I was the very last scheduled "event" before the faculty broke for the summer, they were attentive and re-sponsive throughout. Their questions were good, and several stayed on to chat when I was finished. Though the school has been all-boys since its founding nearly a century ago, the headmaster and his administrators told me that their all-boys composition has until recently felt more like an inheritance than a convinced intention. They are thus my favorite audience, as that was also the condition of University School when I came to teach there a half century ago and the condition of most of the boys' schools that have since embraced a more purposeful mission since the founding of our international Coalition.

Good feelings all around, I think. Alex, the headmaster, invited my back to address the faculty again as the new school year begins. They have all been issued copies of *Reaching Boys / Teaching Boys* and *I Can Learn from You* to read before we reconvene—sales, no less!

June 7, 2017: Another hour of piano for the elderly at the Project Independence facility in Middlebury. I decided to vary my routine a little from name-that-tune / show / movie guessing games and the inevitable closing sing-along of my previous sessions. As it happens today was the 50th anniversary of the Beatles' Sergeant Pepper album, and I thought I might see who besides me among the septuagenarians and octogenarians in the room might recall those wonderful tunes. I should not have been surprised, but was, that all of them did. I have remarked before on the narrowing gap between my age and that of the listeners consigned to this adult day care program, but I am slow and perhaps resistant to let it register fully. Something in me wants these officially "old" people to be my late parents' ages and thus to be delighted that the young man (me) brought in from the outside world actually knows "their" repertoire: the enduring standards spanning the past century's war years, the unforgettable sign off anthems of the Big Bands. How extraordinary, I want them to think, that I can somehow play the popular music of my parents' and *grandparents'* era. Something like this was indeed the case when I used to play the piano in the afternoon for my parents' fellow residents in the Great Room in their retirement home, but it is no longer the case for the Project Independence elderly. Most of them gamely mumble along as I chord through "Don't Sit Under the Apple Tree" and "I'll be Seeing You," but it is more, I suspect, out of a resigned willingness to go with what must seem to many of them a bewildering program rather than any inclination to sing out putative old favorites.

In any event the Beatles went down well—in fact better than any of my prior musical offerings. After a few bars of "I Get High With a Little Help From my Friends" an elated gentleman in the front row rose to his feet and danced energetically through the length of the song.

June 8-11, 2017: My Middlebury College classmates convened on campus for our 50th Reunion. Counting spouses there were about two hundred of us, a good turnout I think, considering that of our class of 400, nearly half the males flunked out or left after our freshman year, and fifty of us have died.

As mentioned in prior entries, the college targets the 50th reunion class for special attention in anticipation of substantial gifts and pledges. Toward that end two alumni office staff members worked pretty much full time for over a year to shepherd us forward to the festivities: lavish banquets every evening, audiences with the college President and other campus dignitaries, tours of facilities, faculty and student presentations, hikes, picnics, yoga sessions. Those of us who had written books or painted pictures or sewn quilts were invited to display and discuss our work. A substantial "yearbook" composed of essays by, pictures of, and extensive biographies of class members was handsomely produced and distributed by the college.

My initial concern was with the Memorial Service, which kicked off the weekend and which I had volunteered to organize. It has been a long time, in fact since my headmaster days, since I have had to rely on other people to deliver promised services in order for an event to come off. The memorial service I envisaged combined reminiscences from the chapel pulpit, literary readings, photo montages, including undergraduate photographs of the deceased classmates, and two songs, not hymns but in the spirit of hymns, sung by all and accompanied by me. I proposed this material and solicited participation mostly by email. I did not know some of the people I asked to present well enough to know if they were reliable. I did not know if they would show up for the single rehearsal. I did not know if there would be adequate technical support for the projected images and the amplification necessary for speakers and musicians. In all there was a lot to worry about, and I did, but I needn't have. Everybody showed up. Every utterance was considered and touching. The musical offerings were splendid. Voices and instruments rang out with a distinct solemnity in the darkly paneled vaulting of the old college chapel. A great relief to have it go well. Thus unburdened I was able to lighten up a bit. There were dozens of people I remember liking and had not seen for a half century. I was not prepared for how moving these reconnections proved to be.

The memorial service was followed by a group session moderated by two therapist classmates who invited us to reflect on life-changing events in our lives—good and bad—and how we had managed the passage. I recalled that something along these lines had been planned for a previous reunion and that it had been dominated by a few people impervious to the tedium they created for the larger group. But this session was not like that. The sharing this time was widely distributed, and the challenges and crises offered up compelled interest. A classmate I remembered as an edgy, outspoken political radical let us know that he had all but decided not to attend the reunion because he had just lost his wife of fifty years and was still grieving. He told us he had married an African American woman, confident in the heady political climate of the late 1960s that he and his wife were more than up to the challenges of an interracial marriage. He said the challenge for him was not meeting social opposition but, to his surprise, understanding what being black in the United States actually felt like and how his own confident preconceptions had dissolved. He managed to convey in just a few minutes the depth of his love for his late wife and a moving humility in acknowledging the rigidity of his undergraduate convictions.

There were other touching revelations, including a few accounts of seeing difficult aging parents through their final years. I was struck by one man's account of tending to his angry and verbally abusive mother for decades. His mother had made a ritual of disapproving of his tastes, ridiculing his career choices, belittling his pleasures and achievements. He said his mother referred to him as "a son of a bitch" many times each day and that, despite his efforts to shrug it off, her aggression and meanness hurt him. He reported feeling great relief when it occurred to him to answer being called a son of a bitch with a heartfelt "you are absolutely right, mother." Thoroughly demented at the end of her life, she had a few surprising moments of clarity, in one of which she thanked him for his care and acknowledged her awfulness to him, concluding with "thank you, and I love you."

A woman recounted tearfully the ordeal of her husband's advancing Alzheimer's symptoms and the pain she felt at his estrangement. Beverly, a poet whom I had asked to read at the memorial service, shared the experience of dying and returning to life. She and her husband had moved after their graduation to the Wyoming wilderness where they made a rugged life in a house they built themselves off the power grid. The rural hospital she went to when her first child was about to be born was not equipped to deal with the complications of the birth, and as a result she hemorrhaged so badly she lost consciousness. When she no longer registered a pulse, someone, she was told, said to the attending doctor and nurse that if she was going to come back to life, somebody better turn her upside down, because if her brain did not get some blood soon, she would be a vegetable. She did revive, due, she feels, to the upending. Like others of my acquaintance who have experienced near-death or return-from-death episodes, Beverly said she experienced nothing stressful or painful in the ordeal. She said she felt surrounded by loving presences and was completely unafraid, eager for whatever would happen next.

There was an hour and a half of this. The collective mood made it comfortable to share with and respond to one another. The session was shot through with affection, consolation, and even high humor. It worked, I think, because all of us are past seventy and past having to keep up impressive appearances. For better and worse, we are what we have become. What a deep pleasure to acknowledge that, to feel that together.

There were a half dozen classmates—artists, professors, writers—I especially wanted to catch up with and managed to do so in the course of the extensive drinks hours and other casual gatherings. I was interested in the presentations of classmates' creative work—their books, their art work, in two cases their inventions—and enjoyed sharing mine, managing even a few unexpected sales. As in some of the planning sessions months earlier, I found that intimate talk and otherwise close adjacency to classmates I had been closely involved with in my undergraduate days revived *intact* strong feelings ranging from admiration to hilarity to erotic stirring.

Without quite bringing it to conscious realization, I had carried with me into the reunion weekend a notion that I would at some point find myself at a piano and that certain classmates—the right ones—would join me and we would sing and reminisce into the small hours. With an eerie inevitability that very thing transpired on the final evening of the festivities. After an evening concert of a new classical composition for saxophone and piano composed by my gifted classmate John Plant, a dozen or so of us decided to assemble in one of the dormitory lounges designated for common socializing. The room contained an unlocked Steinway grand piano, in tune. I began playing, and people gathered around, and for three hours we played and sang, plumbing the depths of our personal repertoires, pretty much exhausting the standard Broadway musicals, Cole Porter, Gershwin, and Rogers and Hart favorites, then remembered '50s rock and roll, the Beatles, Motown, Ray Charles—whatever would suddenly come to mind. The singing was not always tuneful, but it was spirited and loud. I was struck looking out over the body of the Steinway to see my friend Karl engaged in an intense tête-à-tête with his college girlfriend, Anne. I felt I knew exactly what he was experiencing—the intensity of not just remembering but of *reliving* feelings long submerged. When, hours later, they rose to part, their embrace ended with a prolonged reluctance. Karl and Anne's communion seemed to me completely continuous with the uninhibited closeness we experienced around the piano. When we first assembled, a large bottle of Maker's Mark bourbon was placed on an end table, along with several bottles of wine people produced from the singers' dormitory rooms. While vaguely aware that various people kindly refreshed my glass from time to time, I paid little attention to what I managed to drink in the intervals between songs, but at two or three a.m., when we at last quieted and said our goodbyes, all the bottles were empty.

June 24-28, 2017: The International Boys Schools Coalition Conference convenes in Baltimore. We are hosted by the Boys Latin School in posh suburban Roland Park and are bused to Johns Hopkins University and other city venues for special presentations. Again I am struck by the growth of the coalition and of its increasingly international composition. There about a thousand of us representing hundreds of schools in twenty-some countries, and we are billeted at various harbor side hotels in the central city. Having worked with the faculty of the Boys Latin School a few years ago, including a few days in early summer, I anticipated with remembered dread the intense heat and humidity of Baltimore in June, but in the event there was a miraculous stretch of clear, crisp days never exceeding 80 degrees. Not much was required of me this time. I was one of three "founders" asked to present to the full conference for about an hour on the Coalition's quarter century trajectory and continuing mission. Speaking from very rough notes, I felt relaxed to the point of enjoying myself. The questions and comments from the floor were gratifying, but afterward and throughout the conference I felt a twinge of guilt in not contributing more. I was put up in a large, extravagantly appointed suite at the top of a grand Hyatt overlooking the harbor. The Coalition provided travel and all meals, including evening banquets. My biography was featured prominently in the conference's printed program, and while it is undeniably a boost to be given VIP status at such gatherings, this year I felt had sung rather too little for the supper offered. I tried to compensate by making an extra effort to get to know new delegates and to attend as many of the featured presentations as I could possibly attend.

The blur of new acquaintance and reacquaintance and dutiful attention to conference business was engaging enough, but I could not shake the feeling that I am now at best a familiar senior presence whose past contributions have been more than sufficiently honored: that, in truth, the enterprise is proceeding robustly with little need of anything I can provide. I felt this especially as conferees were enthusing about next summer's conference in Queensland, Australia. My thoughts raced ahead to what, if anything I might contribute, then to what now feels like the effrontery even to *propose*, for the twenty-fifth consecutive time, holding forth from a podium and being thus gathered into the Coalition's ever larger, ever less familiar fold—at their considerable expense.

A long but comfortable train ride back to Vermont provided the best possible context for a frank personal assessment about when it is best to step away from former activities and associations—and when it is no longer suitable to offer myself for such.

July 13-20, 2017: This morning Celeste and I drove to pick up Lulu who has just completed her first extended stay away from home: two weeks in the woodsy seclusion of Camp Roosevelt Firebird in central Ohio. Parents of former attendees assured Celeste and me that it was a safe and wholesome enterprise, established by a former high school teacher with a vision of instilling in younger children pacific values and a commitment to a sustainable environment. A few of Lulu's friends have attended in past summers and liked it, so we decided to give it a try.

The winding and precarious unpaved road that led into the camp from a rural highway was all but impassable—and actually impassable if an entering vehicle encountered an exiting vehicle. The campground itself opened up to a glittering lakeshore and a hodge-podge of rickety, cheerfully painted cabins and outbuildings. Out of the car and stretching my legs, I thought it looked just right.

A dozen or so families were in the process of gathering their children and their gear, and as Celeste set about finding a toilet, I struck out in the direction of the cabins. Lulu and I spotted each simultaneously, and she broke into a run to greet me. The campers were not allowed while there to communicate by cell phone or other devices, and though handwritten letters were encouraged, Lulu composed very few; Celeste received one, I none over the course of two weeks.

Lulu was glad to see me and ecstatic about her experience. In the course of walking me through the facilities, she chattered non-stop about her days, her new friends, and the many surprises and novelties she had experienced: her care of the camp's chickens, adventurous kayak excursions, making friends with children from Mexico City and from Ukraine. As she told me this, my mind raced with speculation about how parents in Mexico City or Ukraine could possibly find out about, much less find, the modest and isolated Camp Roosevelt Firebird. Lulu's infectious pleasure in her time away continued through our two-hour car ride back to Cleveland. I could not help contrasting her exuberance with my one and only camp experience as a boy: two weeks, when I was ten, at Camp Rodney Kroehler in northern Wisconsin.

While sixty years in the past, Camp Kroehler still evokes strong images and even smells, none of them good. As a child my mother had always wanted to go to Girl Scout camp, but Great Depression circumstances made that impossible for her parents. That unfulfilled longing I believe motivated mother to seek out a summer camp for me, though all I wanted to do in the summer was to stay at home with my friends with whom I was happy to fill the daylight hours playing Little League baseball and swimming at the town pool. But off I was sent.

It was an all-boys camp, and the prevailing tone was decidedly martial and, for me, punishingly schedule-driven. There was quite a bit of required swimming in murky lake water on too-cold mornings, unappealing food completely discontinuous with anything I had previously eaten. Out of the counselor's view and with their seemingly tacit permission, there was a good deal of bullying on the part of older boys assigned to be in charge of the cabins. There was a Camp Kroehler tradition of "pantsing" unsuspected campers thought to be odd, small, or otherwise vulnerable. Pantsing consisted of an ambushed camper having his blue jeans and underpants pulled down to his ankles to the hyena-like derision of the pantsers as he put himself back together. One could be pantsed in his cabin or on a wooded pathway on the way to the next activity.

The two weeks I was there were punctuated by a series of "special" events, including an endless and talent-less talent show and a "last campfire" intended to evoke fond memories. I don't believe I was "home sick" as much as suspended in a state of barely endurable dread as I counted the days before I could leave the Camp Kroehler world behind me. I remember that, whether due to slogging through tall dewy grass to attend pre-breakfast announcements at the flag pole or due to being caught outside in the rain, all the sneakers and clothes my mother had packed were wet after a few days and, no doubt because I stuffed them into my suitcase at the end of the day, they remained damp and uncomfortable throughout my stay.

Not at all Lulu's experience. Camp Roosevelt Firebird's sulphurous drinking water, spiders in the shower, bats in the cabin rafters were to her wondrous, funny. Happy that she had enjoyed herself but struck by her apparent absence of home-sickness, I asked her what would she have thought if the camp director had asked her this morning if she would like to stay on for a third week. "Oh my god," she said. "Yes!"

July 21-22, 2017: Back home in Ripton, waking each day to soft air and the swaying greens of the forest across the river. It has been a hauntingly beautiful summer in New England. Some historians are comparing it to the eerily lovely summers of 1914 and 1939, each of which was shattered by the onset of World Wars.

The high summer days call Karl and Gary and me to golf. What John Updike called the allure of "green shimmering distances" beckons from the Middlebury College course. My play is neither especially good nor bad—or rather it *is* especially good or bad. Chest swelling pleasure in a series of impressive drives dissolves after a pitifully duffed one slides off the heel of the club into the foliage just off the tee. I sink a long, snaking put from the fringe of the green, and on the following hole three-put from four feet away. All the while it feels right to be striding through the course, toting my clubs up and over gentle rises of fairway, everything faintly, agreeably effortful. I feel myself irrationally energized by the prospect of the next shot soaring, rising, alighting *just where I wanted*, putting for a *birdie* — the infrequency of such outcomes no obstacle to their enlivening anticipation. Having now, at seventy-two, shed anything but a playful sense of competitiveness along with my boyhood dread of being shamed, I surrender to bright sky, enveloping greenery, the violet mounds of mountains on the horizon, and the bracing, unselfconscious *fellowship* of these golf days.

July 28, 2017: M and I drive an hour and a half south to Woodstock, Vermont, where I have been invited to read from and talk about *The Three Lives of Jonathan Force* as part of Bookstock, the town's annual celebration of books and writers. While it was nice to be asked, I had a foreboding about the event. I have already done three reading events from the book in Vermont, and the core of readers and friends acquainted with me and my writing have already done their duty. What other people, I wondered, are likely on a brilliantly sunny Saturday afternoon to turn up to hear a writer unknown to them who has written a long, fairly cerebral book of literary fiction? I was given some hope in that the two sessions prior to mine, one on nature writing and the other on crime fiction, were impressively attended, all the chairs in the library gallery filled. But just twelve or fourteen folks showed up for mine, an audience modestly above failure level. In it, to my surprise, was a former University School colleague and his wife, and it was a pleasure reminiscing with them afterwards. I suppose the reading went well enough, and the exchange of questions and comments afterward was lively, but driving home I felt the heaviness of a day spent with too little consequence, further confirming my sense that my writing and other public utterances are pitched to prior audiences with prior interests, that my creative moment, such as it was, has passed.

August 1-21, 2017: Late last autumn, reflecting back on the summer just past, I decided that, like so much of my life now, the season had passed in a shapeless blur. What I did, where I went, while neither taxing nor disagreeable, had been determined by what was somehow required of me by others. No particular plans of mine were thwarted, because I had made no plans.

My prevailing assumption has been that each day will be spent in Ripton. I rise when I feel like it, usually in midmorning after reading several papers, answering whatever emails have come in, and perhaps doing the NYT crossword puzzle and some on-line scrabble moves. In good weather I have a light breakfast with M, then go upstairs to my study where I work on writing projects until 1:30 or 2, then down for a light lunch, then out for an hour or so of exercise and errands, then back to my study till half-past five when I set the table and prepare the evening meal. At six I will have prepared a drink for me and M, and we will watch an hour of public television news before dinner. After dinner M retires to her studio to meditate. I play the piano or otherwise divert myself for an hour or so until she returns, and then we watch an episode, if not episodes, of an engaging series or, better, a good movie.

Then to bed, where I will read usually for an hour, occasionally more, before turning off the light.

That is my day's template, and I have spent thousands of them since retiring to Ripton. But their succession is broken, as my past entries document, by calls away —to speak, to teach, to perform, to read from a recent book, to visit children, to attend meetings of organizations I belong to, show up for all manner of ceremonies and social occasions. Being called away so often is, as I have reported, occasionally exhausting, sometimes taking a toll on my health. It also creates an impression of being especially "busy," but there is something flaccid and passive in this kind of busy-ness. The events and invitations are generated by others. I merely consent. When feeling stressed, usually in the course of complicated or botched travel, I vow to myself to consent less, but never really do. The invitations come from nice people, sometimes dear friends, and I increasingly find it is more than "nice to be asked"; those commitments and performances reassure me that I am still in the social and productive swim, not yet forgotten. I matter.

But after the unsatisfying summer of 1916 I determined to make a change. I would not merely alternate between the Ripton template and keeping commitments away from home. I would plan something new, something substantial. Rather than be summoned elsewhere, I would gather friends and family —to me. And I would do so in a splendid, memory-making place.

I waited for an image to come to mind, and then it did: I pictured one of the grand seaside houses overlooking Buzzards Bay in Marion, Massachusetts, the town where I had spent more than forty summers of my adulthood with M's family. And while my in-laws' commodious house was indeed on the water closely adjacent to the Gatsby-like structures I had in mind, it was not one of them. Moreover, as I have written earlier, it has been razed to pasture, the land donated to a conservation trust.

I began scanning vacation rental postings in Marion on the internet. Sure enough, a few of the rambling, gabled properties I recalled from my kayaking about the harbor were listed. I decided that a residence of at least three weeks would be necessary to realize my vision; I determined that my one-and two-week getaways in the past were paltry, the kind of choices made by people of not just limited means but small imaginations. Though a little voice insisted that, imagination aside, I was a person of limited means, I ignored it. I would if necessary (and of course it would be necessary) sell securities from a modest fund I had inherited from my father and which, since it helped me meet necessary annual expenses, I knew it was foolish to deplete.

But there was one house listed, at the end of Water Street on the village side of the harbor, that was exactly what I had imagined: a sprawling mansion of weathered shingles, the ells of its three gabled stories housing more than a dozen bedrooms. The ground floor sitting rooms opened into sunrooms furnished with overstuffed sun-bleached sofas and armchairs. The kitchen was fitted out to serve restaurants full of people. The broad lawns sloped down to a stone pier and private beach. The house was wrapped around on three sides by broad covered porches, from which I saw myself, in shorts and boating moccasins, sun-stung at day's end, savoring a chilled martini in the company of a cluster of beloved friends. The problem was not just that the house rented for $8,000 a week—I would have spent it, I *would*—but that it was unavailable for three consecutive weeks.

Checking further, I saw another promising listing, a handsome three story colonial house of historic note at the intersection of Main Street and Water Street, next to the Yacht Club. The photographs showed water views from all rooms and from the back terrace. A widow's walk above the third floor looks out over the harbor and the grand mansions of Water Street. In the eighteenth century the house had served both as the village's first school house and, later, its post office. The large ground floor rooms looked airy and elegantly appointed. It was available for the first three weeks of August for $4,000 a week, a rate that seemed almost exciting—not because I had $12,000 (plus a $3,000 security deposit) at hand, but because it was just *half* the staggering sum I had emotionally committed to the larger, unavailable house.

So I booked it, retirement capital be damned, and set about arranging for our daughters and their families to be there at the same time, a delicate negotiation given their various working commitments. At length we managed to make the middle week the all-Hawley family week, so I could set about filling the rooms in the adjacent weeks with friends. M's sister Lea was attentive to my scheme from the outset and let it be known that she was eager to be in residence for at least two of the weeks. Because we are fond of her and because she insisted on being a paying guest, she became a fixture in what became a complex extended house party.

As it happened it was not the kind of house party I had imagined, though, as the novelist Anthony Powell might have put it, it was "not without all satisfactory features." That I was inescapably an impostor in such a grand house was underscored the moment I entered it. The listing agent told me the key to the residence would be placed inside the closed gas grill on the back terrace. When I made my way to the back of the property to find it, it was not there. Moreover, by some freakish oversight, the gas grill had been left on and had heated itself to 450 degrees. Merely touching the lid blistered my thumb painfully for over a week. Undaunted by the pain and missing key, I tried all the doors at the rear of the house, and one of them was unlocked. I stepped inside to the earsplitting howl of a burglar alarm. I fled the racket and from the driveway phoned the agency to report my situation. The agent I had dealt with was not in. I was relaying a message when two squad cars pulled up in front of the house. Still talking on the phone I waved to the uniformed officer approaching to signal that I was a benign, confident, non-criminal presence. He was not readily convinced. He asked for my name, my home address, and my driver's license, and until his fellow officers in the squad cars verified my car was mine and I was who I claimed I was, showed no interest in what I was trying to explain about renting this house and the key not being where it was supposed to be. I suppose it is understandable that he was not interested in my account of the gas burner and my blister.

When he was sure that I was harmless and probably the rightful renter of the house, he went inside with me where, deafened by the wailing alarm, he tried to help me turn it off. At length I located a notebook set out for renters with instructions for managing various house functions. In it was listed a handyman to call if anything was broken or amiss. The officer brightened when he saw the name. He said he knew him, and that he was a good man. As it turned out he was a good man. He answered his phone when I called and said he would be right over. Minutes later he showed me the code to turn off the alarm—such peace—and disconnected the gas from the dangerously overheated grill. All was well. And stayed well for the duration of our residence.

Once past my rattling first entry, I could see that it was a wonderful house. Its interior had recently been remodeled in a not-too-austere contemporary way. The back of the house overlooked the harbor, and the harbor-facing walls on all three stories were nearly all windows, floor to ceiling. The entire interior was painted white, so that from first morning through sunset the rooms were illumined with gauzy light. In any room I found it impossible to avert my gaze for long from the panorama of the harbor: the forest of masts of the yachts at mooring, the higgledy-pigglety succession of gang planks and piers beyond which the sun sparkled on ripples of open water. Nowhere in the house was the view out more arresting than from the third floor, which had been converted into an enormous master bedroom suite. Its window wall framed the entire harbor and Buzzard's Bay beyond, a prospect that registered to me more like a vast Hudson River School painting than a view out a window.

I retreated up to the restfulness of that third floor panorama several times a day during the course of our stay. I had not been prepared for the jarring complexities of so many people mingling under one roof. I knew that M and I, M's sister, the families of our out-of-town daughters, and the friends I had invited to stay would compose a full house throughout our tenancy, but I had not counted on the appearance of so many others. I had not reckoned on M's sister inviting her older brother down from Maine for a few days, or that M's younger brother and his wife, who live in Marion, would be on hand for much of the day and seemingly all meals. Nor did I realize that Jesse and her family, who live in the village year-round, would also be a daily presence. I probably should have known that Jesse's children Alice, 4, and Leon, 10, would not only enter the house at first light but often find a way to sleep over. It had not entered my mind that many of M's cousins and their families live in Marion, easily a dozen people— *more*. I should not have been surprised that many of them stopped by, often lingering. I had not in the months leading up to our residence in Marion imagined that there would be dinners for 16, that days would pass with no interval between meal preparation and clean up, that between the two-block walk to the Marion General Store and the three-mile drive to the Shaw's supermarket in neighboring Wareham, I would spend hours of each day and thousands of dollars restoring food and drink to the shelves.

In all I failed to come to rest sufficiently to take the measure of how my imagined seaside idyll was going. I could not at any given moment tell if I was enjoying myself. The best of it may have been the rounds of golf with Karl, Gary, and Peter on the eccentric nine-hole Marion Golf Course. I have played this course periodically for a half century, and its oddness—low stone walls cross the fairways and encircle many of the greens—transports me to some place far from the United States: Scotland or Ireland. Doing something decidedly strenuous, consciousness contracted to striking the ball, striding after it in anticipation of striking it again, felt like a restorative corrective to what had become relentless housekeeping routines. The corrective required, really, no more than being outdoors—playing—with my friends.

There were some pleasant day sails on the *Swamp Yankee*, M's brother's 40 foot yawl and on the 12 foot *Vireo*, passed down through generations of M's family to her sister, mild diversions that served to fill time between meals. In various configurations we also walked quite a bit. Marion is a good village for walking. You can walk its circumference—three or four miles—in an hour, varying the route in dozens of ways by alternating side streets. The chief attraction is the houses, the ones on the water opulent and beautifully landscaped. Inland are lovingly restored homes dating from early colonial days when Marion was a fishing and whaling village, predating even New

Bedford down the coast where Melville set *Moby Dick*. Such was my unexpected interpersonal overload that on any given day, even after multiple walks with different configurations of guests, I would duck out of the house for a head clearing solitary stroll.

I have always enjoyed cocktail hours in company, and these were reliably satisfying, if slightly diminished by the requirement of amusing or diverting small children. As cocktail hours go, these were rather long ones, spanning the hours 5 through 7: I spent the half hour prior preparing platters of hors d'œuvres: cheese and crackers, salamis, cold vegetables, shrimp, chips, nuts. I mixed shakers of chilled martinis, set out bourbon and tumblers and ice, uncorked the wine, and prepared juice concoctions for the non-drinkers. By seven the sun would be setting behind the harbor, and a lovely rosy light played on the white walls. As we sat down to eat, there was, I think, an unspoken acknowledgement that we were glad to be together in this place.

At this moment, reflecting back, it is with something between puzzlement and regret that I cannot say I am especially glad to have spent three weeks in this way. I could sense M felt this too—by the number of times she asked me, with a slightly grim set to her face, whether I was having a good time. When I relax directed thought and wait for a positive image to arrive, it is the evening M and I, Karl and Peter and their wives dined out at the Yacht Club, to which I had been given guest passes by one of M's cousins. It was a mild evening, and we were seated under a canopy close to the water. Food and drink were just right, and as we were lingering at the table, a succession of people came to greet us, a few cousins and forgotten Marion acquaintances from summers long past. I cannot explain why it felt heart-opening to see them. It was as if they opened a door to a brilliantly sunny prior life. And then some of Jesse's new teaching colleagues at Tabor Academy, including its Headmaster, came over and introduced themselves because they wanted to tell M and me what a terrific contribution Jesse was already making. Those kindnesses struck a chord of happiness akin to what I remember feeling watching Jesse perform in a show.

About the rest of our time in the rental house, I have an impression of late afternoon light from the harbor irradiating the third floor suite and an accompanying sense of how much there was to contend with below. When our last guests departed, M and I had two days in the house left to ourselves. We decided to drive home instead.

August 29-30, 2017: I am invited back to St. John's High School in Shrewsbury, Massachusetts, to work with the faculty and staff on the opening day of their back-to-school meetings. The teachers had been assigned to read Michael Reichert's and my book, *Reaching Boys / Teaching Boys*, and the non-teaching staff had been assigned our subsequent study, *I Can Learn From You: Boys as Relational Learners*. The plan for the morning was that I would talk for an hour or so about the leading points in each book, after which the faculty would break up by department and brainstorm on possible applications to their classes. In the hour or so while the teaching faculty were doing this, I was to meet with the non-teaching staff to discuss the other book. Then the entire staff was to reconvene and report out what, if anything, they resolved to do differently.

This sequence was explained to me in an email a day or two before my arrival, and I wish the headmaster had contacted me earlier so that I could have raised some basic concerns. The main one being that *both* books were about teaching practice, the first about effective lessons, the second about productive teacher student relationships. I could see little point in assigning the relational book to staff who had little daily contact with students, but more worrying to me was what we could possibly discuss for an hour while the teachers were off in their departments. Though too late, I saw what the problem had been. The headmaster and his colleagues had not first read the books before he asked the staff to read them and in consequence made faulty guesses about who should read what.

In the event, my opening presentation went down well enough. There is a reliable positive energy when school staffs reconvene at summer's end to set the coming school year in motion. But as I anticipated, the non-teaching staff—development officers, secretaries, library monitors, business office clerks—were confused about how they were supposed to respond to the book that bore little relation to their daily work and to the stranger who wrote it. Sensing potential discomfort—an hour of it—I decided to set a relaxed, conversation tone and asked them to share their job descriptions and how, from their respective perches in the school, they encountered boys. I correctly guessed that they had little or no daily contact with students, but they understood that the welfare and forward motion of those boys was at the heart of their jobs. Some of them were parents, and all of them seemed eager enough to share their hopes that the boys in the school would thrive and that the school's program would serve them well. I can't say we accomplished anything beyond an agreeable mood, but when the bell sounded ending the session, I was grateful for that.

As the full staff reassembled in the main auditorium, I realized that I was tired—not sleepy, but exhausted, talked out. I had been speaking more or less continuously for more than two hours, and there was another hour and a half to go. As we set the report-out session in motion, I regretted that I had slept little the night before. The school had once again put me up in a high end hotel a few miles from the school, and as is the case with me now in hotels, I slept fitfully and very little. But more than my fatigue was responsible for the impression that some of the faculty in the And-What-Can-We-Do-Differently session were feeling porky, if short of contrarian. I had anticipated some degree of this, as it is perfectly natural for teachers, especially veteran teachers who are committed to and proud of their pedagogy to resist some new theory or theorist wheeled in to tell them to consider changing. *What does he know about my teaching? What does he know about this school? These boys? Was he a teacher, and was he any good?*

Ten different departments "reported out." Some had given serious consideration to revising practice, and they explained how. The English and history teachers seemed most resistant. They tended to recount the ways their current lessons already reflected what the research indicated was most effective. In the English chairman's opening remarks, I detected a sarcastic dismissal of one of the successful lessons narrated by a teacher in the book. I know the author of that narrative, a superb teacher and a gifted writer. I hope I masked my antipathy for the English chairman.

I left the campus exhausted and with the hindsight conviction never again to preside over a gathering unless I understand and agree to every aspect of the program involving me. A nice woman, the school's Dean of the Faculty and second-in-command, walked me to my car and thanked me for my efforts. This, she revealed, would be her first year at St. John's, and that the design of this morning had been her first assignment. In an instant I could see that the faculty resistance I had begun to sense was grounded in skepticism about this new hire, explaining a certain hesitancy in her tone as she introduced me at the podium and in the less-than-engaged response from the assembled staff as she addressed them. Poor woman.

Now more than exhausted, I got behind the wheel of my car a little past noon and began what would be a twelve-hour drive westward to Cleveland to visit Lulu and her mother.

August 31-September 9, 2017: Made phenomenally good time, though there was an hour or so of periodic self-face slapping in order to stay awake on the Massachusetts leg of U.S. Route 90, arriving in Cleveland Heights a little before ten. Lulu and Celeste were still awake and glad to see me. First impression is that Lulu looked distinctly changed, as much young woman as girl—and she is only twelve.

The "business" mission of this trip is for me to take the measure of Lulu's new school situation. A seventh grader now and midway through her public school's junior high program, she and her classmates were removed from their previous school building in the heart of a leafy residential neighborhood in the heart of old Cleveland Heights to an improvised complex of prefabricated classrooms in an adjacent suburb to the east, the reason being that the prior schoolhouse was in dire need of renovation.

There is reason to be concerned about the adjustment. Apart from the esthetic barrenness of the warren of portable classrooms abutting a busy strip retail thoroughfare, the new configuration combines two large junior high schools on the same site: 1200 children and two parallel administrations and staffs. The combined student bodies include a wide range of tested abilities. The racial composition of the student bodies is mixed, about 60% black and 40% white. Parents last year raised concern about student safety, principally fighting. There was also a verified rape.

Celeste had made an appointment for us to meet with the principal at the start of the day on Monday morning. I was annoyed that in setting up the meeting, Celeste had written to the principal that I was the former Headmaster of University School, highly important, hugely influential, etc., and would be assessing whether the school would be worthy of Lulu's continuing there in light of private school options. It was not hard to imagine the spirit in which the principal would greet such a parent. And I am neither fearful nor worried about Lulu's situation. To the contrary, I—not to mention Lulu and her mother— have been delighted and grateful for all seven prior years of Lulu's schooling in the district. There has been a succession of warm, highly competent teachers who have known Lulu well, encouraged her, very much in tune with what is distinctive about her.

The principal, a tall hefty Irishman, was standing sentinel in the central hallway as Celeste and I entered the complex along with the throng of arriving students. His name is McNichols, and despite his understandable wariness of me as we shook hands, I liked him. We talked for a while in his office, he summarizing the complexities of the temporary quartering of the two junior high schools, I doing my best to sound like an interested, uncritical parent. I liked the fact that he seemed antsy to get on his feet and to show us around the school. Moving through the wide empty corridors, sharing droll quips with passing colleagues and the odd uniformed security guard, he seemed very much the movie Irish cop, understated and in command. While credibly projecting an attitude of cheerful good will, Celeste wanted to register a concern she and I had already discussed: Lulu, who had been designated "gifted" since the requisite tests were first administered had, for some reason, been placed in an English section which was clearly pitched to slower learners. Her former "gifted" classmates had been placed in a different section and were being assigned different, more sophisticated work. Celeste asked how Lulu might be scheduled into the gifted class. The answer was something to the effect of, "Yeah, we can look at that." And while less than a satisfying response, I came away from our conference and tour with an unexpected appreciation for the scope and weight of this principal's daily responsibilities.

The range of his school concerns bore little relation to mine as headmaster of University school. He was a visible presence, along with designated colleagues and security guards, in the corridors and common spaces in the school. Entering the building, Celeste and I had passed through a manned security checkpoint more rigorous than TSA protocols in airports. Signs in every corridor said, "Smile, you are on camera!" so that students would know their out-of-class behavior was being electronically observed. In consequence, even in the bell-driven crush of students between classes, the school felt orderly and safe. From the outside, the featureless lines of the connected portable classrooms gave no indication of their spacious, immaculate and well-appointed interiors. Corridor tiles gleamed. This had taken care, and I was impressed. Mr. McNichols referred to the district's various scholastic programs by acronyms unknown to me, and in doing so seemed, while not exactly showing off, proud of his mastery of the prevailing public school ed.-speak. I left the building in a reverie about the jargon-less directness of my own interactions with students and parents and colleagues in the course of my teaching and headmastering. I believed this to be a positive, superior feature of private school life, but I wonder how that life would appear to Mr. McNichols. He may very well have found my school world overly precious and out of touch.

Together Lulu, Celeste, and I decided to celebrate the onset of the new school year with some special meals, some at the house, others out on the town. I created a freezable store of meatballs in sauce, Celeste cooked impressive Mexican and Indian dinners, and we dined out for the rest, though with curiously poor results. For what was to be our very fanciest night out, including, on Celeste's and Lulu's part, serious dressing up, we chose a highly regarded—even famous!—

bistro in downtown Cleveland called Lola's. My former student and now leading food writer, Mike Ruhlman, had featured Lola's and its chef in an early book about great American restaurants breaking new culinary ground, in consequence making Lola's a destination in Cleveland.

When we arrived downtown on a bustling Saturday night all three of us were in high spirits—and remained in high spirits despite indescribably terrible food. Actually, Lulu's steak and pommes frites were fine, but I was served an eerily rare and gummy pork loin, Celeste some kind of lamb dish in a goopy gravy so salty she had to send it back to the kitchen. Very odd—but the waiters were charming in their apologies and took both entrees off the bill. For some reason, her parents' inedible food notwithstanding, Lulu, in addition to looking gorgeous, was in the happiest of moods, and we managed to make a lively, even hilarious evening of Lola's.

The following evening, my last in Cleveland before the long drive home to Vermont, also included elements of hilarity, this due entirely to what is without question the worst meal I have ever taken in a restaurant. That afternoon as Lulu and I were ambling past the shops and eateries in Coventry Village, a short walk from Celeste's house, we spotted a restaurant newly opened in what had been a big, lively sports bar. The new establishment, spookily lit from within by swirls of blue and white neon, is called Lobster Shake. We looked at a menu in the window and saw that it included all imaginable seafood, including raw oysters, for which at the moment I was more than keen. We decided on the spot to book a table for our evening meal. After the surprising fiasco of our Lola's outing, it seemed we could hardly lose.

But yes, we could. Our dinner at Lobster Shake was with no exaggeration the worst dining experience I have ever had. The interior of the restaurant is a little spooky. There are several adjoining rooms, each of them very dark, the only light projected in cylindrical shafts from above onto the surface of long bare wooden tables—no table cloths, napkins, implements. Okay. Different. Fun, perhaps. I am confused by the menu. As noted earlier, every imaginable variety of fish and shellfish was offered, but you could not order, say, salmon and a salad. You had to order "combos" of various offerings together, the prices of the combos varying with the number of elements selected.

Feeling game and a little whimsical, Celeste and I ordered combos of clams, mussels, crab, lobster, crayfish and shrimp. Lulu, somehow smelling a fish-rat, decided to order the only non-fish offering, a child's helping of chicken tenders. There were drinks, and we chatted. I could not help noticing that to the wall end of our table was affixed a metal housing for a full roll of paper towels. In fact, to the wall end of *every* table was affixed a housing for paper towels.

After a few minutes, a waiter came around offering us large white plastic bibs, which he helped tie around our necks. He also instructed us to put on clear plastic gloves. A few minutes later, Lulu was presented with her chicken tenders, and two steaming, odorous plastic bags of something fishy were plopped down in front of Celeste and me, along with what looked like tin waste baskets. It took a minute and some looking around to the tables of other diners to figure out that we were supposed to reach into the steaming plastic bags with our gloved hands and pick out the contents, pull the shelled bits apart, and, without aid of silverware, put what was edible into our mouths. Celeste and I did our best to get into the spirit of the thing. All the contents of the bags were mushed together in a soupy brown broth, which streamed down over our plastic gloves and onto the tabletop. We made immediate and continuous use of our roll of paper towels. Because of the tangy—Cajun?—broth, everything in the bag tasted the same, whether a chunk of lobster, crab claw, or mussel. The little crayfish had been cooked to inedible, meatless skeletons and had to be discarded intact into the trash tins. A cursory visual scan of the smeared, glistening faces of the other diners suggested that they, like us, were cautiously enduring the challenge before them. I was barely a quarter way into my bag when my stomach clamped shut, an emphatic refusal. When we paid up and left the table, the remaining heap of refuse—bibs, gloves, bags, trash tins mounded with shells—covered the tabletop. I noted that we had used the entire roll of paper towels.

Happily for Lulu, next door was a favorite ice cream shop in which artisans create the ice cream from scratch on frozen granite wheels as the customer looks on. A gladdening antidote to the murky interior of the Lobster Shake and our fish bags. I prepared for bed with an agreeable realization that throughout the outwardly disgusting dining episode, we had enjoyed ourselves, enjoyed each other, the worst of it an occasion for jokes and silliness. I would not be surprised if this evening and others like it do not compose a central place in Lulu's remembered story of this time in our lives.

September 10, 2017: Claire held a party on this radiantly sunny Sunday afternoon to celebrate baby Levi's first birthday. Apart from M and me and the in-law parents who drove up from Massachusetts, the other guests were all peers, mostly college friends of Claire's and Nick's. All were married couples and had a least one child between one and three years old. The renovations have not begun yet on Claire's and Nick's farmhouse, so it was good that we could be outdoors on the newly mown lawns.

A huge quilted blanket sprinkled with toys was laid out on the grass, and at any given moment a half dozen or more wriggling infants were scooting about its surface, tentatively fingering the playthings and each other. The parents sat languidly around the periphery of the blanket, making lazy conversation, occasionally untangling a child from an unwanted embrace.

Claire's property is unenclosed and handsomely landscaped, the lawns opening to acres of rolling green fields, forest and then smoky blue serrations of mountain on the far horizon. Soft breeze, bright sun, no insects. With little to say, I stroll about the grounds, then take a lawn chair a few yards apart from the parents clustered around the blanket. Lounging and at ease, Claire's women friends are so like her in dress and disposition. They are in their mid-thirties, but to my unreliable eye they could be teenagers, each of them fit and pretty. One of them, Louisa, sitting nearest me, has a swirl of red hair clipped up in a loose twist, the sunlight playing in it like fire. For minutes at a time my mind empties of thought. I am agreeably wordless. I am almost an absence here. If I closed my eyes, I would sleep.

September 13, 2017: My old University School friend Keith emailed last night to say that, due to a late night of conversation with an overnight visitor, he had to cancel a luncheon date we had made for tomorrow in New Hampshire, near the campus of Dartmouth College, which is roughly midway between his flat in Maine and Ripton. He did not believe he could manage the three-hour drive having been so sleep-deprived.

The change in plans troubled me. Would it take *two* days to get back to his daily rhythm? For most of the years of our acquaintance Keith had been a problematic drinker, willfully abstaining for as long as he could, then given to reckless binges. For the past twelve years he has been sober. He said that on the wearying night in question he had drunk two cups of tea, while his companion talked into the small hours.

I don't believe he begged off our get together for a brighter option. He had set up the lunch date, and our prior Dartmouth meetings have been lively with humorous reminiscence. What unsettles me in his declining to meet is that, at age 74, he feels impaired to the point of incompetence after a late night. More simply, he feels old, *is* old, an incidental confirmation that I am too, that life must proceed differently now.

September 15, 2017: Yet another piano hour with the elderly clients of Project Independence in Middlebury. The pattern and feel of these outings have grown so familiar to me and to my audience that I no longer feel much nervousness as I prepare what I hope will be an engaging program. This time I ask them to name the billboard top hits between 1940 and 1960, telling them after they guess correctly a little about the background of the song. With fifteen minutes or so left in the hour, song books are passed around and we sing together old chestnuts most of them probably learned when we were in elementary school: *When The Saints Go Marching In, Over There, I've Been Working on the Railroad.* When I entered the hall, there was a spontaneous cheer of welcome, then a rousing round of applause when I got up to go. I felt unhurried and physically comfortable throughout the hour. Banter came easily. There were lots of smiles. Then it sank in: we had become friends. I was one of them.

October 1, 2017: A day that would not cease unfurling. M and I began in Provincetown where I had agreed to spend a few days with our old friend and my former University School colleague Linda so that she and I could complete a draft of a document about how best to relate to elementary school boys. The aim here was to transfer to the teaching of elementary school boys what I had learned over the course of two international studies about how older boys thrive in school. Linda is an ideal collaborator in this work because she was, in her sixteen years teaching University School fourth graders, no less than a genius in relating to and motivating the full variety of boys in her charge. Prior to my arrival in Provincetown Linda had composed a series of narratives of how various boys had progressed through their fourth grade year. I included four of these in the manuscript we are preparing for publication. The boys profiled were interesting and to some extent problematic and challenging, but by any measure successful by year's end and, I hope, illustrate the possibilities for improvement and growth when a teacher is able to create and maintain a warm, attentive relationship.

Provincetown has been a favored summer destination for M and me for years, but it was especially fine to revisit it in autumnal light without the throngs of summer tourists. Linda and I managed to alternate productive sessions of desk work with invigorating walks through town and along deserted beaches at Race Point and Herring Cove. Most of the best restaurants were still open for business, so at workday's end, M and I, Linda, and her partner Jane dined at leisure as late hazy sun declined over the water. Linda and I concluded our work on a note of optimistic high hope, and after an early Saturday breakfast M and I drove north of Boston to what we knew was going to be a very sad and probably uncomfortable commitment: the interment and memorial service for M's cousin Debbie, who earlier in the week had taken her life.

Debbie was more than a cousin to M. She was next door neighbor and summer playmate in Marion from infancy through their coming of age. When Debbie's father retired from his headmastership of the Phillips Academy at Exeter to take over the Peace Corps in Nigeria, Debbie stayed behind and lived with M and her family. Both girls boarded at Milton Academy. In the summer of 1968 M and I and Debbie and her husband were married on the same rise of ground overlooking Marion Harbor. We saw Debbie and her family at least annually in the course of the intervening half century. Debbie was short, sturdy, outwardly cheerful, something of an extrovert. Peter, the man she married, was a distinct east coast WASP type: St. Paul's, Harvard, well-to-do enough not to have to devote himself to a profession, although he did some junior college administrative work north of Boston and, tiring of that, got a law degree and practiced intermittently. Despite her outward chirpiness, Debbie was, like many of her forebears, visited by intense bouts of depression, some of them in her last years requiring residential care and shock treatments. Whether worn down by her depression or otherwise diverted, her husband divorced her a few years ago, and in the ensuing solitude Debbie, despite immersing herself in choirs and other musical ensembles, succumbed to despair and hanged herself in her empty house.

We drove two and a half hours under lowering skies and light rain to Salem, Massachusetts, where Debbie's ashes were interred in an ancient plot full of her Saltonstall forebears. The interment was a family-only gathering and preceded the funeral proper, which was in Wenham, Mass., nearby. Because of the drizzle we huddled under a canopy where a clergyman said prayers, a desultory hymn was sung, and Debbie's eldest sister Joey, hovering on the brink of dementia, read a much too long excerpt from a journal she kept, the selected passage about how she had managed her own serial losses. Her tone throughout was hectoring and self-congratulatory, to the point that I considered asking M if, having done our familial duty here, we could skip the funeral.

I am glad we didn't. Because I had not seen much of Debbie at home over the years and given what I knew about her struggle with depressions and recent divorce, I assumed she had led a closely held, relatively solitary life. As it happens, I was completely mistaken. The large stone church in Wenham was overflowing with mourners when we arrived a quarter hour before the service began. Debbie had been actively involved with two choirs, a recorder ensemble, and latterly as a kind of lark, a ukulele group. All of them were on hand for the service, the choirs combining impressively for a choral tribute. In addition to a short, affecting eulogy by the church pastor, who apparently knew Debbie well, there were seven or eight reminiscences from Debbie's son and daughter, brothers, sisters, and friends. I had not known any of the friends but each spoke warmly about their longstanding relationship with and affection for Debbie. M read a Mary Oliver poem suggested by Debbie's daughter and managed with effort not to cry.

So Debbie had been anything but solitary over the course of her adult years. The tributes to her were full of anecdotes of her uninhibited humor, spontaneity, openness to adventure. The portrait revealed was of an extrovert, a doer, but nonetheless a woman who throughout her adult life was visited by periodic bouts of depression that plunged her into depths from which she could not ascend without medicines and, in emergencies, residential care and electro-convulsive therapy. Her children did not soft peddle the struggle with depression. Instead they marveled at the positivity and resolve with which their mother contended with it. Her daughter read from post-it notes Debbie left about the house coaching herself to stay on task, look to the bright side.

Dating from my sister Binky's suicide nearly a half century ago, I have been uncomfortable when invited to formally "mourn" a suicide. Images of the actual circumstances of the death—in my sister's case asphyxiation in a garaged car, in Debbie's, hanging from a rope in her empty house—intrude horribly on the procession of consoling gestures, wakes, funerals, the visible presence of draped caskets and funerary urns. Like, I suppose, most people, I have no difficulty wanting to think well of the dead and in most cases actually do, but with suicides, again beginning with my sister's, I cannot stop myself imagining the suicide's state of mind, the intensity and quality of her feeling in the moments preceding the act. Imagining this creates for me a kind of mental noise or pain incompatible with decorous rituals. A good deal of the awfulness I expected to feel did not happen in the service for Debbie. For one thing, as I have said, her "problem" was not sidestepped or euphemized; it was front and center in all the spirited tributes. What was celebrated was the energy and warmth and positivity of the 70 years Debbie had got the best of her demons. She had, despite the obstacles before her, lived well.

Church receptions after funerals are for me obligations to be dutifully met, respects paid, with no lingering. The reception after Debbie's service so overfilled a large hall that for minutes at a time movement in any direction was impossible. I felt myself wanting to stay. I waited to greet Debbie's children, Debbie's and M's cousins. I wanted to thank and praise the friends who had offered tributes from the altar. After about two hours the crowd began to thin. M and I were among the last to leave.

In late afternoon through drizzle with low hanging gloom overhead, we drove southeast to Providence, Rhode Island, where daughter Jesse and husband James were showcasing a new theater piece at an avant garde performance space called The Wilbury. Since the performance was scheduled for 9:30 p.m., we had arranged to meet our friend Kerry Brennan, a longstanding booster of Jesse's theater work, at an Italian restaurant for dinner before the show. Not really familiar with Providence's inner city, I put our journey in care of Google's Siri and the global positioning technology that directs her soothing instructions. It was dark when we entered the outer limits of Providence and proceeded through a prolonged series of turns, stops and starts through what seemed to be endless neighborhoods of abandoned warehouses.

But in the manner of urban redevelopment I remembered from visiting Jesse and James in nether reaches of Brooklyn, I had reason to believe that restaurants and theaters and residential lofts do spring up in such outwardly barren urban wastes. At length, the restaurant appeared, a blazing neon oasis surrounded by chain link fence, abandoned factories and pot-holed parking lots. A block away another eruption of blinking neon announced the presence of a Gentleman's

Club. Kerry had heard positive things about the restaurant, as apparently had others. Its warren of connecting rooms were packed solid with clinking, barking millennials, so that we felt lucky to find a table. It was good to be seated and still, and despite the clamor and din, the cocktail was soothing, the food was excellent, and I felt myself coming to rest.

The Wilbury Theater was even harder to find and the neighborhood more desolate than the restaurant's. A greeter outside the hall indicated that we could park around the block in an abandoned lot he assured us was safe and designated for the purpose. When we returned to the theater entrance we were told we could go inside a small vestibule but could not enter the performance space because another production, Harold Pinter's *The Caretaker*, was in progress. It was nearly ten by the time the *Caretaker* people filed out and we made our way to the elaborate miniature set Jesse and James had created for their show: a high ceilinged, densely textured living room with damask hangings, oriental carpet, an arrangement of shabby seating and tables filled with complicated gadgets, including an old fashioned turn-table record player. As we seated ourselves on stools facing the set, James, dressed in a sad, horizontally striped cardigan sweater worn over a shirt and tie, busied himself mixing drinks—"Nor'easters"—which, along with an array of hors d'œuvres spread out on a coffee table at the foot of the playing space, he offered to anyone who expressed interest. This unexpected expression of hospitality—had the show started?—encouraged some of the audience to wander up onto the set, mulling through records and books and other props.

At length, James welcomed the attendees formally, and when they had taken seats began a long and, to me, interesting monologue about being new to the area and various obstacles to making a satisfactory adjustment. At the back of the set, behind a diaphanous screen, Jesse—James' wife in the show as in life—could be seen and heard moving about. At length she enters the room and at once establishes an ominous mood, and so begins the opening scene between George and Martha of Edward Albee's *Who's Afraid of Virginia Woolf?* In the hour or so of subsequent business Jesse and James drop their George and Martha characters and assume roles they have created for themselves: Helen and Lloyd. Helen and Lloyd at various points talk earnestly about their relationship, bicker, and twice dance wildly. At one point Jesse sings—quite affectingly—a bluesy ballad, accom-panied by James on the guitar. At another Jesse moves into the audience and engages a woman in an impromptu exchange about their most embarrassing moments. Toward the end of the show, Helen and Lloyd have descended into a raw despair that seems to have been foundational to their disorienting prior business. The performance concludes as both of them exit behind the diaphanous screen at the rear of the set and are seen in silhouette as Jesse plaintively sings the old country tune "Some People Get Married" accompanied by James on the banjo.

They first told me about this project almost a year ago. I knew enough from their previous productions in New York as The National Theater of the United States of America not to expect any sort of straightforward narrative. In May M and I had attended a Wilbury Theater benefit in which a snippet of this show, which is now is titled *House Warming,* was featured, so we already had some idea of the show's eccentric thrust. This evening our fellow audience members, albeit a decidedly bohemian lot, greeted the full show enthusiastically, and though small in number gave it a hearty ovation. Personally, I was riveted throughout and not, I think, because Jesse is my daughter. A heightened pitch of expectation is aroused by such surprising but convincingly enacted transitions of thought and mood. There were moments of raw emotional confrontation as well as touches of pure whimsy, as when in the course of a fervent exchange of views between Helen and Lloyd, Jesse inexplicably mixes an actual spinach and kale smoothie in a Vitamix blender, decants its vivid greenness into a cocktail glass, and drinks it off in the course of the exchange. The show evoked many laughs, and the musical offerings, however incongruous, were genuinely pleasing. I tend to be ginger about asking Jesse and James about the point or message they hope to convey in their work, aware that confounding standard notions of "point" and "message" is the core aim of avant garde theater. Nevertheless, they were both glad to talk to me about it. As they see it, the show is a distillation of their new circumstances: new jobs in a new region of the country, feeling not quite connected to their new neighbors and colleagues, feeling their way through all manner of uncertainties.

By the time we chatted with Jesse and James after the show, said our goodbyes to Kerry, and headed out to find our car, it was past midnight. M dozed on the drive back to Marion where we were lodging for the night. I was not only wide awake, I felt hyper alert, due I think to a need to integrate the wildly divergent elements of the past day. Over breakfast in Provincetown Linda and I had talked earnestly about our relational teaching project, then hours through the rain to the interment and memorial service for Debbie, more hours driving through rain and darkness into the industrial wastes of Providence, then the vivid, sense-shattering spectacle of Jesse's show. How could this have been a single day? Months have passed with less impact.

October 8, 2017: Weeks ago my friend Karl surprised me in a very touching way by saying he would like to organize an evening hosted by his Unitarian church in which I would read from works spanning my entire writing life. We had talked earlier about a possible reading from *Three Lives of Jonathan Force*, which was then newly out. But Karl was insistent that this be a reading representing the widest possible variety of my work —poems, essays, memoir, fiction. The kindness of this gesture was amplified when I realized he was also distributing posters about town, lining up publicity in the local paper, and arranging for the proprietor of the Vermont Book Shop to be on hand at the church selling books. I know writers who have devoted agents and paid publicists, but who has friends like this?

The proposed reading presented both a concern and a challenge. The concern was about who would come. Old Vermont friends and friends I have made since moving to Ripton number about twenty, and they have already attended multiple readings by me, the *Jonathan Force* events quite recently. I am by no means widely known as a writer, especially in Vermont, and the prospect of people unknown to me venturing out on a Sunday evening to hear me read from my "life's work" seemed highly unlikely. Karl told me to count on his fellow

Unitarian parishioners.

The challenge was to organize an hour-long sequence of excerpted work that might both engage and cohere as some kind of unity. As I began foraging back into earlier and later work, I realized that Karl's invitation was begging a question I had never asked myself: *is* there a unifying theme in my published work? Have I made a Statement, or merely statements. Puzzling over this, I thought of the question ascribed to E.M. Forster: how do I know what I think until I see what I write? Over the course of about a week, the sequence of what I intended to read began not only falling into place, but falling, I thought, *neatly* into place. I felt that I was less compiling than discovering: realizing what I have been thinking by seeing what, over a lifetime, I have written.

By seven o'clock on the appointed Sunday evening, a satisfactory crowd of a few dozen people, most of them unknown to me, showed up to listen. Karl greeted them and introduced me generously and at some length. I began by recounting my earliest intimation that I was a Writer: the sunny Saturday morning when at age five or six I chose not to go outside and play, but instead to seat myself at the dining room table and with a sharpened pencil inscribe "writing" into a spiral bound notebook someone had given me from the Ben Franklin store in town. I only knew how to write a few words: "the," "and," "but," "of," "very," "dad," "mom," and my name, Richard Alan Hawley, and I entered them in my most careful printing onto page after page of the notebook, all the while picturing myself, as if from a vantage point on the ceiling of the room, *writing*—being a writer.

I followed this recollection with my earliest memory of feeling recognized as a writer: the morning when I collected the mail in the vestibule of my flat in Cambridge, England, where I was finishing my graduate work at St. John's College. Homesick since my arrival at the University in the fall, I had been reading and writing a lot of poetry, sending some of the poems to magazines and papers back home. On this morning a letter came back from the *New York Times*, informing me that they would publish a poem I had sent, "Dialogue," in the editorial section of the Saturday edition. The *Times* has long since stopped publishing poetry. At this moment, too, I had a sense of observing myself from above: a Writer holding his acceptance letter and a check for $35:

That fall I had been reading Auden's collected poems, and I was in their thrall. The poems I struggled to write every day were burdened with my effort to capture the historical vision and world weariness of Auden's saddest and best poems. But I had at that point so little historical vision and, far from being world weary, had just begun to wake up to the world. Late one night, justifiably frustrated by the emptiness of my "Audenesque" poems, I wrote very quickly and almost without revision a short poem, "Dialogue," a succession of images from my primary schooling that arose to consciousness unbidden.

> *My teacher had read Dewey.*
> *I read Donald Duck.*
> *Scraping chalk sent shivers up me neck.*
> *She showed us how to draw a finch—*
> *A cinch. Mine perched on a bomber*
> *Bursting into flames.*
> *She stood us in two lines*
> *To spell each other down.*
> *I loved to stand alone.*
> *She taught us world geography.*
> *Spain was orange, so was Greece,*
> *I never knew the names.*
> *Outside she taught us circle games —*
> *But I broke ranks and flew up in a tree.*
> *She left us once to do as we wished,*
> *So I went to the tank*
> *And taught the fish to sing.*

After reading the poem and a few others that I hoped might document my waking up as a writer, I made a transition to my choice of work as a teacher in a school for boys and read excerpts from essays about the experience of being immersed for so long in so much boy-ness. Then I shared something of the impact Jung and other Jungian writers have had on my understanding of the relationship between my personal consciousness and larger existence, illustrating points about soulfulness, the feminine *anima* of males, and the seasons of a male's life with excerpts from memoir and novels. I concluded the talk with the poem that ends my novel *The Headmaster's Papers*. That poem is composed by a beleaguered boys' school headmaster in late middle life who does not believe, in the face of a succession losses and disappointments, that he can continue to live. The valedictory poem he writes, "A Schoolmaster Considers School," concludes with the lines

> *A bright road opening wide to me*
> *Ghost children chanting something*
> *About verbs*
> *They are cheering in waves*
> *Hymns from voices clear and sad*
> *And gone as bells*
> *Hurrying bells, evening bells*
> *School bells banging me back*
> *To school.*

Closing my book and looking out into the faces of the listeners, I realized that what I had just presented *did* reveal a purposeful direction—a *meaning*. The realization deepened as I responded to questions and comments from the audience. In my opening anecdote I recounted a little boy who for no reason he could have explained had seated himself for a bout of *writing*, none of the elements of which he understood or had yet mastered. The gesture expressed a leaning toward something unknown and believed to be great: to be not a boy, but a man, and not merely a man, but a man *writer*. The last excerpts I read were composed by fictional protagonists who were mature male writers, men who had dedicated their life's work—and their writing— to finding the lost and essential nature of boys, including the boys they once were.

The boy reaching out to the not yet realized man and the man reaching back to the yearning boy are me.